*Work and Play: The Production and Consumption of Toys in Germany,
    1870–1914,* David D. Hamlin
*The Cosmopolitan Screen: German Cinema and the Global Imaginary, 1945 to the
    Present,* edited by Stephan K. Schindler and Lutz Koepnick
Germans on Drugs: The Complications of Modernization in Hamburg,
    Robert P. Stephens
*Gender in Transition: Discourse and Practice in German-Speaking Europe,
    1750–1830,* edited by Ulrike Gleixner and Marion W. Gray
Growing Up Female in Nazi Germany, Dagmar Reese
Justice Imperiled: The Anti-Nazi Lawyer Max Hirschberg in Weimar Germany,
    Douglas G. Morris
The Heimat Abroad: The Boundaries of Germanness, edited by Krista O'Donnell,
    Renate Bridenthal, and Nancy Reagin
*Modern German Art for Thirties Paris, Prague, and London: Resistance and
    Acquiescence in a Democratic Public Sphere,* Keith Holz
*The War against Catholicism: Liberalism and the Anti-Catholic Imagination in
    Nineteenth-Century Germany,* Michael B. Gross
German Pop Culture: How "American" Is It? edited by Agnes C. Mueller
Character Is Destiny: The Autobiography of Alice Salomon, edited by
    Andrew Lees
*Other Germans: Black Germans and the Politics of Race, Gender, and Memory in
    the Third Reich,* Tina M. Campt
*State of Virginity: Gender, Religion, and Politics in an Early Modern Catholic
    State,* Ulrike Strasser
Worldly Provincialism: German Anthropology in the Age of Empire,
    H. Glenn Penny and Matti Bunzl, editors
Ethnic Drag: Performing Race, Nation, Sexuality in West Germany, Katrin Sieg
Projecting History: German Nonfiction Cinema, 1967–2000, Nora M. Alter
Cities, Sin, and Social Reform in Imperial Germany, Andrew Lees
The Challenge of Modernity: German Social and Cultural Studies, 1890–1960,
    Adelheid von Saldern
Exclusionary Violence: Antisemitic Riots in Modern German History,
    Christhard Hoffman, Werner Bergmann, and Helmut Walser Smith, editors
Languages of Labor and Gender: Female Factory Work in Germany, 1850–1914,
    Kathleen Canning
That Was the Wild East: Film Culture, Unification and the "New" Germany,
    Leonie Naughton
Anna Seghers: The Mythic Dimension, Helen Fehervary
*Staging Philanthropy: Patriotic Women and the National Imagination in Dynastic
    Germany, 1813–1916,* Jean H. Quataert
Truth to Tell: German Women's Autobiographies and Turn-of-the-Century Culture,
    Katharina Gerstenberger
The "Goldhagen Effect": History, Memory, Nazism—Facing the German Past,
    Geoff Eley, editor

Social History, Popular Culture, and Politics in Germany
Geoff Eley, Series Editor
(continued)

Shifting Memories: The Nazi Past in the New Germany, Klaus Neumann
Saxony in German History: Culture, Society, and Politics, 1830–1933,
    James Retallack, editor
*Little Tools of Knowledge: Historical Essays on Academic and Bureaucratic
    Practices*, Peter Becker and William Clark, editors
*Public Spheres, Public Mores, and Democracy: Hamburg and Stockholm,
    1870–1914*, Madeleine Hurd
*Making Security Social: Disability, Insurance, and the Birth of the Social Entitlement
    State in Germany*, Greg Eghigian
*The German Problem Transformed: Institutions, Politics, and Foreign Policy,
    1945–1995*, Thomas Banchoff
*Building the East German Myth: Historical Mythology and Youth Propaganda in the
    German Democratic Republic, 1945–1989*, Alan L. Nothnagle
Mobility and Modernity: Migration in Germany 1820–1989, Steve Hochstadt
Triumph of the Fatherland: German Unification and the Marginalization of Women,
    Brigitte Young
*Framed Visions: Popular Culture, Americanization, and the Contemporary German
    and Austrian Imagination*, Gerd Gemünden
The Imperialist Imagination: German Colonialism and Its Legacy,
    Sara Friedrichsmeyer, Sara Lennox, and Susanne Zantop, editors
*Catholicism, Political Culture, and the Countryside: A Social History of the Nazi
    Party in South Germany*, Oded Heilbronner
A User's Guide to German Cultural Studies, Scott Denham, Irene Kacandes, and
    Jonathan Petropoulos, editors
*A Greener Vision of Home: Cultural Politics and Environmental Reform in the
    German Heimatschutz Movement, 1904–1918*, William H. Rollins
*West Germany under Construction: Politics, Society, and Culture in Germany in the
    Adenauer Era*, Robert G. Moeller, editor
*How German Is She? Postwar West German Reconstruction and the Consuming
    Woman*, Erica Carter
Feminine Frequencies: Gender, German Radio, and the Public Sphere, 1923–1945,
    Kate Lacey
*Exclusive Revolutionaries: Liberal Politics, Social Experience, and National Identity
    in the Austrian Empire, 1848–1914*, Pieter M. Judson
Jews, Germans, Memory: Reconstruction of Jewish Life in Germany,
    Y. Michal Bodemann, editor
Paradoxes of Peace: German Peace Movements since 1945,
    Alice Holmes Cooper
Society, Culture, and the State in Germany, 1870–1930, Geoff Eley, editor
*Technological Democracy: Bureaucracy and Citizenry in the German Energy
    Debate*, Carol J. Hager
*The Origins of the Authoritarian Welfare State in Prussia: Conservatives,
    Bureaucracy, and the Social Question, 1815–70*, Hermann Beck
From Bundesrepublik to Deutschland: German Politics after Unification, Michael G.
    Huelshoff, Andrei S. Markovits, and Simon Reich, editors
The Stigma of Names: Antisemitism in German Daily Life, 1812–1933,
    Dietz Bering
*Reshaping the German Right: Radical Nationalism and Political Change after
    Bismarck*, Geoff Eley

The *Heimat* Abroad

The Boundaries of Germanness

Edited by Krista O'Donnell, Renate Bridenthal, and Nancy Reagin

The University of Michigan Press   *Ann Arbor*

Copyright © by the University of Michigan 2005
All rights reserved
Published in the United States of America by
The University of Michigan Press
Manufactured in the United States of America
⊗ Printed on acid-free paper

2010   2009   2008   2007   5   4   3   2

A CIP catalog record for this book is available from the British Library.

Library of Congress Cataloging-in-Publication Data

The Heimat abroad : the boundaries of Germanness / edited by Krista
   O'Donnell, Nancy Reagin, and Renate Bridenthal.
      p.   cm. — (Social history, popular culture, and politics in
   Germany)
   Includes bibliographical references and index.
      ISBN 0-472-11491-3 (cloth : alk. paper) — ISBN 0-472-03067-1
   (pbk. : alk. paper)
      1. Germans—Foreign countries.   2. Germany—Emigration and
   immigration.   3. Jews, German—Foreign countries. 4. Population
   transfers—Germans.   I. O'Donnell, Krista, 1967–   II. Reagin, Nancy
   Ruth, 1960–   III. Bridenthal, Renate.   IV. Series.
   DD68.H45   2005
   305.83'1—dc22   2004025472

ISBN 978-0-472-11491-7 (cloth : alk. paper)
ISBN 978-0-472-03067-5 (pbk. : alk. paper)

Acknowledgments

The editors owe thanks to many people who midwifed this project along the way from its beginnings as a panel at the American Historical Association to this more comprehensive volume. Foremost among these is Dr. Hanna Schissler, currently at the George Eckert Institute for International Textbook Research in Braunschweig, Germany. During her visiting professorship at New York University in 1998–99, she organized a conference that brought together our first round of contributors along with trenchant commentators. Among those who enabled us to develop greater coherence for this project in its earliest stages are Volker Berghahn, Alon Confino, John R. Davis, Hasia Diner, Karen Eng, Benjamin Lapp, Daniel Levy, Robert Moeller, Molly Nolan, Martin Schain, and Frank Stern.

In addition, we owe many insights to our German Women's History Group, which, in addition to its much valued sisterly camaraderie, provided forthright suggestions that immeasurably improved work in progress. Ever rejuvenating itself, the group now consists of the following members: Bonnie Anderson, Dolores Augustine, Marion Berghahn, Rebecca Boehling, Jana Bruns, Jane Caplan, Belinda Davis, Lynne Fallwell, Atina Grossmann, Amy Hackett, Deborah Hertz, Maria Hoehn, Young Sun Hong, Marion Kaplan, Jan Lambertz, Molly Nolan, Katherine Pence, and Julia Sneeringer.

We are grateful to Geoff Eley for recognizing the significance of this work for the field of German history and for his wise suggestions and unflagging faith in its ultimate merit. We would also like to recognize our respective institutions for their support of this project: for Krista O'Donnell, the Provost's Assigned Released Time program at William Paterson University; for Nancy Reagin, Pace University, particularly the Dyson Dean's Office, for providing the course reductions that helped to complete the work. We also thank the helpful staff at the University of Michigan Press. We greatly appreciate the thoughtful detailed comments of the two anonymous readers, who compelled us to rethink some of our ideas. Any flaws that remain are due to our own stubbornness.

Contents

List of Abbreviations ix

Introduction 1

PART 1. **The Legal and Ideological Context of Diasporic Nationalism** **15**

CHAPTER 1. Diasporic Citizens: Germans Abroad in the Framing of German Citizenship Law *Howard Sargent* 17

CHAPTER 2. Home, Nation, Empire: Domestic Germanness and Colonial Citizenship *Krista O'Donnell* 40

CHAPTER 3. German-Speaking People and German Heritage: Nazi Germany and the Problem of *Volksgemeinschaft* *Norbert Götz* 58

PART 2. **Bonds of Trade and Culture** **83**

CHAPTER 4. Blond and Blue-Eyed in Mexico City, 1821 to 1975 *Jürgen Buchenau* 85

CHAPTER 5. Jews, Germans, or Americans? German-Jewish Immigrants in the Nineteenth-Century United States *Tobias Brinkmann* 111

CHAPTER 6. German Landscape: Local Promotion of the *Heimat* Abroad *Thomas Lekan* 141

CHAPTER 7. In Search of Home Abroad: German Jews in Brazil, 1933–45 *Jeffrey Lesser* 167

PART 3. Islands of Germanness   **185**

CHAPTER 8. Germans from Russia: The Political Network of
a Double Diaspora   *Renate Bridenthal*   187

CHAPTER 9. When Is a Diaspora Not a Diaspora? Rethinking
Nation-Centered Narratives about Germans in
Habsburg East Central Europe   *Pieter Judson*   219

CHAPTER 10. German *Brigadoon*? Domesticity and
Metropolitan Germans' Perceptions of
Auslandsdeutschen in Southwest Africa
and Eastern Europe   *Nancy R. Reagin*   248

CHAPTER 11. Tenuousness and Tenacity: The *Volksdeutschen*
of Eastern Europe, World War II, and
the Holocaust   *Doris L. Bergen*   267

CHAPTER 12. The Politics of Homeland: Irredentism and
Reconciliation in the Policies of German
Federal Governments and Expellee
Organizations toward Ethnic German
Minorities in Central and Eastern Europe,
1949–99   *Stefan Wolff*   287

List of Contributors   313
Index   317

Abbreviations

AA	Auswärtiges Amt (German Foreign Office)
ADV	Alldeutscher Verband (Pan-German League)
AHSGR	American Historical Society of Germans from Russia
ALR	Allgemeines Landrecht [of Prussia] (General Prussian Legal Code)
BdV	Bund der Vertriebenen—Vereinigte Landsmannschaften und Landesverbände (Union of Expellees—United Regional-Cultural Associations and State Organizations)
BHE	Bund der Heimatvertriebenen und Entrechteten (Union of Expellees and Disenfranchised) (later Gesamtdeutscher Block-Bund vertriebener Deutscher)
BvD	Bund vertriebener Deutscher (Union of Expelled Germans)
CDU	Christlich Demokratische Union (Christian Democratic Union)
CSU	Christlich Soziale Union (Christian Social Union)
DAI	Deutsches Ausland-Institut (German Foreign Institute)
DFP	*Dakota Freie Presse* (*Dakota Free Press*)
DKG	Deutsche Kolonialgesellschaft (German Colonial Society)
DNP	Departamento Nacional de Povoamento (National Population Department)
DOD	*Deutscher Ostdienst* (*German Eastern Service*)
DPO	*Deutsche Post aus dem Osten* (*German Post from the East*)
DVM	Deutsche Volksgemeinschaft in Mexiko (German Volksgemeinschaft in Mexico)
EU	European Union
FDP	Freie Demokratische Parte: (Free Democratic Party)
FstR	Forschungsstelle des Russlanddeutschtums im Deutschen Ausland-Institut (Research Office of the Russian Germandom of the DAI)
GDP	Gesamtdeutsche Partei (All-German Party)
GSWA	German Southwest Africa (now Namibia)
JCA	Jewish Colonization Association

KAM   Kehilat Anshe Maarab (Men of the West Congregation)
LDR   Landsmannschaft der Deutschen aus Russland (Regional-
        Cultural Association of Germans from Russia)
NATO   North Atlantic Treaty Organization
NSDAP National Sozialistische Deutsche Arbeiter Partei (National
        Socialist German Workers' Party [Nazi Party])
PDS   Partei des Demokratischen Sozialismus (Party of
        Democratic Socialism)
RWA   Reichswanderungsamt (Reich Emigration Office)
SIBRA Brazilian-Jewish Cultural and Beneficent Society
SPD   Sozialdemokratische Partei Deutschlands (Social
        Democratic Party [of Germany])
UHRA   United Hebrew Relief Association
VDA   Verein für das Deutschtum im Ausland (Association for
        Germans Abroad)
VDR   Verband Deutscher Reichsangehöriger (League of German
        Citizens)
VdL   Verband der Landsmannschaften (League of Regional-
        Cultural Associations) (formerly VoL)
VFG   Volksdeutsche Forschungsgemeinschaften (Volksdeutsche
        Research Collective)
VoL   Vereinigung der ostdeutschen Landsmannschaften
        (Coalition of Eastern German Regional-Cultural
        Associations) (later VdL)
VoMi   Volksdeutsche Mittelstelle (Volksdeutsche Administration
        of the SS)
VRD   Verband der Deutschen aus Russland (League of Germans
        from Russia) (later Verband der Russlanddeutschen)
YMHA   Young Men's Hebrew Association

Introduction

An idealized German village presented a charming scene for a visitor in 1933: "clean curtains fluttered in front of polished, white-framed windows, and a flower garden bloomed in front of every house. . . . the flowers of grandmother's *Heimat* grew there." Surprisingly, the settlement was in Brazil rather than Bavaria.[1] It just as easily could have been nestled in the deserts of Namibia, the steppes of the Ukraine, or the plains of the Dakotas. How did it get there? Was it really German? If so, what made it German? Communities of German speakers, scattered around the globe, have long believed that they could recreate their *Heimat* (homeland) wherever they moved and that their enclaves could remain truly German. Indeed, the roots of German language and culture developed over a wide sweep of Central and Eastern Europe. Their remnants, strewn among the Eastern European lands, the so-called Germanic *Sprachinseln* (islands of German speakers), have clung tenaciously to the soil of their forebears even as the tides of German borders have ebbed and flowed around them.

The history of Germany is inextricably tied to Germans outside the homeland. Lacking a centralized state and economy until 1871, for centuries Germans faced political and economic pressures to emigrate from Central Europe as colonists to Czarist Russia and the East. Later, Germans came as farmers, traders, and workers to the New World, settling in communities that sometimes withstood acculturation or absorption by predominant Spanish, Portuguese, and Anglo populations. Many of their enclaves maintained cultural, familial, and economic ties with the homeland. Some of the connections were sentimental and symbolic, such as celebrating a "German Christmas," reading newspapers from one's region of origin, or exchanging letters with family at home. Women did much of the work of maintaining German identity behind the scenes, in the domestic sphere. Anecdotes of ethnic German women single-handedly passing on an entire culture to their children are by no means unusual.

She had one passion, it was clear, when she declared that "my children should stay German! Therefore I have to teach them myself. On Sunday mornings we practice reading and writing. . . ." She showed me a thick, well-worn volume—Grimm's Fairy Tales. "The children want to hear these stories again and again," she said. "And then they ask about everything [in the stories] which is unfamiliar to them, because they don't see it here . . . and then I tell them about the German *Buchenwald* and about Christmas in Germany, and how things were in my Heimat."[2]

If the Heimat preserved Germanness through symbols of domesticity, institutional frameworks linking overseas Germans to the metropole were equally important. Together, German men and women overseas strove to maintain symbolic and material ties to Germany, sometimes over many generations. Many exchanges offered practical advantages, including business ties and intermarriage arrangements with Germans at home or education in Germany. Such connections could serve political purposes as well. As a popular Romantic German nationalist movement emerged in the era of Napoleon and culminated in democratic-nationalist revolutions in Berlin, Munich, Vienna, and elsewhere in the failed uprisings of 1848–49, emigrants, many of whom were political exiles, frequently carried with them a longing for the homeland and for German nationhood that tied them politically to the emerging German nation and helped their loyalties endure over generations.

Meanwhile, Prussian history was marked by expansion and conquest, particularly in Eastern Europe, where, for example, much of Polish Silesia was absorbed in the eighteenth century. Indeed, the wars with Denmark, France, and Austria that laid the foundation of the Imperial German nation, Kaiserreich, continued this pattern of territorial expansion, aimed specially at German-speaking populations in French Alsace and Lorraine and Danish Schleswig-Holstein. Austria, with its large German-speaking population, however, remained outside German domination for the time being. After establishing an unimpressive and far-flung colonial empire in Africa and Asia after 1884–85, the German state and private patriotic societies sought to redirect German emigration toward new overseas German territories in Africa and the Pacific. It was in this era that populations of Germans outside the homeland took on new fascination for Germans in the metropole. Nationalist societies lauded and aided the efforts of German settlers in the New World, Russia, and the colonies to retain and express German cultural identity through linguistic, familial, and community practices and institutions, such as private welfare organizations and schools.

The success of the German emigrants, in turn, became a justification for further expansion, even if at times unwittingly so on the part of overseas Germans. Reckless new German nationalist territorial demands in Europe and Africa emerged during military campaigns in World War I and, frustrated by the territorial losses of the Versailles settlement, even more obviously and terrifyingly under Hitler. But even in the post-1945 era, as boundaries and divisions have remained contentious, Germans abroad (especially in Eastern Europe) have made important claims on Germany and vice versa. Historically, it is clear that Germans on the geographical periphery have remained at the center of German territorial ambition, foreign policy, and even national identity.

The chapters in this volume document the dispersal and settlement of ethnic Germans across cultures that span the globe. In the process of this expansion, ethnic Germans experienced varying degrees of acculturation, assimilation, and integration into their host cultures. The concepts of assimilation and integration (and associated metaphors, such as the "melting pot") have had a long and contentious history among social scientists, especially in the United States. A full review of the uses of such terms is beyond the scope of this (or indeed almost any) anthology, since the literature is voluminous and has evolved alongside related political debates in the United States over many decades.[3] But recent work by some historians suggests that there is a consensus among many social scientists that acculturation or integration into a host (or majority) culture occurs on an individual basis; that is, individuals assimilate to varying degrees, while entire ethnic communities generally do not, as a group. And the extent to which individuals from ethnic minority groups can integrate into the majority (or core) culture varies greatly not only on an individual basis but also from one ethnic group to the next, since the majority culture will prove more hospitable (or attractive) to some ethnic minorities than to others. One intelligent summary of such recent work proposes a six-stage model of assimilation, in which individuals from one culture—over a period of generations—pass through (or choose not to pass through or are rejected and unable to complete) a number of stages on the way to assimilation. This author's model discusses phases of contact, acculturation, adaptation, accommodation, integration, and finally full assimilation into a majority or host culture.[4] The nuanced transformations allowed by this analysis well suit the population discussed in this volume.

In this volume, we refer to people who themselves claimed to be Germans as "Germans" and to the cultural markers of ethnic German identity practiced by a community as "Germanness," while recognizing that local norms and the behavior of individuals varied considerably across time and space.[5] Individuals from the German communities discussed in these chapters passed through (or stopped at) varying points on this continuum of Germanness. The largest number of German emigrants during the modern period went to the United States, where it is generally acknowledged that most German speakers melded into the core of American society within a few generations. Their absorption into American culture was accelerated by two world wars in which their country of origin was an enemy of the host country, which put great pressure on German Americans to integrate fully into American society in order to escape persecution. This process also was facilitated by their whiteness, of course. Ethnic Germans elsewhere did not assimilate into their host cultures quite so rapidly.

For example, the German emigrant community in Mexico, the subject of Jürgen Buchenau's chapter in this volume, remained relatively separate from its Mexican host culture for many generations and has only adapted and integrated into mainstream Mexican culture within the last forty years. The Russian Germans discussed by Renate Bridenthal underwent the most halting, complex, and back-and-forth process of assimilation of all the German communities included in this book. Individuals from this community adapted and accommodated to Russian Imperial culture and society, and some of them emigrated to the United States after World War I, where they became acculturated to an even greater degree. But the community itself developed a tenacious and separate group ethnic identity, that of "Russian Germans," and maintained far-flung political and cultural networks. As Nancy Reagin and Doris Bergen show, the varied groups of ethnic Germans scattered across Central and Eastern Europe were idealized by nationalists in Germany as essentialized examples of German ethnic character. However, the reality that German occupation authorities confronted after 1939 included many individuals who had passed through most (or even all) of the six stages of assimilation and whose ethnic identity was indeterminate.

Beyond trying to define who is German and what makes them so, this volume seeks to reconceptualize German identity in global terms. How then should we describe Germans living outside of Germany? Are they migrants? Ex-colonists? Ethnic minorities? Enclaves? A diaspora? So much depends on definition. *Diaspora* is a much-used term these days and could easily serve to contain the variety of groups our contributors describe in this volume. However, current scholarship resists such an inflated use without careful definition. Recent scholarship reminds us of the origin of the word in Greek antiquity: *speiro* (to sow) and *dia* (over), referring to Greek colonists' settling of the ancient world.[6] Its connection to forced exile refers back to the Jewish experience of the destruction of Jerusalem and its temple in 586 BC.[7] Since then, however, the term *diaspora* has been expanded to include many kinds of peoples living outside their country of origin, regardless of whether they immerse themselves in a host culture or maintain ties with their homelands.

Many scholars distinguish migrants in settled enclaves and borderland identities from true diasporas, for which historian Robin Cohen proposes the following typology: victim, labor, imperial, trade, or cultural diaspora.[8] Some groups, he argues, may fit into more than one type; for example, Chinese and Indian migrants may include both traders and laborers, or Jews may be both victims and traders or laborers. Nevertheless, to qualify as a diaspora, the group should share some basic features: dispersal from a common homeland; a collective memory, myth, and idealization of the homeland; a commitment to its maintenance or creation; the development of a return movement; strong ethnic group consciousness sustained over a long time; a troubled relationship with host societies; and empathy and solidarity with co-ethnic members in other countries.[9] As we shall see in the case studies contained in this volume, some ethnic German communities meet this more stringent definition of diaspora, while others fall short. We posit both the historical existence of a German diaspora and its uniqueness. At the same time, we recognize that the German diaspora, like others, does not involve all communities and individuals equally, nor is it unchanging over time.

The importance of maintaining links with one another, but especially with the homeland, is stressed by most scholars of diasporas. Gabriel Sheffer some time ago asked for more research on the triangular networks between homeland, host land, and diaspora population.[10] Recent issues of the journal *Diaspora* confirm this emphasis. One author insists that "(d)iaspora must refer to maintenance of institutionalized ties" and that diasporic culture produces "an imaginary of exile" by perpetuating exchanges with other elements of diaspora.[11] Another narrows this definition even more by claiming that diasporas are "deeply implicated both ideologically and materially in the nation-alist projects of their homelands."[12] The journal's editor requires even more firmly that "the distinguishing diasporic feature" be a multitiered minority led by a small elite committed to mobilizing the rest into a stateless lobby protecting the interests of the group as a whole and pos-sibly also its homeland.[13]

How then are we to understand the various emigrant Germans rep-resented in this collection? The experiences of other displaced people might provide a clue. Perhaps closest to the German is the Italian case. Here Donna Gabaccia's *Italy's Many Diasporas* has provided a fruitful perspective.[14] Like so many of the German emigrants, Italians came from villages not yet incorporated into a nation-state. Consequently, they carried local identities that Gabaccia calls "plural diasporas." Eventually, these village identities merged to form "Little Italies," whose loyalty was contested and reinforced by different organized entities: regional associations, the Catholic Church, international labor organizations, and finally fascist and antifascist political groups. As in German history, Italy's governing classes sometimes dreamed of making an empire of its migrants, and in both cases those enterprises failed, but meanwhile new sorts of plural diasporas had formed. Gabaccia distinguishes other sorts of diasporic pluralism as well, notably those of class and gender. If a single Italian diaspora is to be heuristically possible, she concludes, it resides in the notion of the transnational circulatory character of the migrations from and to Italy.

Here, however, the Italian and German cases diverge, as migrant Germans tended not, as a rule, to circulate back and forth but instead to form lasting institutional ties between foreign enclaves and the homeland. As this volume shows, they set out primarily as economic elites who were occasionally also political and religious exiles (chapters 4, 5, and 7) or as farmers and colonists (chapters 2, 8, and 10), or else, without moving, they found themselves suddenly ethnic minorities in newly created states following the collapse of the Austro-Hungarian and Russian Empires after World War I. Unlike Italians, who Gabac-cia describes as distrustful of the state, Germans were inclined to look toward it: indeed, it was often a welcome preserver of international networks. It is perhaps most obviously Germany's unique approach to citizenship that forged lasting legal ties to its diasporic population even as successive governments aided in promoting institutional ties around the globe.

Sociologist Rogers Brubaker offers helpful conceptualizations regarding the complex relationship between minority ethnic identity and loyalty to a foreign state such as the ties found between Eastern European German speakers and successive historic German states.[15] He refers to the Germans "stranded" under "alien" rule in successor states to the Habsburg Empire and in Poland as enclaves whose relationship to the successive German governments—the German Reich, the Weimar Republic, the Nazi state, and the Federal Republic of Germany—depended on historical contingencies that sometimes led to ethnic mobilization and sometimes did not. Thus, the founding of the German Reich in 1870–71 created a potential external national homeland for the eight million Austrian Germans and later for the Baltic Germans and colonists in the Volga and Black Sea regions threatened by Russification; the Hungarian Germans threatened by Magyarization; and the growing Czech, Slovak, and Slovene national movements in the Habsburg Empire.[16]

Should these German-speaking peoples in Eastern and Central Europe be considered a diaspora? In this volume, Pieter Judson argues that not all of them should be, because the settlers and colonists in the Hapsburg Empire were only imagined as such by German nationalist historians who confused the bounded state with a fictive larger nation residing in Eastern multinational empires. Judson rightly points to the lack of connection between ethnic Germans in the Dual Monarchy and the Imperial German state (1870–1919). In doing so, he confirms the historical importance of cultural definitions of Germanness over biological, territorial, and state-centered notions that this volume's authors propose.

Judson's view also corresponds with that of Brubaker, who contends that it remained for the Weimar Republic to "crystallize" an external national homeland for those identifying as ethnic German citizens in other states. Defeat in World War I and the loss of territory cost the state much of its integrative power, so "nationalism was partially de-territorialized and de-institutionalized." It was reoriented to *Deutschtumspolitik,* further nourished by the flow of ethnic German resettlers (*Auslandsdeutsche*) to Germany from the Baltic states, the Sudetenland, Russia, and Central Europe. This "homeland nationalism" took the form of unashamedly irredentist associations seeking restoration of former territories and colonies, ostensibly private but "discreetly" financed and controlled by the Weimar Republic.[17] The Nazi state appropriated these structures and aggressively transformed them into outright bids for German hegemony in East Central Europe and the Balkans.[18] And it tried to make loyal fifth columns of Germans abroad in distant lands, with varying or limited success.

Before 1871, late by other nations' standards, there was no central German nation of which to speak. Over the past several centuries, ethnic identity rather than citizenship preeminently defined who was German. This accounts in part for the peculiarity of the German diaspora. The shifting German nation-states confronted a complex web of diverse claimants to German ethnicity outside their borders rather than a coherent imagined national community of Germans, to borrow the well-known phrase from Benedict Anderson. Although Brubaker typifies this historical evolution of Germanness, perhaps too simplistically and teleologically, as "an organic cultural, linguistic, or racial community—as an irreducibly particular *Volksgemeinschaft,*"[19] his work has merit in recognizing the singularities in the evolution of German citizenship defined through genealogical descent and the broader ethnocultural basis of Germanness. Other scholars posit a tension between *völkisch* and ethnocultural models of Germanness as early as the eighteenth and nineteenth centuries, in which prestatehood German identity was divergently articulated either as a transnational community of descent or as a *Kulturnation* best characterized by the ideal of high culture (*Bildung*). Völkisch understandings of Germanness lent themselves to a racialized vision of the nation articulated under National Socialism. The second, cultural model represented a national identity that was more democratic and was embraced by many Jewish—and Christian—Germans.[20] In practice, however, these two strands of nationalism were not always clearly distinct, as Norbert Götz's chapter in this volume indicates.

We ascribe to a model of German identity that is less dependent on the nation-state for its definitions and trace the competing racial and cultural criteria delimiting "Germanness" within a web of many strains of nationalism in German history. We argue that successive German states have pursued citizenship and ethnic policies in response to their concerns at the time and, excepting the Hitler dictatorship, generally have been susceptible to the pressures of domestic and international lobbies.

Myriad recent historical writings have demonstrated this complex, dynamic, and ever-changing tenor of German national identity: the ongoing significance of gender, locality, particular interest groups, successive German nation-states, and social classes in enshrining and preserving the competing and overlapping versions of German identity.[21] However, these writings on German nationalism, especially where they privilege local or regional powers and affiliations (Heimat), overlook to a great extent how even local identities extended over the globe and existed within the context of the diaspora, as Lekan's chapter in this volume on the Eifel region's homeland societies elaborates. German speakers within and outside strict political borders often identified themselves and were recognized as Germans, and émigré populations contributed centrally to the formation of German national identity.

Thus, this volume challenges the nation-state as the basis of German nationalism. Overall, the history of Germany has too often ignored the influence of Germans outside of Germany, not only in Central and Eastern Europe but in enclaves, colonies, and diasporic communities around the world. Overseas Germans' visions of themselves and their homeland influenced those of the metropole, where, in turn, they not only fed the national illusion of self but sometimes even reciprocated by idealizing displaced populations. Indeed, the myth of the extraterritorial German, who had been wrongfully excluded through the redrawing of national boundaries after World War I, enlarged Germans' ambitions for global power and played a destabilizing role in German politics after 1918. It is no accident or aberration that the largest volunteer organization in Weimar Germany was the Association for Germans Abroad (Verein für das Deutschtum im Ausland, or VDA), with three million members.[22] The VDA and similar private associations successfully tapped into state funding and power but served their private memberships' purposes as well in inflating their self-importance by aggrandizing German culture around the globe. Moreover, the historical context suggests that the German diaspora continued to destabilize German politics in the postwar era, preventing normalization with the German Democratic Republic in part due to the cold war influence of irredentist groups (*Heimatvertriebenenverbände*), as Wolff's chapter in this volume indicates. The contributors to this volume argue that patterns of migration, particularly those that resulted in a tenacious diasporic network, have uniquely shaped Germanness and, moreover, that a historical approach provides an ideal perspective for understanding how German identity has been forged. We trace how the German state changed in response to the evolving German diaspora. Most importantly, through this history of ethnic inclusion and exclusion, we confront why Germanness has always been and remains a problem.

Part 1 of this volume—The Legal and Ideological Context of Diasporic Nationalism—takes up the vexed question of claimants to German citizenship and state policies toward diasporic communities. Each chapter in turn traces how the existence of the diaspora disrupted debates over citizenship law and established the legal context for constant exchange, due to the still extant legal right of return for extraterritorial Germans. Howard Sargent reviews German citizenship law to 1914, highlighting the disputed 1913 revision to Imperial citizenship policies and evaluating the impact of recent revisions in German naturalization policies in light of this history. Krista O'Donnell then carries the debate forward by considering the tangled claims to German citizenship presented by miscegenation in the overseas colonies before 1914. Norbert Götz continues the discussion of German citizenship policies through the Weimar and Nazi eras with an analysis of the many competing definitions of Germanness and Volksgemeinschaft. Thus, this introductory section outlines the complicated and poorly understood history of German citizenship laws and policies and firmly establishes the overarching centrality of immigration and emigration policy to legal and cultural definitions of Germanness. The three authors suggest to varying degrees the powerful role of private interest groups in shaping state definitions of citizenship and policies toward ethnic Germans living outside German borders.

Part 2—Bonds of Trade and Culture—offers four case studies of diasporic ties between Germany and extraterritorial German enclaves. This section offers a concrete view of German overseas settlements and suggests common patterns for the maintenance and the deterioration of Germanness in these communities. Ethnic colonies held on to their identities not only through the formal bonds connecting them to the German state or cultural bonds of association but also through direct, informal ties: family, travel, trade, and other economic links that led some ethnic Germans to remain closer to home than others. Jürgen Buchenau highlights the basis for the staunch Germanness of the Mexico City colony; Thomas Lekan traces the international influence of the Eifel region's homeland societies on German identity; Tobias Brinkmann outlines the intertwined ethnic, cultural, and religious identities of German American Jews in Chicago; while Jeffrey Lesser examines the German-Jewish influence on Jewish settlement of interwar Brazil. Since the Jewish diaspora was the first and is often perceived as definitive, it is interesting that Jews in the cases presented here all identified closely with the German Kulturnation, as well as in varying degrees with their coreligionists. In many instances, adhering to German ties and identities bestowed practical benefits on German-Jewish enclaves. Moreover, the attraction of Bildung as an inclusive bond of Germanness maintained a sense of "cultivation" and belonging for German Jews abroad.

These chapters detail the complex local accounts of overseas Germans' articulations of ethnic identity through their evolving ideologies and lived experiences. Each author amplifies how various diasporic communities confronted the politics and demands of their host countries and suggests how and why diasporic networks proved advantageous both economically and culturally in some contexts but not in others. In particular, each one examines how German colonies abroad mediated between the attractions and perils of acculturation with host cultures and balanced the demands and challenges in their new locales with their desire to maintain valuable international networks, including political, economic, cultural, and social ties to the metropole. Nationalists deliberately obfuscated gender and tended to keep women out of most of the key institutions within the diaspora; nevertheless, household, marriage, and reproduction are recurring themes in these chapters as vehicles for the transmission and maintenance of national identity. While family and personal ties were important in sustaining diasporic networks, broader cultural and institutional connections had more obvious influence on the evolution of German identity in the metropole, and here, as well, gender played a key, if sometimes submerged, role in defining Germanic cultural norms, particularly within the construct of Heimat.

Part 3—Islands of Germanness—turns to the special circumstances of German settlements in Central and Eastern Europe. First, Renate Bridenthal examines how a network of intellectual elites consciously constructed the "double diasporic" identity of Germans from Russia on three continents. Pieter Judson then discusses how German speakers in the pre– and post–World War I Hapsburg Empire explicitly defined their Germanness through their regional identities and their Austrianness. Next, Nancy Reagin depicts the gendered construction of Germanness as expressed through the domestic practices of Germans in Eastern Europe. Doris Bergen details the logic behind National Socialist efforts to identify and racially categorize ethnic German individuals and communities in the occupied Eastern Territories and presents the difficulties and contradictions inherent in imposing ethnic and racial labels on a diverse population. Finally, Stefan Wolff offers an overview of the efforts of successive German federal governments and various expellee organizations to preserve German minority identities in Poland and the Czech Republic between 1945 and 1999. Judson's piece problematizes the centrality of the minority population's relationship to the German state before 1914 and the use of the term *diaspora* when defined narrowly in terms of the Kaiserreich borders. However, in many ways his chapter supports the others in this section, which show how the complexities of German identity in Eastern Europe, as well as foreign policy in the region historically, have been formulated through the interaction between specific diasporic communities and the metropole. Each case demonstrates the intense conversations that took place between ethnic Germans at home and abroad in negotiating the meaning of German identity through the lens of Heimat. There is an ongoing struggle documented here, in which succeeding German regimes attempted with varying success to define or control "Germanness" abroad in opposition to cultural, biological, or regionally based notions of Germanness maintained in diasporic communities. As a whole, part 3 establishes the persistent basis for the maintenance of German identity over time in illusory symbolic constants that created bonds between private citizens: common landscape, home, and high culture (Bildung).

The enduring cultural tropes that form the basis for German ethnic and national identity make the history of the German diaspora influential within the current German debate over immigration. In the past, Germany sent forth emigrants, but now it takes them in. Since 1990 ethnic Germans from the East, especially from Russia, have employed the right of return to migrate in ever greater numbers into the reunified Germany. Ethnicity, loosely defined, has been the standard and litmus test of German identity and remains stubbornly so even in the global age, for all its claims to multiculturalism. Culture, commerce, democracy, each heavily influenced by American and other Western flavors, became icons of postwar German identity.[23] All of these, ironically, have made present-day Germany a land both attractive to and ambivalent toward foreigners. We have seen a resurgence of Jewish immigration since the fall of the Soviet Union, with Germany being the second largest site of relocation for Jews, after Israel.[24] It is the world's second largest recipient of immigration, after the United States, with 11 percent of the population being foreign born; nonetheless, most Germans persistently consider their nation and their national identity in ethnic terms.[25]

Historian Klaus Bade has noted the difficulty with which Germany now faces her transition from emigrant nation to immigrant destination and consciously advocates the inclusiveness of American society as a model for integration.[26] As Sargent's chapter indicates, sweeping changes in German citizenship and naturalization laws, although limited in scope, nonetheless are resulting in new claimants to citizenship, whose presence undoubtedly will transform German national identity. Since 1990 German investment in Eastern European states and their imminent admission to the European Union have brought about porous boundaries with the former Eastern bloc. Because of these developments, Germany's demographic future no longer lies with its diaspora, and citizenship may no longer pose such a sticky question in the future. The thorniest debates over revising immigration will likely move Germany toward a new definition of citizenship and nationality, whose focus will be naturalization rather than diaspora.

NOTES

1. Maria Kahle, *Deutsches Volk in der Fremde* (Oldenburg, 1933), 13–14. All translations are our own unless otherwise noted.

2. Kahle, *Deutsches Volk,* 13–14.

3. For an introduction to and summary of recent scholarly debates on the use of these concepts, see Russel A. Kazal, "Revisiting Assimilation: The Rise, Fall, and Reappraisal of a Concept," *American Historical Review* 100 (1995): 437–71; see also the succinct summary of earlier work on ethnicity and assimilation in Marion Berghahn, *German-Jewish Refugees in England: The Ambiguities of Assimilation* (London, 1984), 9–20. Finally, Phillip Gleason offers a magisterial overview of the history and usage of such terms as *melting pot, assimilation,* and *minority* since the late nineteenth century in *Speaking of Diversity: Language and Ethnicity in Twentieth Century America* (Baltimore, 1992), 3–151.

4. See Elliot Barkin, "Race, Religion, and Natality in American Society: A Model of Ethnicity from Contact to Assimilation," *Journal of American Ethnic History* 14 (1995): 38–75. Barkin offers clear and comprehensive definitions and descriptions of each of his proposed stages and discusses differences in the degrees to which individuals from varying ethnic groups have been able (or willing) to assimilate into mainstream American culture (e.g., differences in the degrees to which individuals from such minority or immigrant groups as the Amish, the Irish, the Hmongs, the French Canadians, Sephardic Jews, African Americans, Puerto Ricans, and Germans have melded into the broader American culture).

5. Walker Connor, *Ethnonationalism: The Quest for Understanding* (Princeton, 1994), 75, argues that most national groups are "the variegated offspring of a number of peoples . . . but it is not *what is,* but *what people believe is* that has behavioral consequences. A nation is a group of people characterized by a myth of common descent."

6. Robin Cohen, *Global Diasporas: An Introduction* (Seattle, 1997), ix.

7. Cohen, *Global Diasporas,* 3.

8. Cohen, *Global Diasporas,* x.

9. Cohen, *Global Diasporas,* 26.

10. Gabriel Sheffer, "A New Field of Study: Modern Diasporas in International Politics," in *Modern Diasporas in International Politics,* ed. Gabriel Sheffer (New York, 1986), 7.

11. Dominique Schnapper, "From the Nation-State to the Transnational

World: On the Meaning and Usefulness of Diaspora as a Concept," *Diaspora, 8,* no. 3 (1999): 235, 251.

12. Pnina Werbner, "Introduction: The Materiality of Diaspora—Between Aesthetic and 'Real' Politics," *Diaspora* 9, no. 1 (2000): 5.

13. Khachig Tölölyan, "Rethinking Diasporas(s): Stateless Power in the Transnational Moment," *Diaspora* 9, no.1 (2000): 19.

14. Donna R. Gabaccia, *Italy's Many Diasporas* (Seattle, 2000), especially the introduction and chapters 5 and 6.

15. Rogers Brubaker, *Nationalism Reframed: Nationhood and the National Question in the New Europe* (Cambridge, 1996), chapters 5 and 6.

16. Brubaker, *Nationalism Reframed,* 114–16.

17. Brubaker, *Nationalism Reframed,* 117–23.

18. Brubaker, *Nationalism Reframed,* 134.

19. Rogers Brubaker, *Citizenship and Nationhood in France and Germany* (Cambridge, Mass., 1992), 1.

20. Helmut Plessner, *Verspätete Nation: Über die politische Verführbarkeit des bürgerlichen Geistes,* 5th ed. (Frankfurt, 1994); Paul Mendes-Flohr, *German Jews: A Dual Identity* (New Haven, Conn., 1999), 4.

21. Key studies of interest groups and the bourgeoisie include the classic by Geoff Eley, *Reshaping the German Right: Radical Nationalism and Political Change after Bismarck,* 2d ed. (Ann Arbor, Mich., 1991); a dizzying array of recent work stresses regional German identity, including Alon Confino, *The Nation as Local Metaphor: Württemberg, Imperial Germany, and National Memory, 1871–1918* (Chapel Hill, N.C., 1997); Abigail Green, *Fatherlands: State-Building and Nationhood in Nineteenth-Century Germany* (Cambridge, 2001); Jean Quataert, *Staging Philanthropy: Patriotic Women and the National Imagination in Dynastic Germany, 1813–1916* (Ann Arbor, Mich., 2001).

22. Walter v. Goldendach und Hans-Rüdiger Minow, *"Deutschtum Erwache!" Aus dem Innenleben des staatlichen Pangermanismus* (Berlin, 1994), 55, 129; Gerhard Weidenfeller, *VDA. Verein für das Deutschtum im Ausland. Allgemeiner Deutscher Schulverein (1881–1918): Ein Beitrag zur Geschichte des deutschen Nationalismus und Imperialismus im Kaisserreich* (Frankfurt, 1976), 325.

23. Werner Weidenfeld, ed., *Die Identität der Deutschen* (Munich, 1983).

24. Antje Harnisch, Anne Marie Stokes, and Friedemann Weidauer, eds., *Fringe Voices: An Anthology of Minority Writing in the Federal Republic of Germany* (Oxford, 1998), 24.

25. Peter Schuck and Rainer Münz, eds., *Paths to Inclusion: The Integration of Migrants in the United States and Germany,* vol. 5 of *Migration and Refugees: Politics and Policies in the United States and Germany* (New York, 1998), vii–x.

26. Klaus Bade, ed., *Population, Labour, and Migration in 19th- and 20th-Century Germany,* vol. 1 of *German Historical Perspectives* (New York, 1987); Klaus Bade and Myron Weiner, eds., *Migration Past, Migration Future: Germany and the United States,* vol. 1 of *Migration and Refugees: Politics and Policies in the United States and Germany* (New York, 1997).

PART 1

The Legal and Ideological Context of Diasporic Nationalism

Germans' preoccupation with their diaspora predates the existence of Germany as a nation. Indeed, the disunity of the various German states in the early nineteenth century, combined with the growing pressures of internal and overseas migration, compelled individual states to define quite consciously who was a citizen and who was not. Uniquely relying on birth and heritage as key criteria for citizenship, these states sought to maintain ties to extraterritorial Germans even while denying immigrant populations access to state welfare services. The historical evolution of citizenship in Germany shows great continuity over time. From the foundation of the Kaiserreich in 1870 until today, persons demonstrating German extraction who are alienated from the state by geographical boundaries may still legally claim German national citizenship, while many residents lacking German heritage have been denied such citizenship. Moreover, popular German national identity also historically has perceived German ancestry as the essential basis of Germanness and thus has defined the diaspora as part of the nation. Legally and ideologically, then, Germans abroad have always been Germans first and foremost to the homeland. In some ways, diasporic Germans have been symbolically and historically more important than their metropolitan counterparts, not only because they serve to refract and aggrandize popular German self-perceptions within the homeland but also because representing their interests, and even reclaiming this population and its territory, has remained a core principle of German foreign policy and German nationalists' lobbying for as long as there has been a Germany.

This is not to say that, amid the continuity of the diaspora in German awareness, there have not been breaks or shifts in thinking about Germans abroad or their legal status. On the contrary, as the chapters in this section demonstrate, German citizenship policies have undergone major revisions in reaction to new circumstances, most markedly but not exclusively during the Nazi dictatorship. Successive German states in the twentieth century, like other modern nations, have balanced between their own foreign policy objectives and the views of their population. Given the weight of the diaspora on German consciousness, metropolitan Germans' popular self-perceptions have often aligned with nationalists' pressures to foster diasporic ties and to exclude immigrants of other ethnicities from citizenship, especially those of color. As Howard Sargent's chapter on German citizenship law shows, the ideological precursors to Nazi racial and citizenship policies existed in Wilhelmine Germany but did not predominate the debates over emigration, the nation-state's interests, and the push for greater inclusion of diasporic Germans in the 1913 revisions to the German citizenship law. Moreover, legal questions were not the only means of defining Germanness along diasporic lines, as Krista O'Donnell's chapter details. Her discussion highlights the uneasy relationship between race, German citizenship, and colonial population policies in the Wilhelmine period, demonstrating the stark contradictions between the tolerance of German citizenship laws toward biracial individuals and the harsh treatment of Afro-Germans in the colonies and metropole.

Unlike the continuities in legal debates of the Kaiserreich and the late twentieth century, the Nazis recast citizenship laws and policies wholesale to accommodate their racial delusions, military goals, and political expedience with little regard for opposing viewpoints. As Norbert Götz's chapter details, however, the Nazi vision of the supranational German racial community (*Volksgemeinschaft*) undermined the institution of national citizenship laws and often offended overseas Germans with its dictatorial demands, even as it coexisted uneasily with the many divergent views of diasporic Germans articulated in the 1930s. By placing Nazi views of citizenship and German identity in their historic context, the continuities and breaks of the Nazi era are set in stark relief. In the postwar era, the cold war and division of Germany led the Federal Republic to reemphasize their claims on the diasporic population of Germans in Eastern Europe within their citizenship laws and foreign policy, views that helped ensure the strong interests of Germany in soviet Eastern Europe. With the relaxation of these concerns and the most recent revision of German citizenship laws in 2000, which has eased naturalization policies somewhat, whether or not the peculiar importance of the diaspora will continue to define the legal and ideological meaning of Germanness in the future remains to be seen.

CHAPTER 1

Diasporic Citizens

Germans Abroad in the Framing of German Citizenship Law

Howard Sargent

The state's relationship to ethnic Germans abroad, as expressed in German citizenship laws, went through a substantial evolution during the nineteenth and twentieth centuries. This chapter can only present an overview of these developments, but I hope to suggest which societal developments most influenced citizenship legislation and shifting definitions of the national community in the long term. Changing patterns of immigration and emigration have been central to shaping Germany's unique citizenship policies, often in unintended ways. In addition to outlining the successive legislative attempts to define Germanness, this chapter highlights situations in which closely held understandings of German identity came into conflict with each other as a result of new population challenges. Examining the history of debate over citizenship reminds us of the lack of uniformity that historically has characterized Germanness.

The debates over citizenship nevertheless also demonstrated great continuities. Legal discourse generally privileged the inclusion of overseas Germans and encouraged the exclusion of newcomers to Germany from citizenship. Historically, most scholars have agreed that blood descent has been privileged over ethnicity in the legal determination of Germanness. Moreover, although their content has changed significantly, competing biological and cultural definitions of Germanness continue to influence citizenship law in the present, which works against the naturalization of new immigrants. Tracing the continuities in debates over citizenship serves to demonstrate the similarities as well as the differences between the issues involved in the 1999 amendment of the citizenship law—intended to ease naturalization—and reform efforts in the past.

This chapter discusses German citizenship in the sense of the word *Staatsangehörigkeit,* the legal condition of belonging to a (nation-) state.[1] In German, there are other terms to describe participatory citizenship and nationality. The semantic differences emphasize how state building, nationalism, and democracy—which were crystallized in the French case by the Revolution—followed different paths in first the regional German states (*Länder*) of the German Confederation and later unified Germany. The ongoing development of Staatsangehörigkeit as a legal category reflects Germany's transition from a loose union of autonomous states to a centralized federal state, as well as successive governments' responses to the new problems posed by shifts in immigration and emigration over two centuries.[2]

Three time periods have been most crucial to the evolution of citizenship in the territories that later formed Germany. The first was the early nineteenth century, as individual Länder first outlined the local, preunification conditions of citizenship in the German states during the state-building efforts that spanned from the French Revolution to the eve of German unification. The second era began a generation later, following unification, when massive overseas emigration began to undermine existing citizenship laws. Over the course of the nineteenth and early twentieth centuries, as Germans' mobility expanded from interstate to intercontinental migration, the challenge shifted from regulating the movement of ethnic Germans between the German states to redefining the legal relationship between the new nation-state and its overseas citizens. The subsequent rise of massive internal migration to industrial centers, the foundation of Germany's colonial empire, and the development of a strident middle-class nationalism each, in turn, further complicated the problem of regulating citizenship. The citizenship debates of the Wilhelmine era culminated in the new German citizenship law of 1913, which remained in force until the Nazi era and was reinstituted after 1945. Finally, in the postwar era, the contentiousness of the most recent revisions to citizenship law in Germany reveals that many of the conflicts and tensions that dominated the discussion at the beginning of the nineteenth and twentieth centuries persist into the twenty-first.

Citizenship Laws in the German Länder before Unification

Throughout the period from 1815 to 1870, the standards for citizenship in a German state remained contentious: Should citizenship be determined by individuals' ethnic and cultural heritage or restricted to those who had given active service to their state of residence? Not only migration between German states but, even more problematically, the increasing transatlantic outflow complicated this equation. When an individual moved from one state to another, problems developed as former states sought to determine the legal privileges and obligations of absent citizens. Länder asserted that when their expatriated citizens failed to perform their civic duties, such as military service, they abrogated the social contract and jeopardized their status as citizens. As the Länder came to define citizenship primarily through descent, resolving the legal contradictions that absentee Germans and non-German residents posed became more pressing. Germans living overseas represented the greatest challenge, since ethnically and culturally they met the key criteria of citizenship. The problem was compounded by the growing numbers of immigrants who were not of German descent yet performed the duties expected of citizens.[3]

In describing the historical development of the Prussian state in the era between the promulgation of the reformist General Prussian Legal Code (Allgemeines Landrecht, or ALR) in 1794 and the revolution of 1848, Reinhart Koselleck points out the complex negotiations between revolutionaries, reformers, and political functionaries in revising citizenship legislation. The ALR and the Great Reforms, along with the massive impact of the revolutionary era, set social changes in motion that rendered the old political system impractical. These changes combined with legislative efforts to reshape German society and to force a revision of the approach to state membership, compelling the codification of citizenship law.[4]

The ALR united an enlightened conception of the state and society with guarantees for special legal classes (*Stände*), for example, the nobles and guilds. The ALR's provisions for reforming and strengthening the Prussian state led to a more direct, less mediated role for the state in the lives of its inhabitants. The ALR established the Prussian legal system as a potential vehicle for change, and the Prussian state became the sole legitimate source of the law.[5] With the new code, the Stände lost their special status as feudal corporations, and the bureaucratic enforcement of a general, uniform law for all residents of the state became the norm. This leveling function laid the groundwork for a general civic status to replace the privileges of the old order. Prussian reformers sought to initiate a "revolution from above" that reshaped the Prussian administrative structure, basing it on practical needs rather than traditional loyalties and lines of authority.[6] In Prussia, then, because the privileged orders of the absolutist state laid the foundations of citizenship law—rather than a revolution from below, as took place in France and the United States—the ALR preserved and centralized the feudal corporations. Civic membership in the Prussian state still was mediated through the old Stände.[7]

Beyond Prussia, other German state governments enacted reforms with similar goals: strengthening the state and increasing the loyalty of its citizens.[8] Citizenship laws in states such as Baden and Hesse streamlined the organization of local communities, subordinated home towns and the Stände to the state's authority, and introduced freedom of movement and equal citizenship relations among state members. Citizenship in Hesse, for example, could be gained by birth, naturalization, marriage to a male citizen, or service to the state, as well as lost by emigration, marriage to a male foreigner, or expulsion from the civil service.[9]

The Prussian reforms, however, served as a model for legal definitions of citizenship throughout the nineteenth century in the German states. The centralization of authority through these reforms paved the way for the state to displace the local and occupational prerogatives of the old system. The reforms also set social and economic forces in motion that led the German states to develop an externally exclusive conception of membership, which tended to exclude newcomers and the poor. Particularly as the liberation of the peasants and the advent of occupational freedom loosened the ties of the old order, the combination of rural overpopulation, increased mobility, and the dissolution of the traditional system of poor relief brought about a significant increase in the number of immigrant poor.[10] By removing the protections of the old system, the reforms redefined the states' obligations to their inhabitants.

Prussia and the other German states responded to the migrant poor by defining membership more precisely in order to limit their obligation for support and to deport nonresident beggars and the indigent. German states increasingly shifted definitions of citizenship from territorial criteria to the principle of descent, which offered a more stable basis for membership than residence and effectively excluded dependent newcomers from obligatory welfare relief.[11] In discussing the 1820s and 1830s, historian Andreas Fahrmeir contends that independent persons could achieve naturalization through extended domicile but acknowledges the large number of dependents and paupers who could not do so. The majority of Germans with citizenship in a state gained it from their paternity or marriage. Moreover, he notes that states discriminated against minority religious confessions, especially

Jews, in conferring naturalization.[12] It seems fair to conclude that early forms of state citizenship in Germany tended to employ the principle of descent as the key basis for citizenship not as a biological definition of Germanness but simply to exclude alien immigrants, many of whom were ethnically German.

German states' efforts to coordinate their disparate poor relief and deportation programs came to form the foundation for a common regulation of state membership. The legal term for citizenship, *Staatsangehörigkeit,* first appeared in these treaties between states regulating expulsions. In general, these agreements regarded the descendent of a citizen born in the state as "the state member par excellence." By spelling out who was counted as a state member, the treaties now redefined citizenship to exclude newcomers. The 1842 Prussian citizenship law,[13] introduced along with related laws governing freedom of movement and rights to poor relief, explicitly eliminated the right to naturalization in the Prussian state through extended residence. In addition, the Prussian government also revoked the citizenship of Prussians who emigrated. Former migrants who returned were not welcomed back but were rather feared as potential recipients of poor relief.

The Prussians thus consciously framed the 1842 law as an exclusionary piece of legislation. Exclusion was not based on ethnic or cultural considerations, however, but rather was guided by simple economics and occasioned by greater freedom of mobility. Indeed, foreigners from other German states had to meet the same minimum criteria as non-Germans for naturalization. For example, ethnically Polish citizens of Prussia had the same rights as state members of Prussian descent, while German-speaking noncitizens had no civic rights.[14]

The liberal nationalist revolutions of 1848 challenged the Prussian model. Indeed, the revolutionary ideas that swept through Europe in 1848 had a disproportionate impact on the conception of German citizenship, given the short duration of the liberals' victory. Ultimately, 1848 liberals established an inclusive counterpoint to the more exclusive notions of citizenship contained in the 1842 Prussian law. In 1848 the starting position seemed to have changed from exclusion based on the interests of each single state to a new inclusiveness reflecting societal aspirations to form a unified nation-state. The Frankfurt Assembly's attempt to create a German nation-state required a definition of Germanness rather than local citizenship. Its definitions tended to be more liberal, national, and inclusive.[15] Yet the parliamentarians could not reach a consensus. Two competing criteria emerged: some favored a definition of citizenship in the nation-state based on membership in one of the constituent states, while others embraced a cultural vision of a united German nation. Both parts of this dichotomy shaped the future development of German citizenship. Moreover, the constitution of 1849 created a national tradition of basic rights granted exclusively to ethnic Germans as "fundamental rights of the German people."[16]

The Frankfurt Parliament's inclusive view of state membership did not flourish in the first years after its dissolution in 1849. During the era of Reaction that followed, and until the Wars of Unification in the 1850s and 1860s, the conservative Prussian citizenship law continued to serve as the model for regulating membership in most German states. During these two decades, a second fundamental debate over the German citizenship law emerged in the post-1848 revolution's massive emigration of Germans to the United States. The next section examines connected developments in emigration, colonial expansion, the rise of ethnic nationalism, and changing approaches to citizenship in Bismarckian Germany.

Citizenship and Emigration in the German States and Bismarckian Germany, 1850–90

A fundamental shift in the conception of citizenship and nationhood occurred between 1850 and 1890. Ethnic rivalries on the borders of the German Empire and efforts to retain ties to emigrant Germans were parts of a larger challenge to the state-centered definition of the German nation (*Staatsnation*). Rogers Brubaker theorizes that the contention centered on whether the nation should be understood as ethnonational, an ethnic and cultural community independent of the state, or as state-national, "embedded and inseparable from the institutional and territorial frame of the state."[17] The debate intensified in the later years of Bismarck's chancellorship, as increasingly influential patriotic societies bolstered the ethnocultural position, juxtaposing their vision of a *Nationalstaat*[18] to Bismarck's Staatsnation. The issue became more pressing in the second half of the nineteenth century, as emigration changed the way successive German governments viewed their relationship to former citizens.

Although mobility across borders had been an important factor in establishing new citizenship laws in the 1840s, migration after 1848 was different in scale and scope. Replacing migration among the German states, three great waves of transatlantic emigration captured the imagination of the public and the concern of German state governments. In the first wave, from 1846 to 1857, 1.3 million people left the German states. The second wave, in which nearly 1 million emigrated, began in 1864 and lasted until 1873. The final surge in emigration took the most people from Germany: 1.8 million from 1880 to 1893. Remarkably, 220,000 left in a single year, 1881.[19]

Bismarck's contention that it was not in the state's interest to accept responsibility for German expatriates limited the development of an emigration policy through the 1860s. The millions of overseas emigrants, however, eventually forced the German government to reconsider its relationship to ethnic Germans abroad. The North German Confederation's 1870 citizenship law, which the new German nation, Kaiserreich, adopted after unification, represented an effort to extend the Prussian citizenship law of 1842 to new territories acquired between 1864 and 1866 and to create uniform norms for all of the German states. The 1870 law established a federal citizenship on the basis of membership in one of the constituent states. A citizen of any German state was thus treated as a fellow national rather than as a foreigner in the other German states.[20]

The government's approach to the issue of Germans abroad in the debate over the 1870 law demonstrated the impact that emigration had had on the conception of citizenship. Under the 1842 Prussian law, ten years of uninterrupted residence abroad meant loss of citizenship. The 1870 law retained this clause but qualified it by allowing Germans abroad to retain their citizenship through registration at a consulate. Thus, Germans abroad could retain their citizenship through a simple procedure, yet the state could break its bonds to former citizens who chose to dissolve their ties to their fatherland. With this revision, the national government continued the German states' historical assertion that the contract between the state and its citizens consisted of duties as well as privileges; when Germans abroad failed to perform certain duties, they signaled their intent to break the contract and thereby surrendered their privileges.[21]

As the economic slump of the mid-1870s fueled concern about Germany's strength and as the largest wave of transatlantic emigration began at the end of the decade, emigration came to be seen as both a symptom of and a cure for Germany's malaise. The erstwhile fear of impoverished masses returning to their former state was gradually replaced by an appreciation of the value of Germans abroad for the fatherland. During Bismarck's tenure as chancellor, the image of overseas emigrants evolved from unwanted potential poor-relief recipients to a valuable national resource to be jealously preserved for their possible economic, cultural, and military uses. Patriotic writer Friedrich Fabri and other prominent emigrationists altered the conception of the national community by linking Germany's prosperity and power to its success in maintaining ties to the Germans abroad. These colonial publicists argued that emigrants did not lose their importance once they left the Reich; rather, helping them retain their Germanness was essential to the survival of the nation. Public debate over emigration now expanded the definition of Germanness to include the diaspora, which they incorporated through new national symbols. These new symbols celebrated the diasporic bonds of empire, culture, and language, promoting a "vastly broadened perspective on the definition of national issues as well as on the definition of the national community itself."[22]

Changing conceptions of citizenship that would include overseas Germans became stronger, as popular agitation increased for overseas expansion and redirecting emigration to areas of concentrated settlement where the Germans abroad could retain their Germanness. One result was the organization of a colonial movement among patriotic societies dedicated to advancing an expanded vision of the German nation. Patriotic societies played a vital role in Imperial Germany because they claimed to serve the interests of all Germans, not just the narrow interest of a particular group or party. Such national issues were important sources of unity and cohesion in the fractious Kaiserreich.[23]

With these new popular nationalist movements, the definition of the nation remained a source of dispute, however. While the official nationalism was based on the German state, the presence of millions of Germans outside the borders of the new Reich posed a serious challenge to the symbols of Bismarck's politically defined national community. Although Bismarck was able to enshrine the state as the central symbol of German nationalism, he was not able to prevent the development of new cultural and ethnic definitions of the national community among the citizenry that explicitly embraced overseas Germans. Bismarck's acquiescence to the development of colonies, however grudging, provided for an arena for emigration where migrating Germans could retain their citizenship and political ties to the metropole. Ironically, however, the popularity of the colonies as a nationalist rallying point gave further legitimacy and mass appeal to patriotic groups advocating for an expansive view of German identity beyond the state borders established in 1871.[24] This challenge to the limits of the official, state-centered nationalism inevitably influenced thinking about the citizenship law.

The patriotic and colonial societies advanced an inflated definition of the national community that reflected the ideological distance covered since the Prussian Law of 1842. Under their leadership, the popular conception of citizenship changed from a "transnational"[25] model, designed to discriminate on the basis of class rather than nationality, to an "ethnocultural" definition of the German nation, which defined citizenship as membership in the *Volk*.[26] Increasingly, too, popular nationalists imagined Germanness as racial and biological, as well as cultural. The ethnocultural accommodated the need for new forms of citizenship and new bonds between overseas Germans and the German nation that the waves of emigration, national unification, and colonial expansion had established. The popularization of German nationalism created sources of friction with the German government that became ever more strained over time.[27]

The Path to Reforming the Citizenship Law: The "National" Emigration Law of 1897 and the New Citizenship Law of 1913

German domestic politics and foreign policy were characterized by more aggressive pursuit of advantage overseas after Bismarck's fall in 1890. Kaiser Wilhelm II declared that Germany was a world power and asserted that the nation's ties to Germans abroad were vital to its interests. The kaiser voiced sentiments informed by the half century of emigration waves that had taken Germans to all corners of the globe.[28] This sense of expansion and increased power on the world stage encouraged an inclusive approach to ethnic Germans abroad. New efforts to develop emigration and citizenship legislation appropriate to the Reich's stature were the result.

The broadened definition of the national community that patriotic societies and colonial enthusiasts had advocated during Bismarck's tenure continued to play a central role in Wilhelmine Germany. In the 1890s colonial and patriotic societies like the Pan-German League (ADV) and the German Colonial Society (DKG) led a campaign for a national emigration law to direct Germany's settlement where the emigrants could retain their ties to the fatherland. National emigration policy was based on the belief that the state should help Germans who left their homeland achieve their goals abroad and serve the Reich as well. The patriotic societies' desire to maintain closer ties to the millions of Germans who had emigrated in the course of the nineteenth century illustrated the inclusive aspects of the citizenship reform debate introduced in the revolution of 1848. Their definition of the national community also contained an exclusive aspect, however. Exclusion of Polish, French, and other minorities in Germany, all those not of German descent, was the other side of the coin in deciding who was a German citizen. The more assertive nationalism evident in the Wilhelmine era also heightened tensions in the ethnic conflicts within the Reich's borders. For example, the same parties who sought to retain German nationals abroad viewed the growing Polish-speaking population with dismay.

Perceived as a source of inexpensive labor, Poles were recruited to take Germans' place in the German industrial and agricultural labor force. The anxieties produced by these migrations fed both the immediate policy of preventing immigrants from establishing longer-term residence and broader efforts to exclude them from establishing legal claims to citizenship. The politicized relationship between German transatlantic emigration and Polish migration, especially into the Eastern provinces of the Reich, played a central role in the discussion of the emigration and citizenship laws in the Kaiserreich.[29]

The perceptions of migration flows into and out of Germany in the 1890s, filtered through the more assertive nationalism of the Wilhelmine era, spurred efforts to control these movements through emigration and citizenship laws. Inflammatory statements (often by government officials)[30] promoted negative stereotypes about the immigrants and portrayed the enlarged Polish presence as a threat to German culture. After 1880, anti-Semitic and anti-Slavic prejudices guided not only immigration politics but citizenship policy as a whole.[31] Concern over the growing number of "undesirable" immigrants from the East in the 1890s subtly fed the desire to strengthen ties to ethnic Germans abroad. Perceptions of these migration flows reinforced the patriotic societies' hopes and fears for a new definition of the national community—one at once more inclusive of Germans abroad and more exclusionary toward those not of German descent.

The proposals for a national emigration policy represented a marked change from the German states' efforts to discourage emigration during the first half of the century. Until transatlantic migration proved to be a lasting phenomenon, German states considered emigration more an indication of weakness than something to be managed to fit their interests. Slowly, the government's approach to emigration policy shifted from renouncing responsibility for former citizens toward encouraging emigrants to settle in areas where they could maintain their Germanness and their loyalty to the Reich.[32] Differences remained, however, over what aspects of emigration the government should regulate and what should be left to private initiative. By advocating the creation of central government agencies to guide immigrants to selected "regions of emigration"—where they would be able to retain their ties to their fatherland—the DKG and the ADV worked to gain government support for their vision of an expanded German national community. The government passed an emigration law in 1897 after years of debate between the government and the patriotic societies over their appropriate roles in the matter.[33] The government ultimately refused to take on the burden of protecting emigrants in their new countries or to create a central imperial agency to direct migrants to the German colonies and to specific countries where they would retain their Germanness. While they could not claim to be fully satisfied with the law, the ADV and DKG did approve of the wide-ranging powers granted the chancellor in the law that would help realize many of their aims indirectly, through administrative practice.[34]

With the passage of the 1897 emigration law, the government soon moved to reform the citizenship law of 1870. The government debates over these reforms came after years of agitation by both Germans abroad and patriotic societies. These groups claimed that the existing law had failed to maintain the ethnic ties of Germans around the world and lamented particularly the talent and energy lost because of the 1870 law.[35] The ADV and DKG presented their calls for reform as a logical extension of Germany's expanded overseas presence, as well as the emigration law.

Thus, the goals of the citizenship law reforms were to make it easier for Germans abroad to retain their citizenship and to make naturalization for foreigners more difficult. The most vocal demands for change focused on the first issue, particularly on the elimination of the clause in the existing law that revoked citizenship after ten years of residence abroad. This combination of efforts to include ethnic Germans and to exclude others has been inaccurately labeled the "ethnocultural" model of citizenship,[36] since it is based on descent (*ius sanguinis*) rather than residence in the territory of a state (*ius soli*). The debate over the citizenship law in the Kaiserreich evolved into a fifteen-year discussion of the primacy of national community or the state in deriving citizenship in the German Empire. The crux of the argument was whether passive German ethnicity alone was sufficient basis for retaining citizenship for Germans abroad or whether demonstrated loyalty to the state should serve as the decisive criterion. Thus, the government's approach to citizenship for Germans abroad served as the acid test for the prioritization of nation or state.

Most scholarship to date emphasizes that German citizenship is based on such an ethnocultural model, but my research suggests that the *soli/sanguinis* dichotomy does not capture the core of the debate over the citizenship law of 1913. The question of granting citizenship on the basis of residence was not significant in the reform debate. The real question was to what lengths the government would go to insist that the state's interests took priority over popular nationalist views of German identity. I argue that the tension between the ethnocultural image of nationhood and the opposing conception of the state's interests forms the better framework for analyzing the debate over the citizenship law of 1913. Moreover, while the history of German citizenship law focuses on the issues of exclusion of non-Germans, the documents show that the central point of contention in the debate was how best to retain the loyalties of the Germans abroad while not unduly burdening the state. Excluding residents who were not of German descent was not controversial, particularly given the perception of the cultural menace posed by foreign workers. Simply put, the debate lasted more than fifteen years because the issue of which Germans to include, not which foreigners to exclude, remained so divisive that it prevented accommodation among the ministries.

The government began cabinet-level discussions about reforming the citizenship law in 1898. The chancellory charged the Department of the Interior and the Foreign Office with the task of reforming the citizenship law and suggested that they include the Department of Justice, the Naval Office, and the Prussian Ministries of War, Foreign Affairs, and Interior. The leading nationalist organizations were not parties to these discussions but continued to follow the debate closely.[37] By 1904 the ministries agreed upon rescinding the clause that required registration with an overseas consulate to maintain citizenship abroad beyond ten years. They also concurred on revoking citizenship when a German took another citizenship on his own initiative and on additional policies making naturalization more difficult. They split into two camps, however, over whether Germans abroad who failed to perform military service should be stripped of their German citizenship. The Foreign Office and the Prussian ministries insisted that such a revocation was necessary and just, while the Naval Office and the Department of the Interior, with the urging of the ADV and DKG, argued that it ran counter to the very essence of the reform movement. This camp saw Germans abroad as representatives of the best elements of *Deutschtum,* and they argued that these Germans should not be cut off from the

Reich because of extended residence abroad or for failure to perform military service.[38]

Admiral Alfred von Tirpitz, Imperial Naval Secretary, and his subordinates in the Naval Office, in particular, argued that it made no sense to push away precisely those Germans the Reich was reaching out to in its efforts to reform the law to reflect the needs and capabilities of a powerful empire.[39] The Foreign Office and the Prussian ministries argued, conversely, that it would be dangerous to increase the numbers of German citizens abroad who were of no aid to the Reich but could make demands on its resources. These ministries wanted to guarantee protection to Germans abroad only if they fulfilled their duties to their fatherland, especially military service. The officials who argued this line consistently made a clear break with the ethnocultural definition of citizenship; for them, the interests of the Staat took precedence over membership in the Volk. The point of the argument was precisely that the types of "undesirables" (*unerwünschte Elemente*) described so disparagingly in government documents clearly included Germans abroad.[40] In 1910 Chancellor Bethmann-Hollweg grudgingly agreed to the clause connecting military service and retention of citizenship, ending a bitter battle. In 1912–13 the citizenship bill reached the Reichstag, where the government's proposal passed by a solid majority.

In discussing the reform debate, there are several key points to keep in mind. The 1913 citizenship law did not satisfy those ministries advocating a genealogically based law; rather, central aspects of the law demonstrated the emphasis on the state's interests rather than ethnic images of Germanness. This prioritization disappointed those ministries, and their supporters among the patriotic societies, that had worked for a greater ethnicization of the citizenship law. The principle of descent was expanded, but it was strictly defined as descent from a citizen of the Reich, whatever his ethnicity (at this time, citizenship depended on only the father). Some of the most interesting aspects of the debate took place when there were disagreements about the suitability of the principle of *ius sanguinis* absolutely in particular situations. The competing demands of ideologies and interests within and among the pressure groups and ministries working to reform the citizenship law require a more nuanced explanation than the scholarship to date has provided.

Thus, in spite of the expanded popular vision of the national community that developed in the Wilhelmine era, the state insisted on including a clause in the 1913 citizenship law that in fact limited the number of Germans abroad for whom it could be held responsible. Indeed, the 1870 law's requirement that overseas Germans register with the German consulate every ten years had been replaced with a much more arduous sacrifice, military service, in return for retaining German citizenship.[41] While there were conditions included in the law that eased the requirement that Germans abroad return to the Reich to perform military service, both sides of the debate acknowledged that linking retention of citizenship to performing military service would drastically reduce the number of German citizens beyond the borders of the empire. I would therefore suggest that the picture of a government working to ethnicize the citizenship law behind a shared concept of what it meant to be a German, and of the types of people to be included and excluded in the new citizenship law, bears reconsideration.

In one sense, however, the supranationalist definition of Germanness of the Wilhelmine era prevailed. This vision quite obviously influenced the subsequent Nazi conception of German national community, or *Volksgemeinschaft,* that Hitler hoped to call to arms from around the globe. Norbert Götz's chapter in this volume assesses the use of the term *Volksgemeinschaft* and the Nazi era more fully. However, in the context of citizenship law, January 30, 1933, marks a caesura, as it does for so many aspects of German history. Nazi citizenship policies obviously differed not only in degree but in kind from the law passed at the end of the Wilhelmine era. The Nazis not only sought to prevent certain groups from naturalizing, they deprived citizens whom they considered undesirable on racial grounds of their citizenship. The Nazis stated baldly that Jews and other "racially undesirable" groups could not be full citizens in the Nazi citizenship law of 1935 (*Reichsbürgergesetz*), and later stripped them of their citizenship altogether. The Reich altered the criteria for citizenship thereafter to accommodate Nazi racial delusions and political goals.[42]

Citizenship, 1914–2000: Continuities and New Directions

While defeat in 1945 represented a clean break with the past in certain areas of German life, there was no new beginning in the approach to the citizenship law. The Nazis' racial ideology was discredited, but the Federal Republic retained the 1913 citizenship law, supplemented by Article 116 of the Basic Law. This article defined Germans as anyone who held German citizenship or anyone who had been admitted to the territory of the German Reich within its pre–World War II boundaries (as of 1937), any refugee or postwar expellee of German descent, their spouse, or their descendent.[43]

The task facing citizenship legislation in postwar (West) Germany was twofold: to repair the damage done by Nazi citizenship dictates and to provide a temporary legal framework for the millions of refugees who had come to Germany. To address the first concern, former German citizens who had been stripped of their citizenship on political, racial, or religious grounds were given their state membership back if they applied. The second aspect, personified by the twelve million refugees who flooded into Germany in the years after the war, was resolved in the 1953 expellee law, which defined ethnic Germans (*Aussiedler*) remaining in Central and Eastern Europe and Central Asia as "Status Germans." This legal construct allowed the integration of the German-speaking expellees from Eastern Europe, and it enabled the Federal Republic to claim to represent all ethnic Germans outside its boundaries. The 1953 law thus reflected West Germany's refusal to recognize the legitimacy of the German Democratic Republic. The notion of "Status Germans" consolidated the ethnocultural definition of German identity beyond the limits of the 1913 citizenship law. While officially provisional, the standards set out after the war continued to regulate the Federal Republic's citizenship policy through the end of the twentieth century.[44]

Between 1945 and 1949, expellees and refugees predominated among the in-migrating population. After 1955 the Federal Republic established treaties to recruit temporary workers, so-called *Gastarbeiter* from Italy and other Mediterranean countries. Although government recruitment ended in 1973, official family reunion policies encouraged long-term settlement, as have the endemic poor working and living conditions in migrants' countries of origins. Germany has become a de facto country of immigration, much of it illegal. The number of foreign residents has continued to rise, particularly the largest, Turkish minority. Opposition to this new immigration has sometimes appeared to reprise the anti-immigrant prejudices of the post-1880s era. A joint federation-state commission was set up in 1976 to examine the future direction of West Germany's immigration policies, an effort that ultimately led to a statement about the naturalization guidelines (*Einbürgerungsrichtlinien*) that focused on the applicant's cultural integration into German society and not their ethnicity. These 1977 guidelines reiterated the position that Germany was not a country of immigration, but they were a step toward the more far-reaching reforms that would emerge after unification. Also, a bill to give second-generation foreigners the right to naturalize, sponsored by the liberal Sozialdemokratische Partei Deutschlands (SPD) and Freie Demokratische Partei (FDP) coalition, made it to the Bundesrat chamber of the Reichstag in 1981 before being rejected. After the Kohl government came to power in 1982, however, progress on the issue slowed considerably.[45]

The Christlich Demokratische Union Deutschlands (CDU)/FDP coalition, although less receptive to changes than the previous administration, did allow some relaxation of the exclusive nature of the citizenship law in the 1990s. Naturalization policies had granted a great deal of discretion to government officials in each federal state until the 1993 revision to the Aliens Law that granted applicants for naturalization a right to citizenship if they met certain residence criteria and did not have a criminal record.[46]

Reversing the Kohl administration's restrictive policies on asylum and immigration, in October 1998 the new SPD/Green coalition government announced its first major policy initiative: reforming the citizenship law. Declaring that Germany is "a country of immigrants," the new government proposed German citizenship as a matter of right for children born in Germany who have parents without German citizenship. The proposed reform would have granted citizenship to children born in Germany if one parent was born in Germany or came to the country before the age of fourteen. The government's proposal also would have permitted dual citizenship for children and would have reduced the time a foreigner had to live in Germany before applying for naturalization from fifteen years to eight years; those under eighteen could apply for German citizenship after five years of residence in Germany. Foreigners married to a German for at least two years and residing in Germany for three years could also apply to become German citizens. SPD leaders predicted that legislation implementing these changes would make two to three million German residents into German citizens. Otto Schily, SPD minister of the interior, said that the change in Germany's citizenship law was "long overdue."[47]

The proposed citizenship reform immediately evoked strong responses from the opposition parties, as well as the general population, demonstrating that the "continuities of contention" in citizenship debates still resonated in the German body politic. The CDU/Christlich Soziale Union (CSU) started a campaign against dual citizenship in early 1999, arguing that dual citizenship would mean "that foreigners will have a huge natural advantage over Germans.

Germany will be transformed into a land of immigration, a land of unlimited immigration."[48] The CDU/CSU claimed that dual citizenship would devalue German citizenship and argued that the integration of foreigners required a conscious decision in favor of German citizenship, at the expense of their original citizenship. It is worth noting that this argument about "toll-free" naturalization had not been raised before in the context of ethnic Germans (*Aussiedler*), most of whom keep their previous citizenship after naturalization. Within a few months, the opposition was able to collect five million signatures against the SPD/Green government's proposed reform of the citizenship law.[49]

The campaign against dual citizenship also influenced the state elections in Hesse, helping the CDU/FDP coalition win a close victory. The election of the new government in Hesse changed the balance of power in the German Bundesrat, giving the opposition the votes to block the Schroeder administration's initiatives. The SPD/Green coalition thus could not get its proposed citizenship law confirmed by the Bundesrat. A compromise with the FDP had to be found. The compromise bill ultimately included a modified criteria for citizenship based on residence but no longer contained a general acceptance of dual citizenship. Under the compromise, children with two foreign parents born in Germany receive German citizenship if at least one parent has been a legal resident of Germany for eight years or more and has reached a certain category of residence permit (*Aufenthaltsberechtigung,* or an unlimited *Aufenthaltserlaubnis* for at least three years). Although these children are granted German citizenship at birth, they have to decide whether to keep it and give up their other citizenship between the ages of eighteen and twenty-three. Children born between 1990 and 1999 to foreign parents can acquire German citizenship through the application of their parents, but they also have to choose one citizenship when they are between the ages of eighteen and twenty-three.[50] This compromise passed the German parliament on May 7, 1999, with a majority of 365 votes from the SPD, the Greens, and parts of the Partei des Demokratischen Sozialismus (PDS); 184 members of parliament from the CDU/CSU and the PDS voted against the law; and 39 members abstained. The new citizenship law passed the Bundesrat on May 21, 1999, and came into force on January 1, 2000.[51]

Although Minister of the Interior Schily argued that the reform of the citizenship law brought the German citizenship law up to European standards while strengthening social peace, the law now faces critics on the left and the right. The CDU/CSU opposes the law and argues that the five million signatures collected demonstrate that the majority of the population does not support the reform. The opposition parties have used the opportunity presented by a discussion of an immigration law to advance their concept of a German "primary culture" (*Leitkultur*) that immigrants would be required to emulate. Eberhard Diepgen, Berlin's Christian Democratic mayor, argued that Muslim families had to recognize the cultural values of Christianity and humanism. He stated, "This is not a rejection of the Islamic faith . . . it is a limitation of the Islamic state."[52] On the left, migration advocates complained that the citizenship reform did not go far enough and criticized the Greens for compromising too easily.[53]

What strikes a historian about the most recent debates over the citizenship law is how closely the arguments at the end of the twentieth century resemble those made at the century's beginning. The tension between demonstrated service to the state, on the one hand, and inclusion based on ethnic connections (even where they are tenuous, as in the case of some Aussiedler), on the other, parallels the divisions articulated in the Wilhelmine period. On perhaps a more ominous note, the current government must find a way to address the fears that resonate in its citizens' minds about residents who are not of German heritage, which echo similar anxieties of a century ago. Perhaps the ethnicity of the migrants has shifted, but ethnic and religious minorities in Germany face the residue of a populist German self-definition based on the idea of a community of descent. This self-definition has deep roots, which have shown disturbing resilience in weathering dramatic changes in the political climate in Germany over the past century. The challenge facing Germany today is to nurture the desirable elements of its conception of membership while weeding out historic prejudices.

While the new law contributes substantially to the democratization of Germany's citizenship law, it appears that it will not contribute significantly to the integration of Germany's large foreign population over the next generation. In light of the size of the foreign population and current demographic trends, much more remains to be done. Ultimately, the reform's impact on integration remains to be seen. And what level of legal integration or de facto social integration will take place? Will increasing political integration across ethnic lines afford Germans a chance to break down the divisions in their society, or will debates over the principle of a German Leitkultur continue to divide parties and ethnicities? Will the question of citizenship and national identity spiral downward to a lowest common denominator? As usual, the outcome will probably end up somewhere between the best- and worst-case scenarios. The recent revision is not a cure-all, but in the near term, the return to a citizenship law that places the interests of the Staat ahead of those of an imagined Volk can only have a positive influence.

NOTES

1. Rogers Brubaker, *Citizenship and Nationhood in France and Germany* (Cambridge, Mass., 1992), 51; Dieter Gosewinkel, "Staatsbürgerschaft und Staatsangehörigkeit," *Geschichte und Gesellschaft* 4 (1995): 533–56; and Dieter Gosewinkel, "Die Staatsangehörigkeit als Instrument des Nationalstaats," in *Offene Staatlichkeit. Festschrift für E. W. Boeckenfoerde,* ed. Rolf Grawert, Bernhard Schlink, and Rainer Wahl (Berlin, 1996) are careful to make this distinction. The participatory connotations of *Staatsbürgerschaft* or the association of citizenship with a certain set of civic attitudes are not part of the discussion. All translations are my own unless otherwise noted.

2. Brubaker, *Citizenship,* 50–51; Rolf Grawert, *Staat und Staatsangehörigkeit: Verfassungsgeschichtliche Untersuchung zur Entstehung der Staatsangehörigkeit* (Berlin, 1973), 136–40. Early-nineteenth-century citizenship laws in the German states often referred to state members as citizens (*Staatsangehörige*) as well as subjects (*Untertane*) or "residents" (*Einwohner/Landeseinwohner*). For a list of the variety of possibilities, see Grawert, *Staat und Staatsangehörigkeit,* 172ff.

3. Reinhart Koselleck, *Preussen zwischen Reform und Revolution. Allgemeines Landrecht, Verwaltung und soziale Bewegung von 1791 bis 1848* (Stuttgart, 1975), 13–14.

4. Koselleck, *Preussen,* 13–14.

5. Brubaker, *Citizenship,* 54.

6. Thomas Nipperdey, *Deutsche Geschichte, 1800–1866: Bürgerwelt und starker Staat* (Munich, 1984), 31–32. See David Blackbourn, *The Long Nineteenth Century: 1780–1914* (London, 1997), 81–84, for a summary of the reformers' ideas.

7. Brubaker, *Citizenship,* 61.

8. For Bavaria, see Walter Demel, *Der Bayerische Staatsabsolutismus 1806/07–1817. Staats- und gesellschaftspolitische Motivationen und Hintergründe der Reformära in der ersten Phase des Königreichs Bayern* (Munich, 1983); for Electoral Hesse, see Andreas Fahrmeir, "Nineteenth Century Citizenship Laws: A Reconsideration," *Historical Journal* 3 (1997): 721–55, and Winfried Speitkamp, *Restauration als Transformation. Untersuchungen zur kurhessischen Verfassungsgeschichte 1813–1830* (Darmstadt and Marburg, 1986). Jonathan Sperber's "State and Civil Society in Prussia: Thoughts on a New Edition of Reinhart Koselleck's *Preussen zwischen Reform und Revolution," Journal of Modern History* 57 (1985): 278–96, explores these issues for all of *Vormärz* Germany.

9. Emigration with permission entailed immediate loss of citizenship, while

emigration without it meant citizenship was lost after ten years of continuous residence abroad. Fahrmeir, "Citizenship Laws," 732.

10. Grawert, *Staat und Staatsangehörigkeit*, 133; Brubaker, *Citizenship*, 68; and Mack Walker, *Germany and the Emigration* (Cambridge, 1964), passim.

11. Gosewinkel, *Die Staatsangehörigkeit*, 2; Grawert, *Staat und Staatsangehörigkeit*, 190–92, 213.

12. Fahrmeir, "Citizenship Laws," 738, argues that it was not a question of *soli* versus *sanguinis*, but more a matter of establishing a "domicile," or long-term residence, with the approval of the state, that was the decisive element of prenational citizenship laws.

13. "Gesetz über die Erwerbung und den Verlust der Eigenschaft als Preussischer Unterthan, sowie den Eintritt in fremde Staatsdienste vom 31.12.1842," *Gesetzessammlung für die Königlich Preussischen Staaten* (1843), 15.

14. Grawert, *Staat und Staatsangehörigkeit*, 135; Wolfgang Mommsen, "Nationalität im Zeichen offensiver Weltpolitik. Das Reichs-und Staatsangehörigkeitsgesetz vom 22. Juni 1913," in *Nation und Gesellschaft in Deutschland*, ed. Manfred Hettling and Paul Nolte (Munich, 1996), 131–33.

15. Fahrmeir, "Citizenship Laws," 723, argues that the rule of descent was not even proposed. On 1848, see Brian Vick, *Defining Germany: The 1848 Frankfurt Parliamentarians and National Identity* (Cambridge, Mass., 2002).

16. The exclusion of foreigners from these fundamental guarantees separated German fundamental rights from the tradition of universal human rights. Gosewinkel, *Die Staatsangehörigkeit*, 362.

17. Brubaker, *Citizenship*, 123. *Ethnocultural* is the term he uses to describe his model of German citizenship. I will address the details of this definition in the section on the 1913 law.

18. See Ernst Hasse, *Deutsche Politik* (Munich, 1905), for the Pan-German League's vision of a state including all members of the German Volk within its borders. For a broader description of the problem, see Theodore Schieder, *Das Deutsche Reich von 1871 als Nationalstaat* (Cologne, 1961).

19. Figures from Klaus Bade, "From Emigration to Immigration: The German Experience in the Nineteenth and Twentieth Centuries," *Central European History* 28, no. 4 (1995): 512–13. The vast majority of the emigrants chose the United States as their destination. Of the approximately 4.5 million Germans who moved overseas between 1847 and 1914, nearly 4 million went to the United States. Brazil was the second choice, with 86,000 (Blackbourn, *Nineteenth Century*, 194–97).

20. Grawert, *Staat und Staatsangehörigkeit*, 202–3.

21. The issue of severing ties to Germans abroad was a controversial one even at the time the 1870 law was passed. See the statements of Miquel and Braun during the Reichstag debates at the time, discussed in Burt Howard, *The German Empire* (New York, 1913), and Grawert, *Staat und Staatsangehörigkeit*, 202–3. In this line of thinking, it was not in the state's interest to protect Germans abroad who did not contribute to the well-being of the state. Among other points, critics argued that Germans abroad contributed to German cultural, economic, and diplomatic well-being.

22. Woodruff Smith, "The Ideology of German Colonialism, 1840–1906," *Jour-

nal of Modern History 46 (1974): 641–42, 651; and Roger Chickering, *We Men Who Feel Most German: A Cultural Study of the Pan-German League* (London, 1984), 30.

23. Chickering, *We Men,* 24–26.

24. Chickering, *We Men,* 27–28, 34–35.

25. Gosewinkel, *Die Staatsangehörigkeit,* 363.

26. Brubaker, *Citizenship,* chapter 6 and passim.

27. Chickering, *We Men,* 38–40; Smith, "Ideology," 651.

28. Kaiser William II remarked on the twenty-fifth anniversary of the founding of the German Empire, "The German Empire has become a world power. Everywhere, in the farthest corners of the globe, dwell thousands of our countrymen. It is your part gentlemen, to help me in the task of linking firmly this greater German Empire with the smaller home." Kaiser Wilhelm II, *The Kaiser's Speeches,* trans. and ed. A. Oscar Klaussmann (New York, 1903), 132.

29. There is a great deal of literature on the subject of *Polenpolitik* in the Kaiserreich. A few of the major works are Jack Wertheimer, *Unwelcome Strangers: East European Jews in Imperial Germany* (New York, 1987); Helmut Neubach, *Die Ausweisungen von Polen und Juden aus Preussen 1885/86* (Wiesbaden, 1967); Richard Blanke, *Prussian Poland in the German Empire (1871–1900)* (Boulder, 1981); and William W. Hagen, *Germans, Poles and Jews: The Nationality Conflict in the Prussian East, 1772–1914* (Chicago, 1980); Bade's work, "Emigration to Immigration," touches on the topic as well.

30. See Wertheimer, *Unwelcome Strangers,* 23–25, and Till van Rahden, "Die Grenze vor Ort. Die Einbürgerung und Ausweisung von ausländischen Juden in Breslau 1860–1918," *Tel-Aviver Jahrbuch* 27 (1998): 47–69, for examples of such statements.

31. Brubaker, *Citizenship,* 134–35.

32. See P. Maendl, *Das deutsche Auswanderungsgesetz nach dem Reichsgesetz vom 9. Juni 1897* (Munich, 1899), 4–7, for background.

33. Maendl, *Das deutsche Auswanderungsgesetz,* 6. The Reichstag debated the bill three times between March 16 and May 19, 1897. After the first reading, the bill was referred to a committee, where ADV chairman Hasse tried and failed to shape the bill to meet ADV desiderata. The law went into effect on January 1, 1898. See Maendl, *Das deutsche Auswanderungsgesetz,* 6n3, for Reichstag sessions and *Anlagen* citations.

34. For the Colonial Society, see *Die Deutsche Kolonialgesellschaft, 1882–1907* (Berlin, 1908), 75, and for the Pan-Germans, see "Auswanderung und Erwerb und Verlust der Reichs- und Staatsangehörigkeit" in *Zwanzig Jahre Alldeutsche Kämpfe und Arbeit* (Leipzig, 1910). Both organizations printed dozens of articles in their newspapers as well. The Foreign Office officially took over the operation of the DKG's information offices, which urged prospective emigrants to seek their new home in areas other than the United States. See *Die Deutsche Kolonialgesellschaft,* 117–18.

35. One overview of the volume of literature produced on the loss of citizenship through extended (ten years) residence abroad, including an extended historiographical review, in the years leading up to the ministerial debate is B. Weiss,

"Erwerb und Verlust der Staatsangehörigkeit," *Annalen des deutschen Reichs* (1908): 836–49, 902–16, and (1909): 383–96, 472–94.

36. Brubaker, *Citizenship,* 123. *Ethnocultural* is the term he uses to describe his model of German citizenship.

37. Archival documents, Bundesarchiv Lichtenberg (BA-L), Imperial Department of the Interior (RAdI), 8005, 281, marks the beginning of the government discussion. See Department of Justice, film 5063, for considerations of including a representative from the ADV in the initial government discussions. 75 BA-L, RAdI, 8031, IA 6076.

38. The ten-year clause in the 1870 law stated that Germans abroad lost their citizenship after ten years abroad unless they signed the register at a German consulate. Many Germans did not know about this clause, and others had difficulty, it was argued, making the long trip to the nearest consulate.

39. BA-L, RAdI 8031, Tirpitz's *Stellungnahme* of October 30, 1905, is just one example of a position he and his representatives had advocated since discussions began in 1898.

40. BA-L, Reichskanzlei (Chancellory) Film 12587, among others. One particularly bitter example is the Prussian Ministry of Foreign Affairs (Auswärtige Angelegenheiten) memo of December 30, 1908.

41. BA-L, RadI 8011, contains the terms of the breakthrough for the Foreign Office and the Prussian ministries.

42. Brubaker, *Citizenship,* 167–68.

43. Rainer Münz and Rainer Ohliger, "Long Distance Citizens: Ethnic Germans and Their Immigration to Germany," in *Paths to Inclusion: The Integration of Migrants in the United States and Germany,* ed. Peter Schuck and Rainer Münz (New York, 1998), 170.

44. Brubaker, *Citizenship,* 168–69; Münz and Ohliger, "Long Distance Citizens," 170.

45. Hans Heinrich Blotevogel, Usula Müller-ter Jung, and Gerald Wood, "From Itinerant Worker to Immigrant? The Geography of Guestworkers in Germany," in *Mass Migration in Europe: The Legacy and the Future,* ed. Russell King (London, 1993); Simon Green, "Naturalization Policy in Germany," paper submitted for the International Conference on Nationality Law, Paris, 1998, 8–9. Green's article presents a good overview of the political aspects of citizenship legislation in the postwar era and has since been published in *German Politics* 9, no. 3 (2000): 105–24.

46. Greg Kvistad, "Segmented Politics: Xenophobia, Citizenship, and Political Loyalty in Germany," in *Identity and Intolerance: Nationalism, Racism, and Xenophobia in Germany and the United States,* ed. Norbert Finzsch and Dietmar Schirmer (Cambridge, 1998), 57–58.

47. "Germany: Citizenship Changes," *Migration News* 5 (November 1998).

48. "Germany: Citizenship Changes."

49. Ralf Ulrich, "The Reform of the German Citizenship Law," Policy Brief for the American Institute for Contemporary German Studies, 1999 (January 2001). <http://www.aicgs.org/IssueBriefs/ulrich.html>.

50. Ulrich, "The Reform."

51. European Forum for Migration Studies (efms), Universität Bamberg, "New Citizenship Law Comes into Effect on January 1, 2000," *efms Migration Report,* May 1999 (January 2001). <http://www.uni-bamberg.de/~ba6ef3/dmai99_e.htm> (January 2001); Ulrich, "The Reform."

52. See Roger Cohen, "Is Germany on the Road to Diversity? The Parties Clash," *New York Times,* December 4, 2000.

53. efms, "New Citizenship Law."

CHAPTER 2

Home, Nation, Empire

Domestic Germanness and Colonial Citizenship

Krista O'Donnell

When the Kaiserreich came into being in 1871, its rulers had little pre-
monition that the young country would soon become an empire,
acquiring significant overseas territory in Africa, China, and the
Pacific after 1884. Germany's imposition of power over Kiaochow (a
region in the Shandong Peninsula of China, including the city of Qing-
dao), Cameroon, East Africa (present-day Tanzania), German Samoa,
Togo, and Southwest Africa (now Namibia) took place with minimal
forethought of how to administer or incorporate these lands into the
German Empire. Long after Germany acquired colonies, ordinary
Germans still gave little concerted thought to these far-flung possessions or invested much public discussion in Germany's relationship to
its colonies or the meaning of imperial citizenship.[1]

By the turn of the twentieth century, however, Germans throughout
the empire were forced to confront the fact that German colonists were
imprinting their Germanness not only on tropical territories and cultures but also on a new generation of biracial children, many with
claims to German citizenship as the legitimate offspring of German
fathers. (No parallel case has been recorded that involves descent from
a German woman). Some contemporary Germans argued outright
that individuals with Asian or African heritage could not be German
citizens. The matter was one of great legal controversy, and it had crucial implications for the individuals involved. In order to discourage
such unions, local colonial administrations imposed barriers and even
formal bans against interracial marriage, similar to U.S. antimiscegenation laws. The marriage bans were unique among European
empires. In 1905 German Southwest Africa (GSWA) was the first
colony to bar interracial marriage, sexual intercourse, and cohabita-

tion. In 1907 the territory's highest court further ruled that existing interracial marriages also were invalid and their progeny illegitimate.[2]

However, citizenship was not the sole determinant of social and legal status in the colonies. In GSWA and the other overseas territories, the population was divided into two legal categories that were never officially defined: natives (*Eingeborene*) and nonnatives (*Nichteingeborene*). Natives were subject to a completely separate legal code that imposed numerous discriminations, even against persons with German citizenship. In 1910 the GSWA administration declared that the entire mixed-race population was legally native. Consequently, long-standing colonial families like the Baumanns, Krabbenhöfts, von Bernecks, and others with African forebears who had regarded themselves as part of the settler community suddenly learned that they must now carry native passes and that their mobility was restricted. Among many legal hurdles they now faced, local merchants were forbidden to extend them credit or to permit them to purchase firearms or alcoholic spirits. To avoid imposing too many such hardships, the colonial governor's office encouraged local authorities to turn a blind eye toward enforcing the native legal status of such mixed-race individuals: "However, official investigation into the background of such persons, who until now have been seen as whites, and, in view of their cultivation [*Bildung*] and social position, have stood on the level of whites, is not advisable from the standpoint of the administration."[3] Thus, individuals' legal standing in the colony, as well as determinations of race, depended to a great extent on the cultural norms and domestic practices of a family's household. The ambiguity of the citizenship and legal rights of mixed-race individuals plagued the German Empire in the decades between 1890 and 1914. Although the public debate over miscegenation and mixed marriage in the colonies (*Mischehenfrage*) may have been imperial in scope, the case-by-case resolution of individuals' cultural and racial status by territorial courts and administrators made it a local issue as well.

Because the legal status of mixed-race persons was not easily settled, while their numbers only continued to grow, the ongoing juridical controversy expanded into a popular discussion of empire and race. The discussion revealed Germans' deeper anxieties about the imperial project that exceeded the narrow question of citizenship. The many public and private figures who engaged in the miscegenation debate across the German Empire revealed complicated and contradictory understandings of the racial and cultural bases of German identity. Moreover, as metropolitan Germans distanced themselves from miscegenation, they increasingly detached themselves from their empire. In doing so, they cast doubt on the Germanness of these overseas territories and thus on the entire colonial enterprise. A central element of contention was whether individual colonies could ever be transformed into a German *Heimat* (homeland) and, if so, how. The simple answer for many Germans was through the cultural and/or reproductive powers of German women settlers, but even the supposed solution of increased German women's colonization proved insufficient to stop the growth of miscegenation and its alleged dangers.[4]

Although this chapter refers to other colonies as well, it concentrates on German Southwest Africa because German administrators defined this region as the empire's primary settlement colony. It held the largest European population and drew the most substantial German investment and profits. Surviving written accounts suggest colonial officials and enthusiasts paid much more attention to the territory and intervened more substantially in its reproductive and cultural practices. Moreover, GSWA also had a large existing Afro-European population stemming from eighteenth-century and even earlier colonial settlements, and their numbers grew substantially under German occupation. Finally, GSWA suffered one of the most brutal colonial occupations of the early twentieth century, the genocidal Herero-Nama war of 1904–7, which wiped out as many as 60 to 80 percent of the dominant indigenous populations in the territory. This violent past renders the colony's history and the local unfolding of German racism all the more disturbing and significant. For all these reasons, GSWA offers an excellent arena for study, but even more obviously because German women's colonial settlement projects concentrated their work there, in reaction to miscegenation in the territory, and these efforts serve as an especially revealing source for tracing the unfolding of German colonial culture and identity. A close examination of discussions of race and reproduction in GSWA and the German metropole points to the particular importance that notions of domesticity and Heimat held within Germans' local, national, and imperial identities.

Of course, Germans in the homeland encountered Africans and persons of African extraction without venturing to the colonies. In their interactions with "blacks," Germans drew on popular readings of scientific and literary representations of race and empire. In ordinary Germans' minds, encounters with Africans took on the tenor of "colonial contacts" and informed their understanding of Germanness and empire. Arguably, we can trace the convergence of these literary and anthropological influences on metropolitan Germans' prevalent racial and imperial notions in their broadest and most accessible form through readings of the popular Wilhelmine colonialist magazine, *Kolonie und Heimat*. The journal printed the official bulletins of the Women's Union of the German Colonial Society (Frauenbund der DKG), but the organization did not otherwise produce or edit its copy. Rather, its publishers, a group of male colonial enthusiasts, aimed to create a mainstream "colonial family journal," written by male and female writers for Germans of both sexes, of all ages and social backgrounds, who lived across the empire. Moreover, unlike the less popular colonial periodicals, the publishers maintained an independent journalistic stance that was less reflective of official colonial policies.[5] Furthermore, *Kolonie und Heimat* included writings from both the metropole and the colonies and thus brought German colonists' purported expertise on race to an avid home audience. In the pages of this magazine, published between 1907 and 1919, we can track how the "complex social construction of blackness" informed metropolitan Germans' understanding of the colonies and their place in the empire. The journal offers a lens through which to view "the intricate negotiation between imagination and imperialism that underlies German colonial and racial policy."[6]

Kolonie und Heimat maintained a consistent editorial policy toward miscegenation, advocating legal sanctions against it but also promoting German women's colonization and cultural influence as central to the imperialist project: "One can only underscore that the maintenance of racial purity is the first foundation principle of colonial politics. Hand in hand with formal exclusion of mixed marriage, however, must also go the farthest possible promotion of efforts to make the German woman indigenous [*heimisch*] to the colonies."[7] The use of domestic vocabulary was deliberate in this discussion. A number of recent writings have commented at length on the important spatial dichotomy between the metropole and colonies and have noted the importance of efforts to domesticate the colonies within European imperialism. As one anthropologist has outlined, "As a prop in the politics of colonial domination, the conceptual construction of domesticity was at the forefront of change, as were those who gave it institutional efficacy."[8] The ideal of Heimat, with all its domestic connotations, is particularly important in the German case because of its centrality to popular conceptions of German nationalism. Ties to the local Heimat offered a basis for connection to the German national community.[9] If, as another scholar suggests, colonial miscegenation and cultural hybridity "intercepted nationalist and racist visions" and "expressed a domestic subversion, a rejection of the terms of the civilizing mission,"[10] they were especially disruptive to the domestic ideals at the heart of German national identity.

The rhetorical distance between home and colony is reinforced in the mere title of *Kolonie und Heimat*. Among other striking differences, the image of Heimat was widely perceived as female, whereas, statistically, German colonists were overwhelmingly male and symbolically the colonies were male space. The Heimat also appeared as indisputably German and white, while the colonies represented the exotic, other, and nonwhite. The importation of German women, then, became a literal and figurative program to domesticate GSWA.

Domestication of the colonies was no easy task. In the journal's pages, German-speaking colonists in distant climes seemed remotely German at best; at worst, they were corrupted by the pernicious cultural and racial influences of their locales and cut off from the true source of Germanness in the Heimat. This concept of passive racial defilement is clear in Germans' metaphorical depictions of miscegenation, found in commonplace terms like *Verkafferung* (Kaffirization; *Kafir* is a derogatory name for South African natives). This descriptive, similar to the English phrase "gone native," evoked hapless German men, sexually and symbolically contaminated by native women and culture. Moreover, this attention to foreign regions' influence on German settlers' identities is carried through in the journal's complex dissections of racial politics and reproduction specific to each colony. For example, *Kolonie und Heimat* expounded at length on the Rehoboth Basters, a long-standing Southwest African ethnic group of Khoi, Dutch-Afrikaner, and English descent with several thousand members. The magazine stressed the unique racial considerations this population presented for German rule in GSWA. Specifically, the periodical identified the attractions of Baster women's considerable property in land and cattle; European education, dress, and manners; Christianity; and, most importantly, "their comely appearance, which all pose[d] a certain danger for maintaining the purity of Germandom."[11] By these standards, Baster women's seemingly "white" domestic cultural markers were misleading because they masked their supposedly more real African identities.

Another of the magazine's articles described Baster women's comparative cleanliness and maternalism, characterizing them as "careful and clean mothers, in contrast to other natives."[12] Likewise, Baster men's political reliability and loyal military service to the German colonists signaled a similar "domestication," double meaning intended. The author's purpose was to defuse the danger of the Basters by aligning them with Europeans: arguing that the problematic new generation of mixed-race children of German parentage somehow should be absorbed into the Rehoboth Baster community. Thus, in GSWA, the merging of African with European traditions appears to have produced the potential for a form of idealized domesticity and political connection to Germany—one that might neutralize the racial dangers presumed in miscegenation. However, this possibility for an African Heimat that combined the characters of Germans and Africans is very atypical of most colonial writings. Moreover, this mixed-race German domestic community was only to be realized in separation from Germany. After all, the Basters' most valued qualities, those that marked them as European and domesticated, "paled" in comparison to actual Germans.

The specificity and nuance that characterized *Kolonie und Heimat*'s treatment of colonial citizenship and miscegenation in each colony reflected the understanding that overseas territories were each distinct from Germany in their own way but were also in the perpetual process of becoming German through the influx of German settlers and culture. Of course, this process could never be complete because the colonies, by their very nature, were cut off from the source of true domestic Germandom in the Heimat. Indeed, this isolation cast doubt on the colonials' continued Germanness, let alone the overseas lands and their indigenous peoples. Moreover, the German metropole apparently took little active part in this African or Asian struggle for a German colonial domesticity and nationhood. Indeed, the writers of *Kolonie und Heimat* claimed that German colonists' vigilant efforts to control their community's sexuality "alone [could] maintain the claim to lasting German hegemony and cultural leadership in the German colonial lands."[13] Miscegenation, in a sense, became the literal and figurative target for metropolitans' wider doubts about the Germanness of the colonies and the future of the empire.

Outside the pages of *Kolonie und Heimat,* German colonial enthusiasts sought to erase these uncertainties by attacking miscegenation in several concrete ways: first, the colonial administration fully cooperated with the DKG's private campaign of massive voluntary resettlement of over two thousand German women to GSWA between 1898 and 1914, which also entailed the support of racially segregated maternity homes and dormitories for them. Second, German colonial supporters founded cultural and educational institutions and public displays aimed at imparting and inculcating Germanness on the territory and separating the German community from the Africans. When all else failed, the German colonial administration colluded in the creation of local legal sanctions and barriers designed to discourage miscegenation and deny German citizenship to mixed-race individuals. In GSWA, district administrators were responsible for taking measures to identify, discourage, and punish miscegenation in their localities. Fighting miscegenation remained not only a colonial problem but a parochial one, and the metropole could only engage in its solution from afar.[14]

As previously noted, the application of colonial citizenship law was itself local and varied across the empire. In 1896 the German courts had not ruled conclusively on the nationality of African or part-African dependents of German males, and this legal ambiguity evoked fears that GSWA might one day be ruled by *Bastards,* a corruption of the name Baster, intentionally misapplied to biracial individuals to label them as illegitimate black Germans. German colonial administrators in GSWA resolved this dilemma by refusing to register interracial unions performed by Christian clergy as official, state-recognized marriages, even before the formal ban in 1905. Under unofficial pressure from the German administration, most clergy refused to perform such ceremonies at all after 1897. Racial extremists feared that Afro-German nationals might emigrate to Germany, take up residence as citizens, and even marry German women and reproduce. Indeed, for the metropole, the miscegenation debate was largely about preserving the exclusivity of German citizenship. The Berlin colonial administration pressured local administrators to discourage miscegenation through territorial measures, but to do so without contravening German citizenship law.[15]

As suggested earlier, German citizenship was no guarantee of equal treatment in the colonies. The GSWA administration discriminated arbitrarily against some biracial individuals and not others, based on community perceptions of them as racially white and evaluations of their level of "cultivation." Their recognition as "whites" in GSWA hinged in great part on the cultural standards of their household. However, it appears that domesticity had a very different meaning on the Namibian frontier than it did in between the covers of *Kolonie und Heimat.* Like many mixed-race communities at the turn of the century, the disproportionately male German society in GSWA generally viewed long-term interracial relationships as respectable unions, especially if they involved women of biracial backgrounds who had been raised with European customs in established settler households. The

German ex-soldier and settler Friedrich Heuer wrote in 1897 that he wished to "marry the daughter of a [well-established British-Baster] family in whose Heimat my whole future lies."[16] In the logic of Heuer and others like him, only women had the power to create a real home. To them, Southern Africa was the homeland of Baster and Dutch-Afrikaner women rather than new German women migrants, who were without essential knowledge or talent for creating a Southwest African Heimat in the colonies.

Colonial men's negative attitude toward European women as wives and homemakers can be seen in some German settlers' responses to the plan to transport German women to GSWA. An administrator in the more remote south of the colony—Keetmanshoop district commander (*Bezirksamtmann*) Dr. Angelo Golinelli, a much-respected old-timer in Africa who later became the Colonial Office's advisor on GSWA—attacked the organized immigration and employment of German maids.[17] Golinelli insisted that there was no local shortage of "white or almost white girls" (*weißen oder fast weißen Mädchen*) and that German colonists did not want or need German women as servants or wives because their domestic standards reflected their own homeland rather than an African settler home.

> The African woman follows her husband into a hut and gladly shares with him a life of privation, which she has known since childhood. Of the girls who grew up in the homeland, only the exception would bear this burden with satisfaction. The bulk would always feel unhappy and not sweeten the companionate marital life of their husbands. The average settler in this district does not have the income to keep a German woman according to the standards expected at home. In addition, the German girl is completely ignorant of colonial relations and cannot offer local settlers the help of an African woman, who is experienced in an African household and in dealing with [*Behandlung*] the people and animals.[18]

Thus, Golinelli outlines the domestic ideal of an imagined GSWA settler household that could and did allow the blending of races and cultures without necessarily impelling men's degeneration. Colonial Germans continued to voice similar opinions until the end of colonial rule in GSWA in 1915. The GSWA colonial administration tacitly acknowledged the settler community's understanding of a hybrid colonial "domesticity" through its arbitrary enforcement of racial standards in the colony. This compromised vision did not find space in *Kolonie und*

Heimat, however, which advocated strong antimiscegenation measures, including the marriage bans.

Wherever possible, the magazine presented a fictive vision of colonial unity against miscegenation across the empire that was far from the political reality. In 1912 a small and unlikely array of feminists, eugenicists, clergymen, and prominent politicians, including radical feminist Helene Stoecker and future chancellor Matthias Erzberger, objected to all such state-imposed bans as hypocritical, discriminatory, and unlikely to discourage interracial sex. The matter came to a head on May 8, 1912, when a loose coalition of Social Democratic, Center (Catholic), and Polish Party representatives, as well as a number of deputies from other parties, joined together in the Reichstag to pass a controversial measure that demanded that the Reich establish uniform legal provisions for recognizing mixed-race marriages in Germany and its overseas territories. While the autocratic imperial state took little notice of the unenforceable legislative decision, the Reichstag's firm stand nonetheless received extensive coverage in the press and gave rise to great consternation among large segments of the German public, particularly members of the popular radical nationalist movement. *Kolonie und Heimat* responded with a scathing piece entitled "Racial Purity!" by extreme nationalist Leonore Niessen-Deiters, labeling the vote an insult to German women. She insisted German women were the only proper colonial wives because they were the only agents capable of imparting Germanness to GSWA settlers' homes and families.[19]

In its condemnation of the Reichstag vote, *Kolonie und Heimat* went so far as to assert a universal consensus across the empire to ban interracial marriage: "All official representatives of the settler populations as well as the central colonial administration have unanimously and unreservedly declared themselves against the legal sanction of marriage between the white and black race." However, upon detailing the particulars of each of the various colonial administrations in Africa, the article's author was forced to acknowledge a powerful point of dissent from GSWA. The text of the official resolution of GSWA's settler council (*Landrat*) demanded full recognition of all interracial marriages before 1905, "where the lives of the parents and the raising of the children conforms to the general demands of custom and morality. Those affected should be given certification which states that so and so counts as white."[20] The selection offers no further comment on the colony's proposal, but other issues of *Kolonie und Heimat* depicted the Reichstag vote as the metropolitan betrayal of colonial Germans because it undermined racial separation in the empire. The magazine also warned that the vote might cause the loss of racial purity and superiority in Germany and its colonies, "seen in its most frightening form and reality in today's Portugal and its East African colony."[21] Yet another article cautioned that, if enforced, the Reichstag's deliberate devaluation of German women inherent in sanctioning mixed-race unions might lead to the mass rape of white women in the German colonies, as its author contended it had in British South Africa.[22]

Since Germany was self-consciously the only empire to ban mixed-race marriages and concubinage in some territories, international comparisons of its racial policies with the other European empires offered a means to justify the Germans' hard-line stance. However, despite this striking legal singularity, the tone of *Kolonie und Heimat*'s discussion of miscegenation and its dangers overlaps both in content and symbolism with similar contemporary discussions of other European empires decrying colonial intermarriage and miscegenation. In the Dutch and French colonies, observers fretted obsessively over the "slippage" between national identity, race, and culture presented by mixed-race colonial citizens—what anthropologist Ann Stoler refers to as "internal frontiers."[23] Germany's restrictive citizenship and marriage laws established the highest "internal frontiers" of all the empires yet still could not resolve the inconsistencies and contradictions that the growing mixed-race population presented. Consequently, we find *Kolonie und Heimat* demanding the policing of the metropole's *external* frontiers, both literally and figuratively, as the key boundary of Germanness. Markers of domesticity and symbols of Heimat became one such border to be guarded jealously against racial contamination.

As racial anxiety demanded metropolitan Germans' cultural distance from blacks, derogatory terms like *Schwarzer Europäer* (Black Europeans) and *Hosennigger* (trouser niggers) began to appear as epithets in the publication. These labels deplored the adoption of "European" dress and culture among African subjects overseas, as well as among persons with African heritage visiting or residing in Germany. Undergirding the magazine's consistent scorn for Africans' imperfect adoption of European language and manners is the overt fear that this superficial veneer of culture or civilization—the very characteristics that were necessary to forge a Heimat of the German colonies—might encourage dangerous African familiarity with Germans. Among several discussions of the alleged affront that colonial subjects of whole or partial African descent present to national identity appears the suggestion that Africans' very presence in Germany was disturbing and corrupting and that their interaction with German girls was a "public nuisance."[24] Underlying this concern is the repeated assumption that the *colonial* problem of miscegenation might be exacerbated by permitting African subjects to enter the Heimat.

Historians have no exact figures of the number of Africans and their descendants in Wilhelmine Germany, but we know that most arrivals came from the possessions of Togo and Cameroon and migrated as personal servants, skilled and unskilled laborers, and members of traveling ethnological exhibits called *Völkerschauen.*[25] By 1909, faced with only the most minimal contacts between Germans and colonials in the metropole, the journal *Kolonie und Heimat* consistently demanded an end to their immigration and a complete change in German racial attitudes: "No more negroes [*Neger*] from the colonies be allowed to come to Germany, and those here be sent back."

> Certainly, racial consciousness is lacking among wide circles of our people, and not only among the uneducated. The fanaticism of the public for "black princes" dates from a time when they were brought to official functions and "society." From the time that niggers [*Nigger*] were addressed as "royal highness," cultivated families took them in as children and the army placed them as superiors to white soldiers. Even today there are people known for bringing in black [*schwarze*] servants from the colonies.[26]

The basis for the journal's vehemence was a North German newspaper's "Warning to German parents and guardians" against the alleged dangers of allowing German youths and colonial subjects to become pen pals. The article asserted that the curiosity of young men and German girls' romantic desire to send a letter and a photograph to a "black prince" lured them to forget their disparate cultural positions. Unaware of the corruption they allegedly caused, German adolescents enjoyed the thrill of the exotic, while beleaguered colonial Germans paid for their folly. How disturbing for a colonial settler to enter a native abode and find the photo of a young German girl of a "better class" next to a "'black beauty' of unknown origins!" The author expostulated, "Young girls in the homeland must be brought to consciousness how much they lose through such correspondence with natives of the colonies, and how much more difficult they make the work of the colonial administration to civilize [*erziehen*] the natives."[27] By juxtaposing the distinct processes of raising German children and African natives, the article calls for the reeducation of both to the duties of a new racial consciousness rather than a common mission of metropole and colony to bring Africans closer to European cultural ideals. Instead, the journal contends that interracial contacts between Germans and colonials must be strictly limited in the future, lest seemingly harmless cultural interchanges encourage colonial Africans' desire for white women, resulting in miscegenation, which inevitably would lead to the end of colonial rule. Thus, the responsibilities of Germany's overseas empire created the necessity to break sharply, even violently, with past practices in order to keep cultures as well as populations distinct.

Kolonie und Heimat fixated especially on the image of the "trouser nigger," the disruptive Europeanized African who challenged white supremacy by mimicking but never truly attaining German standards of dress and culture. One of the magazine's virulent critics of colonial exhibitions suggested that they were a breeding ground for the "trouser nigger" by giving colonial subjects exaggerated notions of their self-importance.

> [The official], when faced with the return of the "exhibition niggers" [*Ausstellungs Niggern*] from the Berlin Exhibition, in 1896 should have beaten each one with 25 strokes, in order to take issue in a "striking fashion" with any illusions over their personal worth learned in Berlin. . . . These fellows, naturally, were partway to becoming trouser niggers in the capital of the German empire . . . and may have done lasting damage to the development of the young colony.[28]

Strict racial sensibilities were to erase lax metropolitan attitudes and practices and to restore racial order through violence as well as reeducation. Indeed, the magazine called for "a Colonial Society campaign to enlighten the German public on racial questions," complete with slide projections of "images to frighten people with a spark of racial feeling, to show what a worthless development the European trouser nigger is, undeserving of social intercourse with upstanding Germans." Lest fear not succeed, however, the publication also repeatedly demanded increased police restraints on social intercourse between the races in Germany.[29]

To readers of *Kolonie und Heimat,* the increasingly cosmopolitan culture and population of German cities, especially Berlin, represented the foreground of the nation's impending racial and cultural contamination through her colonies. By labeling Africans and Afro-Germans as colonial, metropolitan Germans could assert their danger to the domestic peace and demand their removal from the Heimat. In 1912 *Kolonie und Heimat* cited the object lesson of Johann Mbida, a colonial émigré who wrote from Germany to his parents in GSWA allegedly describing his plans to marry a white girl. The magazine foretold great danger for German women in the colony, if blacks were not placed under greater control in the metropole. Complaints in the magazine against colonial elements often classified any and all foreign elements with nonwhites. The article further raised the specter of "certain Berlin dance halls,"

> where blacks and whites give in to the joys of dance under the eyes of the police. So far has the racial pride of many girls in the capital city fallen! Which forces on us the question, what are so many blacks doing in Berlin? There should be the legal means to force them to return where they belong, German blacks to the colonies, foreigners to their respective motherlands.[30]

Similarly, a Nuremberg reader who had recently returned from the African colonies remarked against the recent influx of African American and other varied foreign entertainments in his city, scorning "black and white variety shows" featuring American and English dances, "colored" circus performers, and black "honky-tonk" ladies (*Tingeltangeldamen*).[31] Among the undiscerning public, then, the multiple contaminations of sexual license, blackness, and foreignness apparently were indistinguishable. The growing alarm over racial familiarity in urban centers was tied to much broader nationalist anxieties in the metropole that confused colonialism and blackness. French historian Yael Simpson Fletcher finds similar patterns of overlapping tensions in interwar Marseilles, a major site of colonial trade, where colonial transplants disproportionately bore the brunt of the public's concern for interracial prostitution and sexual disorder. Thus, racial and sexual anxiety directed against foreigners in general could feed upon colonial imagery in ways that further undermined the validity of the imperial project.[32]

Even the most assimilated and entrenched Afro-Germans could not escape the colonial label as a means of delegitimizing their presence in the metropole. In 1912 the journal criticized the privileged employment of Richard Manga Bell, the educated son of a Cameroonian "prince" received with full honors by the kaiser in 1902. His one-year attendance in a gymnasium, excellent references, and training as a salesman helped

secure him a supervisory position over one hundred German employees in a lumber concern in the Gross-Lichterfeld district of Berlin.
Kolonie und Heimat published a scathing criticism of his employment,
referring to Bell as a "savage" (*Wilder*).

> The main point is that we have to protect the homeland [*Heimat-
> land*] from a racial mish-mash, and therefore blacks don't belong in
> Germany. But God forbid that the negroes who are here now and
> allowed loose around Germany should be allowed, for purely racial
> pedagogical reasons, in positions of authority over whites. The dan-
> ger exists, if a German worker should obey a black, that the simple
> man will easily lose his feeling that he belongs to a higher race and
> will find nothing against it if his daughter should find such a negro
> desirable.[33]

The tirade repeats the notion of domesticity under siege, as the homeland's figurative racial pollution endangered its essential Germanness,
signified in the danger of miscegenation as the contamination of German homes and daughters. The cultural attainments of Bell stand as
irrelevant beside the overarching danger his presence represented.

The complete distancing—which some Germans believed was necessary—between the Heimat and her colonies is perhaps best captured in
the magazine's facetious proposals for halting the pernicious spread of
European garb altogether among colonial Africans and Asians by
encouraging overseas subjects to wear the costumes native to their own
homes, just like German peasants' *Volkstrachten* (regional dress).

> In the Heimat, one strives mightily for the proper regard of Volks-
> trachten, since the old dress of Black Forest or Vierländer peasant
> looks better and is healthier than modern fashions. Shouldn't the
> same stand true for the colonies? Here and over there, the question
> has economic meaning, since it is closely tied to stability [*Boden-
> ständigkeit*]. Wouldn't our ethnographers, who are delighted by
> every attractively worked leather loincloth, find it a rewarding exer-
> cise, provided there's still time, to found a Society for the Preserva-
> tion of Volkstrachten in the Colonies with the slogan: "Down with
> the trouser nigger"?[34]

Underlying the mocking tone, this remark throws the inconsistencies
of colonial propaganda against miscegenation in sharp relief. By face-
tiously equating native costumes with Volkstrachten, the remark inad-

vertently restores the German colonies' position as the Heimat of their native inhabitants and unthinkingly displaces the colonial settlers as rootless interlopers. Such writings reflect the confusion over the boundaries between race and culture. They hint at the uncertain Germanness of the African colonies, at some underlying doubt in the process of "Germanization" or "civilization" to be carried out by German settlers, and at growing acknowledgment of the dangerous contradictions and attractions of the Germanized African in the metropole. Persistent false images of the Afro-German as displaced colonial persisted well into the postcolonial era and the Third Reich.[35] Even today, most Germans unconsciously equate Germanness with whiteness, while many Afro-Germans feel like outsiders in Germany, although it is their Heimat, too.[36]

The German debate over miscegenation, as captured in the pages of the popular magazine *Kolonie and Heimat,* went beyond questions of race and citizenship to disrupt Germans' interconnected visions of home, nation, and empire. German metaphors of Heimat, because they were locally fixed, privileged the understanding of each overseas German community and colony as unique. Metropolitan Germans assumed that colonial settlers would adopt German cultural practices in their households as an expression of the civilizing and domesticating missions of empire and would extend German cultural practices to Africans. Colonists on the ground were to recreate German identity in their communities through daily household practices, without direct intervention of the metropole. The growing incidence of miscegenation in GSWA and the other colonies threatened not only metropolitan German notions of race and citizenship but also the domestic and cultural standards that defined the German Heimat. The German homeland could aid indirectly in the domestication of Africa through assisting the colonization of German women but ultimately regarded colonists' fight against miscegenation as a local struggle. In the view of the metropole, increased miscegenation undermined the colonies' standing as part of the homeland and nation and delegitimized the idea of empire. For their part, colonial Germans in GSWA articulated racially and culturally hybrid domestic ideals that fit local circumstances and disparaged the domestic standards of the homeland. Furthermore, they asserted the power to draw the boundaries between colonizers and natives in their African Heimat on the basis of these ideals, whereas the metropole rejected hybridized domesticity and demanded that the empire maintain unambiguous lines between the races in their reproduction, domestic practices, and citizenship.

Indeed, the physical separation of the German colonies from the metropole distanced them from the German homeland and nation. When GSWA and other colonies failed to maintain the nation's "internal frontiers" between races, cultures, and citizens, the metropole constructed barriers against African immigration and sought to keep out African cultural influences. Professing to safeguard the racial divide for colonial Germans, in the pages of *Kolonie und Heimat,* metropolitans demanded greater racial awareness among the German public and expulsion of colonial subjects. They encouraged violent suppression of Africans in the metropole. They even lampooned Africans who adopted German language and dress, characterizing colonial space as Africans' Heimat rather than colonists'. As the Heimat repulsed the influences of empire and discarded the civilizing mission, even metropolitans' "colonial contacts" with blacks came to represent sexual license and foreign contamination. In rejecting colonial miscegenation, metropolitan Germans privileged the Heimat and nation over empire. In the process, they negated and erased the Germanness of Afro-Germans, despite their legitimate claims to residence and citizenship.

NOTES

Research for this chapter was conducted with funding by the Fulbright Foundation and the German Academic Exchange Service (DAAD). I thank the German Women's History Group and the William Paterson University College of Humanities and Social Sciences Seminar for their editorial suggestions.

1. Woodruff Smith, *The German Colonial Empire* (Chapel Hill, 1978).

2. Pascal Grosse, *Kolonialismus, Eugenik, und bürgerliche Gesellschaft in Deutschland 1850–1918* (Frankfurt, 2000); Lora Wildenthal, "Race, Gender, and Citizenship in the German Colonial Empire," in *Tensions of Empire: Colonial Cultures in a Bourgeois World,* ed. Frederick Cooper and Ann Laura Stoler (Berkeley, Calif., 1997), 263–83; and Franz-Josef Schulte-Althoff, "Rassenmischung im kolonialen System: Zur deutschen Kolonialpolitik im letzten Jahrzehnt vor dem Ersten Weltkrieg," *Historisches Jahrbuch* 105 (1985): 52–94.

3. Directive from the governor's office, Windhoek, February 28, 1914, to the Bethanien Regional Office, Bundesarchiv Koblenz, Bestand Deutschsüdwestafrika (hereafter DSWA), Personenstandssachen: Mischehen, 666.F.IV.r.2, Bd. 2, Bl. 31ff; Bd. 3, Bl. 61. All translations are my own unless otherwise noted.

4. Grosse, *Kolonialismus,* 168–76. Grosse provides the last available population statistics for the empire (1914), which stated that the mixed-race population in the colonies had grown to 3,600 compared to 25,000 whites (151).

5. Lora Wildenthal, *German Women for Empire, 1884–1945* (Durham, N.C., 2001), 146.

6. Tina Campt, Pascal Grosse, and Yara-Colette Lemke-Muniz de Faria, "Blacks, Germans, and the Politics of Imperial Imagination, 1920–1960," in *The Imperialist Imagination: German Colonialism and Its Legacy,* ed. Sara Friedrichsmeyer, Sara Lennox, and Susanne Zantop (Ann Arbor, Mich., 1998), 206; see also Susanne Zantop, *Colonial Fantasies: Conquest, Family, and Nation in Precolonial Germany, 1770–1870* (Durham, N.C., 1998).

7. "Die rechtliche Beurteilung der Mischehen nach deutschem Kolonialrecht," *Kolonie und Heimat* (hereafter *KH*) 2, no. 23 (1908–9), N1.

8. Karen Tranberg Hansen, "Introduction," in *African Encounters with Domesticity,* ed. Karen Tranberg Hansen (New Brunswick, N.J., 1988), 5.

9. Helen Callaway, *Gender, Culture, and Empire: European Women in Colonial Nigeria* (London, 1987), was one of the first authors to explore this issue. Subsequent scholarship suggests that the domestication of the empire was an important process in all European colonial cultures. See, among many works, Julia Clancy-Smith and Frances Gouda, *Domesticating the Empire: Race, Gender, and Family Life in French and Dutch Colonialism* (Charlottesville, Va., 1998). For the expansive literature on Heimat and nationalism, see, for example, Celia Applegate, *A Nation of Provincials: The German Idea of Heimat* (Berkeley, Calif., 1990).

10. Ann L. Stoler, "Sexual Affronts and Racial Frontiers: European Identities and the Cultural Politics of Exclusion in Colonial Southeast Asia," in *Tensions,* ed. Stoler and Cooper, 198–237 (quote is from 226–27).

11. "Die südwestafrikanischen Bastards," *KH* 1, no. 13 (1907–8), 6, and "Die südwestafrikanischen Bastards. Betrachtungen der Rassenfrage," *KH* 4, no. 13 (1910–11), 2–3.

12. "Die südwestafrikanischen Bastards. Betrachtungen der Rassenfrage."

13. "Die deutschen Kolonisten werden, so schliessen diese Ausführungen, ihr Geschlecht in einträchtigem Zusammenhalten zu einem wahren Herrengeschlecht erziehen, das allein die deutsche Oberherrschaft und Kulturführung in deutschen Koloniallanden auf die Dauer zu behaupten ist," in "Wider die Mischehen," *KH* 5, no. 46 (1912–13), N1.

14. For more background on women's colonization in GSWA, refer to my dissertation, "The Colonial Woman Question: Gender, National Identity, and Empire in the German Colonial Society Female Emigration Program" (Ph.D. diss., SUNY Binghamton, 1996).

15. Helmut Bley, *Kolonialherrschaft und Sozialstruktur in Deutsch-Südwestafrika* (Hamburg, 1968), trans. Hugh Ridley, *South-West Africa under German Rule, 1894–1914* (Evanston, Ill., 1971), 212–13, examines mixed-race persons' grounds for claims to German citizenship.

16. Letter from colonist Friedrich Heuer, Otjimbingwe, addressed to the imperial district office for Otjimbingwe, September 28, 1897, DSWA, Personenstandssachen: Mischehen, 666.F.IV.r.2, Bd. 1, Bl. 9.

17. GSWA government circular, dated February 28, 1898, DSWA, Besiedelungssachen, 1079.L.11.k.1, Bd. 1, Bl. 11.

18. Letter from Angelo Golinelli, Keetmanshoop, to the governor's office, Windhoek, date not legible, spring 1898, DSWA, Besiedelungssachen, 1079.L.11.k.1, Bd. 1, Bl. 19–21.

19. Helmut Walser Smith, "The Talk of Genocide, the Rhetoric of Miscegenation: Notes on Debates in the German Reichstag Concerning Southwest Africa, 1904–1914," in *Imperialist Imagination,* ed. Friedrichsmeyer, Lennox, and Zantop, 107–24. The lengthy transcripts of the debate appear in the *Stenographische Berichte über die Verhandlungen des Reichstages,* Bd. 285, 53–56 Sitzungen, May 2–8, 1912, Bl. 1648–747. The resolution passed 203 to 133. Leonore Niessen-Deiters, "Rassenreinheit! Eine deutsche Frau über die Mischehen in den Kolonien," *KH* 5, no. 36 (1911–12), N1.

20. "Die Stellung der Kolonien zur Frage Mischehen," *KH* 4, no. 15 (1910–11), N1.

21. "Wider die Mischehen."

22. "Auch ein Beitrag zur Reichstagsresolution über die Mischehen," *KH* 5, no. 37 (1911–12), N1.

23. Stoler, "Sexual Affronts," 199.

24. "Schwarze Europäer," *KH* 4, no. 17 (1910–11), 13–4; "Oeffentliches Aergernis," *KH* 5, no. 49 (1911–12), N1; "Der Schwarze as Vorgesetzter," *KH* 5, no. 53 (1911–12), N1; "Der 'Hosennigger,'" *KH* 5, no. 22 (1911–12), 2. I have translated the German terms *schwarz* and *Schwarze* as "black"; *farbig* as "colored"; *Neger* as "negro"; and *Nigger* as "nigger," throughout.

25. Campt, Grosse, and Lemke-Muniz de Faria, "Blacks, Germans," 214n6.

26. "Eine Mahnung an deutsche Eltern und Erzieher," *KH* 3, no. 4 (1909–10), N1, reprints an article from the *Norddeutsche Allgemeine Zeitung.*

27. "Eine Mahnung an deutsche Eltern und Erzieher."

28. Otto Stollowsky, "Schwarze Europäer," *KH* 4, no. 17 (1910–11), 13.

29. "Oeffentliches Aergernis"; Ein widerlicher Beitrag zur Rassenfrage," *KH* 5, no. 46 (1911–12), N1.

30. "Ein widerlicher Beitrag zur Rassenfrage."

31. "Oeffentliches Aergernis."

32. Yael Simpson Fletcher, "Unsettling Settlers: Colonial Migrants and Racialized Sexuality in Interwar Marseilles," in *Gender, Sexuality, and Colonial Modernities,* ed. Antoinette Burton, Routledge Research on Gender and History, no. 2 (New York, 1999). The connection between anti-Semitism and prejudice toward blacks is not obvious but seems implied here. George Mosse, *Nationalism and Sexuality: Middle Class Morality and Sexual Norms in Modern Europe* (Madison, Wis., 1985), 133ff, provides a useful framework connecting negative attitudes toward foreigners, so-called inferior races, and fear of their lack of control over their passions. For more on colonial imagery and anti-Semitism, see Wildenthal, *German Women,* 57ff, and Andrew Zimmerman, *Anthropology and Antihumanism in Imperial Germany* (Chicago, 2001), especially 242ff.

33. "Der Schwarzer als Vorgesetzer."

34. Quoted from "Der 'Hosennigger.'"

35. Campt, Grosse, and Lemke-Muniz de Faria, "Blacks, Germans," 228.

36. May Opitz, Katharina Oguntoye, and Dagmar Schultz, eds., *Showing Our Colors: Afro-German Women Speak Out,* trans. Anne V. Adams (Amherst, 1991).

CHAPTER 3

German-Speaking People and German Heritage

Nazi Germany and the Problem
of *Volksgemeinschaft*

Norbert Götz

It has become commonplace to describe the utopia of German National Socialists in their own words as *Volksgemeinschaft*. English-speaking authors quite often do not translate the word as "national community" or "people's community" but rather keep it in the original German. This practice intentionally stresses the specifically German character of the concept and particularly its inextricable association with the ideas of National Socialism. This makes sense, even though the term does exist in other languages, such as the Scandinavian languages or Finnish, and despite the fact that democratic political parties in Germany before the Nazi rise to power also commonly used the phrase. In the 1930s Volksgemeinschaft became a key concept within National Socialism, omnipresent in political, legal, and scientific discussions, as well as in administrative and everyday language. From the National Socialists' point of view, the Volksgemeinschaft consisted of all Germans not excluded for racial, hereditary, behavioral, or political reasons. Since the expansionist National Socialist worldview flatly rejected the German Reich's post–World War I borders, the following questions arose: Which Germans were to be included in the Volksgemeinschaft, and where were they located?[1]

In light of the territorial ambitions of the National Socialists, a discussion of the Volksgemeinschaft in the 1930s and 1940s cannot be limited to the state of Germany. Not only the Nazis, but also German-speaking people of completely different political views in and outside of Germany, staked out relative positions of power and hegemonic spheres in their debate over the meaning of Volksgemeinschaft. In general, the German diaspora was neither able nor willing to resist the use of this powerful terminology.

However, the idea of Volksgemeinschaft could mean different things to different people. Among overseas populations of German speakers or German descent, one can distinguish three different conceptualizations: supranational, national, and subnational notions of Volksgemeinschaft, only partially compatible with each other. Volksgemeinschaft could stand for the democratic idea of citizenship or for Nazi racialism and expansionism. It could be used to support existing political boundaries or to draw new ethnocultural boundaries of Germanness completely at odds with existing national borders. German Nazis had a strong tendency to claim territory outside of the German Empire, but they were rather flexible in how they applied their concept of Volksgemeinschaft. Their definitions of the notion are characterized by ambiguity and vary case by case. Most importantly, the term *Volksgemeinschaft* did not just stand for different notions; it became a vehicle for the struggle over different worldviews among people of German extraction. With some noticeable exceptions, the Nazis were quite successful in their battle to equate German heritage with membership in the National Socialist Volksgemeinschaft. However, they lost the larger war, which was their campaign to translate their definition into practice.

This chapter provides an overview of the broad international discourse surrounding the concept of Volksgemeinschaft as it concerned Germans abroad. The empirical examples that I present reflect the ideas of the largest groups, those in closest geographical proximity to Germany and those whose ideas were most representative of the different concepts of Volksgemeinschaft. Due to this study's methodological orientation toward conceptual history, I also have given preference to cases where the names of institutions or titles of publications actually use the term *Volksgemeinschaft.*[2] Therefore, Mexico and Brazil, where such organizations and writings were prominent, are discussed much more frequently in what follows than, for example, the United States, despite its larger population of German heritage. The lesser importance of the notion of Volksgemeinschaft in North America appears to reflect its lack of appeal for the region's populations of German descent, which I argue is a result of their greater integration and acculturation into mainstream society.[3]

Of the three conceptualizations of the Volksgemeinschaft mentioned previously—the supranational, national, and subnational—the first was most important. The supranational concept was suggestive and aggressive, the one that demanded *Anschluss* and provoked an answer: yes or no. This concept became a catch phrase that compelled Germans abroad, especially those living in regions subject to potential German invasion or other interference, to react.

National Socialists in Germany and German-speaking sympathizers abroad primarily employed the supranational concept of Volksgemeinschaft, which they thought of as a primordial community of common descent ideologically reconstructed by the Nazi movement. Quite often individuals with this supranational viewpoint still displayed nationally grounded points of view on such matters as foreign policy tactics, but in essence they claimed to be the core of an exclusive worldwide population numbering in the hundreds of millions (*Hundertmillionenvolk*). The inclusion of people living outside the borders of Germany became an essential feature of the Nazi notion of Volksgemeinschaft. By means of this supranational concept of Volksgemeinschaft, the Nazis laid claim to the ideological loyalty of citizens of foreign countries to the German Reich. A Brazilian author of German descent indignantly concluded: "Logically and practically, nothing less than German citizenship itself is demanded of us."[4] At the same time, the idea also legitimated the Nazi policy of territorial expansion.

In the supranational view, the institution of the national state served as a frame of reference, upon which the Nazis aimed to imprint the supranational reality. In this context, specific geographical and political conditions were of great importance. The proclaimed Hundertmillionenvolk consisted of the sixty-five million people who lived within the German state's borders. The Nazis saw this state as a "rump Germany" (*Restdeutschland*), and their efforts sought to make it a "core Germany." There were an additional fifteen million German-speaking people in contiguous regions of Belgium, Luxembourg, Switzerland, Austria, Czechoslovakia, and Poland adjacent to German territory— adding to what the Nazis portrayed as "adjoining area of German settlement" (*geschlossener Volkssiedelboden*). There were another four million people with German-speaking background residing in other parts of Europe and sixteen million overseas, mainly living in the United States.[5]

In the language of the 1930s, Nazis proclaimed the supranational Volksgemeinschaft as follows: "Even he, who is not a citizen of the German Reich, but of some other state, or a stateless person, belongs to the German Volksgemeinschaft, if he belongs to the German *Volkstum* [national character]." Such assertions went on to pronounce that

ties to Germany would not disrupt "loyal obedience to all legal responsibilities [of Germans abroad] toward the foreign state of residence
[*volkstumsfremd*]."[6] Often, the question of citizenship of ethnic Germans who were foreign nationals remained vague, but this did not rule
out concrete political measures.

> The German Volk is not defined by the borders of the Reich, but a
> *Volks- und Schicksalsgemeinschaft* [community of the people and of
> destiny] spread out over the whole earth, but bound together by
> blood and race. . . . Since the National Socialist rise to power in 1933
> the welfare of the Germans abroad has become an essential part of
> the Volksgemeinschaft. . . . All the efforts aiming at developing
> closer connections between Germans abroad and the Volksgemein-
> schaft should in a broader sense be considered as welfare measures.[7]

However, with the onset of German territorial expansion and World
War II, Nazi efforts to incorporate extraterritorial Germans assumed
dimensions beyond welfare.

In wartime, the German states' praxis of Volksgemeinschaft far
exceeded humanitarianism and came to include duties assigned to
"national comrades" from adjacent countries and the German diaspora. The following quotation from a juridical work (written during
the period of total mobilization for war) gives a good illustration of the
National Socialist way of thinking and also reflects the replacement of
state legislation by party law, which incorporated arbitrary measures
and which were potentially in conflict with the general principles of
state legislation.[8]

> The party is the elite of the German Volksgemeinschaft; therefore its
> law is the law of the Volksgemeinschaft and is valid for this German
> Volksgemeinschaft. All German *Volksgenossen* [national comrades]
> belong to the German Volksgemeinschaft, no matter if they live
> within or—and this is exactly the crucial point of the National
> Socialist Volksgemeinschaft—outside of the borders of the Reich.
> Concerning *Volksdeutsche* [ethnic Germans] of foreign citizenship,
> bilateral considerations do not allow an expansion of the party rule;
> but there are no restrictions against extending the party's regula-
> tions to stateless members of the German Volk, as well as to such
> members of the German Volk, whose foreign citizenship in the near
> future will be canceled and replaced by the citizenship of the Ger-
> man Reich (e.g., all resettlers).[9]

In general, as the self-proclaimed agent of the Volksgemeinschaft, the National Socialist Party asserted itself as the highest legal authority for all of these people. In practice, the party, in consideration of international relations, refrained from exercising its claims on the citizens of foreign countries. However, under the condition of war, the party no longer felt it necessary to regard combatant nations' claims and therefore claimed the loyalty of those individuals in annexed territories who were considered a part of the German Volksgemeinschaft. Obviously, then, the Volksgemeinschaft was a highly flexible ideological construct, and Nazi Party officials made use of this notion as it suited them.

The instruments of the supranational Nazi Volksgemeinschaft policy consisted of different organizations that were ostensibly etatist in that they gave lip service to extraterritorial Germans' obedience to foreign regimes but unofficially spread a subversive message. Among these, the noteworthy are the Volksbund für das Deutschtum im Ausland (People's Union for Germanness Abroad) and the Auslandsorganisation der NSDAP (Foreign Organization of the NSDAP).[10] The latter pretended to consider as Germans abroad only the two or three million "persons of German blood living outside the borders of the Reich as conscious Germans and possessing German citizenship."[11] In Nazi terminology, the *Auslandsdeutsche* (German citizens abroad) together with the so-called Volksdeutsche (ethnic Germans) made up the *Deutschtum im Ausland* (Germans abroad). Officially, only the German citizens abroad were to be incorporated into the party as a sort of virtual district (*Gau*) through the Foreign Organization of the NSDAP.[12]

Although a contemporary observer at one point in time noted that, for a couple of months, the speeches of the leader of the Foreign Organization of the NSDAP, Ernst Wilhelm Bohle, had not addressed the German Volksgemeinschaft and the Volksgenossen abroad but instead the "German citizens abroad," a clear distinction between these two groups was usually avoided.[13] The discussion of the Volksgemeinschaft did not stop, and even if sometimes the impression appeared that the term referred specifically to the community of German citizens, this narrower meaning was in conflict with the more inclusive concepts of Volk and ethnic Germans, which Nazis also employed. Apart from the deliberate use of vague and contradictory language, the militant images of the Foreign Organization of the NSDAP were quite revealing, for example, the statement that the Germans abroad had "discovered the distant great German Volksgemeinschaft, and feel themselves to be its most exposed outpost."[14] Obviously, all the concepts the Nazis used were highly ambiguous and contained different messages for representatives of foreign states and for persons they considered to be Germans in these states. Nazis sought to calm the former with etatist references while mobilizing the latter with rhetoric featuring tribal imagery.

One offshoot of the Nazi Foreign Organization was the Deutsche Volksgemeinschaft in Mexiko (DVM, or German Volksgemeinschaft in Mexico; in Spanish, Centro Aleman). The second annual report of this organization ended with the following words: "By means of our unity in Mexico, we want to prove to our German fatherland that it always can rely on its brothers abroad. We are willing to assume the heaviest burdens for the well-being and best interests of the great Volksgemeinschaft of all Germans. Heil Hitler!"[15] Even if this organization consisted of German citizens residing in the host country of Mexico, the organization addressed Mexicans of German descent as well, as a Christmas message of the German envoy showed: "Loyal to the orders of Adolf Hitler, the DVM refrained from interference in the political matters and the views of the country we live in. It therefore did not give any legitimate cause for complaint, and enabled even those Mexican citizens of German descent to hold onto German ways and customs without violating their loyalty to the land of their citizenship."[16] Despite such claims to sensitivity to their host country, the concept of Volksgemeinschaft suffered serious problems when the Liga pro cultura alemana, an organization of left-wing German exiles, explained to the Mexicans that the Foreign Organization of the NSDAP considered them to belong to an inferior race.[17]

The intentions of the Foreign Organization of the NSDAP came through more clearly in its cultural products than through the double-speak of official announcements. A good example is a serialized novel that appeared in the journal of the DVM. In this supposedly "true wild west story" the DVM finances the resettlement of a ragged orphan over the great ocean "once crossed by his father to find a home in Mexico, to Germany . . . to the fatherland . . . to the land of his ancestors, where he should find a home in the *Hitlerjugend* and in the German Volk." In the story, a consul regards the German Volksgemeinschaft as "the highest aim of the Führer." The novel further describes a sense of German comradeship that stretches out far beyond the circle of German citizens.

"We all belong together, Freese, you and I and the poor settlers in the countryside, and the German workers in the mines, and the employees on the plantations, and even the feudal masters, who one day will realize as well, and those who are still vagabonds at the moment. . . . All, all of us have the same Führer now. . . all of us are now bound together by destiny more than ever. . . ." said Mr. Heymann, who had begun as a lowly employee on an isolated plantation many years ago and by means of hard work and ability eventually acquired a warehouse, where he specialized in selling German products. . . . "We . . . WE, Freese, will achieve this, when every German sees in his Volksgenossen first a German, a national comrade, and tries to help to reconcile, to *gleichschalten* [force into line]—as they say over there nowadays—differences of rank or class or birth or wealth."[18]

As this quote makes clear, the real goal of the organizations dealing with the Germans abroad was the complete transfer of their loyalties from their nations of residence to the Volksgemeinschaft: disintegration, Gleichschaltung, relocation, and reintegration of all people of German descent or language. Promoting this agenda was an obvious aim of *Deutsches Wollen* (German will), the propaganda journal of the Foreign Organization of the NSDAP.

At the same time, the Nazi conception of the people and the Volksgemeinschaft as independent from state ties led to the discovery of alien Volksgemeinschaften within the German Reich. The Nazi Party viewed the Danish minority in Schleswig and the Polish minority in Prussia as citizens but also saw them as part of a non-German Volksgemeinschaft.[19] The members of the so-called Jewish blood community and Volksgemeinschaft (*Bluts- und Volksgemeinschaft*) were given an inferior citizen status with the Nuremberg citizenship laws in 1935, in spite of most of them having German as their mother tongue. The Sinti and Roma were treated in the same way. As a publication of the Reichsausschuß für Volksgesundheitsdienst (Reich Committee on Public Health Service) shows, people with one Jewish parent could be considered part of the German Volksgemeinschaft (they could get regular citizenship as well) but not of the Blutsgemeinschaft (blood community), which was more narrowly defined but not of the same legal importance.[20] Those belonging to the Masur-, Sorb-, Czech-, and Frisian-speaking minorities within the German borders were declared to be part of special regional variations of the German Volksgemeinschaft, while minority populations of Lithuanians and Kashubians were dismissed as irrelevant because of their small numbers.[21] The German policy of expansion in World War II led to further complications in the definition of the Volksgemeinschaft and to a further decrease of the significance of spoken German as a determinant of membership or exclusion in the Volksgemeinschaft. When Norwegian volunteers had to be recruited for the German Waffen SS there was even talk of a "European Volksgemeinschaft."[22] More typical were the five ranks of the German *Volksliste* with their cultural-racial measures of proximity to Germanness. (Doris Bergen's chapter in this volume examines the use of the Volksliste in more detail.) This list was a register that people in some occupied territories could sign if they believed they had characteristics making them suitable for German assimilation—thus, officially, it was a program for re-Germanization. Inclusion was subject to political criteria, as well, since the party regarded the political enemies of National Socialism as having placed themselves outside the Volksgemeinschaft.[23]

The notion of a supranational German Volksgemeinschaft also existed outside Nazi ideology, although in this connection there was more emphasis on a community of culture and language, or Volkstum, rather than on race. Unlike the Nazis, representatives of this view—for example, the Deutscher Verband zur nationalen Befriedigung Europas (German Association for National Peacekeeping in Europe), which united prominent members of German minority groups in Eastern Europe—did not just address the supranational distribution of ethnic Germans but also accepted this situation. In an appeal to all Germans, the association lamented that the Nazis' elevation of "party consciousness to a determinant of Germanness . . . had destroyed the concept of Volksgemeinschaft."[24]

National conceptions of Volksgemeinschaft based on notions of state-specific citizenship rather than genealogy were not compatible with any of these supranational conceptions. Members of strong German-speaking groups outside the state of Germany (for example, in Switzerland, Austria, or Czechoslovakia) preferred these constructs, and even members of typical immigrant societies such as Brazil sometimes found them more attractive than supranational ideology. In Austria and Czechoslovakia these national concepts, which always carried social connections to one's fellow citizens at the same time, were challenged. A German-speaking Brazilian observer contrasted his community's feelings with those of other German minorities, especially those living in Eastern Europe: "We are not Brazilians against our will," he wrote, "like they are Czechs, Poles, Italians against their will. Maybe they can be called 'Auslandsdeutsche' in 'everyday language.' We, however, are no 'Auslandsdeutsche' in similar 'everyday language.' Or, would you call the German-speaking people of Switzerland 'Auslandsdeutsche'?"[25]

The man who wrote these lines was Franz Metzler, editor of the Catholic newspaper *Deutsches Volksblatt* in Porto Alegre. Under pressure from the Nazi vision of an all-inclusive Volksgemeinschaft, Metzler in 1936 arranged a contest for essays on the questions "*Was ist Volkstum? Was ist Volksgemeinschaft?*" (What is German character? What is Volksgemeinschaft?). Besides asking for an answer to the basic question regarding the difference between these concepts, the contest called on participants to define Brazilian understandings of these notions and to compare these with their German counterparts. Metzler himself was one of the twenty-seven participants in the contest, reviewed by an independent panel of three.[26]

Metzler summarized the contest results as follows: "All the essayists believe in German Volkstum and German Volksgemeinschaft. All their entries recognize the Brazilian Volksgemeinschaft. Concerning Brazilian Volkstum, most entrants believe that it has not yet developed to a phenomenon pulsating extensively and uniformly throughout the whole life of the individual and of the whole Volk. But its promising beginnings are recognized by all but three, who flatly deny a Brazilian Volkstum."[27]

Sympathy with Metzler was clearly found in those essays stressing differences between Volkstum and Volksgemeinschaft. According to him, Volkstum had to be seen as a "supranational social reality," a loosely defined cultural concept with a marked tendency toward hybridization. Volksgemeinschaft, in contrast, had to be seen "as a phenomenon associated with the existing constitutional and international order of law." If one leaves aside the problem of dual citizenship, Metzler and his fellow authors' shared notion of Volksgemeinschaft was an exclusively national (in their case Brazilian) concept.[28]

The award-winning essay, whose author preferred to remain anonymous, depicted the notion of Volksgemeinschaft in this sense: "A Brazilian Volksgemeinschaft exists of all the Brazilian citizens living inside the Brazilian borders, just as in Germany. It is here and there a state-oriented, civic *Rechtsgemeinschaft* [community of law]." As this author saw it, some individuals, however, could belong to several Volksgemeinschaften in cases of multiple citizenship.[29] In his own contribution, Metzler referred not only to the Volksgemeinschaft but also to a *Staatsvolksgemeinschaft* (a community of people within a state).

Moreover, he criticized National Socialism for conjuring up "a monstrous, mythical concept of Volk, spreading in the territories of other peoples and demonstrating its own absurdity by claiming Volksgemeinschaft on the basis of real similarity of the blood, whereas the superior form of Volksgemeinschaft is concretely based in the rule of the state." Metzler went on to accuse the Nazis of seeking to "completely abolish the exiting borders of the Volksgemeinschaft that had been forged by the state, in favor of a new, imaginary border without any theoretical or practical value, apart from the auto-suggestive effect its large numbers exercises on people."[30]

The contest seems to have caused a major stir among the German-speaking people in Brazil, and an open letter of response was published under the pseudonym Furor Teutonicus. Its basic accusation was that the award winner—not the least with his understanding of Volksgemeinschaft—was "an outsider far from any generally acknowledged views" who did not consult "the profound literature regarding this question." The German Brazilian, Furor Teutonicus stated, was "racially part of the German Volksgemeinschaft in the whole world, regardless of the public community he lived in or his political interaction with the Lusobrazilians and other ethnic groups in Brazil." In this view, National Socialism had realized the trend toward the Volksgemeinschaft.[31]

In spite of Metzer's attempts to counter the Nazi interpretations, there was altogether little opposition against National Socialism among Brazilians of German heritage or most other German communities abroad.[32] Further evidence of the attraction of the Nazi notion of Volksgemeinschaft is offered in the writings of the editor of the Blumenau *Urwaldbote* (*Jungle Messenger*), Arthur Koehler. In a letter to the local representative of the Nazi Party from August 1933, he warmly welcomed the fact that Hitler's government "set great store on giving the word *Volksgemeinschaft* a much broader meaning" than earlier had been the case in the Weimar Republic and the Kaiserreich.[33] In one instance, a pastor responded to criticism of his spread of Nazi ideas among boys in his community in the following way.

[I]t was not necessary to tell him that the boys were Brazilian citizens, and he himself educated them to be loyal citizens, but otherwise as bearers of German blood, the boys belonged to the German Volksgemeinschaft. And the whole German Volksgemeinschaft, not stopping at the borders of nations and countries, today just had . . . one Führer, which it must listen to, whose name is Hitler; it gathered around one symbol, the swastika, and one song was holy for it, the song of the martyr of the [Nazi] movement, Horst Wessel. It is completely impossible and not in the least conceivable to see the [ethnic German] people here as comprising their own, separate German Volksgemeinschaft.[34]

In fact, Brazilians of German heritage widely accepted the Nazi equation of Nazism with Germanness, of a Nazi-German Volksgemeinschaft. Thanks to the distance from Germany, however, Hitler did not take advantage of these sympathies.

In Switzerland, however, the situation was quite different. During World War II, Switzerland was like a small independent island in a European sea controlled by the Nazis and their allies. Despite the fact that two-thirds of its population spoke a German dialect as their mother tongue, Switzerland had a long tradition of keeping the German state at a distance. Because of the strategic situation, Hitler accepted Swiss neutrality, at least for the moment.

In Switzerland the concept of Volksgemeinschaft seems to have been much less controversial in relation to its national identity than in any other country. The term already had been used in Switzerland before World War I, and once the Nazis achieved power in Germany the term played a crucial role in the political debate. The Volksgemeinschaft became the key concept underlying the so-called spiritual defense of the country—that is, the antitotalitarian Swiss rhetoric of community in the 1930s.[35]

Oliver Zimmer argues that two rival movements, both founded in 1933, especially propagated the concept. One of them was the bourgeois left, unionist Die Nation, whose positions were articulated by the newspaper with the same name and who supported the "Volksgemeinschaft as social democracy." The other one was the middle-class Neue Schweiz (New Switzerland), which advocated a corporative "Volksgemeinschaft as an authoritarian democracy of bonds" between citizens. The rise of the Neue Schweiz was as rapid as its fall, and it was dissolved by the end of 1936, by which time its concept of Volksgemeinschaft had been increasingly delegitimatized and marginalized. Zimmer interprets this failure as strong evidence in support of Reinhart Koselleck's hypothesis "that disputes about the legitimate semantic coinage of political key concepts can develop into a struggle for the existence or extinction of social groups." He argues that the primary reason for the failure of this organization was the limited tradition and circulation of authoritarian and racist discourses in Swiss society on which to build momentum.[36] For our purposes, however, it is even more important to note that, although references to heredity were fundamental to the arguments of the Neue Schweiz, their racial definitions were not grounded in Germanness but rather were based on the notion of an "Alpine man," which included the whole Swiss population "between the Alps and the Jura mountains."[37] Even the right-wing Neue Schweiz viewed the German, the French, the Italian, and the Raeto-Romanic parts of the population as a unified whole.

In contrast to the Neue Schweiz, with its ambivalent position toward National Socialism, the editorial board of *Die Nation,* in accordance with its subtitle—*Independent Newspaper for Democracy and Volksgemeinschaft*—distanced itself clearly from the German regime: "A central concept of National Socialism is the Volksgemeinschaft. But this concept receives a new meaning [in National Socialism]. It is not defined spiritually, but naturally, through the Volk, racially. The Volk is not the unity of common culture and knowledge. Volksgemeinschaft does not mean closeness in history and political principles, but rather community of blood and language."[38] In contrast, *Die Nation* advocated a "League of Nations in miniature," combining cosmopolitan universalism and *Heimatbewußtsein* (awareness of one's homeland), and undertaking an active economic policy of crisis management and the "extension of social inclusion to encompass the left." Zimmer depicts a model of Volksgemeinschaft that was based on patriotic allegiance to the national constitution (*Verfaßungspatriotismus*) and rejects the hypothesis (which would come easily to those with traditional left-wing views) that the labor movement had been co-opted through the idea of national unity and induced to pursue bourgeois ends.[39] According to Kurt Imhof, the Swiss concept of Volksgemeinschaft did not function "as a strait-jacket for a status quo, but rather as a vehicle of contentious political bargaining, leading to a weakening of the policy of deflation and to the realization of a minimum consensus—which was still insufficient—on social and economic policy," on which Switzerland's wartime economy and postwar welfare state could be based.[40] Interestingly, Volksgemeinschaft in the Swiss context can indeed be seen in this way. While the concept of Volksgemeinschaft certainly does not entirely explain modern Switzerland's political distribution of power, it demonstrates that there was an alternative frame of reference available, which was substantially different from the German one. This was a potentially democratic usage of the term, lost in most interpretations outside of Switzerland.

In the case of Switzerland, it would be interesting to develop more precise analysis of the role played by the concept of Volksgemeinschaft in the labor movement, to investigate pan-German or perhaps particularistic German-Swiss notions that may have arisen in Nazi circles, as well as to examine the reception of the concept in the French- and Italian-speaking parts of the country.[41] Although the use of the concept of Volksgemeinschaft in Switzerland had a democratic tradition and history, its connotations there today are generally colored by the German Nazi experience.[42]

In Austria, the concept of Volksgemeinschaft was more precarious. There was a certain tradition of assigning Austrians and Germans to one and the same Volksgemeinschaft, whose justification stemmed not only from the common language but also from a shared history of political union that endured from the origins of the Holy Roman Empire until the breakup of the Germanic Confederation in 1866. The subsequent foundation for a *kleindeutsche* (small German) empire was orchestrated by Bismarck, who—in the interests of Prussian domination—deliberately excluded Austria from the German Kaiserreich in 1871 in the face of nationalists' criticism. This sense of historic omission became the basis for popular demands for a latter-day *großdeutsche* (greater German) political reintegration. When the Habsburg Empire dissolved after World War I, only the victorious powers prevented the remaining German-speaking Austrians from merging with the state of Germany. Indeed, the plausibility of a common German-Austrian union served as an ideal justification for revisiting the Treaty of Versailles, which opened the door to the even more ambitious revisions that the Nazis intended.

During World War I, Otto Gierke, a German professor of law, had referred to German Austrian Volksgemeinschaft; the conservative Deutschnationale Volkspartei (German National People's Party) included the concept in its postwar program; and between 1923 and 1925, when the National Socialist Party was banned in Germany, its cover organization, the Großdeutsche Volksgemeinschaft (Greater German People's Community), even took it as a label.[43] In Austria in 1921 a German women's association formed, calling itself "Volksgemeinschaft." But the existing separate Austrian state became increasingly popular during the 1930s, and with the banning of the Nazi Party, the organization experienced substantial losses in membership. However, when the Germans invaded Austria in March 1938, the Austrian group offered to integrate (*Gleichschaltung*) with Nazi women's organizations. Once having reached its goal, the leadership saw itself in the role of "nameless soldiers again."[44]

As in other places, even in Austria there were uses of the notion of Volksgemeinschaft that did not imply ethnic unification but rather social integration within the country, such as preserving the distinct Austrian national framework. As Austrian minister of agriculture in 1931, Engelbert Dollfuß stated that the nation's farmers had reached their present position in public life "only by means of their functional and systematic cooperation within the framework of democratic Volksgemeinschaft."[45] Dollfuß—who later as chancellor eliminated the constitution, founded the so-called Austrofascist movement, and put down a socialist uprising in February 1934—subsequently "warmly welcomed the good workers into our Volksgemeinschaft." Contrary to the politics of the labor movement, Dollfuß apparently also saw the working classes as "necessary parts of our Volksgemeinschaft."[46] The difficulty of distinguishing a separate Austrian path during this time was reflected in Dollfuß's rhetoric, which maneuvered back and forth between references to "German" and "Austrian." One speech, which discussed the "German fatherland Austria," demonstrated perfectly the problematic context within which the national Austrian question was discussed.[47]

After Dollfuß died in an attempted Nazi putsch, his successor, Kurt Schuschnigg, continued to define the Volksgemeinschaft as a domestic Austrian phenomenon. A collection of his speeches features chapters on "Woman and Volksgemeinschaft" and the "Armed Forces and Volksgemeinschaft." Schuschnigg considered the Austrian military in particular "to be one of the first and most important schools of the state capable of educating [its people] to a living Volksgemeinschaft."[48] His minister of political education, Walter Adam, advocated "concentrating on the realization of the idea of social justice, and, moreover, on the establishment of a real Volksgemeinschaft and the maintenance and extension of charitable institutions."[49]

In contrast, the German Nazis used the concept of Volksgemeinschaft against Austria to legitimize their own power politics. This culminated in the annexation of Austria, but Nazi intentions were clear long before 1938. In the mid-1930s, some Germans accused the Austrians of using political Catholicism to promote the division of ethnic Germans in Southeastern Europe, especially in Southern Tyrol, Yugoslavia, and Hungary, "into Germans and Austrians abroad." Such Germans maintained that "any means" were justified in opposing the "separatism preached within [ethnic German] communities," since these "efforts aimed to tear ethnic German groups to pieces and make the development of the Volksgemeinschaft among [ethnic] Germans abroad impossible."[50]

In his speech of March 18, 1938, on the occupation and annexation of Austria, Adolf Hitler asked rhetorically: "What satisfaction could make a man prouder in this world than having led the people in his own Heimat [homeland] into the greater Volksgemeinschaft!"[51] A few days before, at the so-called liberation rally in Vienna, he had shouted at the crowd: "This country is German, it has understood its mission, which it will fulfill, and it shall never ever be outdone by anybody in its loyalty to the greater German Volksgemeinschaft." However, he paid a certain tribute to the special status of Austria on this occasion, talking of the "German-Austrian man in the framework of our great Volksgemeinschaft."[52] The regime attempted to erase this hybrid identity later, when Austria was renamed Ostmark (Eastern Marches).

In Czechoslovakia, where the so-called Sudeten Germans made up a quarter of the population, the situation was similar to Austria in at least one aspect: the Sudeten Germans had great psychological and political difficulties in becoming accustomed to their new home state, which had been built from the ruins of the Habsburg Empire. Moreover, they had lost their previous position as a regional ruling elite and were even denied influence proportionate to their size or self-administration in the homogenous German-speaking areas of Czechoslovakia. This social and political demotion was a breeding ground for Nazi notions of Volksgemeinschaft that questioned existing national borders.

It is not surprising, then, that Czechs viewed the idea of Volksgemeinschaft with alarm. As reported in a memorandum of the Verband der deutschen Volksgruppen in Europa (League of German Communities in Europe), led by the Sudeten German Nazi leader Konrad Henlein, the Czechs considered "any education that promotes German Volksgemeinschaft . . . as an attack on the state, and [they] spare no effort to combat the different forms of German youth education, including labor service."[53] The subtitle of a newspaper on the occasion of the Sudeten German supplementary election, staged by the Nazis on December 4, 1938, was "*Your 'Yes' to the Leader of the Greater German Volksgemeinschaft.*"[54] Hitler had already issued a similar appeal on their behalf to their German counterparts in the Reich in October of the same year, after the German invasion of Czechoslovakia: "We have to include these people in the circle of our Volksgemeinschaft and help them."[55]

Even among ethnic Germans in Czechoslovakia, however, there was a democratic usage of the term *Volksgemeinschaft* after 1933 among the so-called Volkssozialisten (People's Socialists), a fraction within the Social Democratic Party. This notion was put forward most aggressively in an article by Josef Hofbauer, who was sympathetic to the People's Socialists and editor of the theoretical journal of the Sudeten German Social Democrats, *Der Kampf* (The Struggle). Hofbauer contrasted the bourgeois usage of the notion, represented by "today's nationalist Volksgemeinschaftler" Hitler and Henlein, with the dream of a Volksgemeinschaft consisting of free men, in the spirit of the suppressed tradition first articulated by Johan Gottlieb Fichte. Such men would be neither nationalist nor opposed to other nations. As he continued, Hofbauer drew on the classical repertoire of the labor movement.

> Those trying to mislead the workers about the fact of class conflict by means of deceitful talk of Volksgemeinschaft, which aims at the maintenance of the rule of Germans over Germans, prevent the development of Volksgemeinschaft. The goal of the proletarian class struggle is the elimination of class rule, the abolition of classes, and thus precisely the realization of Volksgemeinschaft! Whoever wants Volksgemeinschaft has to stand for class struggle, to pave the way for the perfection of the nation.[56]

The People's Socialists did not advocate class struggle but rather a cross-class alliance of industrial workers with agricultural workers, peasants, and the middle class against Henlein's pro-Nazi Sudetendeutsche Partei (Sudeten German Party). Wilhelm Sollmann, former secretary of the interior, was the only important member of the Social Democratic Party of Germany (SPD) in exile who sympathized with the strategy pursued by the People's Socialists. Richard Löwenthal expressed the majority opinion among the exiled SPD leadership, arguing that the Social Democrats had "to deal with this tendency as the incursion of the enemy's political ideology within our ranks."[57] His harsh reaction is partly explained by concern about contacts between prominent People's Socialists and the leftist faction of the German Nazi Party centered around Otto Strasser, which was also in exile.[58]

This is not the place to discuss the complex and differing motives that might underlie such dubious contacts. It will suffice here to note that there were People's Socialists who in the course of the dismemberment of Czechoslovakia turned into Nazis and there were others who did not and fled. An example from the first group is Emil Franzel, who became editor of the journal *Vorposten* (Forward Post) and one of the spiritual leaders of German Nazism in Prague. In postwar Germany he made a career as the editor of the *Bayerischer Staatsanzeiger,* the official newspaper of the state of Bavaria.[59] An example from the latter group is Wenzel Jaksch, the author of the best-known publication of the People's Socialists and vice chairman of the Sudeten German Social Democrats. He fled to London but later would emerge as one of the leading and more sensible expellee politicians in the Federal Republic of Germany. It was not generally odd for a Social Democrat to support the idea of a people's community. In the Weimar period, Social Democrats had frequently tried to promote their own understanding of Volksgemeinschaft, for example, in the party program of 1921 and in chairman Otto Wels's speech in Parliament on March 23, 1933, in which he rejected the Nazi's assumption of power.[60]

The People's Socialists explicitly favored Swedish social democracy (which was also a popular model in America during the New Deal), and they contrasted a Germany internally torn apart with a Sweden that showed "the organic growth of a genuine Volksgemeinschaft in its political structure."[61] Wenzel Jaksch characterized his program concisely through reference to Sweden: "To explain, once and for all, what is meant by the term 'People's Socialism,' which was occasionally used in the book *Volk und Arbeiter* [Jaksch's book, *People and Workers*], the answer is: Sweden!" In his view, the failure of German social democracy was due to its "unnatural coupling of dogmatic theory with a partly realistic, partly opportunistic practice," which resulted in ideological fossilization and the consequent isolation.[62]

In his book, Jaksch even discussed an atomizing "fascist 'Volksgemeinschaft'" and "the yearning of an unfinished nation for a full and solid form of life," which struggled unremittingly for expression "in the bloodily violated concept of Volksgemeinschaft." He concluded that there was "just one form of real Volksgemeinschaft, i.e., the integration of the whole nation in the process of manufacturing, in a meaningful organized system of production and distribution of goods."[63]

The Saar region was a special case, where the national concept of Volksgemeinschaft under National Socialism mirrored the term's use in supranational contexts in seeking and achieving territorial expansion. Here, the decision to unite with the German Reich was made in a referendum supported by international law and without the violation of national borders. The regional Nazi Party cover organization, Deutsche Front (German Front), whose journal shared its name and bore the subtitle *The Newspaper of the German Volksgemeinschaft,* threatened that anyone who did not join the German Front "would be expelled from the German Volksgemeinschaft and treated as traitors after the return." Such intimidation had the opposite of its intended effect and was halted.[64]

Finally, there was a subnational conception of Volksgemeinschaft; "subnational" here refers to a Volksgemeinschaft rooted in a particular ethnic community that formed a minority group within a multiethnic nation. The subnational Volksgemeinschaft was usually linked to dual loyalties on the national and the supranational level. Concentrating attention narrowly on one's own group and its institutions while ignoring broader questions posed by supranational Germanness and citizenship could reduce the conflicts produced by these competing loyalties. Nonetheless, although the subnational notion of Volksgemeinschaft could be forced into compatibility with both of the other usages of the term, it was far from neutral. The use of the term *Volksgemeinschaft* in the sense of an independent ethnic community within a certain state had stronger affinity to the supranational concept of an ethnically founded Volksgemeinschaft than to the notion of citizenship deriving from residence in a particular state. Thus, the idea of the greater Volksgemeinschaft advocated by Nazi propaganda was, as one observer writes, "almost predetermined" by the work of German cultural organizations in Eastern Europe.[65]

The institutionalization of the subnational concept of Volksgemeinschaft was probably begun first in Latvia. In this country, the upper class traditionally had been recruited from a small German minority, even under czarist rule. When Latvia became independent after World War I and the Russian Revolution, the social and cultural position of this German ruling class was challenged.

Representatives of the German-speaking minority proposed a "Law on national-cultural autonomy of the German Volksgemeinschaft and on the use of the German language in Latvia" in 1922 to counteract their loss of power. According to the draft of a "Law on the German Volksgemeinschaft" presented in the following year, all those labeling themselves Germans in a census were to be placed together in a compulsory public cooperative with the right to govern their own taxation. The law did not pass, and eventually it became clear that a Volksgemeinschaft under public law was not a realistic goal. As a substitute, an organization called German-Baltic Volksgemeinschaft in Latvia was founded as the private umbrella organization for all German-Latvian associations.[66] Obviously this name only refers to a specific German minority within a certain state, thus representing a subnational conception of Volksgemeinschaft. However, when the German Nazis asked for the resettlement of the German-speaking group in Latvia in connection with the Hitler-Stalin agreement after the beginning of World War II, the president of this Volksgemeinschaft asked his people to leave their "three-quarters of a millennium of construction work" in Latvia in favor of the tasks asked for "by the great *Gesamtvolk*," the all-German people. The overwhelming majority moved and settled in recently conquered areas of Poland.[67]

In Romania, about 7 percent of the population belonged to the German-speaking minorities, which were concentrated in two main areas of settlement. There is some evidence that the statutes of the Verband der Deutschen in Rumänien (League of the Germans in Romania) founded in 1919 already aimed to further the association's goal of uniting the areas settled by ethnic Germans into a living Volksgemeinschaft.[68] The newspaper *Süd-Ost* (Southeast), a "Daily of the Volksgemeinschaft of the Germans in Romania," was begun in 1926 in Hermannstadt (Sibiu). Its subtitle, *Deutsch-Schwäbische Volksgemeinschaft Sathmar* (German-Swabian Volksgemeinschaft of Sathmar), points to a clear subnational frame of reference. National Socialism seems to have been accepted more rapidly in Romania than in the Baltics: a journal article published in the Reich in 1934 warns against false comparisons between the Baltics and Transylvania, because in the latter case the Romanian wing of the movement could "almost be equated with the term *Deutsche Volksgemeinschaft in Rumänien*" (German Volksgemeinschaft in Romania).[69] In spite of its characterization as an institution "in" Romania, the National Socialist organization was internally fragmented. The group proclaimed: "Bearing in mind our commitment to the great Volksgemeinschaft of a hundred million Germans, we want and will create a living Volksgemeinschaft of all Germans in Romania, who, grown from the same blood, are firmly embodied in the soil. Our individual members will serve this Volksgemeinschaft with all their strength."[70] From this standpoint, the small ethnic community and its organization were just elements of the greater worldwide Volksgemeinschaft, with its greater plans and commitments.

To sum up, there was enormous variation in the use of the term *Volksgemeinschaft* as it was deployed to describe people of German heritage or language outside the state of Germany. Examining the questions of what type of Volksgemeinschaft the users of this concept aimed to achieve and which territories and groups of Germans were to be encompassed illuminates the many conflicting definitions of the term in the interwar era and World War II. There were three ideal models that proved useful for the classification of the different conceptualizations: the supranational, the national, and the subnational notion of Volksgemeinschaft. Whereas the subnational concepts in general were compatible with the other two usages, the national and supranational concepts were mutually exclusive. In fact, they marked irreconcilable opposites. A contemporary observer described the consequences appropriately, noting that "According to the National Socialist dogma, it is the blood that substantiates the Volksgemeinschaft. By applying this principle, a lot of German citizens have been excluded from the German Volksgemeinschaft, on the other hand, many who already have felt at home in another Volksgemeinschaft have been included in the German Volksgemeinschaft."[71]

The title of this volume, *The* Heimat *Abroad,* is as ambiguous as the term *Volksgemeinschaft.* It can refer either to the old Heimat in Germany or to the new Heimat in the area of settlement. The Nazi approach was to equate Heimat with Germany (and at the same time to equate National Socialism with Germany) and to proclaim this to be permanently true, even for subsequent generations—naturally depending on racial criteria. Germans abroad, according to the Nazis, simply lived in the wrong place. Thus, a huge program of resettlement was started in World War II, aimed at increasing German control over both occupied territories and what was considered the larger Volksgemeinschaft. By contrast, the Nazis would have found unthinkable the very idea that the term *Heimat abroad* could also be used to describe a homeland outside of Germany for people of German heritage. A new Heimat would only leave a limited space for identification with Germanness—and certainly not any identification with a German Volksgemeinschaft. To them, such a concept as *Heimat abroad* was utterly suspect and only reserved for other nationalities, particularly for Jews or those they considered to be Jewish. Applied to German people, the latter understanding of the Heimat abroad, by definition, works as an antifascist notion.

NOTES

I would like to thank the editors of this volume as well as two anonymous readers for the University of Michigan Press for their invaluable help in improving my English and for comments and questions that made this chapter better. All translations are my own unless otherwise noted.

    1. The conceptual history of Volksgemeinschaft in the twentieth century is

treated in depth in my dissertation, "Ungleiche Geschwister: Die Konstruktion von nationalsozialistischer Volksgemeinschaft und schwedischem Volksheim," Die kulturelle Konstruktion von Gemeinschaften Series No. 4 (Baden-Baden, 2001). This chapter provides a more thorough analysis and documentation of the problem of Volksgemeinschaft in the Nazi era as it applied to German-speaking people outside the borders of the German state and considers the ideas of both the National Socialists and these groups. For an account of the use of the concept in Sweden, see Norbert Götz, "The Swedish *Folkgemenskap:* Democratic vs. Fascist Conceptions of National Community in the 1930s," in *Collective Identity and Citizenship in Europe: Fields of Access and Exclusion,* Report 3/99, ed. Theodor Barth and Magnus Enzell (Oslo/Jerusalem, 1999), 49–62.

2. Cf. Melvin Richter, *The History of Political and Social Concepts: A Critical Introduction* (New York and Oxford, 1995); Reinhart Koselleck, *Futures Past: On the Semantics of Historical Time* (Cambridge, Mass., 1985).

3. Cf. Mattias Lau, "Im Kampf um ihr Deutschtum: Die *Volksgemeinschaft* in Abwehrstellung: Zwei deutschsprachige Zeitungen in Nordamerika im Vergleich (1935–1939): Der Deutsche Weckruf und Beobachter und die Deutsche Zeitung für Canada," John F. Kennedy Institut Abteilung für Geschichte, Working Paper 101 (Berlin, 1997).

4. José Carlos Englert, "Beitrag des Herrn Stud. jur. José Carlos Englert, Porto Alegre," in *Volkstum und Volksgemeinschaft: Was ist Volkstum,- was Volksgemeinschaft? Das Ergebnis eines Preisausschreibens,* ed. Franz Metzler (Porto Alegre, 1937), 92.

5. Horand Horsa Schacht, "Volksdeutsche Erziehung: Unser Grenz- und Auslanddeutschtum im Unterricht," in *Deutsche Erziehung im neuen Staat,* 2d rev. ed., ed. Friedrich Hiller (Langensalza, 1936), 268–73. A different distribution of the Hundertmillionenvolk is given in an illustration in *Der Schulungsbrief* (1938), 124, reprinted in Jost Dülffer, "Hitler, Nation und *Volksgemeinschaft,*" in *Die deutsche Nation: Geschichte—Probleme—Perspektiven,* Kölner Beiträge zur Nationsforschung, vol. 1, ed. Otto Dann (Vierow bei Greifswald, 1994), 101.

6. Günther Küchenhoff, "*Volksgemeinschaft* und Reich (Gemeinschaftsgedanke und Staatsgestaltung)," in *Handwörterbuch der Rechtswissenschaft,* ed. E. Volkmar (Berlin, 1937), 8:788.

7. H. Weidenstrass, "Auslandsdeutsche, Fürsorge für—II.Völkische Wohlfahrtspflege im Ausland," in *Handwörterbuch der Wohlfahrtspflege,* 3d rev. ed., ed. Hermann Althaus and Werner Betcke (Berlin, 1939), 117f.

8. Cf. Ernst Fraenkel, *The Dual State: A Contribution to the Theory of Dictatorship* (New York, [1941] 1969).

9. Edgar Randel, *Die Jugenddienstpflicht* (Berlin, 1942), 55f.

10. Concerning VDA philosophy, see Hans Schoeneich, "Der volksdeutsche Gedanke im neuen Reich," *Das Junge Deutschland* 27 (1933): 176–80. The thesis put forward here, that "a 'Gleichschaltung' of our thought was not necessary," is undoubtedly accurate (178).

11. Emil Ehrich, *Die Auslandsorganisation der NSDAP,* Schriften der Deutschen Hochschule für Politik 2, no. 13 (Berlin, 1937), 7.

12. Ernst Wilhelm Bohle, "Auslandsorganisation der NSDAP," *Jahrbuch für Auswärtige Politik* 4 (1938): 17.

13. Franz Metzler, ed., *Volkstum und Volksgemeinschaft: Was ist Volkstum,— was Volksgemeinschaft? Das Ergebnis eines Preisausschreibens* (Porto Alegre, 1937), 165.

14. Ehrich, *Die Auslandsorganisation,* 22.

15. *Jahresbericht der deutschen Volksgemeinschaft in Mexiko* 2 (1936).

16. Frh. Rüdt von Collenberg, "An die deutschen Volksgenossen und Volksgenossinnen in Mexiko," *Mitteilungen der Deutschen Volksgemeinschaft in Mexiko* 1, no. 11 (1938): 2.

17. "Stellungnahme der Deutschen Gesandtschaft," *Mitteilungen der Deutschen Volksgemeinschaft in Mexiko* 1, no. 10 (1938): 11.

18. Franz Ketelhut, "Eine wahre Wildwestgeschichte: Schluß: *Volksgemeinschaft,*" *Mitteilungen der Deutschen Volksgemeinschaft in Mexiko* 1, no. 10 (1938): 23f.

19. Letter of the Association of German Communities in Europe (Werner Hasselblatt) to the Reich Minister and Head of the Reichskanzlei (Heinrich Lammers) of December 19, 1936, Ministry of the Interior, Bundesarchiv Berlin [hereafter cited as BA] R 43 II/512, 47–49.

20. *Organisationsbuch der NSDAP,* 2d. ed. (Munich, 1936; reprint, 1937), 531; "Reichsbürgergesetz" and "Erste Verordnung zum Reichsbürgergesetz," in *Gesetze des NS-Staates,* 3d ed., ed. Ingo von Münch (Paderborn, 1994), 119, 121f .

21. "Niederschrift über eine Besprechung am 12. Februar 1937 betr. Behandlung fremder Volksgruppen im Reich in den Durchführungsbestimmungen zum Gesetz über die Hitlerjugend," in the Ministry of the Interior, BA R 43 II 512, 93–96.

22. "Standarte Nordland—Regiment der Waffen-SS: Die Bestimmungen für den Eintritt in die neue Freiwilligeneinheit," *Deutsche Zeitung in Norwegen,* Jan. 15, 1941, 2.

23. Cf. Bohle, "Auslandsorganisation der NSDAP," 18.

24. "Deutscher Verband zur nationalen Befriedung Europas," *Alarm* 1, no. 2 (1937): 1–3.

25. Metzler, ed., *Volkstum,* 168. Correspondingly, Metzler propagated the term *Deutschbrasilianer* (German Brazilians) in contrast to the Auslandsorganisation der NSDAP, which preferred the term *Brasildeutsche* (Brazilian Germans) (34f.).

26. Metzler, ed., *Volkstum,* 8–11.

27. Metzler, ed., *Volkstum,* 8–11.

28. Metzler, ed., *Volkstum,* 158–61.

29. "Die Preisarbeit," in Metzler, ed., *Volkstum,* 39 (quote is from 45).

30. Metzler, ed., *Volkstum,* 139, 146, 149, 151.

31. Furor Teutonicus, *Was ist Volkstum! Was ist Volksgemeinschaft!* (Porto Alegre, 1937), 2–8 (quote is from 7).

32. Rene Ernaini Gertz, "Politische Auswirkungen der deutschen Einwanderung in Südbrasilien: Die deutschstämmigen und die faschistischen Strömungen in den 30er Jahren" (Ph.D. diss., Free University of Berlin, 1980), 138.

33. Letter of Aug. 29, 1933, BA R 59/1191, cited in Gertz, "Politische Auswirkungen," 124.

34. Metzler, ed., *Volkstum,* 19. A blatant example of a Christian, extremely anti-Semitic fanatic of Volksgemeinschaft is Friedrich Wilhelm Brepohl, *Nationalsozialistische Revolution und Volksgemeinschaft,* Die nationalsozialistische Revolution 1 (Ponta Grossa, 1933).

35. Kurt Imhof, "Das kurze Leben der geistigen Landesverteidigung: Von der '*Volksgemeinschaft*' vor dem Krieg zum Streit über die 'Nachkriegsschweiz' im Krieg," in *Konkordanz und Kalter Krieg: Analyse von Medienereignissen in der Schweiz der Zwischen- und Nachkriegszeit,* Krise und sozialer Wandel 2, ed. Kurt Imhof, Heinz Kleger, and Gaetano Romano (Zürich, 1996), 19–83 (especially 20f., 46).

36. Oliver Zimmer, "Die '*Volksgemeinschaft*': Entstehung und Funktion einer nationalen Einheitssemantik in den 1930er Jahren in der Schweiz," in *Konkordanz und Kalter Krieg,* ed. Imhof, Kleger, and Romano, 85–109 (quotations are from 98, 101f).

37. *Neue Schweiz* 11, no. 10 (1935), cited in Zimmer, "*Volksgemeinschaft,*" 100.

38. *Die Nation* 27, no. 10 (1933), cited in Zimmer, "*Volksgemeinschaft,*" 95f.

39. Zimmer, "*Volksgemeinschaft,*" 95, 99, 101 (quotations are from 98n45, 104).

40. Imhof, "Das kurze Leben," 21.

41. An example of the reception in the French part of Switzerland is Gonzague de Reynold, "Les bases de notre communauté nationale," *La Suisse* 6 (1935): 20–37.

42. Hansjörg Siegenthaler, "Konkordanz und Kalter Krieg: Marginalien anstelle einer Einleitung," in *Konkordanz und Kalter Krieg,* ed. Imhof, Kleger, and Romano, 9–17.

43. Otto von Gierke, "Der deutsche Volksgeist im Kriege," in *Der Deutsche Krieg* (Stuttgart, 1915), 46:26; "Deutschnationale Volkspartei, Grundsätze 1920," in *Deutsches Handbuch der Politik,* vol. 1, *Deutsche Parteiprogramme,* ed. Wilhelm Mommsen (Munich, 1960), 536; material of the Großdeutsche Volksgemeinschaft is kept in BA NS 26/857.

44. Paula Krauß, "An unsere Mitglieder!" *Die deutsche Frau* 15, no. 98 (1938): 1f.

45. Engelbert Dollfuß, "Speech of Dec. 8, 1931," in *Dollfuß an Österreich: Eines Mannes Wort und Ziel,* Berichte zur Kultur- und Zeitgeschichte 10, ed. Edmund Weber (Vienna, 1935), 203.

46. Engelbert Dollfuß, "Speech of March 4, 1934," in *Dollfuß an Österreich,* ed. Weber, 171.

47. Dollfuß, "Speech of March 4, 1934," in *Dollfuß an Österreich,* ed. Weber, 211.

48. Kurt Schuschnigg, *Österreichs Erneuerung: Die Reden des Bundeskanzlers* (Vienna, 1935–37), 2:106 (citation from his speech of September 1, 1935).

49. *Protokolle des Ministerrates der Ersten Republik,* sec. 9, vol. 3: *Kabinett Dr. Kurt Schuschnigg: 31. Mai 1935 bis 30. November 1935* (Vienna, 1995), 278.

50. Fritz Bauer, "Auslandsdeutsche und 'Auslandsösterreicher,'" *Wille und Macht* 4, no. 5 (1936): 23f. Separatism here is not a political concept connected to a respective state but rather an ideological position defining extraterritorial individuals' relationship to the German Reich. It becomes very clear through this text that the notion of Germans abroad was not limited to the citizens of the Reich; otherwise the problem with Austria would not have arisen in the first place.

51. Adolf Hitler, *Reden und Proklamationen 1932–1945: Kommentiert von einem deutschen Zeitgenossen,* ed. Max Domarus (Wiesbaden, 1973), 1–2:830.

52. Domarus, ed., *Hitlers Reden,* 824.

53. Memorandum of 1937 concerning "Jugendorganisationen der deutschen Volksgruppen in Europa," BA R 43 II/512, S. 73/14.

54. "Wahlaufruf: Zum großen Appell," BA NS 26/2120.

55. Domarus, ed., *Hitlers Reden,* 952.

56. Josef Hofbauer, "Von deutscher *Volksgemeinschaft," Der Kampf* 2 (1935): 201–3.

57. Paul Sering [Richard Löwenthal], "Was ist der Volkssozialismus?" *Zeitschrift für Sozialismus* 3 (1936): 1106. Of the members of the Sudeten German social democratic movement, even Karl W. Deutsch, later renowned as a political scientist, discussed the idea of People's Socialism. See his "Emil Franzels konservativer Sozialismus," *Der Kampf* 3 (1936): 408–16. Cf. the review of Wilhelm Sollmann, "Volksrevolution und Volkssozialismus: Zu dem Buche von Wenzel Jaksch 'Volk und Arbeiter,'" *Neuer Vorwärts,* January 23, 1936. Cf. also Wilhelm Sollmann,"Sozialistische Machtpolitik," *Zeitschrift für Sozialismus* 2 (1935): 758–65.

58. Cf. Martin K. Bachstein. "Der Volkssozialismus in Böhmen: Nationaler Sozialismus gegen Hitler," *Bohemia* 14 (1973): 340–71.

59. *Munzinger-Archiv,* December 11, 1976.

60. See more details in Götz, *Ungleiche Geschwister,* 90–94.

61. Cf. the editorial text introducing Willi Vogel, "Schweden bändigt die Krise: Von den Leistungen einer Arbeiterregierung," *Sozialdemokrat,* April 21, 1935, 5f.

62. Wenzel Jaksch, "Konservativer Marxismus?" *Der Kampf* 3 (1936): 428, 432.

63. Wenzel Jaksch, *Volk und Arbeiter: Deutschlands europäische Sendung* (Bratislava, 1936), 93, 127f.

64. Ernst Kunkel, *Die Sozialdemokratische Partei des Saargebietes im Abstimmungskampf 1933/1935* (Saarbrücken, 1956), 52.

65. Karl Dietrich Erdmann, *Deutschland unter der Herrschaft des Nationalsozialismus 1933–1939,* 9th ed., Gebhardt Handbuch der deutschen Geschichte 20 (Munich, 1980; reprint, 1993), 122.

66. Wolfgang Wachtsmuth, *Von deutscher Arbeit in Lettland 1918–1934,* vol. 1, *Die deutsch-baltische Volksgemeinschaft in Lettland 1923–1934* (Cologne, 1951), quote from p. 117, see also 66f, 69f, 99.

67. Alfred Intelmann, "Deutsche Volksgenossen!" *Rigasche Rundschau,* October 9, 1939, cited in Dietrich A. Loeber, *Diktierte Option: Die Umsiedlung der Deutschbalten aus Estland und Lettland 1939–1941* (Neumünster, 1972), 163.

68. Helmut Wolff, ed., *Ein Jahr Volksgemeinschaft der Deutschen in Rumänien unter Fritz Fabritius* (Hermannstadt, 1936), 5.

69. "Falsche Vergleiche zwischen Baltikum und Siebenbürgen," *Das junge Deutschland* 28 (1934): 89.

70. Helmut Wolff, "Schlußwort," in *Ein Jahr Volksgemeinschaft der Deutschen in Rumänien unter Fritz Fabritius,* ed. Helmut Wolff (Hermannstadt, 1936), 68.

71. Englert, "Beitrag," 83.

PART 2

Bonds of Trade and Culture

The German diaspora was not simply a "seeding" of German people from a motherland. Rather, it was a way of seeing the dispersed German-speaking communities, which emerged long after the multiple migrations discussed in this volume's introduction. The descendants of these dispersed communities were sought out by German nationalists after World War I, who hoped that the German diaspora could prove to be a deterritorialized nation in order to counteract the territorial losses of the German Reich. How members of this diaspora viewed themselves depended on many factors: the status of emigrants, the time they emigrated, conditions in the receiving country, and that country's relations to the politically transformed German state. Nowhere is this variety more keenly recognizable than among the German communities in the Western Hemisphere, which differed from the colonies of German's short-lived empire as well as from the German-speaking minorities stranded by the receding Austrian-Hungarian Empire.

The four chapters in this section illustrate the predominance of cultural, rather than racial, identity among Germans in Brazil, Mexico, and the United States. With local variations, one of the forms their connection with Germany took was feelings of superiority to native and other immigrant societies. While this could easily tip over into notions of biological superiority, it rarely and only briefly did so.

Thomas Lekan argues that, from the late nineteenth century and well into the twentieth, immigrant Germans not only tried to re-create their home landscapes but generally claimed superior stewardship of land, with implicit moral lessons about humanity's relationship to nature. However, they remained impervious to Nazi appeals of "Blood and Soil," which claimed, besides lands contiguous to Germany, a genetic predisposition of Germans to be the best caretakers of any land.

Tobias Brinkmann shows that nineteenth-century German Jews in Chicago pioneered Reform Jewry, streamlined its rituals, and used German in services because they identified modernity with Germanness. Similarly in Brazil, according to Jeffrey Lesser, German Jewish refugees from Hitler felt themselves to be carriers of German high culture, which differentiated them from earlier Jewish immigrants of East European origin and from the majority of Brazilians and brought them closer to the Brazilian elite.

Jürgen Buchenau traces almost two centuries of Germans in Mexico City and depicts most vividly the transformations induced by political change. Here a merchant community of "trade conquistadors" at first segregated themselves from Mexican society, out of feelings of cultural superiority. The Wilhelminian state sustained the elitist separatism by subsidizing the local German school. The enclave supported German national interests in World War I, partly in hope of expanding its own market share of international trade. Later, the community embraced Nazism but was forced to abandon it when Mexico allied with the United States in World War II. Finally, the arrival of new immigrants, including Jews and other refugees from Nazism, introduced more political complexity into the German Mexican enclave. Today trade conquistadors who come from Germany to Mexico to work for transnational companies don't relate much to the old colony, which has largely assimilated to Mexican language and cultural norms.

CHAPTER 4

Blond and Blue-Eyed in Mexico City, 1821 to 1975

Jürgen Buchenau

Mexico City has long been home to a small but influential community of mostly wealthy German immigrants. Giving an affirmative answer to the question of whether there is a German diaspora, this chapter discusses the negotiation of national identity in the German "colony" in Mexico City. This colony defines itself as those Germans and their descendants who pursue "respectable trades" and subsidize German-language institutions in Mexico City. Composed mainly of merchant families, this colony began with fifty individuals in the 1820s, only to grow to three thousand people by 1939.[1]

As the usage of the word *colony* illustrates, foreign merchant communities in Latin America lived in a Mediterranean tradition transferred by Iberian conquistadors to the New World. Merchant colonies date back to the cities of Renaissance Italy, where merchants formed "trade diasporas"[2] according to their city of origin. While these colonies remained separate from the elites in the host city, they interacted socially with them. Thus, a colony in a Latin American city consists of "those who seek to maintain their own racial and cultural integrity although living in an alien land which has an independent government."[3] This effort involves a sense of superiority over the host society, the spirit of belonging to a close-knit community, and a "territorial consciousness"[4]—the notion that the colony constitutes an integral part of the home country. Members of a colony remain alienated from the host culture, they plan to return to their home country, and they develop institutions designed to promote the home culture for the benefit of their children.

This chapter challenges the existing dichotomous notions on German trade diasporas in Latin America. Often influenced by modernization theory, older accounts praised German merchants for helping

85

to spearhead the painful but necessary modernization of the region.[5] Influenced by dependency analysis, later scholars lambasted the same newcomers as contributors to the imperialist exploitation of Latin America or even as eager supporters of Nazi expansion in the Hitler era.[6] Both of these models portray foreign diasporas as enclaves that operate as instruments of the sending society and that refuse to incorporate any influence from the host society. The German colony in Mexico, however, does not fit this monolithic picture. In the first place, the enclave phase represented only a relatively brief period in the history of the diaspora. Second, like their U.S. counterparts, studied in Thomas Lekan's chapter, many Germans in Mexico refused to become lackeys of either the Kaiser's or Hitler's geopolitical interests. Finally, the Germans gradually came to accept Mexican culture. Therefore, an approach that stresses the ambiguities of the immigrant experience, such as transnational theory, comes closest to matching the German experience in Mexico City.[7]

As a window on the German presence in Mexico in the context of increasing U.S. influence, this chapter contributes to the recent postcolonial scholarship on foreign cultural and economic influence in Latin America.[8] The history of the German community in Mexico City demonstrates the fluidity and contested nature of citizenship and national identity. It not only qualifies previous analyses that have portrayed European trade diasporas in Latin America as mere outposts of imperial rivalry, but it also questions such worn dichotomies as local versus foreign and insiders versus outsiders.[9] It sheds light on the formation and disintegration of a foreign community in a nation that, unlike the United States, did not foster the assimilation of ethnic enclaves. Thus, the German colony in Mexico City yields a close-up view of what Mary Louise Pratt has called a "contact zone," a social space "where disparate cultures meet, clash, and grapple with each other, often in highly asymmetrical relations of domination and subordination."[10]

This chapter examines three stages of national identity in the German colony. The formative phase (1821–94) created a proto-diaspora: a sojourner community characterized by the remigration of "trade conquistadors"[11] after a few successful years in Mexico. During the enclave phase (1894–1945), the Germans created a "*Heimat* abroad" in Mexico that included a German school and a host of other social and cultural institutions. Finally, the assimilationist phase has marked the gradual absorption of the German colony into the Mexican elite and middle classes since 1945.

Despite repeated efforts by the Mexican government to encourage a "whitening" of the Mexican population by mass immigration from Europe, Mexico attracted few of the traditional immigrants that characterized German diasporas elsewhere in the Americas. In particular, farmers did not express interest in Mexico. Rugged and mountainous, the country possesses precious little farmland of the kind that once encouraged European rural people to stream to Argentina, Brazil, Canada, Chile, and the United States. The mountain ranges, deserts, steppes, pine forests, and tropical jungles that mark the country's unparalleled natural beauty make up more than 85 percent of Mexico, a figure that was even higher before the war with the United States (1846–48) cost the country half of its territory. Much of the arable land requires hard work and irrigation to yield enough crops, and by independence, the best lands were in the hands of a landed elite. To top it off, the Mexican government did not grant assistance to rural colonization projects, which doomed any but the best-funded agrarian immigration scheme.[12] Prospective farmers therefore found themselves in the sad predicament typical for a country without a class of yeoman farmers. Existence as rural wage earners doomed them to compete for jobs with the Mexican peasantry—hardly the ideal for a European seeking a better life.[13] For artisans, low wages and a glut of skilled craftspeople made a migration to Mexico similarly unpalatable.[14] Until the coronation of the Habsburg prince Maximilian as emperor of Mexico in 1864, German immigration consisted of several hundred merchants, miners, and intellectuals who fled the stifling political climate in Holy Alliance Germany.

Initially, the country's problems made life difficult for German merchants. A protracted conflict, the Wars of Independence (1810–21) left the economy ruined and central authority severely weakened. In the succeeding decades, Mexico experienced four major foreign invasions due in no small measure to the fact that caudillo warlords successfully disputed central authority in Mexico. Mexico also posed specific obstacles for immigrants that kept the total number of Germans in the capital well below six hundred, including a constantly changing legal framework and discrimination against Protestants. During the 1830s and 1840s, Mexican commerce hit rock bottom, as banditry threatened overland trade and the departure of most of the Spanish retail merchants deprived Mexico of its system of distribution. In addition, the country lacked a base of customers for foreign goods. The Mexican peasantry—a group that accounted for 70 percent of the population—did not spend its scant income on foreign-made goods, and the urban middle class remained too small to stimulate imports.[15] As a result of the risks involved, most wholesale merchants operated only on a commission basis, a practice that limited them to doing business with "trustworthy" retailers in larger Mexican towns. Dating from colonial times, the typical wholesale store in early- and mid-nineteenth-century Mexico remained the *almacén:* the warehouse owned by a scion of a European export business clan. In addition, various Mexican administrations had experimented with the idea of outlawing foreign ownership of retail businesses, an idea that could only further discourage foreign capitalists.[16]

By the middle of the century, however, rewards beckoned for German merchants. During the 1840s, most of the British almacén owners withdrew from the import business in favor of investing in mining and banking. As a result, German and French immigrants took over most of the almacenes. The political climate also became more favorable. During the 1850s, the Liberal Reforma attempted to foster free trade and individual ownership of land.[17] Initially, the Liberals' struggles with their Conservative rivals precluded an implementation of many of these measures. Ironically, it was the Habsburg emperor Maximilian, called onto the scene by a French-Conservative alliance, who ensured the triumph of their program. In a betrayal of his backers, Maximilian supported the Reforma, and he ended discriminatory legislation that had discouraged immigration. Enticed by the prospect of living under a German-speaking ruler, German immigrants flocked to Mexico in increasing numbers. Once there, Germans found out that Mexicans held Europeans in high regard. Indeed, they enjoyed a social prestige higher than that of many wealthy Mexicans.[18]

Most German wholesale merchants in Mexico City came as trade conquistadors, and they therefore represented a special case among immigrants to the Americas. Many immigrants were migrants of necessity, as they fled persecution or poverty in their home country. Trade conquistadors, on the other hand, were migrants of opportunity, who desired to get rich quickly in order to return to a position in their father's business. Not surprisingly, most of these men considered themselves temporary residents rather than immigrants in the true sense. Since most businessmen anticipated a stay in Mexico of relatively short duration, they sent their profits home rather than commit significant capital investments to the host society. They typically did not take families with them; instead, the typical merchant arrived as a bachelor in his early to mid-twenties. Sharing the predominant view that "whiter" was better, he consorted primarily with fellow merchants from the country of his birth and segregated himself from the society around him in the process.[19] Like the German Jews in Chicago, described in chapter 5 by Tobias Brinkmann, he identified modernity with Germanness or at least with being European. However, there were exceptions to this trend, such as the Hagenbeck and Pöhls families from Hamburg, who intermarried with the Mexican bourgeoisie. At a meeting of the descendants of the original Pöhls immigrants in 1998, only one-third of those present spoke any German at all.[20]

This self-segregation assumed three forms. Most importantly, the foreign resident avoided private contact with Mexicans and often even with residents from other countries than his own. In addition, he stuck to people from his own social class, religious denomination, and profession. Finally, the resident did nothing to make his stay in Mexico appear permanent. He usually did not marry while overseas, he did not invest in local production or manufacturing, and he did not seek Mexican citizenship. Giving up his native citizenship would have deprived him of the recourse of diplomatic protection, a recourse that was quicker than going through Mexican courts. Because merchants made up the greatest part of the European communities in Mexico City, they therefore marked them as predominantly male, segregated, and conservative.[21]

There were good reasons for foreigners not to seek assimilation into Mexican society. Many of them enjoyed considerable power and wealth precisely due to their status as outsiders, that is, their connection to overseas producers. Paradoxically, both xenophobia and xenophilia played important roles as well. Popular xenophobia resulting from European and U.S. interventions in Mexico helped immigrants justify their self-segregation. At the same time, centuries of colonial rule had imbued Mexicans with an inferiority complex with respect to Europeans and, later, white North Americans. Even many elite Mexicans thought of Europeans as representing the highest level of civilization.[22] According to popular lore, they held the French and the Germans in particularly high regard: in the words of twentieth-century U.S. novelist Katherine Anne Porter, the Mexicans "loathe the Americans . . . hate the Spaniards, distrust the English, admire the French, and love the Germans."[23] As the nineteenth century progressed, the influence of positivist and social Darwinist thought only accentuated this trend. As the Porfirian-era adage "Mexico: mother of foreigners and stepmother of Mexicans" indicates, foreign merchants enjoyed a high social prestige.[24]

Moreover, creole efforts at maintaining their dominance in a multi-ethnic society encouraged constructions of identity that were not conducive to the assimilation of immigrants. While a castelike division between the Spanish and Indian worlds had marked early New Spain, miscegenation soon produced a growing group of mestizos who challenged the established division between the *república de españoles* and the *república de indios.* As the mestizos assumed their position in the middle of the Mexican social pyramid, class and cultural distinctions began to replace racial categories (as one of Mexico's oldest adages goes, "money whitens"). In the absence of a rigid system of racial categories, the creoles asserted their superiority by imagining themselves as the representatives of a Spanish, Roman Catholic nation on Mexican soil as embodied in the Virgin of Guadalupe.[25] Even as the creoles defied the political power of the peninsulares in identifying themselves as *americanos,* they recognized the perils of relinquishing the association with the Spanish heritage.[26] In this view, all those not of Spanish culture ("Indians" as well as foreigners) remained outsiders, while the mestizos gained acceptance by rising to economic and military significance during the bloody history of the nineteenth century.

Linguistic conventions further discouraged assimilation, as the Spanish language does not lend itself easily to describing hyphenated identities such as the ones common in English or German.[27] In Spanish, a woman may be either a *francesa* or a *mexicana* but never a *francesa-mexicana,* and even the more graceful *franco-mexicana* sounds more cumbersome to Mexican ears than *franco-mexicaine* does to French ones. Likewise, the son of a German immigrant would refer to himself as a *Deutschmexikaner* (German Mexican) in German, but he would face the stark choice between *alemán* and *mexicano* in Spanish. When foreign immigrants came to Mexico, they thus faced a cultural divide: one was either a Mexican or a foreigner but not a hyphenated product of both worlds. This dichotomy between Mexican and foreign extended to succeeding generations, so that most children of non-Spanish-speaking parents still considered themselves foreign.[28] Interestingly, the same language that discouraged hyphenated identities encouraged the Hispanization of names, especially where a German umlaut was involved. For example, hardware merchant Robert Böker called himself Roberto Boker upon his arrival in Mexico City. His brother Heinrich became Enrique, and his son Franz became Francisco, all without any paperwork. The Bökers switched between Spanish and German versions of their names strictly as a matter of convenience.[29]

Not surprisingly, the foreigners in nineteenth-century Mexico City formed expatriate communities. Made up of well-to-do, temporary migrants with a limited personal stake in the host society, these communities were transient and male dominated. Most of their members remained in Mexico for less than a decade, and bachelors and young couples outnumbered families. The social life of the expatriate communities took place in males-only clubs. In the absence of other associations such as schools, churches, athletic clubs, and beneficent associations, these communities did not fulfill the functions of ethnic enclaves until the turn of the century.[30]

About three hundred strong at the time of Robert Böker's sojourn, the German colony serves as a good example of such an expatriate community.[31] Three out of four of the Germans were male, most were Protestant, and almost all of the women were married. Although deep social divisions marked the German community, merchants dominated the scene. Because most of these merchants had made plans to return to their native country before starting a family, their interest in social life remained slight. As their only significant social club, the Casino Alemán, or Deutsches Haus, became the central meeting point of all Germans in Mexico City, a club founded in 1848 in an effort to unify German expatriates divided in their political loyalties. The Protestant German entrepreneurs expressed little interest in intermarrying with the Catholic Mexican elite.[32] Instead, the Germans (like the British and the handful of U.S. citizens who lived in Mexico) belonged to the most segregated foreign communities in pre-1867 Mexico.[33] In contrast to British and U.S. immigrants, however, the Germans could not count on a powerful nation-state to back their interests. It took the two processes of Mexican modernization and German unification to create a genuine diaspora. Taken together, Benito Juárez's triumph over Maximilian in 1867 and Prussia's triumph over France in 1871 thus signaled watersheds in the history of the German merchant colony.

With the final victory of the Liberals, Mexico entered an era of export-led economic growth that contributed to greater political stability during the dictatorship of Porfirio Díaz (1876–1911). Juárez and Díaz seized the opportunity afforded by the rapid industrialization of the North Atlantic economies. Despite periodic economic contractions, these economies emerged as major markets for Mexico's products, as well as sources of foreign capital. During the Díaz era, the Porfirians built a network of railroads, which led to a revival of the mining industry and a surge in the production of tropical products.[34] Like Juárez's

Liberals, they also dreamed of "whitening" Mexico by a mass agrarian immigration—a project doomed to failure due to the continuing social conditions in the countryside. Porfirian modernization involved a change of elite values and ideas—ideas that affected foreign merchants almost as much as the new political and economic parameters. As much as Anglo models dominated Mexican economic ideas of the time, French positivism influenced social thought. Most members of the Francophile Porfirian governing elite desired to model Mexico after the Third Republic: a society that combined the conservative idea of order with the liberal notion of material progress.[35] Thus, don Porfirio and his advisers sought to learn the best that Europe and the United States had to offer in order to elevate Mexico from tradition into modernity. Rather than a specific set of economic or political ideas, Porfirian thought was a persuasion: a widespread notion that Mexico would one day share the limelight with the world's most "advanced" nations such as Britain, France, Germany, and the United States.[36]

Meanwhile, German unification created the conditions for political and economic expansion into Latin America. Much as the Industrial Revolution had paved Otto von Bismarck's way to the unified German Empire, the elimination of internal borders in turn fostered industrialization and, subsequently, the search for export markets. In Mexico, German industrialists found a willing buyer of hardware, weapons, and chemical products, and the diplomats of the new centralized state soon identified it as a key area in which German exporters could displace their British and French competitors. This effort met with limited success. During the 1880s and 1890s, Germany lost lucrative banking and arms concessions to the French yet became the fourth most important exporter to Mexico. While German exports to Mexico finally came to surpass both of their European rivals during the 1900s, Imperial Germany joined the other European powers in losing out to the United States, which by 1910 was the origin of 70 percent of Mexican imports.[37]

The Porfirian/Imperial era changed the way German merchants did business in Mexico. With political stability and the existence of an export-oriented infrastructure, the Porfirians had created the potential for the kind of national market that benefited specialty stores. While the French monopolized the sale of expensive imported textiles, and the Spaniards continued to dominate retail trading and the sale of dry goods, the German merchants specialized in hardware, drugs, dyes, and musical instruments. German hardware stores sold cutlery, tools, machinery, agricultural and mining implements, carriages, and sewing machines—in sum, the equipment necessary to build an infrastructure in Mexico. Despite the fact that Germany had arrived belatedly on the industrial stage, merchants from Hamburg, Bremen, and Remscheid emerged as the primary hardware wholesalers in Mexico City.[38] The German hardware merchants soon found themselves at the cutting edge of building the infrastructure of the presumed "prosperous Mexico,"[39] and they realized large profits in a relatively short period of time. To a lesser extent, other German merchants specializing in drugs, jewelry, and musical instruments also succeeded in finding their niche in the booming Mexican import economy.

The German colony therefore became a part of the cosmopolitan elite in Porfirian Mexico. To the dismay of the German Imperial government, German businesses cooperated with their colleagues from other countries. For example, in 1877 several German merchants signed a petition of "American residents" to U.S. president Rutherford B. Hayes that demanded that he not recall the U.S. consul from Mexico City, an action that threatened imports of U.S. hardware.[40] In 1888 the eminent hardware importers Roberto Boker y Cía. even allowed the U.S. consulate in Mexico City to conduct financial transactions via the company.[41] Therefore, national allegiance mattered less than the ultimate goal of making money in a setting friendly to foreign economic interests.[42] While two-thirds of all German merchant houses failed in the period from 1867 to 1880—a failure due to greater competition from the United States and Mexico's former enemies—those that remained raked in profits so great that its owners could retire comfortably in Germany after a decade of work in Mexico.[43]

By the turn of the twentieth century, the German sojourner community had transformed itself into an ethnic enclave. According to a census by the German consul, the German population in the capital numbered 1,236 individuals, not counting Austrian, Swiss, or naturalized Mexican citizens. Females made up 32 percent of the adult population (up from 25 percent in 1865), and, even more importantly, the census counted more than 400 children. Therefore, the nuclear family had surpassed the single trade conquistador in importance within the German community.[44] This larger and more socially diverse population spawned the emergence of a host of new German institutions. In 1912 a German travel guide to Mexico listed a German newspaper, the *Deutsche Zeitung von Mexico,* as well as fourteen associations, including sporting clubs devoted to rowing, horseback riding, swimming, and gymnastics; two Masonic lodges; the Women's Association; and a German school.[45]

The school constituted the key institution that aided the transition from loose diaspora to ethnic enclave. In 1894 the Deutsche Schule von Mexico/Colegio Alemán de México opened its doors, a school financed by German businesses and a generous subsidy from the German Empire. While the school initially offered instruction in the first six grades only, gradual expansion allowed it to offer secondary education as well. In 1918 the Colegio Alemán graduated its first high school class, and four years later it became the first school outside Europe to win the approval of the German authorities for the *Abitur* degree.[46] The Colegio Alemán pursued a threefold mission: to educate German children in the tradition of their ancestors, to teach Germans what they needed to know about Mexico, and to acquaint Mexicans with German culture. Since the school could not attract enough German students, it offered two different tracks—one for native speakers and one for Mexicans who studied German as a foreign language. From the very beginning, students in the Mexican track outnumbered those in the German track. Teachers imparted knowledge of both cultures, and essay topics for a comprehensive examination included "Mexican customs and habits"; "The influence of Porfirio Díaz on the development of Mexico"; and "What captivates Germans about Mexico."[47] Beginning in 1913, the wave of jingoism that engulfed the European nations swept up the Colegio Alemán. The new principal, a career administrator who knew nothing about Mexico until his arrival, saw the school as a mouthpiece for German propaganda and desired to keep it separate from Mexican society. By 1915 the principal had firmly integrated the school into the German war effort. In a speech to the school's administrative council, he enjoined all those present to "remove everything within us that is not German, and to resist the internationalist disintegration of our thoughts." Final examinations reflected exactly such efforts; for example, an essay question asked students to "describe all that has been done by the German colony in Mexico to help their native country in the European War." By 1919 a new mission statement proclaimed that the goal of the school was to "practice German discipline . . . and to open eyes and minds of its charges to the German character and German knowledge."[48]

Efforts to promote German churches experienced far greater difficulties than those to promote the school. With the option of worshiping in Mexican churches, German Catholics did not organize until the late 1910s, and by then the revolutionary state's attack on the organized church did not allow the foundation of a German Catholic Church. The Lutherans, a majority among the Germans in Mexico

City, experienced somewhat greater success. Since 1861 they had congregated in a variety of buildings, including a monastery, the British Episcopal Church, and a concert hall, where, as the German pastor reported, "lewd decorations featuring Venus and lovebirds threatened the quiet devotion of . . . visitors." In 1930 the Lutheran umbrella organization in Berlin began to provide financial backing for the construction of a church building, as well as a subsidy for the pastor. Because the merchant elite lacked interest, however, the building project languished until 1957.[49] Not even the fact that the U.S.-based Missouri Synod began to woo Lutherans away from the German Lutheran congregation in the mid-1920s could encourage the majority of the German merchants to give up their indifference toward the church.[50]

The development of the Colegio Alemán and the Lutheran Church epitomized the change in foreign expatriate diasporas in Mexico City. As these communities grew in size, and as the home societies that helped sustain them fought a global war, they isolated themselves from each other. The foreign enclaves also widened the gulf that separated them from Mexican society at large. In the words of one member of the German colony, the Germans led a "Leben unter der Käseglocke," which can be loosely translated as "life under the bell jar."[51] Until the 1950s this life engulfed the "old" German families to such an extent that German, and not Spanish, remained the first language even of those born in Mexico. In most merchant families, the children were not allowed to speak Spanish inside the family home, apart from necessary communication with the Mexican servants that tended to the family's needs. The existence of a sizable German colony with its own cultural and social institutions therefore allowed the merchants to raise their children in an expatriate German environment.[52]

Nothing describes this cloistered existence better than the observations made by U.S. sociologist Ethelyn C. Davis about the typical Mexican-born child of foreign parents. The following passage reflects her own experience growing up in Mexico City.

His contacts with Mexicans seldom exceed those of his parents. He usually attends the American school; if he does find Mexican playmates they speak English and are learning his ways. . . . He is cared for by a maid over whom he soon learns to assume authority; he is not required to do anything for himself and becomes dependent upon servants for his needs. So long as he remains in Mexico he is not in a position between the two cultures and there is little conflict in his situation. It is when he leaves Mexico that he finds conflicts because life there has not equipped him to meet the conditions which he finds in the United States. It is when he leaves Mexico that he finds himself in a marginal position.[53]

The "life under the bell jar" typified the foreign enclaves in Mexico City. With the exception of the Spaniards, who intermarried with the Mexican elite, these colonies cultivated a sense of separateness, both from one another and from Mexican society.

World War I only accentuated the forces that militated in favor of self-segregation. After many decades during which the Germans had coexisted with other immigrant communities in Mexico City, the war drew a line between the German speakers and the small Turkish community on the one hand and the British, French, and U.S. colonies on the other hand. In addition, the German Imperial government enlisted its citizens abroad in the war effort. In 1915 the German legation sponsored the creation of the Verband Deutscher Reichsangehöriger (VDR, or League of German Citizens). The VDR not only collected contributions to the German war effort and spread pro-German propaganda in the Mexico City press; along with the *Deutsche Zeitung von Mexico,* it also helped enforce political conformity among the German colony. According to the slightly paranoid U.S. ambassador Henry P. Fletcher, VDR members even trained Mexican Boy Scouts in the goose step made famous by the Prussian army.[54] As a result, the German colony appeared, at least to the outside, united in its support for Kaiser Wilhelm II. The sons of many merchants enlisted in the German military, and the colony greeted each notice that one of them had died with cries of patriotic pride. Finally, blacklists barred the nationals of each of these countries from trading with the enemy, and an important incentive for international cooperation thus disappeared.[55]

Despite this groundswell of nationalist fervor, the Mexican Revolution of 1910 might have ended the self-segregation of the German colony. Beginning as a broad opposition movement against the dictator Díaz, the revolutionary coalition disintegrated soon after its triumph in 1911, which led to six years of factional fighting among agrarian movements, upper- and middle-class nationalists, urban workers, and counterrevolutionaries. To the disgust of the foreign merchants, who soon wistfully bemoaned the passing of a golden age, the revolutionaries shared a desire to end the privileges that wealthy foreigners had enjoyed in Porfirian Mexico. Moreover, the turmoil forced the foreign colonies to cooperate: while their sons killed each other in the trench war, merchants from seventeen different countries formed an

International Committee to ward off ransackers and forced loans.[56] Finally, the revolutionary constitution of 1917 contained provisions such as the nationalization of land and subsoil and the idea that foreign diplomats could not protect their citizens to the extent that such a protection exempted foreigners from Mexican law. If carried out to the letter, this new constitution would have posed a serious challenge to the German enclave.

A discussion of Mexican immigration law, however, demonstrates that foreign enclaves weathered the nationalist aspects of the revolution with relative ease. Porfirian immigration law respected the fact that most immigrants did not wish their children to become Mexicans by virtue of their birth in Mexico. Although the constitution of 1857 espoused the principle of *ius soli,* the law stipulated that a Mexican-born child of foreign parents would retain his or her father's citizenship if the father desired it. Not until 1933 did an immigration reform close this loophole, and even then the German practice of *ius sanguinis* allowed dual German-Mexican citizenship. While propertied newcomers continued to enjoy an open door in Mexico, the new legislation sought to keep out lower-class immigrants of modest means, who after 1918 made up the bulk of immigration. In 1936 President Lázaro Cárdenas signed a law designed to promote the miscegenation of the foreign communities by waiving immigration requirements for those who married women of "Mexican origin."[57] These measures, however, were not successful. By the eve of World War II, the German colony had more than doubled in size, as immigration restrictions in the United States forced an increasing number of lower- and middle-class migrants to look elsewhere for a new home. Intermarriage remained the exception rather than the rule, and most Germans continued to cling to their identification with the homeland. There was a good reason for such an attitude, as the postrevolutionary governments continued to give red-carpet treatment to foreign residents. Sadly, even the carnage of World War I, which should have given Mexicans a good reason to question the supposed superiority of European ways, did nothing to allay this situation.[58]

Thus, the revolution in fact did not harm the position of German merchants in Mexico City. To be sure, the widespread political chaos made wholesale trading difficult, and during the worst years of fighting, retail sales slumped to between 1 and 5 percent of pre-1910 levels. Once the German merchants had endured these difficult years, however, better days lay ahead. New president Venustiano Carranza favored German investments as a counterweight to the rapidly increasing capital flow from the United States. In fact, Carranza expressed such pro-German sentiments that U.S. and German diplomats believed that he might enter a Mexican-German alliance. Hence, the ill-fated Zimmermann Telegram, which proposed such an alliance and helped bring the United States into the war against Germany, and U.S. ambassador Henry P. Fletcher's frequent tirades against German influence in Mexico.[59] In addition, once the most intense fighting had ended, merchants charged for their wares in gold pesos, taking advantage of the fact that many Mexicans had hoarded gold coins during the time of worthless paper money.[60]

Ironically, the revolution contributed to a process that strengthened rather than weakened the German colony. For all German merchants, the years of turmoil precluded a return to their home country in the foreseeable future and thus increased their stake in Mexico. In 1917 several German merchants pooled resources to fund El Anfora, a highly successful stoneware factory. While their purveyors in Europe and the United States battled to survive the crash, Mexican manufacturers such as El Anfora began to fill the gaps and ultimately helped these merchants overcome the consequences of the Great Depression.[61] An increasing commitment to buying real estate complemented this trend to invest in Mexico. By 1930 most affluent Germans had purchased a private residence, and some merchants even owned the building that housed their business. With so much capital invested in Mexico, the German merchants took a greater interest in their colony and expended a considerable amount of time and money to help the enclave succeed. While most Germans still envisioned an eventual return, Mexico had emerged as the focus of their life.

Not surprisingly, the lives of Germans in Mexico differed from those of their countrymen. While the Germans in Mexico enjoyed prosperity and a high social status despite the revolution, most of Germany saw the same period as a time of war, hunger, national humiliation, runaway inflation, and sluggish economic growth. As a result of this discrepancy, the old German families cherished an image of a mother country that no longer corresponded to reality. Perhaps inevitably, this desire to cling to past greatness contributed to an almost unanimous rejection of the Weimar Republic among the German merchant colony in Mexico City.[62] The issue that best demonstrated this conservative opposition to the Weimar Republic was the *Flaggenstreit,* or debate over the German flag. The official flag of the Weimar Republic was black, red, and gold, since the Napoleonic Wars the flag of German democrats. The vast majority of Germans in Latin America refused to recognize these colors, preferring the black, white, and red flag of the empire.[63] In 1922 a poll taken by the VDR manifested the attitude of most Germans in Mexico: eighteen hundred Germans favored the imperial flag, and only two preferred the black, red, and gold.[64] The old merchant families felt so strongly about this issue that they did not mind affronting the government in Berlin. In 1920, for instance, the German owner of the building that housed the German consulate took down the consulate's black, red, and gold flag and hoisted the black, white, and red one instead. Unable to find a German landlord who supported him in the Flaggenstreit, the consul moved his offices to the German legation.[65]

Also not surprisingly, the Germans in Mexico reacted with undisguised glee to the news that Adolf Hitler had been appointed chancellor. As early as 1930 not only had they hoped for a right-wing coup d'état, but many of them had expressed overt Nazi and anti-Semitic sentiments.[66] Merchants supported Hitler for a variety of reasons, including the humiliation of Germany after the lost world war, the promise of the radical right to assist German commercial outposts, fears of communism in both Mexico and Germany, and a firebrand "idealism of the expatriate German" for an ideology that created a strong cultural and political bond between the fatherland and the German diaspora. In many ways, the German colony in Mexico City had long operated as a microcosm of what the Nazis desired to accomplish among all ethnic Germans (*Volksdeutsche*). Moreover, Germans of Jewish descent did not hold prominent positions in the organizations of the colony. Finally, if anyone among the old merchant clans had doubts about the Nazis, their company's dependence on German imports made them think twice before opposing Hitler in public.[67]

Nonetheless, Nazi efforts to unify all Volksdeutsche encountered limited success. Hitler's minister, Baron Rüdt von Kollenberg, had little trouble bringing the expatriate Germans into line with Nazi policies, and at least 150 Germans joined the Nazi Party.[68] In particular, recent immigrants, who made up almost half of all Germans in Mexico City, enthusiastically supported the Nazi cause. By 1939 all institutions of the German colony answered to the Foreign Organization of the NSDAP. The Foreign Organization of the NSDAP also supervised the activities of the small local branch of the Nazi Party, attempted to bribe Mexican politicians, and helped German intelligence operations.[69] These same totalitarian policies, however, created a dissident German-speaking diaspora, as more than two thousand German exiles, among them many intellectuals, artists, and leftist politicians, soon joined a small number of German antifascists in Mexico. These new immigrants—which included a large number of Jewish refugees from similar social backgrounds to those studied by Jeffrey Lesser in chapter 7 of this volume—wasted no time attacking Hitler's totalitarian state.[70] Given this new diversity in the German population, the Nazi goal of ideological conformity among German speakers in Mexico remained elusive.

To the chagrin of von Kollenberg, cooperation in economic and political matters proved even harder to achieve. While his efforts to eliminate the sale of U.S., British, and French goods in stores owned by native Germans succeeded, the old German businesses balked at such limitations. Even more importantly, the owners of many of these enterprises would neither lay off their Jewish employees nor join the Nazi Party. Not only did these companies depend on their long-standing cooperation with U.S. enterprises, but their directors also knew that an exclusive reliance on German products would guarantee their inclusion in U.S. blacklists in case of war. Instead, companies like the Casa Boker officially divested themselves of their German shareholders.[71] When war broke out, wary German merchants also resigned their offices in the organizations of the colony.[72] In general, the greater an individual's stake in the Mexican economy, the less he or she complied with the dictates from the German legation.

World War II dealt a crushing blow to these efforts. Before the German attack on France, the Nazis in the German colony had enjoyed relatively free rein in their activities. Aware of the fact that most Mexicans favored a strict position of neutrality, President Lázaro Cárdenas, who was strongly antifascist, declared in May 1940 that his government did not worry about a fifth column in Mexico. But when the German armies attacked Western Europe, he promised the U.S. government to support the coordination of hemispheric defense in return for a favorable resolution of pending U.S.-Mexican disputes. By early 1941 his successor, Manuel Avila Camacho, had permitted U.S. agents to launch an intelligence campaign that destroyed the influence of the Nazi Foreign Organization.[73] Finally, the state of war between the United States and the Axis powers led to a U.S.-Mexican alliance, as Avila Camacho declared that the war pitted democracies against dictatorships.[74] In December 1941 his government froze the assets of Axis nationals as well as of all Mexicans who traded with the Axis, and six months later Mexico declared war on Germany following the sinking of two Mexican tankers by German submarines.

The existence of the German, Italian, and Japanese colonies, however, precluded a complete harmonization with U.S. interests. The Mexicans did not desire to punish its nationals whose only sin was to speak, look, or act German, Italian, or Japanese. The Mexican government also refused calls for the deportation of Nazi agents, whom it interned in an old fortress, and it did not expropriate German property as Guatemala, Brazil, and other Latin American countries had done. Moreover, it allowed Germans born in Mexico to declare themselves Mexican citizens. These acts of insubordination rankled many Department of State officials, one of whom criticized the Mexican government for its failure to crack down on nationals of "Germanic extraction whose known sympathies are pro-Axis."[75]

Having foiled German geopolitical designs in Mexico, U.S. diplomats focused on the destruction of the German colony. In this effort, the "Proclaimed List of Certain Blocked Nationals," which forbade U.S. citizens all commercial transactions with those on the list, proved most effective. Containing more than two thousand names, the list ushered in a U.S. witch hunt in Mexico that ruined many legitimate small businesses. For example, the Division of War Trade Intelligence added a young photographer to the list because he had *requested* German film for his studio.[76] With Mexico a belligerent, the "Proclaimed List" achieved its desired effect. In June 1942 Avila Camacho placed all Axis firms and institutions under the supervision of a special committee, the Junta de Administración y Vigilancia de la Propiedad Extranjera. Although the Mexican government returned most of the German companies after the war, the German colony never recovered from this blow. Because of the Junta's seizure of the Colegio Alemán and other German cultural institutions, World War II irretrievably shattered the bell jar that separated the German enclave from Mexican society.[77]

The postwar era witnessed a blurring of the formerly sharp lines between the German colony and Mexican society. Mexican society had changed too much to accept the continued self-segregation of foreign colonies. Industrialization produced a formidable Mexican middle class, whose members did not accept the artificial barriers existing between foreign enclaves and Mexican society. More Mexican families began to enroll their children in the schools of the foreign colonies—schools that enjoyed an excellent reputation for their stringent curriculum and their bilingual education. Finally, within the German colony, the arrival of employees of multinational concerns marginalized the old merchant families. As most of these newcomers planned a relatively brief stay in Mexico City, they further fragmented an already divided community.

The immigration restrictions of the Mexican state played an important role in this process of assimilation. The end of the nineteenth-century policy of "whitening" Mexico had been long in coming, as a series of immigration reforms beginning in 1908 had sought to exclude first Asian, then poor, and finally almost all immigrants. The economic nationalism and xenophobia that accompanied the revolution shifted the momentum toward encouraging the natural growth of the population and the naturalization of foreign immigrants. Soon the rapid growth of the Mexican population and the increasing clout of the middle sectors—the prime competition for foreign immigrants—made the government clamp down further on immigration. After the immigration reform of 1973, most immigrants only qualified for temporary visas, and obtaining permanent residency in Mexico became more difficult than receiving a green card for the United States.[78] Since only a continuing flow of immigrants could make up for the loss of people to remigration and (increasingly) miscegenation, these changes threatened the foreign colonies and particularly the German community. The immigration and naturalization of German nationals remained forbidden until the resumption of diplomatic relations in 1952, and Mexican law continued to curtail the activities of existing German residents. Not surprisingly, the majority of Germans born in Mexico belatedly declared that they wished to be considered Mexican citizens, a step that allowed them to bring family members from Germany.[79]

Changes in Mexican society also encouraged assimilation. The Mexican elites and middle classes had gained self-confidence from victory in the war, and the abyss of totalitarianism had at last discredited the supposedly superior German ways. In addition, following the lead of the United States, Mexico began to produce mass culture appealing to the children and grandchildren of foreign immigrants. When young Mexicans used the new mass media to articulate their own version of the wave of counterculture made in the United States, their peers from foreign families discovered that it was "hip" to be Mexican.[80] Meanwhile, import-substitution industrialization produced a sizable group of urban nouveaux riches who soon discovered the value and prestige of the foreign institutions such as the German Club and the Colegio Alemán. Formerly exclusively German, the Club Alemán underwent a thorough Mexicanization· of fourteen current executive officers of the club, only four speak German as their native language. As Mexico City grew from a city of one million to a megalopolis of twenty million, the German colony became increasingly marginalized and the use of Spanish more important. Today almost all ethnic Germans born in Mexico—whether of the first or the sixth generation—consider Spanish their native language, and most of those who have learned German speak it with a Spanish accent. Finally, the last thirty years have witnessed an increasing number of mixed marriages between Germans and Mexicans, usually alumni of the German school.[81]

The Colegio Alemán mirrored these changes. After the Junta's takeover in 1942, the school did not offer instruction in German until its reprivatization in 1948. As a result, the Mexican share of the student population increased to almost 75 percent, and Spanish became the language of currency among the students. In 1950 Rudolf Brechtel, the new principal of the Colegio Alemán, attempted to reverse the trend by mandating the exclusive use of German in the two kindergarten grades as well as in the first grade. While this mandate led to a better command of German, Brechtel could not dictate the language the children used on the school grounds, and Spanish remained dominant there. This trend only grew stronger during the 1960s and 1970s, as the teachers contracted in postwar Germany increasingly failed to connect with their conservative German and Mexican students. According to Blanca Huici, the former secretary of the Colegio Alemán, "slovenly dressed Hippie teachers" provided a poor advertisement for German culture. To make matters worse, these teachers earned up to twenty times the salary of their colleagues contracted in Mexico, including those who spoke perfect Spanish and German and thus possessed the best qualifications to teach in this bicultural school. Nonetheless, Mexican elite families, including those of former presidents Luis Echeverría and José López Portillo, continued to send their children to the German school.[82] Wealthy Mexicans still believed that knowledge of German culture improved the moral fabric of their children.[83]

While it could not dissuade either Mexicans or Germans from attending the Colegio Alemán, the issue of the Hippie teachers highlighted the crisis in confidence that World War II left in the German colony. The citizens of Imperial and Nazi Germany had held their heads high at a time when German science and military power jockeyed for world dominance, and they had often regarded the Mexicans as an inferior people. With German unity shattered and the two successor states a pair of pawns on the cold war chessboard, however, segregating oneself from Mexican society was hard to justify. Moreover, the colony fell to infighting and mutual recriminations. The Nazi past divided those who had actively participated in the dictatorship from those who had passively observed the situation, only to loudly proclaim their anti-Nazi leanings as soon as the war was over, not to mention the refugees from Hitler's terror. A further gap existed between these three groups and returnees from Germany, who had lived through five years of aerial bombings and bitterly complained about the materialist attitude of the Germans in Mexico. In the view of these returnees, the German colony had enjoyed an easy ride in Mexico despite the Junta and U.S. hostility.[84]

Today, the old German colony has itself become marginalized within the community of German speakers in Mexico City. Between 1960 and 1990, almost seventeen thousand Germans came to Mexico, a third of them to the capital, and Germans ranked fourth on the list of immigrants, behind U.S. citizens, Spaniards, and Guatemalans. "Industrial nomads" on three- to five-year contracts, most of these newcomers work for multinational companies such as Volkswagen and plan to return to Germany at the conclusion of their contract. Secure in their jobs and better paid than most members of the old colony, these "potato Germans" (*Kartoffeldeutsche*)—a term that refers to the supposed German predilection for potatoes rather than rice, beans, and tortillas—are more alien to the members of the old colony than the Mexican alumni of the Colegio Alemán. Therefore, beyond the classroom, only tenuous links connect pre-1945 immigrants and their children to the German industrial nomads, who often show little interest in Mexican society.[85]

It was not surprising, then, that the Asociación de Ayuda Social de la Colonia Alemana (Social Assistance Association of the German Colony) recently changed the last two words of its name to "Comunidad Alemana" (German community). Today, the German colony exists in name only, and the word *community* best expresses the looser ties that prevail among German speakers in Mexico City.[86]

For those who have cast their lot with Mexico—the members of the former enclave and their descendants—the road toward assimilation has not yet reached its conclusion. Even today it remains advantageous to the German community to retain ties to German culture. Not only does bilingualism confer advantages to any individual, but things "American" and "European" also still retain a flavor of superiority in Mexico. Moreover, many Mexicans still consider the blond, blue-eyed descendants of German immigrants as foreigners, despite their impeccable Spanish accent and Mexican mannerisms. Likewise, many German Mexicans continue to feel privileged by their ethnicity, and some of them still treat Mexicans with disdain.[87]

In a sense, the Germans in Mexico have come full circle: just as in the nineteenth century, the greater part of the German community looks forward to a brief stay in an exotic land, planning to return to Germany wealthier if not wiser. Just as the trade conquistadors, the industrial nomads maintain their social world in Germany and consider their stay in Mexico at best an exotic adventure and at worst a necessary evil for professional advancement. Neither the trade conquistadors of the nineteenth century nor the industrial nomads of the late twentieth century sought to live their lives under the bell jar. Ultimately, the enclave phase, the paradigmatic period of the German colony according to the historian Brígida von Mentz,[88] was an exception, a product of an ultranationalist era in world and German history. And even in the enclave phase, the conservative, nationalist German merchants refused to support either the imperialism of the German Empire or Nazi aggression at the expense of their business interests.

Why have German families in Mexico City taken longer to acculturate than the much larger German communities in Argentina, Brazil, and the United States? Despite the efforts following the Mexican Revolution, Mexican national identity remains particularistic rather than inclusive (the traditional U.S. ideology of the "melting pot" serves as an example of the latter). In nineteenth-century Mexico, the dominant constructions of national identity excluded both the indigenous population (as "dark" and provincial) and U.S. and European foreigners (as "white" and cosmopolitan). Language and physical appearance served as the common denominators in this equation. In this fashion, the Spanish-speaking creoles and mestizos considered themselves the "real Mexicans." While the *indigenistas* propaganda after 1920 sought to exalt all Mexicans as a "cosmic race," the failure of the postrevolutionary regimes to live up to this idea undermined its credibility. Today the same idea of the nation that oppresses indigenous people still benefits the foreigners: the "real Mexicans" consider themselves above the "Indians" but below Europeans and U.S. Americans. As a group privileged in terms of both class and ethnicity, the German colony has therefore taken its good time becoming a part of Mexican society.

NOTES

1. Marianne Oeste de Bopp, "Die Deutschen in Mexico," in *Die Deutschen in Lateinamerika: Schicksal und Leistung,* ed. Hartmut Fröschle (Tübingen, 1979), 491. All translations are my own unless otherwise noted.

2. For this term, see Philip D. Curtin, *Cross-Cultural Trade in Global Perspective* (Cambridge, 1984).

3. Ethelyn C. Davis, "The American Colony in Mexico City" (Ph.D. diss., University of Missouri, 1942), ii.

4. Silke Nagel, "Integration oder nationalistische Abgrenzung? Deutsche Einwanderer in Mexiko-Stadt" (M.A. thesis, Free University of Berlin, 1991), 5.

5. A good example is Wilhelm Pferdekamp, *Auf Humboldts Spuren: Deutsche im jungen Mexiko* (Munich, 1958).

6. For the Germans in Mexico, consult Brígida von Mentz et al., *Los pioneros del imperialismo alemán en México* (Mexico City, 1982); idem, *Los empresarios alemanes, el Tercer Reich y la oposición de derecha a Cárdenas,* 2 vols. (Mexico City, 1987); and Luz María Martínez Montiel and Araceli Reynoso Medina, "Imigración europea y asiática, siglos XIX y XX," in *Simbiosis de culturas: Los inmigrantes y su cultura en México,* ed. Guillermo Bonfil Batalla (Mexico City, 1993), especially 336–65.

7. For representatives of this diverse theory, see Linda Basch, Nina Glick Schiller, and Cristina Szanton Blanc, *Nations Unbound: Transnational Projects, Postcolonial Predicaments, and Deterritorialized Nation-States* (Langhorne, Penn., 1994); Arjun Appadurai, "Global Ethnoscapes: Notes and Queries for a Transnational Anthropology," in *Recapturing Anthropology: Working in the Present,* ed. Richard G. Fox (Santa Fe, N.M., 1991), 191–210; and Gabriel Sheffer, "Ethnic Diasporas: A Threat to Their Hosts?" in *International Migration and Security,* ed. Myron Weiner (Boulder, Colo., 1993), 263–86.

8. Most of this exciting work is in the area of U.S.-Latin American relations. For an anthology of some of the best examples of this scholarship, see Gilbert M. Joseph, Catherine C. Legrand, and Ricardo D. Salvatore, eds., *Close Encounters of Empire: Writing the Cultural History of U.S.-Latin American Relations* (Durham, N.C., 1999).

9. Gilbert M. Joseph, "Close Encounters: Toward a New Cultural History of U.S.-Latin American Relations," in Joseph, Legrand, and Salvatore, eds., *Close Encounters,* especially 15–16.

10. Mary Louise Pratt, *Imperial Eyes: Travel Writing and Transculturation* (London, 1992), 4.

11. The term is Walther Bernecker's in *Die Handelskonquistadoren: Europäische Interessen und mexikanischer Staat* (Stuttgart, 1988).

12. George D. Berninger, *La inmigración en México, 1821–1857* (Mexico, 1974).

13. Bernecker, *Handelskonquistadoren,* 566–67.

14. Oeste de Bopp, "Die Deutschen in Mexico," 483–84; Hendrik Dane, *Die wirtschaftlichen Beziehungen Deutschlands zu Mexiko und Mittelamerika im neunzehnten Jahrhundert* (Cologne: Böhlau, 1971), 53–64.

15. Bernecker, *Handelskonquistadoren,* 460.

16. David A. Brading, *Miners and Merchants in Bourbon Mexico* (Cambridge, 1971), 97–99; Pferdekamp, *Auf Humboldts Spuren,* 55–60.

17. Richard N. Sinkin, *The Mexican Reform, 1855–1876: A Study in Liberal Nation-Building* (Austin, Tex., 1979).

18. Moisés González Navarro, *Los extranjeros en México y los mexicanos en el extranjero,* vol. 3 (Mexico City, 1993), 460.

19. Walther L. Bernecker and Thomas Fischer, "Deutsche in Lateinamerika," in *Deutsche im Ausland—Fremde in Deutschland: Migration in Geschichte und Gegenwart,* ed. Klaus J. Bade (Munich, 1992), 200–210.

20. Interview with Herbert Bostelmann, Mexico City, June 13, 2000.

21. von Mentz et al., *Los pioneros del imperialismo alemán,* 333–62; Bernecker, *Handelskonquistadoren,* 581–93.

22. Moisés González Navarro, *Los extranjeros en México y los mexicanos en el extranjero,* vol. 1 (Mexico City, 1993).

23. Katherine Anne Porter, *Ship of Fools* (Boston, 1962), 79–80.

24. Charles A. Hale, *The Transformation of Mexican Liberalism in the Late Nineteenth Century* (Princeton, 1989).

25. David A. Brading, *Los orígenes del nacionalismo mexicano* (Mexico City, 1979); and Jacques Lafaye, *Quetzalcóatl and Guadalupe: The Formation of Mexican National Consciousness, 1531–1813,* trans. Benjamin Keen (Chicago, 1976).

26. Alan Knight, "Racism, Revolution, and *Indigenismo:* Mexico, 1910–1940," in *The Idea of Race in Latin America, 1870–1940,* ed. Richard Graham (Austin, Tex., 1990), 72–73; Benedict Anderson, *Imagined Communities: Reflections on the Spread of Nationalism* (London, 1983).

27. For a similar argument comparing the issue of hyphenation in Argentina and the United States, see Donna Gabaccia, "Race, Nation, Hyphen: Italian-Americans and American Multiculturalism in Comparative Perspective," in *Are Italians White? How Race is Made in America,* ed. Jennifer Gugliemo and Salvatore Salerno (New York, 2003), 44–59.

28. von Mentz et al., *Los empresarios alemanes,* 328–29.

29. For a history of the Boker clan, see Jürgen Buchenau, *Tools of Progress: A German Merchant Family in Mexico City, 1865–2000* (Albuquerque, N.M., 2004).

30. Bernecker, *Handelskonquistadoren,* 567–93.

31. Friedrich Ratzel, *Aus Mexico: Reiseskizzen aus den Jahren 1874 und 1875* ([1878] Stuttgart, 1969), 379.

32. Bernecker, *Handelskonquistadoren,* 573–76.

33. Oeste de Bopp, "Die Deutschen in Mexico"; Bernecker, *Handelskonquistadoren;* von Mentz et al., *Los pioneros del imperialismo alemán.*

34. This analysis of the Porfiriato follows François-Xavier Guerra, *Le Mexique de l'Ancien Régime à la Révolution,* vol. 1 (Paris, 1986).

35. Mauricio Tenorio Trillo, *Mexico at the World's Fairs: Crafting a Modern Nation* (Berkeley, Calif., 1996), 20; Charles A. Hale, *The Transformation of Liberalism in Late Nineteenth-Century Mexico* (Princeton, N.J., 1989), passim.

36. The term *Porfirian persuasion* comes from William Beezley, *Judas at the Jockey Club and Other Episodes of Porfirian Mexico* (Lincoln, Neb., 1987).

37. Friedrich Katz, *Deutschland, Diaz und die mexikanische Revolution* (Berlin, 1964).

38. von Mentz et al., *Los pioneros del imperialismo alemán,* 77; Bernecker, *Handelskonquistadoren,* 562.

39. Paolo Riguzzi, "México próspero: las dimensiones de la imagen nacional en el porfiriato," *Historias* 20 (1988): 137–57.

40. American residents to Hayes, May 7, 1877, National Archives, Washing-

ton, D.C., and College Park, Md. (hereafter cited as NA), RG 59: General Records, Department of State, Consular Dispatches, Mexico City, microcopy M 296, reel 8.

41. More to Rives, Mexico City, June 6, Oct. 10, and Dec. 31, 1888, Apr. 1, 1889; More to Wharton, Mexico City, July 1, 1889, NA, RG 59, Consular Dispatches, Mexico City, microcopy M 296, reel 10.

42. Wangenheim to Bülow, Mexico City, Dec. 6, 1905, Bundesarchiv Berlin, R 901: Auswärtiges Amt, R 12299, 5–6.

43. Fernando Rosenzweig, "El comercio exterior," *El porfiriato: Vida económica, Historia moderna de México,* ed. Daniel Cosío Villegas, vol. 7 (Mexico City, 1965), pt. 2, 693–710; Katz, *Deutschland, Diaz und die mexikanische Revolution,* 95–98.

44. F.C. Rieloff, "Liste der in Mexico D.F. lebenden Deutschen," June 10, 1914, Politisches Archiv, Auswärtiges Amt, Bonn, Germany (hereafter cited as AAB), Archiv der ehemaligen deutschen Gesandtschaft in Mexico (hereafter cited as ADGM), packet 45, vol. 1.

45. Erich Günther, *Illustriertes Handbuch von Mexico mit besonderer Berücksichtigung der deutschen Interessen* (Mexico City, 1912), 354.

46. Matthias Wankel, *Reflejo de la historia de dos pueblos: el Colegio Alemán de México/Spiegelbild der Geschichte zweier Völker: Die deutsche Schule in Mexiko, 1894–1942* (Mexico City, 1994), 81.

47. *Jahresbericht 1912,* 10; Archivo Histórico, Colegio Alejandro von Humboldt, Mexico City (hereafter cited as AHCA), box 2.

48. *Jahresbericht 1915,* 11, 18; *Jahresbericht 1919,* 3; AHCA, box 2.

49. Nagel, "Integration oder nationalistische Abgrenzung," 135–71.

50. "5 Jahre deutsche evangelische Kirchengemeinde in Mexico," Evangelisches Zentralarchiv, Berlin, 5/2827, 66–75; Gabriele Buchenau, interview by author, June 2, 1992, Warleberg, Germany.

51. Gabriele Buchenau, interview by author, June 5, 1992, Warleberg, Germany. As residents of Mexico since 1865 and citizens since the early 1900s, members of my family provide important oral history sources for this study of the German colony.

52. Richard Eversbusch, interview by author, June 8, 1998, Mexico City.

53. Davis, "The American Colony in Mexico City," 18.

54. Friedrich Katz, *The Secret War in Mexico: Europe, the United States, and the Mexican Revolution* (Chicago, 1981), 446–48; Fletcher to American Consular Service, Mexico City, May 30, 1917, and George T. Summerlin to George A. Chamberlain, Mexico City, Aug. 2, 1917, NA, RG 84, Records of the Foreign Service Posts of the Department of State, Mexico City Consulate, 1912–1936, vol. 312, file 711.3, 1917; Duems to von Lübeck, Mexico City, July 1, 1918; NA, RG 84, Mexico City Embassy, 1912–1936, vol. 587, file 820.02, 1918; "Alphabetical List of Subjects of the Teutonic Powers," Sept. 8, 1917, NA, RG 165, box 2031, file 9140–668/3; W. F. Herring to Chief Military Censor, Feb. 17, 1919, NA, RG 165, box 3775, file 10915–201/77.

55. Chamberlain to Secretary of State, Mexico City, Oct. 31, 1917, NA, RG 59, 763.72112/5323; Summerlin to Secretary of State, Mexico City, Jan. 8, 1918, NA, RG 59, 763.72112/6414; Chamberlain to Summerlin, Mexico City, July 31, 1917, NA, RG 84, Mexico City Consulate, 1912–1936, vol. 312, file 711.3, 1917; War

Trade Board, Confidential List, Apr. 4, 1919, NA, RG 165, box 3802, file 10921–2/26–4.

56. John M. Hart, *Revolutionary Mexico: The Coming and Process of the Mexican Revolution,* 2d ed. (Berkeley, Calif., 1997); Luise Böker to Maria Pocorny, Mexico City, Feb. 26, 1915, and Franz Böker, "Versuch über mein Leben etwas aufzuzeichnen," Archivo Boker, S.A., Mexico City, Fondo Memorias.

57. Moisés González Navarro, *Población y sociedad en México,* vol. 2 (Mexico City, 1974), 34–56.

58. Nagel, "Integration oder nationalistische Abgrenzung," 52–70.

59. As an example, see Fletcher to Secretary of State, Mexico City, May 24, 1918, NA, RG 59, 862.20212/1261. For U.S. myopia about the German threat in early-twentieth-century Mexico, see Nancy Mitchell, *The Danger of Dreams: German and American Imperialism in Latin America* (Chapel Hill, N.C., 1999).

60. Franz Böker, "Schicksal von Kapital und Arbeit im Hause Böker," Archivo Boker, S.A., Mexico City, Fondo Memorias, 5.

61. Gabriele Buchenau, interview by author, June 5 and 6, 1992, Warleberg, Germany; von Mentz et al., *Los empresarios alemanes,* 155–57.

62. von Mentz et al., *Los empresarios alemanes,* 2:203–48; interview with Gabriele Buchenau, Warleberg, Germany, June 2, 1992.

63. Stefan Rinke, *"Der letzte freie Kontinent": Deutsche Lateinamerikapolitik im Zeichen transnationaler Beziehungen, 1918–1933* (Stuttgart, 1996), 379–91.

64. Montgelas to Auswärtiges Amt, Mexico City, Jan. 23, 1922, AAB, R 79645.

65. Montgelas to Auswärtiges Amt, Mexico City, Sept. 16, 1920, AAB, R 79645.

66. So much so that Jewish immigrants to Mexico felt threatened by this rhetoric. Interview with Marianne Frenk-Westheim, Mexico City, June 20, 2000.

67. von Mentz et al., *Los empresarios alemanes,* 143–70; Gus T. Jones, "The Nazi Failure in Mexico," Stanford University, Hoover Institution Archive, collection Gus T. Jones, 4–13. A list of German organizations in Mexico City can also be found in Jones.

68. A list of four hundred Nazi Party members published in a Mexican newspaper contained more than two hundred members who had joined in Germany, as well as about fifty individuals who, according to party documents in the Berlin Document Center, were not party members. *El Popular,* Oct. 19, 1941.

69. Jones, "The Nazi Failure in Mexico," 1–2.

70. Patrik von zur Mühlen, *Fluchtziel Lateinamerika: Die deutsche Emigration, 1933–1945; politische Aktivitäten und soziokulturelle Integration* (Berlin, 1988), 160.

71. Gunther Boker to Miguel Alemán, Mexico City, Mar. 29, 1948, Archivo General de la Nación, Mexico City, Ramo Presidentes, Miguel Alemán Valdés 562.11/9–8; idem, "Unsere Geschaefte waehrend und nach dem Kriege," Archivo Boker, S.A., Fondo Memorias, folder "Familiengeschichte," 3–5.

72. See list of officers of German Casino, Riding Club, and Rowing Club prepared by the FBI (probably Gus Jones), Feb. 13, 1942, NA, RG 165: Military Intelligence Division, box 2460, folder "NSDAP vol. 19." Immediately prior to Mexico's entry into World War II, most officers of these organizations were recent arrivals who had little to lose from their activities.

73. Blanca Torres Ramírez, *México en la segunda guerra mundial* (Mexico City, 1979), 9–66; *Excelsior,* May 23 and June 4, 1940.

74. Text of broadcast enclosed in McGurk to Secretary, Mexico City, Dec. 11, 1941, NA, RG 59 812.00/Avila Camacho, Manuel/171.

75. Welles to Messersmith, Washington, D.C., May 23, 1942, NA, RG 84: Records of the Foreign Service Posts of the Department of State, Mexico City (Mexico) General Records, 1937–52, box 152. For the thesis that Mexico only reluctantly cooperated with the United States, see María E. Paz, *Strategy, Security, and Spies: Mexico and the United States as Allies in World War Two* (University Station, Penn., 1998).

76. Summary for Interdepartmental Committee, "Brehme, Hugo," May 1, 1942, NA, RG 353: Division of World Trade Intelligence, box 22, folder III.

77. For the activities of the Junta, see Junta de Administración y Vigilancia de la Propiedad Extranjera, *Informe sintético de su actuación durante el período comprendido entre el 15 de junio de 1942 y el 15 de junio de 1947* (Mexico City, 1947).

78. M. D. Mónica Palma Mora, "Inmigrantes extranjeros en México, 1950–1980" (Ph.D. diss., Universidad Nacional Autónoma de México, 1999), 83–132.

79. Oeste de Bopp, "Die Deutschen in Mexico," 522; Archivo Histórico de la Secretaría de Relaciones Exteriores, Mexico City, Archivo de Concentraciones, Constancias de Nacionalidad.

80. Eric Zolov, *Refried Elvis: The Rise of the Mexican Counterculture* (Berkeley, Calif., 1999); Carlos Monsiváis, "Tantos millones de hombres no hablaremos inglés? (La cultura norteamericana y México)," in *Simbiosis de culturas,* 500–513.

81. Dennis Brehme, interview by author, May 25, 1999, Greenville, S.C.; Renate Boker de Hernández, interview by author, June 1, 1998, Mexico City; Pedro Boker, interview by author, Oct. 2, 1999, Mexico City.

82. Most recently, however, the Colegio Alemán has fallen a bit out of favor. Ex-president Carlos Salinas de Gortari, for example, sent his children to the Japanese school. See Jane Bussey, "Salinas de Gortari, Carlos," in *Encyclopedia of Mexico: History, Society, and Culture,* vol. 2, ed. Michael Werner (Chicago, 1997), 1332.

83. Blanca Huici "Los años cincuenta," *Noticias Humboldt,* nos. 4–5 (June 1999): 79–82; Veronica Kugel, interview by author, June 9, 1998, Mexico City; Blanca Huici, interview by author, Oct. 8, 1999, Mexico City.

84. Oeste de Bopp, "Die Deutschen in Mexico," 497; Gabriele Buchenau, interview by author, June 5, 1992, Warleberg, Germany; Helmut Buchenau, interview by author, Oct. 18, 1997, Hattiesburg, Mo.; Ulrich Buchenau, interview by author, May 16, 1996, Julich, Germany.

85. Palma, "Los inmigrantes extranjeros," 173–79; Veronica Kugel, interview by author, June 9, 1998, Mexico City.

86. Klaus Boker, AASCA president, interview by author, June 8, 1998, Mexico City.

87. A leading employee in a prominent German Mexican firm, for instance, told me that the Mexican-born owners "look and act German" (Alvaro Gómez, interview by author, May 23, 1998, Mexico City).

88. von Mentz et al., *Los empresarios alemanes,* passim.

CHAPTER 5

Jews, Germans, or Americans?

German-Jewish Immigrants in the
Nineteenth-Century United States

Tobias Brinkmann

Traditionally the history of Jewish migration to America has been
divided into three periods. The first Jews in America were descendants
of Jewish refugees from Spain and Portugal. They reached the shores
of North America in the seventeenth century and founded small communities on the East Coast in harbor cities such as Charleston,
Philadelphia, New York, and Newport, Rhode Island. Their numbers
remained low. In 1800 approximately three thousand Jews lived in the
United States. After the Napoleonic Wars in Europe the "Sephardic"
period gave way to the so-called German period, with the migration of
at least one hundred thousand Jews from Central and Eastern Europe
to the United States until 1880. Triggered by anti-Jewish pogroms in
Russia the third and decisive Jewish migration brought more than two
million Jews from Eastern Europe to the United States between 1880
and 1920. The introduction of restrictive quota laws in the early 1920s
brought this third Russian or Eastern European period of American
Jewish migration history to a sudden end.[1]

In recent years the tripartite model has come under attack. Studies
on the colonial period have shown that most Jews who arrived before
1800 were Jews from Eastern and Central Europe. Although Sephardic
Jews played a dominant role in most Jewish communities before 1820,
terms such as *colonial Jewry* or *Jewish communities of the early republic* have replaced the labels *Sephardic era* or *Sephardic Jewry*.[2] A similar reevaluation is currently under way for the hitherto little studied
second or German period.

For decades scholars working on American Jewish history have paid
scant attention to the German period. Most authors designated these

immigrants as German Jews, without examining the term's origins or the exact meaning of the attribute *German.*[3] Recently, however, Hasia R. Diner has questioned the usefulness of the terms *German Jews* and *German Jewish period.* In her general study on the second migration, part of a five-volume study on American Jewish history, she emphasizes that many Jewish migrants who arrived before 1880 came from a number of territories outside of Germany, such as Hungary or Poland. And even most Jews who had lived in German territories such as Bavaria or Baden, Diner claims, had had little contact with German culture prior to migrating literally "out of the ghetto" to the United States.[4] But Diner does not deny that "many American Jews who themselves—or their parents—had hailed from the lands of the east described themselves as 'Germans,' an identity thought to be prestigious, and ignored their Polish or other roots."[5]

Most scholars of German immigration to North America in the nineteenth century rarely mention Jewish immigrants, although Jews played visible roles within German American communities and German-language papers extensively reported on Jewish congregations and associations. A notable exception is Stanley Nadel's study on German immigrants in nineteenth-century New York City.[6] Nadel is one of the very few scholars working on German migration to the United States who has included Jews in his analysis. He discovered many Jewish immigrants ranging from workers to millionaires who were active in German associations, often in leading positions. For Nadel these Jewish immigrants were "German Jews" because they formed an integral part of Little Germany in New York before 1880.[7] In his recent survey on Jewish immigration from Germany to the United States between 1820 and 1914, Avraham Barkai suggests yet another interpretation. He claims that, until 1880, German Jews in the United States formed a branch of German Jewry.[8]

This chapter, based on a social and cultural study of Chicago Jewry between 1840 and 1900 with a focus on Jews who arrived before 1880, examines the relationship and boundaries between Germanness, Jewishness, and Americanness for nineteenth-century Jewish immigrants to the United States from Central and Eastern Europe. The concluding section returns to the different meanings of the term *German Jews* and reexamines the positions of Diner and Nadel in light of the presented material.

"German" Immigrants in Nineteenth-Century America

After the end of the Napoleonic Wars a growing number of Jews in Central Europe left their home villages for the United States. According to the traditional view of Jewish migration to the United States before 1880, Jews fled anti-Jewish persecution and discrimination. More recent studies have highlighted the impact of socioeconomic factors on the Jewish migration.[9] The largest group of Jewish immigrants emigrated from the South German states, especially from Bavaria but also from Baden, Württemberg and Hesse. Many Jews also left the Prussian duchy of Posen. Smaller groups came from Bohemia and from several regions in Eastern Europe. Due to the clear-cut separation of religion and state in the United States, Jewish migrants were not counted as Jews. Therefore estimates of the number of Jewish migrants to the United States between 1820 and 1880 range widely from one hundred thousand to two hundred thousand.[10] The large majority of Jewish immigrants moved to large cities. Jews who arrived between 1820 and 1880, however, often spent several years in small cities and towns before moving on to larger cities.[11]

The Jewish migrants were but a small part of a huge migration wave that brought 5.5 million "German immigrants" to North America between 1815 and 1914.[12] The term *German immigrants* is, like *German Jews,* hard to define. The German nation-state was only founded in 1871. The decision for *Kleindeutschland* excluded millions of German speakers, such as Austrians, while including a number of national minorities such as Poles and Danes. Immigrants who considered themselves or were described as Germans were by far the largest but also the most heterogeneous immigrant group in nineteenth-century America. They came at different times for different reasons over an extended period. Their identification with their home region, such as Bavaria or Mecklenburg, was sometimes stronger than that with the emerging national state. Religious differences, especially between Protestants and Catholics, were a divisive force.[13] Nevertheless, most German immigrants shared a common language and an orientation toward German *Kultur.*

In large American cities, German immigrants and their descendants formed not one homogeneous and institutionally organized community but rather loose and fluctuating networks of numerous *Vereine* (associations), congregations, and lodges. On certain occasions, members of these groups interacted as "Germans." In nineteenth-century Chicago, for instance, almost all of the German associations came together once, for the large victory parade in 1871 celebrating the German unification.[14]

The use of German as a spoken language and the participation in so-called German associations are reliable criteria for identifying immigrants in nineteenth-century America as "German." And indeed, most

Jewish immigrants in New York, St. Louis, Cincinnati, Chicago, and many smaller cities spoke German, and many joined German associations in the period before 1880. But a closer analysis based on Chicago Jewish history suggests a more cautious approach and also casts doubt on the widespread use of the label *German Jews*—but not for the reasons Diner stresses, that is, the origin of Jewish immigrants in non-German territories and the slight contact of Jewish immigrants from the German states with German culture before the migration.

Jewish Immigrants and "Germanness" in Chicago

Chicago was one of the centers of the German migration in the United States. During the second half of the immigration wave, German-speaking migrants represented the largest immigrant group in the rapidly growing metropolis of the American West. But Chicago also attracted large numbers of Irish, Czech, Swedish, and, increasingly after 1880, Eastern European Jewish, Polish, and Italian immigrants; therefore the German presence in Chicago was never as dominant as in Milwaukee, Cincinnati, and St. Louis.[15]

Until the 1870s most Jews in Chicago were German speakers.[16] The *Illinois Staatszeitung* covered events in the Jewish community into the 1890s, an indication of a substantial Jewish readership. Even internal Jewish controversies were sometimes reported by the *Staatszeitung.* Several rabbis, especially Bernhard Felsenthal, wrote for the paper on theological and cultural subjects, addressing Jews and Gentiles alike.[17] Jews were often identified as "Germans" by outside observers, although they may not have considered themselves as such. Early in the 1850s an English visitor observed in Chicago that "most Jews here are Germans and speak that language."[18] The publication of two weekly English-language papers for the Jewish community after 1878 illustrates the fading of German as a spoken language. One of the two papers, the *Jewish Advance,* still had an extended German section.[19]

Chicago's leading Jews, in particular, were closely connected with the German community on a social level until the 1880s, and in a few individual cases even longer. Two biographical compilations of leading Germans in Chicago contain the names of famous Jews.[20] The involvement of most Jewish leaders in the upper echelons of German community circles suggests a broad membership of Jews in German associations before the 1870s. In his article "German-Jewish Identity in Nineteenth-Century America," Michael A. Meyer argues convincingly that German associations offered Jewish immigrants acceptance when they were still outsiders in America.[21]

Jews who were leaders of Jewish associations were equally active in German associations. Rabbis and leading Jewish businessmen were especially involved in German associations between 1850 and 1880: in 1853 Jews helped to establish the leading German philanthropic association, the Deutsche Gesellschaft—later known as the German Aid Society—which supported needy immigrants from Germany. The lawyer Julius Rosenthal acted as one of its early presidents. He was a member of the board during the disastrous 1871 fire. Jacob Baiersdorf also served as president of the German Aid Society for some time.[22] During the Fourth of July parade in 1862 Henry Greenebaum and Edward Salomon led the German cohort. While one can assume that other Jews participated in the German cohort, Jewish associations and congregations did not march.[23] Between the mid-1850s and early 1870s Greenebaum and, to a lesser extent, Salomon belonged to the ethnic leadership of the Germans of Chicago.[24]

In Emil G. Hirsch, who became the rabbi of the Sinai congregation in 1880, the Germans in Chicago found an intellectual of grand stature, one who was always ready to give speeches in English and German, one who could speak for the Germans of Chicago.[25] All these men also played leading roles within Jewish organizations in Chicago. These leaders could not have acted against the will of the members of Jewish congregations and associations. It was only after 1917 that the limits of involvement with the "German" cause were clearly drawn for Jewish community leaders. Emil Hirsch almost lost his position at Sinai in 1918 after he had repeatedly expressed his support for the German war effort.[26]

The large German community in Chicago was never cohesively organized, but often Jews led the efforts to bring all the Germans in Chicago together. The organization of the victory parade of 1871 was largely in the hands of Jewish community leaders. The parade was organized in the office of Julius Rosenthal and led by Henry Greenebaum; both were counted among the most respected Jews and Germans in Chicago. Yet, as in 1862, Jewish associations and congregations did not participate in the victory parade.[27] Another issue that united the Germans in Chicago (and elsewhere) was the call for the imposition of strict controls on the use and sale of alcohol. Debates over prohibition were battlegrounds of class conflict and ethnic tension in nineteenth-century U.S. cities. As early as 1867 Rabbi Isaak Chronik of the Sinai congregation had invited leading Germans to his house to organize a drive against Sunday drinking laws.[28] In the early 1870s native-born businessmen again instrumentalized the alcohol issue to strengthen their political position. After the fire of 1871, when renewed attempts were made to introduce prohibition laws in Chicago, Henry Greenebaum helped the candidate of the anti-prohibition People's Party win the mayor's office by unifying the large majority of German and Irish voters. But success was short lived. Once the threat of prohibition was removed, the political union of Germans broke down.[29]

Jews were prominently represented among the leading Germans of Chicago, but these leadership positions resulted more from social commitment to a large and dispersed community of groups than from real power over a tightly organized community. Why did Jewish leaders invest so much energy into organizing a German community? The German community in Chicago was open and inclusive for Jews. German immigrant leaders did not discriminate against Jews. In Chicago and elsewhere, many German ethnic leaders were Forty-eighters, liberals who had found asylum in the United States after the failed revolution of 1848–49. One of the leading Forty-eighters in Chicago was Lorenz Brentano. Before his emigration, Brentano, a leading left-wing liberal member of the second chamber of the Baden assembly, had persistently called for the emancipation of the Jews in Baden.[30] After the rise of modern anti-Semitism in Imperial Germany in the late 1870s, the Chicago-based *Illinois Staatszeitung* and many other German papers in the United States took a firm line against anti-Semitism, criticizing even Bismarck in strong terms because he sought to instrumentalize the anti-Semitic movement for his own ends.[31]

While there is plenty of evidence for the involvement of prominent Jews in the German community, there are, especially for the early period, almost no documents available that clearly prove widespread Jewish involvement in the German community.[32] After 1880 only a few Jewish leaders, notably Emil Hirsch and Henry Greenebaum, identified themselves with German associations in Chicago. Although as late as 1890 at least 10 percent of the contributors to the German Aid Society were Jewish, they were passive donors and were not represented on the board as they had been earlier in the century.[33] The commitment to philanthropic organizations outside of the Jewish community was influenced by Jewish tradition (discussed later), but it was also important for the Jewish leaders to counter anti-Jewish prejudices and to prove their willingness to open up to society. It is very likely that many Jews below the leadership level had social contacts with other

German immigrants in the 1850s and 1860s and even in the 1870s. But apart from the memories of individual immigrants, little material survives to corroborate this assumption.[34]

The Jewish Community

The wide coverage of Jewish matters in the *Illinois Staatszeitung* and the fact that most Jews spoke German should not be taken as proof for a close relationship between German-speaking Jews and Gentiles in all fields of social life. In the 1850s and 1860s Jews in Chicago organized their own community around a central philanthropic organization. The driving force was Chicago's first lodge of the Jewish fraternal order, B'nai B'rith (Sons of the Covenant).

The Independent Order B'nai B'rith had been founded by twelve Jewish immigrants in New York in 1843 as America's first secular (but not antireligious) Jewish association. The B'nai B'rith was an early response to the diversity of Jewish life in the United States. Jewish immigrants came from different regions in Central and Eastern Europe carrying different cultural baggage. Differing religious orientations, but also cultural and social differences between established and newly arriving immigrants, presented a serious problem for Jewish communities in the making. The B'nai B'rith, modeled after existing fraternal organizations, intended to unite Jewish men with different backgrounds. Especially religion, a source of potential conflict, was "off limits" within the B'nai B'rith.[35]

The history of the B'nai B'rith, especially its role in the local context, has hardly been examined. But my research for Chicago and other cities indicates that between 1860 and 1880 local B'nai B'rith leaders were the movers and shakers of Jewish communities in the making. Chicago's first B'nai B'rith lodge, named after the birthplace of Samuel, "Ramah," was formally installed in 1857. Within the lodge Jews with different backgrounds successfully worked as "brothers" for the establishment of an institutional core that would tie most Jewish congregations and associations in Chicago together.[36]

Jewish immigrants in the United States had to define Jewish communities on their own. This was a challenge for immigrants who came from close and clearly defined communities in Europe. In the German states, Jewish communities (*Gemeinde*) were strictly regulated by the state. As a consequence of the forced isolation and lower legal status of the Jews, the traditional Jewish Gemeinde become semiautonomous. It had taken over many tasks that transcended religious services, such as the collection of taxes, limited jurisdiction, and a number of social responsibilities, such as education, caring for the sick, and philanthropy. Although the autonomy of the Gemeinde was dismantled after 1800, Jews in the German states were obliged to belong to the one state-regulated Jewish Gemeinde at a given city, town, or village even after the Emancipation of 1871. The Gemeinde continued to direct many social tasks outside of the religious sphere. It represented the Jewish community.[37]

In the United States, due to the clear-cut separation of state and religion guaranteed in the Constitution, membership in congregations and associations and thus in the overreaching community was and is strictly voluntary. Many "indifferent" Jews decided not to join any Jewish congregation or association, without actually converting to Christianity. And in the United States, a strong institutional Jewish tradition or established patterns for the organization of Jewish communities did not exist, because very few Jews had settled in North America before 1800. Therefore, community building presented a difficult task for Jewish immigrants who arrived after 1820 in the United States.[38]

In Chicago the first step toward the organization of an overreaching Jewish community was the founding of the United Hebrew Relief Association (UHRA) in 1859, which B'nai B'rith leaders initiated. The UHRA brought most Jewish congregations and associations as corporate members under its wings. In the United States, Jewish philanthropy became the most important institutional symbol of "Jewishness." It served as a platform connecting Jews of very different backgrounds: modern Jews with the Jewish tradition, Reform Jews with orthodox Jews, rich Jews with poor Jews, religious Jews with secular Jews, "Bavarian Jews" with "Polish Jews," Jews from different parts of a city, and even Jews from different countries. Jewish philanthropy, rooted in the Jewish tradition of "tzedakah" (social justice), provided an opportunity to identify with "Jewishness" without shedding one's orthodox or Reform beliefs. Jewish philanthropy was also a response to anti-Jewish stereotypes or, rather, to fears of such stereotypes. Jewish leaders in Chicago repeatedly stressed that poor Jews did not become a public charge. Most importantly, however, Jewish philanthropy was the constant attempt to overcome the loss—in a retrospective, often idealized, sense of community—of a *Gemeinschaft* in the ghetto.[39]

In the 1860s and 1870s, new Jewish congregations and associations were founded, which became corporate members of the Chicago

UHRA, especially newly formed lodges of the B'nai B'rith and also several chapters of the Young Men's Hebrew Association (YMHA). In 1869 the Standard Club, a prestigious club for Jewish businessmen, was organized, probably because Jews were excluded from non-German Gentile clubs. Jewish women also formed numerous organizations. In 1874 they organized the first Chicago chapter of the Unabhängiger Orden Treuer Schwestern (Independent Order of True Sisters).[40]

After the 1870s many leading Jewish families had become wealthy, a prerequisite to participating in the social life of the well-to-do in the city, and German circles were increasingly replaced by those of the established urban society. These developments corresponded with residential mobility; in the 1850s most Jews had lived in the southern part of the Loop, Chicago's central business district. In the 1860s Jews began to move to the near and far South Side, the elite section of Chicago. Smaller groups lived on the West Side and the North Side. Before the disastrous fire of 1871, which wiped out the North Side and the Loop, well-to-do Chicagoans preferred the West Side. After the fire the West Side gradually declined and was replaced by the South Side as the neighborhood of the middle and upper classes. While most of the older Jewish Chicagoans had left the West Side for the South Side by the 1890s, the near West Side became the center of the so-called ghetto, where thousands of new immigrants from Eastern and Southern Europe (among them many Jews) settled after 1880. On Chicago's proletarian North Side, where most German-speaking immigrants settled before and after the fire of 1871, the Jewish presence was relatively marginal before 1900. Although many Jews lived in close proximity to each other, they shared these neighborhoods with many native-born Gentile neighbors. Large numbers of Jews seem not to have lived in German middle-class neighborhoods.[41]

The German community in Chicago was a loose ethnic network, and prior to 1880 the Jewish community had a number of close connections with it, especially at the upper level. At no time, however, did the small Jewish community belong to the large German community. In 1867 Jews organized a large parade to the construction site of the future Jewish hospital of Chicago. The parade included all the Jewish congregations, lodges, and associations, as well as Chicago's mayor. The *Illinois Staatszeitung* covered the event in detail and printed the speeches, but it was obvious that the hospital project was important for the Jewish community and its standing in the city of Chicago. Except for the language, "Germanness" was not an issue.[42]

American Patriotism: Germans and Jews in the Civil War

The involvement of Chicago immigrants in the Civil War illustrates
how Jews and Germans could simultaneously be closely involved yet
remain clearly distinct. During the 1850s anti-immigrant agitation by
the so-called Know-Nothings had received wide support in the Northeastern and Midwestern states. Therefore the Civil War presented a
chance for immigrants to prove their loyalty to their new home country.[43] In Chicago hundreds of German and Irish immigrants immediately volunteered for the Union army in 1861. When President Lincoln
called for troop reinforcements in the early summer of 1862, leaders of
the large immigrant groups in Chicago quickly responded.[44] Jewish
leaders organized a mass meeting on August 13, 1862. Within minutes
six thousand dollars had been collected to furnish an all-Jewish company. The *Chicago Tribune* and the *Illinois Staatszeitung* praised "our
patriotic Israelite fellow citizens" for their determined action.[45] One
day later even more Jews attended a second mass meeting. This was the
first time that almost all Jews in Chicago came together as Jews, as they
formally decided to put aside their numerous differences, particularly
with regard to religion, for the time being. Henry Greenebaum
addressed the Jewish crowd in German and reminded them "that they
[the Jews] owe the Union loyalty, because it gave them social and political freedom, a freedom they did not enjoy in Europe." And his call
was heeded: all Jews present agreed in their resolution "that we, at this
time, feel compelled—driven by our deep patriotic feelings, and by our
adherence and love to the fatherland of our choice—to undertake as a
community an effort for our fatherland that had adopted us." More
donations were collected, and a company of almost one hundred Jewish volunteers was organized that evening, fully equipped by the Jews
of Chicago. The size of the company is remarkable, since only around
two thousand Jews lived in Chicago in 1862. The Jewish "Company C"
became part of the Eighty-second Illinois Regiment. This regiment was
led by the famous Forty-eighter Friedrich Hecker and was composed
mostly of German immigrants.[46]

On August 20 another meeting took place to celebrate the formal
entry of the Jewish company into Hecker's regiment. The Jewish
women of Chicago donated the regiment's flag to Colonel Hecker, who
attended the meeting along with Lorenz Brentano and other prominent
Germans. The small but influential group of the Forty-eighters was the
only other group of Germans in Chicago that owed its freedom to the
United States, like the Jewish immigrants. In his impressive speech
Hecker drew a parallel between the struggle for Jewish emancipation in

Germany in 1848 and the fight for the emancipation of the black slaves in the South: "I fought in my former home country for the civil rights of Jews, defending them against intolerance and race hatred. You have repaid to me today. Just as emancipation was inscribed on our flags then, this flag will be the symbol of emancipation."[47]

The Jews of Chicago were praised for their quick response, and they were proud of themselves. Although Chicago's Jews were closely involved with other immigrants from Germany, not least as soldiers of the same regiment, the Jewish war effort clearly illustrates that Jews considered themselves as a separate ethnic group. Later in 1862 the directors of the UHRA of Chicago declared in their annual report:

> The very existence of that good Government, to which the Israelite especially is indebted for the enjoyment of political equality, and religious liberty, is threatened. . . . The Stars and Stripes, that emblem of justice and free institutions, has been trampled under foot by traitors at home, while the act, if not openly commended, is secretly cheered by Despots and Crowned heads of tyrannical Europe. . . . And nobly, yes thrice noble, and patriotically did the Israelites of Chicago respond in the emergency. With a burning love for country and freedom did they arise . . . and praise resounded throughout the land for their support of the war.[48]

The Jewish company and its soldiers did well in the war, although it suffered heavy casualties. Many soldiers were decorated and returned as officers. During the war Edward Salomon succeeded Hecker as commander of the regiment and was promoted to brigadier general.[49] For Jews in Europe such careers were not even imaginable.

American patriotism proved to be a unifying force for the loose community of Jewish immigrants, because it transcended all religious, regional, and other differences. But the other important driving force for the decisive Jewish action was the rise of anti-Jewish prejudice during the Civil War. Unlike most Jews in the European states all American Jews were free and equal citizens. But legal equality did not confer social acceptance. Already in late-eighteenth-century America anti-Jewish stereotypes were widespread, although only a few Jews lived in North America at the time. Historians of anti-Jewish prejudice in the United States consider the Civil War as a turning point, because of the widespread use of anti-Jewish stereotypes in the public arena. Several leading members of both legislatures and a number of leading officers on both sides took their anti-Jewish prejudice into the public.[50]

Two events in particular indicate that Jews were not fully accepted:

General Grant's infamous Order Number Eleven expelling all Jews from the military department under his command in Tennessee and the army chaplain question. On both occasions, Rabbi Bernhard Felsenthal of Chicago's Sinai congregation wrote protest letters to politicians in Washington. Felsenthal was one of many Jews who called for the lifting of Grant's order.[51] In the army chaplain question, Felsenthal's protest to Senator Wilson of Massachusetts may have been decisive. Wilson accordingly sponsored a bill to change the law on army chaplains from "ministers of some Christian denomination" to "ministers of some religious denomination."[52] These two events were setbacks for American Jewry, but the outcome also offered some encouragement.

After the war, Rabbi Liebmann Adler published a number of patriotic speeches he had given in 1865 as sermons to his congregation. Adler's sermons were delivered in German, but they prove that Jewish immigrants from the German states were patriotic Americans.[53] The religious sphere has been interpreted as a bastion of ethnicity by immigration historians.[54] But although the Jews of Chicago spoke German in their services and were inspired by the Jewish Reform movement in Germany and by Germany on a cultural level, in the synagogue they emphasized early on that they were free Americans and proud of it. On the occasion of Lincoln's second inauguration, Adler declared: "Thank you, o God, for saving this free land. . . . Do you, you people, want to love a country and do what you can to keep it strong, when you are so powerful?"[55] Adler spoke in German to a Jewish audience, but he was not addressing the Jewish people in this paragraph; rather, he was addressing the American people. The important theme of the suppression of Jews in Germany and Eastern Europe and the consequent need to defend the freedom of America was not an issue in these sermons. Adler spoke as an American to Americans, and he praised the democratic republic of the United States while condemning the monarchies of Europe.

"We American-German Jews": The Origins of Reform in Chicago

American Jews had a particularly close relationship with Germany and German Jewry on a cultural and religious level before 1880. Before the rise of migration from Eastern Europe in the 1880s, most American Jews who belonged to a congregation identified with the Jewish Reform movement. Many American Jews, and in particular Reform Jews, identified with Germany and German Jewry on a cultural level because they considered Germany as the motherland of modern Judaism.

Until recently, most historians of modern Jewish history have treated Germany as the epitome of the modern Jewish experience. Recent historiography on modern Jewish history, however, has criticized the German-centered approach (with some justification) for ignoring Jews outside of Germany, for instance, in Amsterdam or in port cities like Trieste, who also developed modern concepts of Jewishness. But even the critics acknowledge the sustained impact of the German Jewish "response to modernity," in Michael A. Meyer's phrase, on Jews all over the world in the nineteenth century.[56]

Until the late eighteenth century the Jewish minority in the German states was forced to live separately from the majority of the population. Jews had a lower civil status, their movement was restricted, and they could not engage in many occupations. Most Jews were poor. With the impact of the Enlightenment on state bureaucracies in the late eighteenth century, and especially with the advance of Napoleon's armies into Central Europe, these limitations were gradually eased. Although numerous setbacks hampered the emancipation process—all Jews in Germany were only fully emancipated in 1871—many restrictions had been lifted in the first decade of the nineteenth century, particularly in French-occupied states under Napoleon. Jews were not passive objects of these emancipation policies. Jewish philosopher Moses Mendelssohn became the early role model of the modern Jew. He engaged in an intense dialogue with Enlightenment thinkers, some of whom he befriended outside of the ghetto. Soon other intellectual Jews followed in his footsteps. On the religious level, however, Mendelssohn remained a traditional and observant Jew.[57]

The opening of the ghetto presented a major challenge for traditional Judaism, which had dominated Jewish life in the ghetto. Around 1800 several famous Jews, among them also children of Mendelssohn, converted to Christianity; others called for the adaptation of Christian forms into the Jewish service, while many opposed any changes. In this context, during the first half of the nineteenth century, Jewish Reform emerged as a genuinely Jewish response to the opening of the ghetto and the ideals of the Enlightenment. Its theology was strongly influenced by the emergence of *Wissenschaft* (critical and rational sciences) in Germany. Jewish Reformers opposed external reforms or adaptations without theological underpinning. Rather, they called for a theological reevaluation of Judaism based on scholarly research of its origins and development.[58]

Traditional Jews opposed such efforts, but many realized that traditional Judaism would not survive outside of the ghetto. As a consequence, different theological concepts emerged. Some Jewish theologians attempted to mediate between traditional Judaism and the demands of modern society and scientific progress. Zacharias Frankel, in particular, is considered the forerunner of contemporary Conservative Judaism. Others were more radical. Abraham Geiger, who has been called "the founding father of the Reform movement," stressed that texts, including the Torah and the Talmud, had no absolute authority but were, rather, sources that had to be interpreted and analyzed with the methods of critical Wissenschaft. Geiger and other Reformers also rejected the notion of the Jewish return to Zion and national aspirations inherent in Judaism. Influenced, among others, by the leading German historian Leopold von Ranke, Geiger interpreted Judaism in its specific historic context as a progressive religion. Judaism had changed its forms, but its underlying spirit had persisted—the belief in the one God, a strong emphasis on ethical values, and the vision of peace for mankind. Geiger and other Reformers regarded external changes as necessary, if forms such as parts of the liturgy did not convey the religious spirit of Judaism in the present circumstances.[59]

On a cultural and social level the German ideal of *Bildung* also had a major impact on German Jews on their way out of the ghetto. The late George L. Mosse argued that, during the emancipation, Jews in Germany replaced traditional Judaism with Bildung. Bildung was an open and inclusive ideal; it can be defined as constant spiritual self-education with a strong emphasis on universal principles like freedom, equality, and openness. Bildung became the ideology of the emancipating German bourgeoisie, and it was embraced by many Jews who sought entry into the bourgeoisie. The trailblazers and heroes of Bildung were leading writers such as Goethe, Schiller, and Lessing and artists such as Beethoven. Mosse writes, "Surely here was an ideal ready-made for Jewish assimilation, because it transcended all differences of nationality and religion through the unfolding of the individual personality."[60] Bildung, especially its emphasis on openness and universalism, exerted a strong influence on Jewish Reformers.

Although German Jews in Germany developed ambitious concepts of modern Judaism, the framework for Jewish life did not change accordingly. Repressive state authorities closed down early Jewish Reform congregations. Even after 1871 Jewish Reformers were forced to reach compromises with traditional Jews within the state-regulated

Gemeinden. In the United States, on the other hand, the state did not intervene, traditional Jewish elites did not exist, and, more importantly, Jews could split over religious issues and form separate congregations. Therefore, the conditions for Reform in the United States were much more favorable, and in the second half of the nineteenth century America rather than Germany became the land of "classical" Reform Judaism, as Michael A. Meyer has stressed.[61]

Conflicts over Reforms of the service developed in many American Jewish congregations after 1850, in a number of congregations even earlier. But before 1860 such debates were largely about external Reforms of the service rather than over the agenda of German Reform. In the late 1850s, however, Chicago became one of the early centers of the German-oriented Jewish Reform movement in the United States.

Only a few years after Jews in Chicago had organized their first congregation in 1847, called Kehilat Anshe Maarab (KAM, or Men of the West), the language of the service caused tensions. Several new members demanded that German be introduced as the language of the service, because nobody could understand Hebrew prayers.[62] In the mid-1850s German became the language of the service.[63] Behind the conflict over the introduction of German were differing views on Judaism within the congregation: the founders of the congregation were rural Jews from Franconia and the Palatinate who clung to traditional forms of religious observance.[64] Early in the 1850s a number of younger, better-educated men, some trained at German universities, reached Chicago and called for a modernization of the service at KAM. Leopold Mayer, one of these youths, remembered fifty years later in 1899 that the services at KAM did not appeal to them because "religion is for the living and not for the dead."[65] Two problems demanded immediate action: not only did the traditional service seem completely out of place and embarrassing to younger immigrants who had social contacts with Gentiles, but many Jews simply stayed away from services and severed their ties with the community in the making.[66]

After long debates a number of external Reforms were introduced: a choir was organized and—much to the distress of older members—an organ was acquired.[67] After severe struggles the Reform faction even managed to install an outspoken Reformer as president.[68] The ensuing Reforms boosted the reputation of the Jews in Chicago: in 1859 a visitor reported to Chicago's leading paper: "I understand that the new board of Administration has caused all th[e] change in the mode of service; . . . some time ago, a stranger, who visited their synagoues [sic], would hardly believe that he was among a civilized people . . . [but now

the service is] so nice . . . that all prejudice against these, our fellow citizens, must give way."[69] The Chicago Reformers may have been
flattered by these remarks, but the passage indicates also that anti-Jewish stereotypes were still widespread. The Gentile observer hinted quite
clearly that prejudice against traditional Jews was justified.

Up to this point the developments at KAM reflect the general trend
toward external Reforms in most American Jewish city congregations.
However, most of the young Reformers were not satisfied with the concessions they had won from the older members, but they did not have
a clear agenda. In this situation, the struggle over Reforms at KAM
became part of a conflict between two men who offered two different
visions for the young American Reform movement, the move of Isaac
Mayer Wise toward Americanization and David Einhorn's call for
Germanization.[70]

In the early 1850s Wise, a young Cincinnati rabbi from Bohemia, set
himself the goal of organizing Judaism in the United States under one
roof. He frequently visited many distant and small Jewish communities; in 1854 he began to publish a weekly, the *Israelite,* and one year
later he started a German-language weekly for women, *Die Deborah.*[71]
Wise saw himself as an Americanizer, and he called for the introduction of English as a spoken language. As the founding of *Die Deborah*
indicates, however, he had to use German in order to convince Jewish
readers to switch to English.[72] Wise was a Reformer, but he never
developed a consistent theology. His interest in Reform was more a
matter of decorum. He was willing to make concessions as long as
other Jewish leaders accepted his leadership role and supported his
project of uniting American Jewry. Therefore, it is not surprising that
Wise was well informed about the situation in Chicago. In July 1856 he
visited the city for the first time.[73] He expressed support for Reforms
and criticized the "ultra-conservative" faction. Chicago Jewry seemed
to be safely in his pocket: he claimed that many of the one thousand
Jews in the city read his *Israelite* and *Die Deborah,* and he emphasized,
"no opponent here."[74]

In the same year that Wise visited Chicago, David Einhorn came to
America to begin his tenure at Har Sinai congregation in Baltimore.
Einhorn was the first leading German Jewish Reformer to come to
America. He immediately challenged Wise's attempts to become the
leader of American Jewry by publishing the *Sinai,* a German-language
monthly, and attacking Wise, often in strong terms.[75] Einhorn was
offended by Wise's approach to Reform and his willingness to compromise on religious matters.[76] Wise called for an accommodation of

the Jewish service to the "present age," that is, external changes to the service, while Einhorn demanded a thorough modernization of Jewish theology.[77]

In 1856 Einhorn received a letter from another recent immigrant, Bernhard Felsenthal, in Madison, Indiana, who wished to contribute articles to the *Sinai.* Felsenthal was not an ordained rabbi, but he had university training and extensive knowledge of Jewish theology. Einhorn was enthusiastic to have found a correspondent for his paper who possessed thorough Bildung.[78] In 1857 Felsenthal himself moved to Chicago and quickly emerged as the spiritual leader of the Reformers. Felsenthal then helped to organize the so-called Jüdischer Reformverein (Jewish Reform Association), where the Reformers developed their program, and he published the manifesto of the early Reform movement in Chicago, titled "Kol Kore Bamidbar: Über jüdische Reform" (A voice calling from the wilderness: On Jewish Reform), which grew out of a series of articles for Einhorn's *Sinai.*[79]

In the religious sphere Felsenthal, like Einhorn, was a Germanizer; he argued that German Reform Judaism had to serve as the model for American Reform Judaism. Germany was important to him and to Einhorn as a cultural center and as the motherland of modern Judaism. Felsenthal emphasized in 1865: "We must not distance ourselves from German Judaism and its influences. As in medieval times the sun of Jewish Wissenschaft was shining in the Spanish sky, this sun is now shining in the German sky sending out its light to all Jews and Jewish communities, who live among the modern cultured peoples. Germany has replaced Sefard."[80] In 1859 he stressed: "The German people are still the first among the cultured peoples of the world, and we bow our heads in reverence before its spirit, its literature, its language. . . . We American-German Jews want to keep German in our synagogues."[81]

For Felsenthal the Germanization of Jewish theology in America was synonymous with the thorough modernization of Judaism. He argued that Reforms of the service leading to greater decorum, such as the introduction of an organ, were useless unless Judaism was redefined as a modern religion consistent with intellectual progress in the sciences and humanities. Felsenthal was clearly influenced by leading German Jewish Reformers like Geiger. Felsenthal interpreted Judaism as a progressive religion centered around monotheism. Traditional religious practices that did not convey the essential religious truths were to be abandoned, and new elements had to be added, especially the sermon in the German language, which would be understood by all congregants. It did not make sense, Felsenthal argued—and Einhorn praised him for it—to introduce copied versions of the Christian service by external Reforms or by turning the Jewish service into a show (*Schaugepränge*) with choirs and music. Radical Reform was a matter of spiritual Bildung rather than superficial accommodation to the "present age" along the lines proposed by Wise. Felsenthal did not oppose music as such in the service, but the congregants had to be affected in their inner spirit and "religious feelings" rationally rather than emotionally.[82] Another example for Bildung was the Sabbath: it was wrong to rush from the store to the service on Saturday for one hour or not to attend the service at all, Felsenthal declared. But it was also wrong for Jews to obey the Talmudical rules without intellectually recognizing the important religious truths guiding them. Yes, one could smoke a cigar on the Sabbath or, even better, attend a drama by Schiller or walk in the park to listen to a symphony by Beethoven. To educate oneself in this way was better than robotlike obedience to hollow laws without recognition of their inner spirit.[83] Felsenthal's remarks on the observance of the Sabbath in this passage perfectly illustrate Mosse's argument that German Jews replaced traditional Judaism with Bildung.

It was also very characteristic for "radical Reformers" like Felsenthal to question the notion of authority as such—the authority of "holy" texts like the Talmud that had regulated religious observance and the daily lives of Jews for centuries; the authority of religious elites who had controlled religious affairs in the old ghetto; and the authority of the state, which had interfered with the religious affairs of Jewish communities. In America there was no state interference in religious affairs, and Felsenthal often praised religious freedom in the United States.

Numerous quotes on the importance of spiritual Germany could be added, and Einhorn was even more outspoken on this matter. But the hymns Einhorn and Felsenthal sang to Germany can only be understood in their very American context. While Einhorn himself may have never felt at home in America, he was well aware that the Reforms he was calling for had a chance to be realized only on American soil.[84] Felsenthal was very frank about this in *Kol Kore Bamidbar*. In the United States (as opposed to Europe) Felsenthal argued convincingly that every individual Jew was "free" to evaluate Judaism and opt for Reforms. The American Constitution guaranteed the separation of religion and state; there were no old, established religious elites; and religious factions within a congregation could split from each other and form new congregations. He addressed the Reformers in Chicago: "Do you want to expel them [the traditional Jews]? Do you—and we speak to American Israelites—do you want to dictate to others how they have to pray to their God? Let us not fight, we are brothers, let us separate."[85] The words "we are brothers, let us separate" read like a paradox, but the call for separation illustrates that the call for Germanization was American in its very roots, since only in America could Jews split peacefully over religious matters, form their own congregations, yet remain united as Jews on a higher level, in secular and philanthropic associations like the B'nai B'rith or the UHRA of Chicago, founded in 1859, that represented most Jewish congregations and associations in Chicago. For Felsenthal America was a cultural desert, a land of spiritual superficiality. He praised Germany on a spiritual and cultural level, but politically, he emphasized, Germany was "miserable" (*elend*). And, indeed, in 1859 not a single German state had emancipated its Jewish subjects, while Jews in America were equal citizens.[86]

In January 1860 Wise came to Chicago again, after visiting the city at least once in 1859.[87] Earlier Einhorn had warned Felsenthal that Wise would try to interfere in Chicago in order to take over the Reform faction.[88] Wise met with a reception that was not hostile, but he felt that the Reformers around Felsenthal were busily preparing to establish their own "German" congregation. Wise again promoted modest external Americanization of the service: "Judaism changes not, but its forms, its outside has changed very often and must change again to suit our age and land, our taste, views, demands and wants." Wise could not admit that his position in Chicago was weakening and claimed not to have met any of these "radicals": "there is nothing in existence of it [radical Reform] except a pamphlet that starts with rationalism and ends in kitchen and stomach, with the extreme nonsense between. . . . This party will never succeed in Chicago." He described Felsenthal scornfully as "a pedantic and fantastic man . . . [and a] ship-wrecked egoist." Much to his dismay, Wise had an encounter with Felsenthal at a meeting of the local B'nai B'rith lodge. Felsenthal took the opportunity to challenge Wise to a debate, but Wise left in disgust: "This gave my pedantic spectacled and ship-wrecked opponent an opportunity to criticise, scold, lament, decry, laugh, cry, and practicing German grammar, of course when I was gone."[89] These descriptions were harmless compared to what Wise printed a few weeks later in his paper. Felsenthal was characterized in this way: "[a] long hook-nose upon which rest a pair of large silver spectacles, covering a couple of glass-like eyes . . . [like an] elephant . . . the famous . . . Chicago pamphleteer of radicalism."[90] Wise's scorn and sarcasm were only an indication of Felsenthal's success, otherwise Wise would have ignored the Reformers, as he had done in September 1859 when "radical Reform" in Chicago was mentioned only once as a threat for Jewish congregations there.[91] In 1860 a growing number of Reformers joined the Jüdischer Reformverein (Jewish Reform Society). Einhorn was now openly and enthusiastically referring to Felsenthal as "our Felsenthal."[92] In 1861 the new congregation, named Sinai after Einhorn's journal, was established when the Reformers split from KAM congregation.[93]

Some of the Reform measures introduced at Sinai congregation show that Chicago Reformers were inspired by the German model but that they were American Jews when it came to Reforms: from the beginning, mixed seating of men and women was introduced at Sinai congregation.[94] Leading German Reformers such as Abraham Geiger were alienated by such Reforms.[95] A Jewish traveler from Germany was also offended by the "reform madness" (*Reformwuth*) in Chicago in 1861.[96] German remained important as the spoken language in the service until the late 1870s, retaining its highly symbolic meaning until the turn of the century. Several Chicago congregations advertised for positions in the 1880s that required the ability to deliver sermons in German.[97] The language requirement had little to do with day-to-day activities at the congregation, but it remained a symbol for the Bildung of the spiritual leader of the congregation and demonstrated religious progress. In this light, Avraham Barkai's thesis that "German Jews" in America formed a branch of German Jewry before 1880 is convincing.[98] And yet, Felsenthal's call for separation shows that early on "Americanness" as a metaphor for democracy and freedom became a crucial part of the self-image of Jewish immigrants in the United States.

Conclusion

The term *German Jews* was widely used only after 1881, when thousands of Jewish immigrants from Eastern Europe, the so-called Russian Jews, arrived in the United States and faced established Jews, many of whom were assimilated and embraced Reform Judaism. To this day, many scholarly works reflect the perspective of the newcomers.[99] It is hardly surprising, then, that the term *German Jews* carries notions of arrogant, assimilated "uptown Jews." But why was the term *German Jews,* rather than *American Jews,* used after 1881, in a period when German as a spoken language had already lost its importance even in Reform synagogues and when there were fewer contacts between Jewish and Gentile immigrants from Germany?

For Reformers the term *Germany* carried a special meaning as the birthplace of modern Judaism. Even after 1880 the term *German Jews* stood for perceived cultural superiority, for progress and openness. By contrast, Jews living in Eastern Europe were regarded by assimilated Jews in America and Germany as backward and traditional—as the very opposite of the educated and open-minded "German Jew." In his book *Brothers and Strangers,* Steven Aschheim describes how assimilated Jews in Germany constructed negative images of Eastern European Jews in order to distinguish themselves from traditional Judaism and thus from their own past.[100]

The conflict between "Germans" and "Russians" in the United States had its roots in the decades before 1880. Power conflicts between these immigrants from different regions in Europe and religious differences were part of the Jewish experience well before 1880. Already in the 1840s such conflicts were fought on an East-West platform, for instance, between "Bavarians" and "Pollacks." In Chicago and many other cities the relationship between "Bavarians" and "Poles" was difficult.[101]

During the 1860s growing numbers of Jewish immigrants came from the Russian Empire—the Jewish philanthropic association in Chicago mentioned the term *Ostjuden* (in an otherwise English text) as early as 1864.[102] The established and assimilated Jews, perceived by the newcomers as "Germans," viewed poor newcomers as "other Jews" not just on a religious level but also in social terms as a different class.[103] With the increase of Jewish immigration from Eastern Europe in the 1870s and especially after 1881 the rift between established Jews and newcomers deepened. *German Jews* became a synonym for an established status group, while *Russian Jews* served as a metaphor for traditional Jewish newcomers and outsiders. Both terms were heavily charged images; the respective content depended on the perspective of each group. For many "Russians," the "Germans" were assimilated and arrogant Jews who denied their Jewishness. Many "Germans," on the other hand, looked down upon the "Russians," because they were perceived as "too Jewish." Established "Germans" feared that the presence of traditional (that is, visible) Jews in American cities strengthened anti-Jewish stereotypes.

The labels *German Jews, Ostjuden,* and *Russian Jews* reflect, therefore, complex and fluctuating images that do not clearly refer to the actual origin of Jewish immigrants. Not all "Germans" came from the German states—quite a few originated in Bohemia and even Russia—while some "Russians" were actually Jewish immigrants from Germany.[104]

Should the term *German Jews* therefore be dropped, as Hasia R. Diner has suggested? This chapter has shown that, superficially, Stanley Nadel's argument seems indeed striking: most Jews in Chicago spoke German until the 1870s, they read German papers, and the Chicago-based *Illinois Staatszeitung* covered events in the Jewish community well beyond 1880. In fact, Jews acted as organizers and even leaders of the German community project in Chicago. But they did so individually. Jewish associations and congregations did not belong to the German community. While Jews participated in German parades, even as leaders, Jewish congregations and associations did not march. In 1867 Chicago Jews organized their own Jewish parade. These examples indicate that the emerging Jewish community remained clearly distinct from the German community. The B'nai B'rith's drive to establish the UHRA and the Jewish effort during the Civil War are clear indicators for the ethnicization of Jewish immigrants on American, not "German," terms. Even the radical Reformers who called for a Germanization of the Jewish service acted explicitly as "American Israelites," as Felsenthal stressed in his call for separation. Therefore the term *Jewish German-Americans* describes the involvement of Jews in ethnic German associations better than *German Jews.*

However, Hasia R. Diner's argument is also problematic because the geographic origin did not automatically determine the ethnic identification of Jewish immigrants in the United States. In nineteenth-century Central and Eastern Europe, state and nation were not identical entities. Citizenship did not automatically predetermine the ethnic identity of immigrants from this part of Europe. For Jewish immigrants in the United States the adjective "German" did not relate to a state that did not even exist before 1871 but rather to a spiritual and cultural concept of modernity. Felsenthal and Einhorn, described by Diner as elitist German Jews, are a case in point. They did not identify with Germany on a political level but exclusively on a cultural one. And as this chapter has shown, their calls for Germanization can only be understood in their very American context.[105]

The research for Chicago indicates that the term *German Jews* for Jewish immigrants in nineteenth- and early-twentieth-century America should indeed be handled carefully because it has at least four distinct layers. First, *German Jews* is used to describe the involvement of Jewish immigrants with other German-speaking immigrants. Second, *German Jews* is used because many Jewish immigrants who arrived before

1880 originated in the German states. Third, *German Jews* describes the strong cultural identification with Germany, in particular with the origins of modern Judaism in Germany, especially by adherents of the Jewish Reform movement in the United States. For Jewish Reformers like Felsenthal, *German Jews* was a synonym for "modern Jews." More important for the use of the term by contemporary historians, however, is the fourth layer: The term *German Jews* was rarely mentioned in the sources before 1881. After 1881, however, *German Jews* became a synonym for "established Jews"—Jews who had arrived before 1881—at a time when very few of these Jews still spoke German or were active in German associations. It is this latter use of the term—which often reflects the perspective of the newly arriving Jews from Eastern Europe upon arrogant "uptown Jews," who refused to deal with the new immigrant—that has survived to this day.[106]

Eventually, the meaning of *Germanness* extended even beyond Jews who had arrived before 1881. For the newly arrived Jews from Eastern Europe, *Germanness* conferred social status and a high degree of assimilation. Observations made by the noted urban sociologist Louis Wirth, who researched the residential mobility of Eastern European Jewish immigrants in Chicago in the 1920s, prove this point: In the beginning of the 1920s a growing number of immigrants moved from the area of first settlement, the so-called ghetto district near the center of Chicago, to a slightly upscale West Side neighborhood, called Lawndale. The Jews in the ghetto referred to Lawndale in Yiddish as Deutschland. Wirth points out that for the ghetto residents, many of whom were orthodox, the term *Deitchuk* (the German) represented the image of assimilated Jewish immigrants from Eastern Europe who moved out of the ghetto, did well economically, and did not strictly adhere to Jewish laws.[107]

Diner, who identifies herself strongly with Eastern European Jewish immigrants and concedes that for her "German Jews" were the "other" (that is, arrogant uptown Jews),[108] points out correctly that many of the established "German Jews" (who arrived before 1880) actually originated in Eastern Europe. But she neglects the important third layer—the strong, cultural identification of American Jews, who regarded themselves as modern Jews, with a spiritual "Germany" and, even more importantly, with German Jewry in Germany. Many Jewish immigrants from Central and Eastern Europe became modern and thus "German" only in the United States, for instance, when they joined radical Reform congregations in the 1860s and 1870s.

After 1880, however, "Germanness" increasingly represented images of Jews who had achieved social status and acceptance, often at the cost of their Jewishness, regardless of where they or their parents originated in Europe. The actual core meaning of "Germanness" in this specific Jewish context—that is, its relationship to Wissenschaft, Bildung, and modern Judaism—was greatly diminished. After 1880 "Germanness" increasingly conferred social status. Indeed, in the American context, *German Jews* corresponds with *Ostjuden,* a similarly loaded and problematic term that refers to complex and shifting images of unassimilated Jews.[109] The complex cultural baggage of the term *German Jews* makes it necessary to reflect on its actual meaning in the respective historic context by decoding the image, or images, to which it refers. Since the term itself was rarely used before 1880, it is of limited use for the historical analysis describing Jewish immigrants in the United States before 1880.

NOTES

This chapter is based on my monograph, "Von der Gemeinde zur 'Community': Jüdische Einwanderer in Chicago, 1840–1900" (Studien zur Migrationsforschung 10), Osnabrück, 2002.

1. Hasia R. Diner, *A Time for Gathering: The Second Migration, 1820–1880* (Baltimore, 1992), 1–5.

2. Eli Faber, *A Time for Planting: The First Migration, 1654–1820* (Baltimore, 1992).

3. See especially Naomi Cohen, *Encounter with Emancipation: The German Jews in the United States, 1830–1914* (Philadelphia, 1984).

4. Diner, *Time for Gathering,* 232–33. The term "out of the ghetto" was coined by Jacob Katz; see *Out of the Ghetto: The Social Background of Jewish Emancipation, 1770–1870* (Cambridge, 1971).

5. Diner, *Time for Gathering,* 49.

6. Stanley Nadel, "Jewish Race and German Soul in Nineteenth-Century America," *American Jewish History* 77 (1987): 6.

7. Stanley Nadel, *Little Germany: Ethnicity, Religion, and Class in New York City, 1845–1880* (Urbana/Chicago, 1990), 99–103; see also Nadel, "Jewish Race and German Soul," 6–26.

8. Avraham Barkai, *Branching Out: German-Jewish Immigration to the United States 1820–1914* (New York, 1994), 228. Barkai and Nadel have used German-language sources extensively.

9. For the traditional view, see Naomi Cohen, *Encounter with Emancipation,* 4–17. For recent studies, see Barkai, *Branching Out,* 9–10; Cornelia Östreich, *"Des rauhen Winters ungeachtet . . ."—Die Auswanderung Posener Juden nach Amerika im 19. Jahrhundert* (Hamburg, 1997); and Stefan Rohrbacher, "From Württemberg

to America: A Nineteenth-Century German-Jewish Village on Its Way to the New World," *American Jewish Archives* 41 (1989): 142–71.

10. Jacob Toury, *Soziale und politische Geschichte der Juden in Deutschland, 1848–1871* (Düsseldorf, 1977), 43, gives the figure of one hundred thousand for the years 1815–80. Barkai, *Branching Out,* 9–10, estimates two hundred thousand from 1830 to 1914.

11. The history of rural Jewry in the United States has hardly been researched; see Lee Shai Weissbach, "The Jewish Communities of the United States on the Eve of the Mass Migration," *American Jewish History* 78 (1988): 79–108.

12. Klaus Bade, "Migration Past and Present: The German Experience," in *People in Transit—German Migrations in Comparative Perspective, 1820–1920,* ed. Dirk Hoerder and Jörg Nagler (Cambridge, 1995), 400.

13. Walter Kamphoefner, "German Emigration Research, North, South, and East: Findings, Methods, and Open Questions," in *People in Transit,* ed. Hoerder and Nagler, 19–34; Klaus J. Bade, "Die deutsch überseeische Massenauswanderung im 19. und frühen 20. Jahrhundert: Bestimmungsfaktoren und Entwicklungsbedingungen," in *Auswanderer—Wanderarbeiter—Gastarbeiter, Bevölkerung, Arbeitsmarkt und Wanderung in Deutschland seit der Mitte des 19. Jahrhunderts,* vol. 1, ed. Klaus J. Bade (Ostfildern, 1984), 259–99. On religious differences, see Nadel, *Little Germany,* 91–103.

14. Kathleen Conzen, "Ethnicity as Festive Culture: Nineteenth-Century German America on Parade," in *Invention of Ethnicity,* ed. Werner Sollors (New York, 1989), 44–76. For Chicago, see *Illinois Staatszeitung* [Chicago] (hereafter cited as *ISZ*), Jan. 31, Mar. 3, and May 26, 1871; Eugen Seeger, *Chicago: Die Geschichte einer Wunderstadt* (Chicago, 1892), 131–32; Hartmut Keil, "Introduction," in *Deutsche Arbeiterkultur in Chicago von 1850 bis zum Ersten Weltkrieg: Eine Anthologie,* ed. Hartmut Keil (Ostfildern, 1984), 6. All translations are my own unless otherwise noted.

15. On immigrant groups in Chicago see the essays in *Ethnic Chicago: A Multicultural Portrait,* ed. Melvin G. Holli and Peter d'A. Jones (Grand Rapids, Mich., 1995). On German immigrants in Milwaukee, see Kathleen Conzen, *Immigrant Milwaukee: Accommodation and Community in a Frontier City* (Cambridge, 1976). On Cincinnati, see Bruce Levine, "Community Divided: German Immigrants, Social Class, and Political Conflict in Antebellum Cincinnati," in *Ethnic Diversity and Civic Identity: Patterns of Conflict and Cohesion in Cincinnati since 1820,* ed. Jonathan Sarna and Henry D. Shapiro (Urbana, Ill., 1992), 46–93.

16. Bernhard Felsenthal, *Kol Kore Bamidbar: Ueber jüdische Reform —Ein Wort an die Freunde derselben* (Chicago, 1859), 24. Felsenthal estimated that 90 percent of all American Jews would either only speak and write in German or prefer German.

17. Compare the bibliography in Emma Felsenthal, *Bernhard Felsenthal: Teacher in Israel* (Oxford and New York, 1924).

18. "Bericht eines englischen Conseils über den Stand der Juden in Chicago," in *Erzählungen meiner Erlebnisse,* ed. Salomon Ephraim Blogg (Hannover, 1856), 43.

19. The papers were *The Chicago Occident* and the *Jewish Advance* [Chicago].

The *Advance* was discontinued after 1881. In 1869 Rabbi Isaak Löb Chronik published and edited a short-lived German Jewish monthly in Chicago, called *Zeichen der Zeit* (Signs of the Times); the last remaining copy is kept at the University of Maryland Library.

20. See biographies of leading Jews in Emil Dietzsch, *Chicago's Deutsche Männer* (Chicago, 1885), 36, 129, and 193. See also *Chicago und sein Deutschthum* (Cleveland, 1901–2).

21. Michael A. Meyer, "German-Jewish Identity in Nineteenth-Century America," in *Toward Modernity: The European Jewish Model,* ed. Jacob Katz (New Brunswick, N.J., 1987), 252.

22. Article taken from *Der Westen* [Sunday edition of the *ISZ*], November 1909 [day not known], in Folder 129, German Aid Society, Historical Collections, Library of the University of Illinois at Chicago; obituary of Julius Rosenthal, *Chicago Legal News,* May 21, 1905; Dietzsch, *Chicago's Deutsche Männer,* 36, 129, and 193; *Cooke's City Directory for Chicago: 1859–60* (Chicago, 1860).

23. *ISZ,* July 4, 1862.

24. *ISZ,* Jan. 31, Mar. 3, and May 26, 1871; Seeger, *Wunderstadt,* 131–32.

25. On Hirsch see Hyman L. Meites, *History of the Jews of Chicago* (Chicago, 1924), 141. On one of his most patriotic speeches praising the German war effort during World War I, see *Jahrbuch der Deutschen* (Chicago, 1916), 31–33.

26. *Chicago Tribune,* Apr. 13, 1918.

27. *ISZ,* Jan. 31 and Mar. 3, 1871; Seeger, *Wunderstadt,* 131–32.

28. *ISZ,* Dec. 9, 1867. In Chronik's house a "Comite gegen Temperenz- und Sabbath-Zwangsgesetze" was organized to combat temperance and blue laws. While many Germans socialized on Sundays, often in beer gardens, Jews who observed the Sabbath opposed Sunday laws because they were forced to keep their shops closed.

29. Karen Sawislak, *Smoldering City: Chicagoans and the Great Fire, 1871–1874* (Chicago, 1995), 255–57.

30. Seeger, *Wunderstadt,* 419; Reinhard Rürup, *Emanzipation und Antisemitismus: Studien zur 'Judenfrage' der bürgerlichen Gesellschaft* (Frankfurt, 1987), 81–83.

31. On this issue, see *ISZ,* Apr. 15, 1881. A survey of the critical stance of German American papers (*Cincinnati Gazette, New York Staatszeitung*) toward anti-Semitism in Germany can be found in *Der Zeitgeist* [Milwaukee], Dec. 9, 1880. For the general argument, see Meyer, "German-Jewish Identity," 252.

32. There are hardly any sources such as membership directories available to document the history of German Americans in Chicago before 1880. One likely reason is that many sources were destroyed by the 1871 fire.

33. *37. Jahresbericht der German Society of Chicago (Deutsche Gesellschaft von Chicago) 1890–91* (Chicago, 1891). Greenebaum devoted much time to setting up the German old-age home (*Altenheim*) on Chicago's West Side; see the numerous references to Greenebaum in Seeger, *Wunderstadt.*

34. One of the old immigrants, Leopold Mayer, remembered in 1899 that in the 1850s "the Germans, Jews and non-Jews, were one"; quoted in Herman Eliassof and Emil G. Hirsch, "The Jews of Illinois: Their Religious and Civic Life, their Charity and Industry, their Patriotism and Loyalty to American Institutions,

From their Earliest Settlement in the State unto Present Time," *Reform Advocate* [Chicago], May 4, 1901, 287.

35. For a general treatment, see Deborah Dash Moore, *B'nai B'rith and the Challenge of Ethnic Leadership* (Albany, N.Y., 1981).

36. See Brinkmann, *Von der Gemeinde,* 149–51.

37. Steven M. Lowenstein, "Die Gemeinde," in *Deutsch-jüdische Geschichte in der Neuzeit,* vol. 3, ed. Michael A. Meyer (Munich, 1996), 123.

38. Jonathan Sarna, "The Evolution of the American Synagogue," in *The Americanization of the Jews,* ed. Norman J. Cohen and Robert M. Seltzer (New York, 1995), 218–22.

39. Tobias Brinkmann, "'Praise upon you: The U.H.R.A.!': Jewish Philanthropy and the Origins of the first Jewish Community in Chicago, 1859–1900," in *The Shaping of a Community: The Jewish Federation of Metropolitan Chicago,* ed. Rhoda Rosen (Chicago, 1999), 24–39. "Tzedakah" is often wrongly translated as "charity." The correct translation is "social justice," that is, the obligation for every pious Jew to support needy Jews (and Gentiles).

40. *Standard Club: Articles of Incorporation, Club Annals, Officers and Directors, By-Laws, House Rules, Roster of Members* (Chicago, 1912). See also Meites, *History of the Jews of Chicago,* 116–17; Second Annual Report of the District Grand Lodge No. 6. of the Independent Order B'nai B'rith (Chicago, 1870); File Johannah Lodge No. 9—Independent Order of True Sisters, Chicago Jewish Archives. Women's associations in Chicago were the last Jewish associations to replace German with English as the official language. The Johanna Lodge of the Unabhängiger Orden Treuer Schwestern introduced English as the official language only in 1895.

41. These observations are based on samples drawn from membership lists of the leading Jewish philanthropic organization in Chicago, the UHRA (founded in 1859), from the 1860s to the 1890s. The data is included in Brinkmann, *Von der Gemeinde.* On the transition of the West Side, see Richard Sennett, *Families against the City: Middle Class Homes of Industrial Chicago, 1872–1890* (Cambridge, 1970), 9–43. On Chicago's Northwest Side, German-speaking Jewish workers seem to have lived in close proximity to non-Jewish German workers in the 1880s; see Hartmut Keil, "Immigrant Neighborhoods and American Society: German Immigrants on Chicago's Northwest Side in the Late Nineteenth Century," in *German Workers' Culture in the United States, 1850–1920,* ed. Hartmut Keil (Washington D.C., 1988), 43.

42. *ISZ,* Sept. 4, 1867. On this parade see Tobias Brinkmann, "Charity on Parade: Chicago's Jews and the Construction of Ethnic and Civic 'Gemeinschaft' in the 1860s," in *Celebrating Ethnicity and Nation: American Festive Culture from the Revolution to the Early Twentieth Century,* ed. Jürgen Heideking and Geneviève Fabre (New York, 2001), 157–74.

43. For the background see Maldwyn A. Jones, *American Immigration* (Chicago, 1960), 157. John Higham, *Strangers in the Land: Patterns of American Nativism, 1860–1925* (New Brunswick, N.J., 1955), 7, 12–14.

44. Theodore J. Karamanski, *Rally 'Round the Flag: Chicago and the Civil War* (Chicago, 1993), 72, 113–14.

45. *ISZ,* Aug. 15, 1862.

46. *ISZ,* Aug. 15, 1862. On the number of Jews in Chicago see *Sinai* [Philadelphia], Sept. 1862, 232.

47. *ISZ,* Aug. 15, 1862, 231 (taken from *ISZ,* Aug. 20, 1862—the copy is probably lost). Like Brentano, Hecker had also served in the second chamber of the Baden assembly until 1848–49.

48. *Third Annual Report of the United Hebrew Relief Association of Chicago* (Chicago, 1862). The determined action indeed made big news "throughout the land"; compare *Cincinnati Volksfreund,* Aug. 16, 1862; *Allgemeine Zeitung des Judenthums* [Leipzig], Oct. 7, 1862.

49. Meites, *History of the Jews of Chicago,* 88–89.

50. Frederic C. Jaher, *A Scapegoat in the New Wilderness: The Origins and Rise of Anti-Semitism in America* (Cambridge, 1994), 196–200; Ira Katznelson, "Between Separation and Disappearance: American Jews on the Margins of American Liberalism," in *Paths of Emancipation: Jews, States, and Citizenship,* ed. Pierre Birnbaum and Ira Katznelson (Princeton, 1995), 167–69.

51. The order was lifted by President Lincoln. Felsenthal file (Letter to B. Felsenthal, Minister of Sinai Congregation, by the War Department, Washington City, Jan. 10, 1863), Chicago Jewish Archives. See also Joakim Isaacs, "Ulysses S. Grant and the Jews," *American Jewish Archives* 17 (1965): 3–15.

52. *Sinai,* Aug. 1862, 200–201, based on an article in the *ISZ.*

53. Liebmann Adler, *Fünf Reden: Gehalten in der Israelitischen Gemeinde Kehilas Anshe Maarab hierselbst an wichtigen nationalen Gedenktagen der Ver. Staaten* (Chicago, 1866), 20.

54. For an introduction, see Edward Kantowicz, "The Ethnic Church," in *Ethnic Chicago,* ed. Holli and Jones, 574–603.

55. Adler, *Fünf Reden,* 6.

56. Pierre Birnbaum and Ira Katznelson, "Emancipation and the Liberal Offer," in *Paths of Emancipation,* ed. Katznelson and Birnbaum, 20–22. One of the classic "German-centered" studies on the origins of modern Judaism is Jacob Katz, *Out of the Ghetto: The Social Background of Jewish Emancipation, 1770–1870* (Cambridge, 1973). Two recent works on the modern Jewish experience outside of Germany are Miriam Bodian, *Hebrews of the Portuguese Nation: Conversos and Community in Early Modern Amsterdam* (Bloomington, Ind., 1997), and Lois C. Dubin, *The Port Jews of Habsburg Trieste: Absolutist Politics and Enlightenment Culture* (Stanford, Calif., 1999).

57. Rürup, *Emanzipation und Antisemitismus,* 13–25; Katznelson, *Between Separation and Disappearance,* 169.

58. Michael A. Meyer, *The Origins of the Modern Jew: Jewish Identity and European Culture in Germany, 1749–1824* (Detroit, 1967), 144–82.

59. Michael A. Meyer, *Response to Modernity: A History of the Reform Movement in Judaism* (New York and Oxford, 1988), 62–99 (quote is from 89).

60. George L. Mosse, *German Jews beyond Judaism* (Bloomington, Ind., and Cincinnati, 1985), 3. See also David Sorkin, *The Transformation of German Jewry, 1780–1840* (New York, 1987).

61. Meyer, *Response to Modernity,* 62–99, 264–95; Maria T. Baader, "From

'the Priestess of the Home' to 'The Rabbi's Brilliant Daughter': Concepts of Jewish Womanhood and Progressive Germanness in *Die Deborah* and the *American Israelite, 1854–1900*," *Leo Baeck Institute Yearbook* 43 (1998): 47–72.

62. Bernhard Felsenthal and Herman Eliassof, *History of Kehillath Anshe Maarab: Issued under the Auspices of the Congregation on the Occasion of its Semi-Centennial Celebration, Nov. 4, 1897* (Chicago, 1897), 23.

63. *The Occident* [Philadelphia], Jan. 1855, 526.

64. Bernhard Felsenthal, "A Contribution to the History of the Israelites in Chicago," manuscript, 1863, Col. Felsenthal, Bernhard. Box 130, Chicago Historical Society.

65. Quoted from Eliassof and Hirsch, *The Jews of Illinois,* 287.

66. On the "indifference" of Jews in Chicago toward religious observance, see *The Occident* [Philadelphia], Jan. 1857, 586.

67. *Die Deborah* [Cincinnati], Aug. 8, 1855; *Israelite* [Cincinnati], July 8, 1859.

68. Felsenthal and Eliassof, *History of KAM,* 31–34.

69. *Israelite,* July 8, 1859 (copied from *Chicago Daily Democrat*).

70. Meyer, *Response to Modernity,* 235–50.

71. Meyer, *Response to Modernity,* 243.

72. *Die Deborah,* Aug. 24, 1855; Nadel, "Jewish Race and German Soul," 9–10.

73. *Israelite,* Aug. 8 and 15, 1856.

74. *Israelite,* Aug. 8 and 15, 1856.

75. *Sinai,* Feb. 1856, 4–10.

76. Meyer, *Response to Modernity,* 245.

77. *Israelite,* Sept. 30, 1859. Wise remarked about the "orthodox" faction in Chicago: "Our orthodox brethren must gradually be educated for the present age."

78. *Sinai,* Feb. 1856, 412.

79. *Sinai,* Mar. and Apr. 1859.

80. Bernhard Felsenthal, *Jüdisches Schulwesen in Amerika: Ein Vortrag gehalten am 13. Dezember 1865 in der 'Ramah-Loge' zu Chicago von Bernhard Felsenthal Prediger der Zionsgemeinde daselbst* (Chicago, 1866), 37.

81. Felsenthal, *Kol Kore Bamidbar,* 25; translation by Michael A. Meyer.

82. Felsenthal, *Kol Kore Bamidbar,* 19–20; David Einhorn, "Felsenthal's Kol Kore Bamidbar," *Sinai,* May 1859, 115.

83. Felsenthal, *Kol Kore Bamidbar,* 22–23.

84. Meyer, *Response to Modernity,* 248.

85. Felsenthal, *Kol Kore Bamidbar,* 14.

86. Felsenthal, *Kol Kore Bamidbar,* 25. Felsenthal's appeal that Jews were "brothers" clearly points to the B'nai B'rith, whose members called themselves "brothers" and were striving to unite Jews outside of the synagogue.

87. *Israelite,* Jan. 13, 1860; *Israelite,* Sept. 30, 1859.

88. Letter from Einhorn to Felsenthal, June 2, 1859, in Felsenthal Papers, American Jewish historical Society.

89. *Israelite,* Jan. 13, 1860.

90. *Israelite,* Feb. 3, 1860.

91. *Israelite,* Sept. 30, 1859.

92. *Sinai,* Nov. 1859.

93. Bernhard Felsenthal, *The Beginnings of the Chicago Sinai Congregation: A Contribution to the Inner History of American Judaism* (Chicago, 1898).

94. Felsenthal, *The Beginnings,* 26.

95. Meyer, "German-Jewish Identity," 260–61.

96. Israel Joseph Benjamin, *Drei Jahre in Amerika, 1859–1862* (Hannover, 1862), 112.

97. In the mid-1880s American-born Joseph Stolz, one of the first graduates of the Reform-oriented rabbinical seminary Hebrew Union College in Cincinnati, exchanged a number of German letters with the Zion congregation in Chicago, whose board was looking for a suitable successor for Felsenthal, who had recently retired. Zion's board eventually invited Stolz to give a German sermon, and this sermon pleased the congregation so much that Stolz was hired. See Joseph Stolz papers, in MS Coll. 242, American Jewish Archives, Cincinnati.

98. Barkai, *Branching Out,* 228.

99. Diner, *Time for Gathering,* xv.

100. Steven Aschheim, *Brothers and Strangers: The East European Jew in German and German Jewish Consciousness, 1800–1923* (Madison, Wis., 1982).

101. Rudolf Glanz, "The 'Bayer' and the 'Pollack' in America," *Jewish Social Studies* 17 (1955): 27–42. For a graphic description of these conflicts between Jewish immigrants from "Germany" and "Poland" in New York, see *Allgemeine Zeitung des Judenthums* [Leipzig], July 27, 1846.

102. *Fifth Annual Report of the Directors of the United Hebrew Relief Association of Chicago* (Chicago, 1864).

103. The UHRA of Chicago differentiated two "classes" of Jewish victims of the disastrous fire that destroyed much of Chicago in 1871. The "other" Jews were described as "that class of our poor, or rather paupers, that enjoyed but little, if any, education. They never were taught that any honest labor is honorable. . . . They have learned of religion but little more than the external ceremonies. Principles are unknown things to them. They have never imbibed the love of truth or the appreciation of honorable actions." The established Jews ("we" as opposed to "them") were depicted as "another class of your people, relatives, friends, and neighbors, men and families, that stood side by side with you heretofore in society, in congregations, in this council." Quoted from the *Twelfth Annual Report of the UHRA* (Chicago, 1872).

104. This issue is treated in detail in Brinkmann, *Von der Gemeinde,* 331–82.

105. Brinkmann, *Von der Gemeinde,* 232–33. On this meaning of the term, see also Baader, "From 'the Priestess of the Home,'" 47–72.

106. See especially the influential book on the complicated relationship between "Germans" and "Russians": Moses Rischin, *The Promised City: New York's Jews, 1870–1914* (Cambridge, 1962), 95–98.

107. Louis Wirth, *The Ghetto* (Chicago, 1928), 246–49.

108. Diner, *Time for Gathering,* xv.

109. Aschheim, *Brothers and Strangers.*

CHAPTER 6

German Landscape

Local Promotion of the *Heimat* Abroad

Thomas Lekan

In 1869 a German factory worker described his experience at a picnic on Chicago's North Side. "Nothing thrills a German more than a festival in the woods under the green leaves of oak trees!" he exclaimed. "This [feeling] has clung to our people since the forest life of our ancestors. I forgot that I was so far, so distant from my homeland celebrating a festival under foreign oaks, [and] I had lively conversations with those around me and was full of happiness."[1] This worker's belief that oak trees could stimulate convivial feelings of homeland invokes one of the most pervasive tropes among Germans abroad: a belief that all Germans, regardless of time and location, had a special affinity for their landscape of origin. Indeed, the concept of *Heimat,* which scholars have usually identified as a local sense of place grounded in emotional attachments to familiar surroundings,[2] was actually a highly mobile rhetorical device, one that provided a touchstone of identity for emigrants from German-speaking lands throughout the nineteenth and early twentieth centuries. American observers often referred to German Americans as a people who had gone "from forest—to forest." Their yearning for a familiar environment made them seize upon woodland areas even in comparatively treeless regions, and they supposedly clung to Old World provincialism despite America's rapid industrialization and urbanization.[3] Germany's status as a "nation of provincials," in which most citizens envisioned their country as a decentralized mosaic of regional landscapes, also shaped the experience of Germans abroad and enabled them to imagine themselves as part of a *Kulturnation* that spanned the seas.

In this chapter, I use German American communities' relationship to the German homeland between roughly 1880 and 1939 as a case study in the transplantation and transformation of Heimat identities on both sides of the Atlantic during a period of unprecedented contestation over the character and boundaries of Germanness. The migration and reinforcement of provincialism were not unique to German Americans; Irish, Italian, and Russian immigrants also identified strongly with specific districts or counties in their home countries. What I believe was unique to German diasporic communities, however, was their belief that they had physically inscribed a particular cultural landscape into their new Heimat. Writings on German Americans claimed that they maintained (or could be stimulated to embrace) emotional ties to the natural features of their homeland; that these attachments resulted in a superior stewardship over the land; and that the distinctive cultural landscapes that had emerged in their home country through centuries of occupation would be recapitulated in a foreign setting. Their concept of landscape resembled that of Wilhelm Heinrich Riehl, whose romantic concept of *Land und Leute* had proposed a belief that each landscape, be it national, regional, or local, represented an aesthetic totality that synthesized natural features and cultural customs into an organic whole, a *Kulturlandschaft*.[4] The Kulturlandschaft did not serve merely material needs, but instead was an *ideal* form that dispensed moral lessons and legitimated historical claims to a particular territory. Germanness, in this sense, was not merely linguistic or cultural; it could be envisioned, even touched, in particular landscapes and natural experiences. And just as the Heimat movement in Germany was largely an urban phenomenon of middle-class associations (*Vereine*) dedicated to researching the rural Heimat and exploring it through hiking and weekend excursions, so too were the regional clubs of America founded in cities like Chicago similarly composed largely of middle-class or skilled working-class members.

The nineteenth-century impetus for promoting such Heimat identities emerged on the German American side. For first-generation immigrants, visions of homeland, whether Rhenish, Swabian, or Saxon, were linked to personal and collectives memories of place. For second- and third-generation German Americans, the Heimat clubs provided a form of urban sociability and a sense of cultural uniqueness in an era in which "Anglo-Saxon" elites looked disapprovingly upon all immigrant groups as a threat to their religious mores and economic status. World War I, however, shifted the locus of Heimat promotion from America to Germany. The decline of German American organizations amid the hysteria of World War I occurred just as the territorial losses of the Versailles settlement and the ensuing conflicts of the Weimar era sharpened the tone of Heimat rhetoric within Germany and made the "loss" of millions of Germans along the Reich's frontiers an area of public concern. To reclaim Germany's stature as a world power would require a new definition of the German *Volk* that was independent of particular state borders. The construction of this new identity, in turn, made the *internal* demarcation of homeland dependent upon the identification and reethnicization of *external* German communities throughout the world. Such rhetoric prepared the way for the National Socialist regime to recast Heimat rhetoric along racist lines and to create more extensive forms of outreach to American's *Deutschtum,* yet the regime was never successful at displacing German Americans' culturalist vision of homeland with a racist one based on "Blood and Soil" (*Blut und Boden*).

Transplanted Homelands: Landscape, Provincialism, and German American Identity before 1914

Scholars have often referred to German Americans as an "elusive" or "incomplete" ethnic group.[5] "Like a skein through the history of German immigrants in American [*sic*]," writes Kathleen Neils Conzen, "runs the complaint of ethnic weakness, ethnic incompleteness, departure from some supposed norm of American ethnic group character."[6] Outside a few rural enclaves, traces of German American influence have disappeared; the once-flourishing Little Germanies of American cities such as New York, Milwaukee, and Chicago, notes Randall Miller, "now exist only in old prints and photographs."[7] This impression is surely not due to a lack of German immigrants to the United States. So many German-speaking individuals arrived on America's shores in the nineteenth century that many observers labeled their migration a second *Völkerwanderung.* By the 1850s Germans made up roughly 37 percent of all immigrants to the United States, and while the proportion of Germans among all immigrants declined thereafter, it still amounted to about 1.5 million persons in the 1880s. The volume of emigrants left an indelible mark on America's ethnic composition, with roughly 29 percent of the U.S. population claiming some degree of German ancestry in the 1980 census.[8] A sense of group consciousness, nevertheless, was lacking. German Americans never seemed different enough from their "Germanic" Anglo-Saxon cousins to constitute a distinct nationality; the boundaries of Germanness, in this sense, were too permeable to create a lasting ethnic identity. Americans of German descent had not only become Americanized, but late-nineteenth-century America had become Germanized, easily embracing the educational values, arts appreciation, and sociability that gave German Americans a distinct presence in American cities.[9]

Historians have offered additional explanations for this lack of a German American ethnic presence. One often-cited factor was a long, drawn-out period of emigration involving Germans of widely disparate social classes.[10] Another factor was the confessional division between Catholic and Protestant Germans. Other historians have focused on German provincialism as a force for disunity; Old World particularism, in this view, remained intact in the New World and "retarded" a unified consciousness. The "motley encyclopedia" of pre-Bismarck Germany left German Americans with no unified national identity to which they could cling during the high tide of midcentury immigration. "Provincial in origin," writes Randall Miller, "Germans remained provincial in practice once in America." As they moved through the continent, "they sought out familiar faces and cultures in their treks. Mecklenburgers congregated in Chicago and Württembergers in New York, for example, and they tried to recreate the full array of Old World institutions and associations, with all their Old World jealousies intact, in the new settings."[11]

Still, forces within urban areas did tend to draw German Americans together as they found common ground in language (despite the lack of high German), cultural patronage, customs, and forms of conviviality. Anglo-Americans and other immigrant groups perceived them as "Germans" regardless of regional origin. German Americans' conspicuous role in eliminating religious instruction from public schools, repulsing the temperance movement, and assuring less oppressive Sunday laws earned them the ire of many puritanical Anglo-Americans.[12] German American communities at the turn of the nineteenth century also engaged in extensive debates about their appropriate role and future within American society. As Conzen has noted, German Americans did not merely react to assimilative norms or other ethnic groups but actively sought to "invent" an ethnicity that provided a core identity for all Germans regardless of class, religion, or regional origin. German Americans embraced a form of "pluralistic integration"; they asserted the "right to enter the melting pot collectively and on their own terms," bringing "special gifts" to the American nation that seemed to be lacking within the dominant culture.[13]

The actual formulation of these gifts was vague but usually centered on Germans' supposedly higher aesthetic and cultural sensibilities. In the numerous histories of German American contributions to America that appeared in the late nineteenth and early twentieth centuries, German Americans appeared as the "idealists" who patronized the arts, insisted on strict standards of morality in business and personal relationships, and enjoyed leisure time in a manner that was alien to the rough, business-minded Yankees of the American scene. As A. D. White wrote in 1909:

> The dominant idea [of idealism] is . . . [t]hat the ultimate end of a great modern nation is something besides manufacturing, or carrying, or buying or selling products; that art, literature, science, and thought, in its highest flights and widest ranges, are greater and more important. . . . In no land has this idea penetrated more deeply than in Germany, and it is this idea which should penetrate more and more American thought and practice.[14]

As purveyors of a higher culture, in other words, German Americans could both remain "German" and help to civilize the young American nation.

German Americans' characteristic attitude toward the natural environment and treatment of the land were some of the most often-cited manifestations of German idealism in the New World. Unlike the Yankee, who was apt to exploit his property to the utmost, cash in on its appreciated value, and move on, the German farmer occupied the land with an eye toward permanent possession and sustainability.[15] In his well-known 1909 survey of German American history, *The German Element in the United States,* Albert Faust argued that Germans tended to occupy land after the first wave of pioneers and chose parcels that guaranteed a long-term investment. In particular, Faust claimed that Germans gravitated toward wooded areas, especially those with oaks, "a sure sign of good land," whereas other settlers, such as the Irish, looked for the more obvious signs, such as well-watered areas near big rivers or the rich soils of prairies.[16] The German farmer patiently cleared the land of stumps and stones, rotated crops to avoid soil exhaustion, and refrained from overworking horses and livestock. Germans' conservationist attitude also extended to forests. "The German farmer has always shown more regard for the trees than the Anglo-Saxon," Faust remarked. "It is recorded of the Pennsylvania-Germans that they were economical in the use of wood, even where it was abundant." Unlike Yankee farmers, a German understood that forests protected homesteads against storms and filtered the water going into irrigated fields, yet he also cherished them for "sentimental" reasons. In Faust's view, it was not surprising that a man of German descent, former minister of the interior Carl Schurz, was the first to propose nationwide forest protection legislation, while another German national, Henry Bergh, led the fight for laws to prevent cruelty to animals.[17]

Faust's depiction of the German farmer as a conservationist by nature, patiently caring for a homestead to ensure long-term yields, stood in stark contrast to a popular negative image of the German as too soft for the frontier. Images of the "Latin farmers," classically educated refugees from the revolution of 1848 unfit for practical labor, still haunted German American settlement efforts. In *The Tragedy of German-America,* John Hawgood invoked a similar image when he wrote of the "German immigrant's weakness for the amenities of civilization, on his cautiousness in locating near to established markets, on his refusal to speculate in land or to gamble on the future of a district, on his preference for partly developed to virgin land."[18] Such characteristics meant that Germans were unfit to be pioneers on the farthest reaches of the frontier; instead, the German preferred to be near markets and navigable rivers and to remain "permanently in the place where he first settled." Faust's text placed such cautiousness in a positive light. "The native [Anglo-]American farmer was wasteful; the German farmer invariably economical. Economy was the rule of his life. He saved even the wood, which seemed so abundant, using stoves instead of huge fireplaces, constructing fences of a kind that did not squander wood."[19] Faust thus equated the frontier ethic with a slash-and-burn mentality inimical to Germans' longing for permanency.

Germans' ultimate goal, according to Faust, was the re-creation of their organic connections to homeland in new soil rather than short-term profit. Given a choice, the German farmer would select that countryside most like those in this place of origin and would raise products similar to those of his native country. Whereas the Scotch-Irish selected well-watered meadow land that resembled that in Ulster County in the north of Ireland, the Germans chose "undulating country of rich forest growth, like that of the Rhenish Palatinate." In Faust's view, then, German attachments to Old World provincialism were not a liability that prevented ethnic cohesion but instead facilitated Germans' success as immigrants by constructing and maintaining a sense of permanency, a Heimat abroad. Faust claimed that even second- and third-generation farmers chose homesteads resembling the one owned in the original locality and, by extension, the farm where ancestors once labored in the German homeland itself.[20] By such means, Germans were able to buy up land slowly, often edging out other immigrant groups in a particular area, and to keep farms within families generation after generation. The result was a distinctive cultural landscape that symbolized the most prized virtues of German character. The architectural style of the German barn, "built first in Pennsylvania, made its way down the Ohio, and can be seen in Wisconsin, or wherever the German abides." Germans built distinctive stone houses, signs of permanent occupancy, rather than vulnerable wooden structures. Indeed, an overall impression of order and harmony symbolized Germans' conservationist ethic.[21]

In charting the transplantation of German homelands into American soil, Faust not only extolled Germans' superior abilities as caretakers of the land but also provided tangible sites for imagining German Americans as both culturally distinct from and actively contributing to an evolving American identity. In answer to critics who claimed that Germans had not made a distinctive mark on American life, Faust portrayed a large proportion of America's agricultural landscapes, particularly the breadbasket of the Midwest, as a product of German initiative.[22] The German cultural landscape was one of stability and permanency, an enduring achievement that countered the materialistic greed of the typical Anglo-American entrepreneur. Faust also implicitly proposed that Germanic settlement, though scattered across the entire country, followed a different pattern of development than the model proposed by the American historian Frederick Jackson Turner in his oft-cited frontier hypothesis.[23] Whereas Turner proposed that European ethnic groups lost their ethnicity along the frontier, absorbed into America's wilderness environment, Germans had given the "stamp of their uniqueness" to the landscapes of the Midwest.[24] Transplanted homelands thus created a space for visualizing Germanness in a culture that denigrated or ignored German American contributions to American society. As the famous Leipzig historian Karl Lamprecht remarked upon passing through Wisconsin from Chicago to Milwaukee: "In the prettiest parts it seems as if we had come into a land such as the German farmer might dream of: an improved Germany, a region of which the poet had a foreboding when he said 'And like a garden was the land to look upon.' Such is the land of the German farmer, the land of German industry."[25] The German Kulturlandschaft was thus a garden that both marked German American cultural superiority and contributed to uplifting America at the same time.

Heimat sentiments shaped not only German Americans' perception of their role in America's rural life but also their emerging networks of sociability in urban areas. German Americans embraced Verein life, and clubs devoted to particular regions—the Rhineland, Hessen, or Swabia, to a name a few—flourished in America's cities between 1870 and 1914. Two-thirds of German-born immigrants were living in cities by 1890.[26] Many of them found their familiar attachments to the former provincial homeland more compelling than the German nation-state created by Bismarck in 1871. This period was the heyday of the Heimat movement within Germany, and German Americans sometimes established local cells of these same societies in the New World.[27] For example, urban professionals in Bonn and Cologne founded the Eifelverein in 1888, which soon became the Rhine province's major hiking club and still exists today. Rhineland urbanites were captivated by the Eifel region's preindustrial beauty and sought to preserve and make it accessible to young people and factory workers from the province's cities. "We need to make Germany's lungs, the Eifel, available to school children," noted the Verein in 1913. "Hundreds, indeed thousands of hikers from the urban barracks surrounding the Eifel were happily accommodated just this past summer."[28] At the same time, the Eifel was one of Germany's poorest areas; until the advent of modern tourism, rugged scenery did not provide the region with a product to sell on national and international markets. Many emigrants to the United States from the Rhineland were thus Eifelers.

In 1911 Jacob Leo Jung and J. C. Cremer, both of whom had emigrated to America during the 1880s, founded a Chicago chapter of the Eifelverein after Jung accidentally came across an issue of the club's journal. The Chicago Eifelverein committed itself to "preserving the love and honor of our Heimat, the familiar Eifel mountains, here in the far west, far from the homeland."[29] By 1914 the club counted over four hundred members, made up almost exclusively of men born in the Eifel or Luxemburg. Chicago Eifelverein members sponsored "Eifel Balls" and "Eifel Picnics" and joined together in singing the "Eifel Song," composed by Jung, which extolled the region's scenic beauty: "There, where small streams flow to the Mosel and the Rhine, through meadows filled with flowers, in fresh Eifel regions, there is where I'd like to be."[30] Here, landscape imagery masked the painful memories of poverty that had driven peasants from the Eifel in the mid-nineteenth century. The appeal of Heimat evoked a time and place that had never truly existed yet could be re-envisioned through an urban lens and the distance of time and space. Heimat sociability was not simply romantic nostalgia, however. Chicago Eifelverein members bought "Eifel Brand" tomato puree from local distributors, provided job contacts for recently arrived immigrants from the region, and dispensed charity to members who were ill or disabled. Homeland sentiments thus maintained the contours of an imagined local community spanning the Atlantic, providing immigrants with social contacts and economic ties that were crucial for survival in an urban environment.

The Chicago Eifelverein was one of hundreds of German American clubs in that city supporting an enormous population of recent German immigrants and German descendents. In 1882 the *Chicago Arbeiterzeitung* estimated that over 104,350 Germans had come into the city in the five-month period between January and May 1882, while the August 1884 article "A Large German City in America" claimed that the city contained 209,631 Germans, as compared to only 143,000 native-born "Americans" and 114,005 Irish.[31] By one estimate, there were approximately 363 German American organizations in Chicago in 1910 compared to 189 within the Bohemian community and 81 among Polish Americans. Chicago's Germans organized themselves into sports clubs, choruses, mutual benefit societies, and professional associations, but some of the most successful were those that maintained a regionalist emphasis and appealed to Heimat identities, such as the Rheinischer Verein and the Saarländer Verein. The most prominent of the provincial clubs was the Schwabenverein, founded in 1878 under the motto "Charity and *Gemütlichkeit.*" The club is still the largest German American club in Chicago. During this period, its membership rose from 164 members in 1878 to a height of 1,361 members in 1918.[32] In 1903 the club celebrated its twenty-fifth anniversary with a *Gedenkschrift* chronicling the achievements of Germany's "oldest tribe" (*Stamm*) in the "new Heimat." The organization both borrowed and reinforced the rhetoric of Heimat to establish linkages to the Old World. "One of the nicest traits of the German American, which jealous people and enemies often inveigh against," noted club member Carl Härtung, "is the loyal devotion he keeps toward his distant place of birth. The children of the various tribes within our people are proud of their mother Germania, but at the same time outdo one another in an effort to keep thoughts of the more intimate Heimat fresh in their minds."[33] By imagining Germany as a mosaic of tribes under the purview of "mother Germania," Härtung rhetorically overcame the barriers of time and space through an appeal to familial ties and the domestic comforts of homeland.

Despite the club's regionalist emphasis, its membership was open to all German Americans: Swabian provincialism, in this sense, opened a pathway to national consciousness rather than fragmenting it. The

Schwabenverein's most important social event, one that it still organizes today, is the annual Cannstatter folk festival, which attracts
Chicagoans to picnic groves on the North Side.[34] Modeled on the harvest festivals of European peasant culture, the *Volksfest* re-created the
outdoor feel of rural life in a tree-shaded venue; at its center stood a
"harvest column" that dispensed Riesling from the "Stuttgart
Hofkellerei."[35] Schwabenverein members designed the folk festival to
promote German culture and to raise funds for charity. In the first few
years of the festival, the club's goal was to obtain donations for a monument to Swabian poet Friedrich von Schiller, noble son of both his
Heimat and German culture as a whole, which was erected in Lincoln
Park in 1886 as the city's first German monument. Over the years, the
Verein also contributed to a statue of Johann von Goethe in the same
park, as well as hospitals, orphanages, old-age homes, and the
Chicago-area Red Cross.[36]

Schwabenverein members thus confirmed the faith in German
Americans' positive contributions to the community yet also provided
an arena for inventing "Germanic" customs in an often hostile urban
setting. Whereas the city's Victorian elites condemned alcohol consumption and Sabbath breaking, the Cannstatter festival embraced
food, song, and beer in an outdoor setting, even on Sunday. For
Chicago's German Americans, picnics offered respite from the Anglo-
Americans' increasingly moralistic disapproval of public celebrations
in the city. These elites viewed picnics as a distinctly German form of
recreation; rather than confining their social life to the domestic parlor,
these self-identified Germans took their celebrations into the great outdoors of Chicago's city parks.[37] German Americans also believed that
such events provided a necessary balance to the much-vaunted American work ethic, thus contributing to the health of the nation as a
whole.[38] The invented tradition of Heimat and outdoor celebration, in
other words, provided referents for fashioning a pluralistic integration,
a *German* Americanness that celebrated cultural uniqueness while
claiming positive contributions to the evolving American experiment.

The Mobilization of Heimat Sentiment in World War I and the Weimar Republic

World War I and its aftermath proved disastrous for the flourishing
German American Heimat clubs, as it did for the rest of German
Americans' social, press, and mutual-aid societies.[39] German American societies initially lobbied to prevent America's entry into the war

on the side of the Allies and even helped the German war effort. In 1914, for example, the Chicago Eifelverein gave the German Red Cross 1,400 marks to aid Germans injured in the war; in 1915 it wrote a letter to President Woodrow Wilson protesting American armament shipments to Germany's enemies.[40] Once America entered the war on the Allied side, however, these activities made German American clubs vulnerable to charges of disloyalty; everything "German," including language, music, and publications, became suspect.[41] The Eifelverein suffered a drastic loss in members and, in 1917, broke off contact with local cells in Germany.[42]

German American Vereine recovered somewhat during the 1920s, but Prohibition made patterns of Heimat conviviality centering on outdoor consumption of beer and wine impossible to maintain. The Schwabenverein declined slowly from a peak in 1918 of 1,361 members to about 1,277 in 1927; by 1935 there were about 1,053 remaining members. Reporting on a Humboldt Park demonstration against Prohibition in July 1925, the Chicago *Abendpost* reported that "the German oak tree is still alive despite some devastating storms."[43] Economic prosperity in the 1920s and the growing dominance of American consumer culture also accelerated the assimilation of second- and third-generation German Americans into the dominant culture and limited the appeal of the "Old Heimat." As Eifelverein president Michael Zender noted in 1932, German American youth "looked for entertainment after the meeting; they wanted to balance the needs of Heimat with sports, dancing and other amusements."[44] By the end of World War II, the Chicago Eifelverein's membership stood at about 100 members, never again recovering its pre–World War I level.

Although the Kaiserreich had not offered direct institutional or financial support to German American organizations before 1914, the Great War and its aftermath unleashed profound anxieties about German character that led German state officials and private organizations to seek out cultural and economic ties with their "brethren" on the other side of the Atlantic.[45] The Reich government had passed the Law on Emigration Matters in 1897 to control emigration affairs and to protect potential immigrants in foreign countries, but the founding of the Reich Emigration Office (Reichswanderungsamt, or RWA) in 1919 signaled a new era of state intervention in managing emigration and maintaining relations with German nationals abroad. Recognizing that Germany's economic woes might force German citizens to seek out opportunities abroad, the RWA offered potential emigrants advice on their intended country of immigration in an effort to protect them from exploitation. Though the Weimar constitution viewed immigration as a personal right and guaranteed German citizens the freedom to emigrate, the RWA actively discouraged individuals from leaving the country. RWA staff members tried to use "moral influence" to show potential emigrants how their departure might hurt Germany's economic, physical, and spiritual recovery or tried to direct them to countries where it was believed they could retain their German cultural heritage and emotional ties to Germany. In a similar vein, the German Foreign Office (Auswärtiges Amt, or AA) believed that the central government should represent the interests of ethnic Germans abroad. The AA tried to create partnerships between state officials, private organizations, and Germans abroad to aid in Germany's economic recovery and to improve its international standing.[46]

Semiprivate and private organizations also played a major role in this drive to mobilize "ethnic consciousness" among Germans abroad. The German Foreign Institute (Deutsches Ausland-Institut, or DAI)—which was supported by the Reich Ministry of the Interior, the AA, the state of Württemberg, and the city of Stuttgart—tried to expand overseas markets for German industrial goods that had been lost during World War I. One method for achieving these economic goals was to investigate and maintain contact with the two million Germans who had emigrated to the United States before the war, since DAI officials assumed these individuals could facilitate trade relationships between Germany and America, heal the damage caused by Allied anti-German propaganda, and defend the interests of recent German immigrants. DAI members argued that the Reich government had not done enough to prevent the assimilation and cultural decline of Germans abroad following the war and created a network of individuals within foreign countries to gather pertinent information and to disseminate literature about Germany. During the 1920s the DAI thereby became a major research and information center on emigration, containing over forty thousand volumes on Germans abroad, as well as photographic images, newspaper files, and journals that could be used by both potential emigrants and ethnic Germans in foreign lands.[47]

The most prominent and well-known private organization that sought to establish relations with German diasporic communities was the Association for Germans Abroad (Verein für das Deutschtum im Ausland, or VDA). Founded in 1908 to promote German-language schools in Austria-Hungary and other parts of East Central Europe, the organization paid little attention to North America before 1914 but during the Weimar era became an advocate for German minority rights and the preservation of German culture and ethnicity across the globe. The VDA was a trenchant critic of the Versailles peace settlement, accusing the Allies of having violated the principle of self-determination by severing numerous German-speaking areas from the German Reich and transferring approximately fifteen million Reich citizens to neighboring countries. The VDA called on German leaders to pressure foreign governments in states such as Belgium, Poland, and Czechoslovakia to recognize the "minority rights" of these German nationals and sought to make the German public aware of infringements of the cultural autonomy of these groups, such as the closing of German-language schools. The VDA prospered during the Weimar era: in 1917 it reported approximately 62,000 members; by 1930 this number had risen to two million.[48]

Like many nationalist organizations during the Weimar era, the VDA advocated revision of the Treaty of Versailles. The VDA writer Hermann Ullmann embraced the Mitteleuropa concept of an expanded German ethnic state in Central Europe, encompassing the German Reich, the border areas severed by Versailles, and Austria. Ullman remarked that "the Germans, wherever they live, are members of one Volk. . . . Mitteleuropa is no utopia, but a form of life that is prescribed by nature to the people between Russia and France."[49] To legitimize Germans' claim to self-determination in Mitteleuropa, the VDA also argued that the expanded state would represent the interests of an estimated 100 million "Germans" living throughout the world. The society's belief that all Germans, regardless of location, were one people soon expanded the VDA's vision of Germandom beyond Europe to include North America, South America, and the former African colonies. The VDA thus attempted to delegitimize the Versailles settlement's territorial provisions by rendering them incompatible with an expanded definition of ethnicity. Anxieties over German identity created by the treaty, in turn, fueled ever-expanding definitions of Germans abroad and a desire to establish contact with them. Indeed, the VDA viewed all Germans, regardless of citizenship, as part of one people's community, or *Volksgemeinschaft;* German ethnicity, in this view, was independent of particular state borders.[50]

Regional Heimat organizations within Germany also participated in the mobilization of ethnic sentiment during the 1920s. The VDA leader Ullmann proposed that "frontier Germans," that is, those living in contested zones such as the Rhineland or the Saar, were the Germans who felt their ties to the Volksgemeinschaft most intensely. Ullman asserted that frontier Germans were best able to lay aside class, religious, and regional differences in an effort to work toward the common good of the Volksgemeinschaft. Germany's borderlands did experience important changes in the ideology and iconography of homeland in this period, and it was in these areas that many local societies shifted their aims from cultivating culture heritage within provincial borders to serving as stewards over nearby "lost" territories. Heimat clubs and provincial officials in the Rhineland, for example, who had hoped for a negotiated peace based on Wilson's self-determination principles, looked on with horror as Belgium annexed the region's westernmost districts of Eupen and Malmedy and French troops occupied the area in 1919. The French supported separatists demanding a separate Rhenish Republic and mounted their own propaganda campaign, known as *pénétration pacifique,* designed to convince Rhinelanders that the region belonged by geography, culture, and race to the sphere of French civilization. The French goal was to create popular support for annexing the Rhineland, thus achieving the nineteenth-century goal of making the Rhine France's "natural" border.[51] The French, in other words, also exploited the rhetorical division between a "people" and state borders by insisting that Rhineland belonged to the French cultural-geographical sphere.

While numerous German statesmen called on the state to stem France's "peaceful penetration" of the Rhineland, the region's provincial officials and Heimat organizations, rather than central authorities in Berlin, assumed the leading role in creating a patriotic *Heimatfront* against French incursions. Like the VDA, provincial Heimat organizations insisted that Versailles had transgressed primordial *völkisch* bonds, determined by centuries of interaction between Land und Leute, which superceded political calculations. To ensure the strength of ethnic bonds between the Rhineland and areas annexed to Belgium, Rhineland officials supported the Eifelverein's decision to maintain organizational cells in the severed districts of Eupen and Malmedy.[52] The Rhineland's Provincial League (Provinzialverband), an organ of self-administration funded largely by municipalities in the region, also supported scientific institutes countering French claims to the region. The Rhenish Regional History Institute (Institut für Geschichtliche Landeskunde der Rheinlande), founded in 1920 at Bonn University, used economic, sociohistorical, and ethnographic methods to show the "Germanic" rather than the "Roman" roots of Rhenish settlement patterns.[53] To prove Rhinelanders' loyalty to the Reich, Heimat publications from the era insisted that the Rhineland border region had served as the cultural axis of the once-proud Holy Roman Empire, able to assimilate and Germanify the many outside influences brought to it by the river and through the area's porous western borders. The prominent historic preservationist Edmund Renard insisted that the Rhine itself created a "unifying power" in the province that enabled common patterns of culture, settlement, and agriculture (especially viticulture) to emerge.[54] In the Weimar era, therefore, the cultural landscape signified a German ethnicity grounded in nature rather than in contingent political borders.

Racial Comrades Abroad: Blood, Soil, and the Greater Heimat of National Socialist Germany

The close relationship between local Heimat stewardship over frontier Germans and the state's interest in maintaining national loyalties in the regions severed by Versailles paved the way for the National Socialist regime to exploit regional Heimat clubs in its own quest to unify the "hundreds of millions of Germans worldwide" (*Hundertmillionenvolk*).[55] Based on their racial ideology, the Nazis made outreach to Germans abroad a priority of the new government. Soon after the Nazi seizure of power, Rudolf Hess claimed to one audience, "You know as well as I do that the one great mistake of the former regime was in not keeping up ties of blood which connect the Germans in their home country with Germans abroad."[56] Though the Nazi regime focused on race rather than geography, language, or culture in defining Germanness, Blood and Soil rhetoric nonetheless assigned the landscape a pivotal role in shaping national character. Hitler wrote that "the German countryside must be preserved under all circumstances, for it is and has forever been the source of strength and greatness for our people."[57] Nazi officials, in turn, insisted that the German landscape was once the primordial *Lebensraum* of the Germanic Volk and deserved better preservation measures and regional planning.[58]

The National Socialists claimed that landscapes mirrored racial character alone rather than a synthesis of geographic, cultural, and historical influences. The Nazi landscape architect Wiepking-Jürgensmann described the landscape as "a form, an expression and a characteristic of the people living within it. . . . It is the distinctive mark of that which a race feels, thinks, creates and does." He insisted that Germans' affinities for plants and "harmonious landscapes" were a result of "biological laws innate in our being."[59] National Socialist ethnologists, historians, and educators also argued that Germans abroad had transplanted distinctive landscape forms and superior land-use practices in their movements across the globe. In his 1938 *Germans Far from Home,* for example, Fritz Wächtler, head of the National Socialist Teachers' Association, documented the achievements of German colonizers in East Central Europe, the Americas, and Africa. Wächtler developed a sliding scale of the "Germanic" impact on cultural landscapes abroad. In East Central Europe, in which the climate, soils, and geographic features were almost identical to those in Germany, Wächtler insisted that German nationals had created "islands of Germanness" (*Volkinseln*) such as the villages of the Siebenbürgen in Rumania, whose physiognomy resembled German towns and villages. "The German cultural landscape in Siebenbürgen is not only an island of Germanness in a sea of foreign peoples because of its inhabitants, but also in its whole design," he wrote. "From this island the [Germans'] superior skills in agriculture and handicraft methods expanded outward into a much broader area."[60] Gothic architecture in towns and cultivated landscapes that preserved woodlands were some of the markers of German *Kultur;* these sites, in turn, provided a geographical locus for imagining an array of benefits—spiritual, material, and artistic—that Germans had bestowed upon the Slavic, Magyar, and Rumanian peoples east and southeast of the Elbe. The rhetoric of Blood and Soil, in other words, recast Germans' reputation as caretakers of the land in a racialist mold, which insisted that environmental consciousness was a product of racial superiority.

In the German settlements farther abroad, such as those in North and South America, Wächtler saw more diffuse contours of Germanness due to different environmental conditions and the tendency among German nationals to marry and procreate with members of other European groups. Wächtler argued that Germans in America had experienced the most "horrific decline" among the world's Deutschtum. German immigrants to North America had generally been "pushed into an environment shaped by Anglo-Saxon culture and lifestyles"; the decline in German language use then "cut the cultural band that tied the Germans far from home with the motherland."[61] Though twenty-five to thirty million Americans claimed German ancestry, Wächtler estimated that only five to seven million still spoke the language and felt linked to German culture. German Americans were victims of the "melting pot"; Americanization, in Wächtler's view, was the adoption of a "foreign" Anglo-Saxon culture and language rather than a neutral process of modernization. Despite German Americans' "Anglicization," Wächtler, like Faust, believed that certain landscapes in America, particularly a handful of compact agrarian settlements in Pennsylvania, still carried traces of German influence. And just as Faust had celebrated Germans' achievements as agriculturalists in the New World, so too did Wächtler claim that German farmers had refused to employ Anglo-American farmers' exploitive practices, which he claimed had made "broad stretches of North America barren." Under a photograph depicting a rolling farmstead in Pennsylvania, with a prominent barn and a rambling home nestled among oak trees, Wächtler noted that "the entire cultural landscape takes on German characteristics." By visualizing Germanic racial elements in cultural landscapes abroad, Wächtler hoped that Germans throughout the world would recognize themselves as one Volk and avoid the "old tragedy of Germans far from home being engulfed by foreign peoples."[62]

To renew "ties of blood" with "racial comrades" in the United States, the Nazi regime fostered or created an array of organizations dedicated to forging institutional bonds between the Reich and America's Deutschtum. While American fascist organizations such as Friends of the New Germany are the best known among such groups, the Nazis' polycentric approach to cultural affairs supported an array of institutions—including the National Socialist German Workers' Party's (NSDAP) Foreign Office, the SS Volksdeutsche Mittelstelle (VoMi), and the VDA—in what became known as "America work": making the country's enormous ethnic German population aware of its racial heritage.[63] Because of high-level support from Hess and Minister of the Interior Wilhelm Frick, the VDA, which changed its name from the Verein to the Volksbund für das Deutschtum im Ausland in 1933, became the regime's leading proponent of America work between 1933 and 1937. Hess and Frick agreed that the VDA should enjoy some measure of outward independence in pursuing its cultural activities, for it maintained contacts with prominent German American individuals and organizations that would not have welcomed direct Nazi propaganda.[64] In a 1937 article, the VDA's America Service called on the country's Deutschtum to unify for the good of Germans around the world. "German ethnic consciousness," the VDA asserted, "is the recognition of the value of the German man, regardless of where he may live or may have been born." In another essay titled "We Conquered the 'Wild West,'" the VDA described Germans in western Canada as the "*Volk ohne Raum*" (people without space) who had taken over the "*Raum ohne Volk.*"[65] Despite these varied efforts, Heinrich Himmler's VoMi absorbed the VDA in 1937, destroying the organization's precarious independence and disrupting its efforts to forge scientific and cultural ties to German Americans.[66]

The VDA had been divided into provincial and state (*Land*) branch organizations since its founding in 1908, with each VDA regional organization responsible for recruiting Germans from its particular Heimat. Despite the National Socialists' tendency to centralize cultural affairs, this organization division of labor continued in the Third Reich. Individual states and provinces organized VDA "Research Offices" in their respective areas, a tendency that allowed provincial officials and regional Heimat networks to assume a key role in developing cultural relationships with German American organizations. These ties often lasted well beyond the VDA's absorption by VoMi. The regional groups packaged the Nazi Volksgemeinschaft along regionalist lines, arguing that the majority of German Americans would respond readily to the familiar contours of Heimat as a stepping stone to broader racial consciousness.

One of the most prominent regional officials who connected provincial Heimat traditions to the Nazi vision of a greater racial Heimat was the Rhenish provincial governor Heinz Haake, who held this position from 1933 to 1945. Haake first focused his attention on the Rhine province's border regions. He argued that the province needed to undertake "ethnic work" (*Volkstumsarbeit*) to establish cultural ties with "ethnically related" groups in Western Europe. In 1933 Haake established a "frontier office" within the provincial administration, which reinvigorated the Weimar practice of funding Heimat activities in territories Germany had lost in 1918, such as Eupen-Malmedy and the Saar region. Haake's use of regional cultural politics to construct an Aryan racial community soon reached beyond Western Europe to encompass racial comrades across the Atlantic. In 1936 Haake established the Research Office for Rhinelanders throughout the World (Rheinländer in aller Welt) under VDA auspices to compile lists of emigrants from the Rhineland (especially those in North and South America) and to encourage them to recognize their racial ties to both the Rhenish Heimat and the German national community. The National Socialists believed that they needed to incorporate emigrants into the larger Volksgemeinschaft and to enlist their support in preventing racial degeneration. As Haake asserted, "The National Socialist view of Volk and state demands that we consider our brothers on the other side of the border, look after them and support them in their battle for the endangered German race." While the emigrant could remain a loyal citizen of his country, he needed also to recognize his German racial character. Haake noted that many German emigrants had "declined" in their new, foreign surroundings, constituting "an unhappy, homeless racial mixture. The danger is especially great wherever the emigrant lives in scattered rather than closed settlements, such as in the big cities of the United States."[67] Under Haake's direction, therefore, provincial Heimat promotion lost its ties to the regional cultural landscape, evolving instead into an instrument for imagining a pan-European identity whose parameters were defined by blood rather than by geography.

Haake believed that emigrants' love of their regional Heimat, which he referred to as the *Stammheimat,* provided a stepping-stone to greater racial awareness. Haake noted that each migrant took with him a particular Heimat experience that was different for Bavarians, Saxons, and Rhinelanders; through the Research Office's work, this experience would "remain lively and strong . . . in the emigrant's heart," thereby "protecting the greater German Volksgemeinschaft along the pathway through the more familiar Stammheimat."[68] To begin the process of contacting these emigrants, the Research Office assembled a list of their addresses and then sent them a so-called letter from home, or *Heimatbrief,* during the Christmas holidays. The Heimatbrief contained Rhenish poetry in dialect, Rhenish songs, and Rhenish recipes, as well as a Rhineland wall map and photographic calendar. Linking modern consumerism to the invention of Heimat identity, the Rhineland Tourist Bureau promised that the map, "The Merry Rhineland," would "infect" observers with "Rhenish cheerfulness" and make them want to discover the area themselves.[69] In the 1939 calendar that accompanied the Heimatbrief, a forward by Haake began, "Dear Rhenish-German People's Comrade! Heimat, a word of unique and magical ring, it awakens the imagination and memories to the sites of youth, to the great, German Fatherland." The calendar consisted of landscape scenes designed to awaken Heimat feelings, showing the viewer the "unforgettable beauties of the Rhenish landscape, mountains and castles, valleys and rivers, as well as men at work and play. The Heimat greets you and comes to you."[70]

The Research Office envisioned sending such letters three to four times a year; those who returned the confirmation card in the letter were assigned a sponsor, who forwarded additional information about the emigrant's hometown or city.[71] The Research Office also enclosed surveys in the Heimat letters that it used for "kinship study," presumably to assist the provincial administration in its heredity maps of the Rhenish population. Haake was especially concerned with establishing "bonds of a blood" with the third- or fourth-generation emigrants, who no longer had the direct experience of Heimat, awakening their national consciousness and encouraging them to remain racially pure.[72] Haake's racialization of provincial Heimat cultivation thus expanded the purview of Rhenish identity beyond the region's borders, encompassing individuals for whom the Rhenish landscape, culture, and history had no personal meaning yet who were supposedly bound by blood to the greater German Volksgemeinschaft.

While Haake's Rheinländer in aller Welt program sought to cultivate ties with so-called racial comrades across the Atlantic, the Heimatbriefe campaign sparked controversy and hostility among many Americans. In a May 1939 article entitled "I Had, One Time, a Lovely Fatherland," the *New York Evening News* condemned German organizations for using Germans' characteristic "sentimental longing for an idealized homeland" as a "wedge . . . to gain information about Americans of German origin which could easily one day be used against them or their relatives or friends, and which most certainly is being used to prejudice them against the country of their adoption."[73] Describing a Heimatbrief from the VDA's Swabian Research Office, the *Herald Tribune* noted that the enclosed pamphlets were "calculated to arouse longing for the homeland. Cities, towns, and villages where the emigrant formerly lived are described in words and pictures in such a manner as to evoke pleasant memories, and at the same time to remind the wanderer that his native Deutschland has never ceased to think of him and care for him and offer a warm welcome to him on his return."[74] The *Evening News* article speculated that the kinship questionnaire might be used to trace Jewish blood or to blackmail families still in Germany with an eye toward confiscating their property. Germans, the editor noted, had learned nothing from the failure of their propaganda during the Great War. The Heimatbriefe would merely arouse resentment against Germany.

While American journalists reacted antagonistically to Nazi Germany's cultural outreach efforts, the reaction among German American Heimat organizations was indifferent rather than hostile. The Chicago Eifelverein, for example, celebrated Eifeler identity throughout the 1930s along traditional lines of regionalism, culture, and landscape, with little evidence of a wider racial consciousness. The *Chicago German Newspaper,* a key cultural organ for the city's German-speaking population, maintained a traditional focus on the Eifel environment, rather than blood, in shaping Eifelers' character.

> The soil scarcely nourishes its inhabitants. Yet the Eifelers cling to their Heimat with a love that seldom can be found. . . . What Nature

has refused the Eifelers in treasures . . . they have found within themselves: a rich collection of legends, a richly developed folk poetry, the love of singing and merrymaking, a firm solidarity in all aspects of life.[75]

Heimat sociability also followed traditional lines. The Chicago Ortsgruppe celebrated its twenty-fifth anniversary in 1937 with a concert and dance at the Englewood Masonic Temple. The festival included the Germania Orchestra under the direction of Mr. Steinmetz, who was also the head of the local men's singing club, "Frohsinn Mozart." The evening included a rendition of the "Eifel Hiking Song," and all members joined together to sing "Rhein und Mosel." A shared identification with the landscape and culture of Heimat, not racial inheritance, formed the basis for the Eifelverein's ties with its American affiliates.

Although Chicago's Schwabenverein embraced German nationalism and a language of "tribe" to describe its members' relationship to Germany, it also remained impervious to Nazi xenophobia. At the 1933 Cannstatter Volksfest, the club celebrated the contributions of "Swabian blood" to Chicago's material progress but noted that this heritage included "pre-Celtic, Celtic and Roman" elements; three-quarters of Swabians were of "mixed blood or dark and squat." Such racial blending, the program asserted, had made Swabians the "best of the Germans." The festival enabled Swabians as well as other German Americans, regardless of class or religion, to "come here together, far from the old Heimat, and think about the land of their ancestors full of pride and nostalgia."[76] At the 1935 festival, the program described Hitler as an admirable leader who had restored Bismarck's vision of German greatness and even spoke approvingly of the Austrian *Stämme* uniting with their South German cousins.[77] Yet there were also limits to this organization's ideological *Gleichschaltung*. The 1933 program commented that participants "look with sadness at the old Heimat, which is torn apart and fragmented by class- and racial hatred." Quoting Schiller, the program admonished Germans of all regions: "Let us be a united people of brothers."[78] Embracing New Deal pluralism, the Schwabenverein encouraged all "racial" groups in America to recognize and cultivate their heritage but insisted that such awareness spurred cosmopolitan toleration rather than racial exclusion.

German regionalism and Heimat imagery thus provided a crucial pathway for sustaining a belief in "Germanness" that crossed European frontiers and the Atlantic Ocean during the Kaiserreich, Weimar, and Nazi periods. The familiarity of "home," particularly local natural landmarks and cultural landscapes, provided tangible sites for imagining a primordial German identity that transcended class and religious differences and was deemed more essential than the vagaries of political events. German American communities embraced this Heimat ideal to fashion identities in America that bridged the old and new. By working the land and creating villages in vernacular homeland styles, German Americans had created orderly and sustainable cultural landscapes that many writers viewed as quintessentially German. Such spaces, in turn, provided German Americans with visual evidence of their ties to the greater Heimat.

The decline of German American communities during World War I coincided with increasing anxieties within Germany over territoriality, concerns that erupted into numerous debates over the character and "natural borders" of Germany during the Weimar Republic. In an effort to spur a revision of Versailles and to reestablish Germany as a great power, the national VDA as well as local Heimat societies created a sharp distinction between *Volk* and *Staat.* In this climate, the identification and preservation of Germanic cultural landscapes were no longer of antiquarian interest, and local Heimat societies linked their activities closely with the state's goal of maintaining political loyalties in Germany's borderland regions. The National Socialists exploited this growing concern over Germans abroad but recast the Heimat concept in terms of Blood and Soil and the rescue of "racial comrades" abroad. This racialized vision of Heimat resided uneasily alongside German American clubs' vision of themselves as part of an extended "nation of provincials," rendering the Nazis' overseas outreach efforts largely fruitless. While German American clubs often spoke of their regional identities in terms of "tribe," this notion coexisted with an array of other coordinates of regional identity, such as local customs, religion, festivals, and, especially, landscape. Nazi racism, moreover, was out of touch with German Americans' goal of "pluralistic integration," a concept that viewed the cultivation of ethnic identity as a contribution to American republicanism rather than racial exclusiveness.

Notes

1. *Der Westen,* July 22, 1869. Cited in Helmut Keil, ed., *Deutsche Arbeiterkultur in Chicago von 1850 bis zum Ersten Weltkrieg: Eine Anthologie* (Ostfildern, 1984), 214–15. All translations are my own unless otherwise noted.

2. On German Heimat movements and the relationship between provincial identities and national memory, see Celia Applegate, *A Nation of Provincials: The German Idea of Heimat* (Berkeley, Calif., 1990), and Alon Confino, *The Nation as a Local Metaphor: Württemberg, Imperial Germany, and National Memory, 1871–1918* (Chapel Hill, N.C., 1997).

3. John A. Hawgood, *The Tragedy of German-America: The Germans in the United States of America during the Nineteenth Century—and After* (New York, 1940), 27.

4. On Riehl's work, see Applegate, *A Nation of Provincials,* 21–30.

5. See Kathleen Neils Conzen, "German Americans and the Invention of Ethnicity," in *America and the Germans: An Assessment of a Three-Hundred Year History,* ed. Frank Trommler and Joseph McVeigh (Philadelphia, 1985), 131; Randall Miller, "Introduction," in *Germans in America: Retrospect and Prospect,* ed. Randall Miller (Philadelphia, 1984), 1.

6. Kathleen Neils Conzen, "Patterns of German American History," in *Germans in America,* ed. Miller, 15.

7. Miller, "Introduction," 1.

8. On immigration statistics, see Conzen, "Patterns," 17; Miller, "Introduction," 1.

9. Miller, "Introduction," 3.

10. Conzen, "Patterns," 16–19.

11. Miller, "Introduction," 5.

12. Richard Hofmeister, *The Germans of Chicago* (Champaign, Ill., 1976), 59.

13. Conzen, "Invention of Ethnicity," 133, 139–43.

14. Cited in Albert B. Faust, *The German Element in the United States* (Boston, 1909), 473.

15. Conzen, "Patterns," 26. This belief in the superiority of German land-use practices over those of the "Anglo-Saxons" also legitimated German colonialist expansion in Africa. See William Rollins, "Imperial Shades of Green: Conservation and Environmental Chauvinism in the German Colonial Project," *German Studies Review* 22 (May 1999): 187–213.

16. Faust, *The German Element,* 34–35.

17. Faust, *The German Element,* 57, 446.

18. Hawgood, *The Tragedy of German-America,* 23.

19. Faust, *The German Element,* 29.

20. Faust, *The German Element,* 35.

21. Faust, *The German Element,* 29–30.

22. Faust, *The German Element,* 2. Beginning in the 1880s, groups such as the Illinois German American History Association also published local histories that described Midwest settlement as the transformation of wilderness into a Germanic cultural landscape. See the speech by Ernst Bruncken in *Deutsch-Amerikanische Geschichtsblätter* 1, no. 2 (April 1901): 3–4.

23. On German and German American interest in the frontier, see Jerry Schuchalter, "Charles Sealsfield and the Frontier Thesis," *German American Studies* 30 (1995): 19–35. For Frederick Jackson Turner's frontier hypothesis, see *The Frontier in American History* (New York, 1947).

24. Wilhelm Bocke, "Werth und Ziel der deutsch-amerikanischen Geschichts-forschung," *Deutsch-Amerikanische Geschichtsblätter,* 1, no. 2 (April 1901): 4.

25. Cited in Faust, *The German Element,* 37.

26. James Bergquist, "Germans and the City," in *Germans in America,* ed. Miller, 37.

27. On German Heimat movements, see Applegate, *A Nation of Provincials,* and Confino, *The Nation as a Local Metaphor.*

28. *Eifelvereinsblatt,* 1913, 203. Cited in *Die Eifel, 1888–1988. Zum 100jährigen Jubiläum des Eifelvereins* (Düren, 1989), 254.

29. *Eifelvereinsblatt,* 1911, 268. Cited in *Die Eifel, 1888–1988,* 289.

30. Cited in *Die Eifel, 1888–1988,* 290–91: "Dort, wo viel Bächlein fliessen, Zur Mosel und Zum Rhein, Durch blumenreiche Auen, in frischen Eifelgauen, Dort möcht ich gerne sein."

31. Hofmeister, *The Germans of Chicago,* 11, 17.

32. Hofmeister, *The Germans of Chicago,* 113–19.

33. Chicago Historical Society (hereafter CHS). Carl Härtung, "Der Schwaben-verein von Chicago," *Fünfundzwanzigstes Stiftungs-Fest Gedenk-Schrift,* March 31, 1903, 5.

34. Hofmeister, *The Germans of Chicago,* 118; Keil, *Deutsche Arbeiterkultur in Chicago,* 211–12, 215–16.

35. Cannstatter Volksfest Program, 1903, CHS.

36. Hofmeister, *The Germans of Chicago,* 118–19.

37. *Chicagoer Arbeiter Zeitung,* June 27, 1883. Cited in Keil, *Deutsche Arbeit-erkultur in Chicago,* 212–13; Faust, *The German Element,* 382.

38. Faust, *The German Element,* 378.

39. Hofmeister, *Deutsche Arbeiterkultur in Chicago,* 60–79.

40. *Die Eifel, 1888–1988,* 309, 311.

41. Barbara Wiedemann-Citera, "The Role of the German American *Verein* in the Revitalization of German American Ethnic Life in New York City in the 1920s," *German American Studies* 29 (May 1987): 107.

42. *Die Eifel, 1888–1988,* 290.

43. Hofmeister, *Deutsche Arbeiterkultur in Chicago,* 79, 119.

44. Michael Zender, *Eifelvereinsblatt,* 1932, 118–20. Cited in *Die Eifel, 1888–1988,* 290.

45. Although there is little evidence that the German government actively engaged in promoting cultural ties with German Americans, several private nationalist organizations did attempt mobilization, but to little effect. On the divi-sions between the state and private associations in nationalist agitation, see Geoff Eley, *Reshaping the German Right: Radical Nationalism and Political Change after Bismarck,* 2d ed. (Ann Arbor, Mich., 1990), especially 42–43, 140.

46. For an informative discussion of Weimar state and private organizations involved in establishing contacts with Germans abroad, see Grant Grams, *German Emigration to Canada and the Support of Its* Deutschtum *during the Weimar Republic* (Frankfurt a. M. and New York, 2001), 1–27.

47. Grams, *German Emigration to Canada,* 7–10. See also Sander Diamond, *The Nazi Movement in the United States, 1924–1941* (Ithaca, N.Y., 1974), 45–64, and

Ernst Ritter, *Das Deutsche Ausland-Institut in Stuttgart 1917–1945* (Wiesbaden, 1976).

48. See Allen T. Cronenberg, "The Volksbund für das Deutschtum im Ausland: Völkisch Ideology and German Foreign Policy, 1881–1939" (Ph.D. diss., Stanford University, 1970), 200–201; Grams, *German Emigration to Canada*, 10–14.

49. Cronenberg, "The Volksbund," 65.

50. Cronenberg, "The Volksbund," 50.

51. On French and German propaganda efforts in the Rhineland, see Franziska Wein, *Deutschlands Strom—Frankreichs Grenze: Geschichte und Propaganda am Rhein 1919–1930* (Essen, 1992).

52. See Archiv des Landschaftsverbandes Rheinland (hereafter ALVR), Kulturabteilung, nr. 11169. See also Karl Bartz, *Das Unrecht an Eupen-Malmedy* (Berlin, 1928).

53. On the Bonn Institute, see Edith Ennen, "Hermann Aubin und die geschichtliche Landeskunde der Rheinlande," *Rheinische Vierteljahresblätter* 34 (1970): 9–42, and Marlene Nikolay-Panther, Wilhelm Janssen, and Wolfgang Herborn, eds., *Geschichtliche Landeskunde der Rheinlande: Regionale Befunde und raumübergreifende Perspektiven* (Cologne, 1994). Geographical determinism in the form of *Geopolitik* also dominated discussions about Germany's future role in Europe. See David Thomas Murphy, *The Heroic Earth: Geopolitical Thought in Weimar Germany, 1918–1933* (Kent, Ohio, 1997).

54. Edmund Renard, "Die Denkmalpflege in der Rheinprovinz," in *Die Rheinische Provinzialverwaltung*, ed. Johannes Horion (Düsseldorf, 1925), 443.

55. This phrase was used repeatedly by the VDA in its publications after 1933. See "Unsere 100-Millionen-Familie: Wir sind nicht nur Reichsbürger des Deutschen 67-Millionen-Reiches—sondern auch Volksgenossen des 100-Millionen-Volkes der Deutschen in aller Welt!" *VDA-Pressemitteilungen*, nr. 519, Dec. 8, 1937, 1.

56. Rudolf Hess, *Reden* (Berlin, 1938), 34. Cited in Diamond, *Nazi Movement*, 49.

57. Quoted in Reinhold Hoemann, "Aufgaben und Pflichten der Führer der Gemeinden betriff. Landschaftspflege und Landschaftsgestaltung (1938)," 1, AVLR 11136.

58. Walther Schoenichen, *Naturschutz im Dritten Reich. Einführung in Wesen und Grundlagen zeitgemässer Naturschutz-Arbeit* (Berlin-Lichterfeld, 1934).

59. H. F. Wiepking, "Der Mensch and die Pflanze," *Gartenflora* 84 (1935): 221–23. On the relationship between "nativism" in landscape architecture and fascism, see Gert Groening and Joachim Wolschke-Bulmahn, "Politics, Planning, and the Protection of Nature: Political Abuse of Early Ecological Ideas in Germany, 1933–1945," *Planning Perspectives* 2 (1987): 137–39.

60. See Fritz Wächtler, *Deutsche Fern der Heimat*, vol. 3: *Deutsches Volk—Deutsche Heimat* (Munich, 1938), 29.

61. Wächtler, *Deutsche Fern,* 13.

62. Wächtler, *Deutsche Fern,* 13–14, 157–58.

63. See Diamond, *Nazi Movement*, 51, 78. See also Susan Canedy, *America's Nazis: A Democratic Dilemma* (Menlo Park, Calif., 1990), and Cornelia Wilhelm,

Bewegung oder Verein: Nationalsozialistische Volkstumspolitik in den USA (Stuttgart, 1998).

64. Cronenberg, "The Volksbund," 100–101, 118–23.

65. *Amerikadienst der VDA-Mitteilungen,* no. 4, March 1938, "Aufruf zur Einigung des Deutschtums in Amerika: Zum Wohl des Gesamtdeutschtums ist der Zusammenschluss der Amerikaner deutschen Blutes notwendig!" 1, ALVR 4667.

66. Cronenberg, "The Volksbund," 174–75.

67. Entwurf für die Rundfunk-Reportage über die Forschungsstelle "Rheinländer in aller Welt," 1–2, ALVR, Nachlass Haake, no. 63.

68. Entwurf, Nachlass Haake. See also Abschrift from Forschungsstelle Rheinländer in aller Welt to Kreisring Volksaufklärung und Propaganda, Feb. 16, 1939, ALVR 4614; Forschungsstelle "Rheinländer in aller Welt," ALVR 4606; Walter Diener, "Rheinische Auswanderer: Ihre Schicksal und ihre Betreuung," *Westdeutscher Beobachter,* Mar. 13, 1939.

69. "Das fröhliche Rheinland: Die Wandkarte der rheinischen Lande als Gast- und Wohnraumschmuck," 1939, ALVR 4617.

70. Heinz Haake, "Lieber deutscher rheinischer Volksgenosse!" Düsseldorf, 1939, ALVR 4617.

71. See requests for *Lesepaten,* ALVR 4605, 4608.

72. Rundfunk-Reportage über "Rheinländer in aller Welt," 4–6, ALVR, Nachlass Haake 63.

73. "I Had, One Time, a Lovely Fatherland," *New York Evening News,* May 13, 1939, ALVR 4605.

74. M. Farmer Murphy, "Reich Hunts Immigrant, Demands Loyalty, Stirs Him Against New Home," *New York Herald Tribune,* May 7, 1939, ALVR 4605.

75. "Silberjubiläum des Eifelvereins—Ortsgruppe Chikago," *Chikago Deutsche Zeitung,* 1937, 36–37, quoted in *Die Eifel, 1888–1988,* 446.

76. Julius Klein, "Deutsche Kulturarbeit der Schwaben," 1, Fifty-sixth Cannstatter Volksfest Program, 1933, CHS.

77. See Fifty-eighth Cannstatter Volksfest Program, 1935, CHS.

78. Klein, "Deutsche Kulturarbeit der Schwaben," 3, CHS.

CHAPTER 7

In Search of Home Abroad

German Jews in Brazil, 1933–45

Jeffrey Lesser

Ethnicity, no matter how narrowly constructed, is by definition unstable. Internal conflicts (political, generational, or other), relations with the majority society, and international factors all create a constant flux. Any kind of ethnic maintenance, then, is a remarkable phenomenon: it is based on group negotiation and acceptance of myriad variables, all of which are constantly changing. The interplay of forces can be seen clearly in the formation of Brazil's German Jewish refugee community in the 1930s, a group that sought to integrate into white elite society while emphasizing its difference from Eastern European Jews who had arrived earlier.

The pattern of Jewish immigration to Brazil necessarily influenced the ways in which German Jewishness was created and contested. While some Jews came to Brazil in the colonial period, the creation of community in the contemporary sense only took place in the late nineteenth century when Jews from North Africa settled in the Amazon during the rubber boom. These Jews were followed in the early twentieth century by significant groups of Bessarabians, who settled in agricultural communities in southern Brazil funded by Baron Maurice de Hirsch's Jewish Colonization Association (JCA). The farming colonies were a failure, but the migration of these Jews into Brazil's major cities set the stage for large-scale Eastern European, primarily Polish, immigration in the 1920s and 1930s. Indeed, in some years almost 13 percent of all the Jews leaving Europe settled in Brazil, making it one of the most important nations of Jewish relocation in the world.[1]

These migration patterns were markedly different from those in the United States, Argentina, and Canada, where nineteenth-century Central European Jewish migration created a corporate base against which all later migrants reacted. One historian, for example, has described the Jews of Buenos Aires in the late nineteenth century as "refined Western European Businessmen who were heirs to the Emancipation [and were] generally committed to the tenets of German reform and its concern for dignified services, sermons in the vernacular and the termination of rules that tended to make Jews appear different."[2] Such comments would be appropriate for the U.S. and Canadian cases as well, and in the latter decades of the nineteenth century, Jewish internal hegemony in communal/organizational life in all three nations can be demarcated as German Jewish based.[3] Such characterizations are not appropriate for Brazil, where formal political Jewish culture was dominated by Eastern European Jews who arrived after the Russian Revolution. While the almost ten thousand German Jewish refugees (see table 1) who arrived in Brazil between 1933 and 1941 had much in common with the elite population of the country, their shared experiences with Jews already in Brazil were minimal. Thus they did not find themselves welcomed from within but ironically became outsiders anew within the Jewish community. This, and an image in Germany of Brazil as a "backward country," helps explain why German Jewry was actively discouraged from immigrating to Brazil until the late 1930s, long after the emigration of Jews fleeing Nazism had begun.

When German Jews began to enter Brazil in the second half of the 1930s, they integrated quickly into an upper- and upper-middle-class culture, which constructed Brazil's economic and social problems as the "fault" of the lower classes. This discourse meshed easily with German prejudices about Brazil, allowing refugees rapid entry into elite culture. Other factors also helped refugees slip easily into the upper classes. Unlike in the United States, where the slow accumulation of capital by immigrant Jews led to entrance into a burgeoning middle class, the absence of just this middle class in Brazil meant that any capital accumulation whatsoever vaulted many refugees into the upper 25 to 30 percent of the population that was not destitute. Finally, many in the Brazilian elite saw that Central Europeans were the most desirable of all immigrants. Urbanized and relatively socially assimilated German Jews with professional- and managerial-class backgrounds were thus, at least discursively, vaulted into the upper echelons of Brazilian society, even when they arrived destitute. Indeed, since German Jews began entering Brazil only fifty years after the abolition of slavery, they (like previous Eastern European Jewish immigrants) accrued status upon arrival simply on the basis of color. Industrialization and urbanization combined with a racial scheme designed to keep people of color at the lowest rungs of the economic and social pyramid to help them move extraordinarily quickly up the economic ladder.[4]

Envisioning Brazil

Brazil first came to the attention of Central European Jewry in 1824 when the country became an empire independent of Portugal. This ended the official persecution of Jews even though the Catholic Church remained established and non-Catholics were not permitted public exercise of their faith. Limitations on religious freedom were relaxed in the later years of the empire to encourage Protestant immigration, and although the census of 1872 recorded no Jewish inhabitants, perhaps two thousand Jews did enter as part of a general European migration, mainly to the capital city of Rio de Janeiro.[5] Indeed, Dom Pedro II, Brazil's emperor from 1841 to 1889, was often described as a philo-semite because of the Hebrew liturgical poems he translated into French and his travels to the Holy Land.[6] The interest in Judaism did not translate into a desire for actual Jews, and the transient nature of the Jewish business community led to the creation of only a few communal institutions, notably cemeteries.[7]

For most Europeans, Jews included, Brazil was a faraway and scary place in the mid- to late nineteenth century. Indeed, the first proposal

TABLE 1.   Jewish Emigration from Germany and Jewish Immigration to Brazil, 1933–41

Year	Total Jewish Émigrés from Germany	German Jewish Émigrés to Brazil	Percent of All German Jewish Émigrés Who Went to Brazil	Percent of All Jewish Émigrés to Brazil Who Were German Jewish
1933	37,000	363	0.9	10.9
1934	23,000	835	3.6	22.0
1935	21,000	357	1.7	20.0
1936	25,000	1,772	7.0	51.8
1937	23,000	1,315	5.7	65.6
1938	40,000	445	1.1	83.9
1939	78,000	2,899	3.7	63.0
1940	15,000	1,033	6.8	27.2
1941	8,000	408	5.1	3.7
	270,000	9,427	3.4	40.3

Source: Werner Rosenstock. "Exodus 1933–39: A Survey of Jewish Emigration from Germany I," *Leo Baeck Institute Yearbook* 1 (1956): 377; and Herbert A. Strauss, "Jewish Emigration from Germany: Nazi Policies and Jewish Responses (I)," *Leo Baeck Institute Yearbook* 25 (1980), 326. "Rapport d'activité pendant la periode 1933–1943—les juifs dans l'histoire du Bresil," HIAS-Brazil, Folder 1, YIVO-NY.

for planned Jewish immigration to Brazil, in 1881, was never even completed because of lack of interest.[8] A decade later more serious thought was given to mass settlement when Tsar Nicholas II expelled all Jews from Moscow as part of his "Russification" plan, an important component of which was the compulsory practice of the Russian Orthodox religion.[9] In Germany, Jewish communal leaders, fearful that the Russian Jews might resettle among them and interfere with the process of acculturation begun so auspiciously under Napoleon's emancipation decree, set out to find some alternate places of residence for the refugees. They quickly set up an agency, the Deutsches Zentral Comitee fuer die Russischen Juden (German Central Committee for Russian Jews), and sent Oswald Boxer, a Viennese journalist and friend of the Zionist leader Theodore Herzl, to Brazil to investigate possibilities for the resettlement of Russian Jewry as farmers.[10] Notions of "return to the land," then popular among European Jewish intellectuals, led many in the Deutsches Zentral Comitee to ignore the fact that most Muscovite Jews were urban tradespeople and not farmers. Regardless of this difficulty, Boxer reported enthusiastically to the committee after visiting São Paulo and Rio de Janeiro in May 1891.[11] The high hopes were dashed when a series of political changes, including the "revolution" that transformed Brazil's empire into a republic and a subsequent coup against the ruling junta, discouraged the Deutsches Zentral Comitee from sending any immigrants to Brazil. The secular nature of the new Brazilian Republic, and the end of all legal distinction of religious affiliation, did not soothe the many fears about Brazil's safety. Indeed, they were confirmed in 1892 when Oswald Boxer died of yellow fever in Rio de Janeiro.[12]

While Brazil remained far from German Jewish consciousness in the forty years after Boxer's death, a number of factors, including a change in Brazil's image and restrictive immigration policies in other American republics, did lead Eastern European Jews to settle in large numbers beginning in the 1920s. Eastern European Jews were economically successful in Brazil, but their increasing presence led conservative elites to embark on an increasingly virulent anti-Semitic campaign that found its most open expression in the early 1930s, just as German Jews began to consider Brazil as an immigration site.

In spite of the fact that the 1920s and 1930s had seen an increase in quotas and restrictive immigration legislation throughout the Americas—most notably in the United States, Argentina, and Canada—German Jews rarely considered Brazil as a place of refuge, even as their situation deteriorated.[13] Indeed, prior to 1936 most German Jews saw Brazil as a country of trouble and misery. According to popular wisdom Brazil lacked educational facilities and was a land of revolution and dictatorship.[14] White-collar refugees were afraid they would be forced to become day laborers and would not have the opportunity to purchase land or homes. This image of Brazil had been in the making for some time. A 1928 conference on refugees held in Buenos Aires had portrayed Brazil specifically, and Latin America generally, as a blue-collar region unattractive for German Jewish merchants, businesspeople, and academics. According to Haim Avni, the *Korrespondenzblatt* (newsletter) of Berlin's Central Office for Jewish Emigration frequently warned German Jewry about the dangers of migration to South America.[15] The portrayal was so negative that between 1933 and 1936, when emigration from Germany was highest, Jews generally went to the United States, Canada, Palestine, or Argentine rather than Brazil, which had virtually no entry restrictions for those entering from Central Europe with even modest amounts of capital.

The most frightening vision of Brazil was produced by Dr. Arthur Ruppin, a German Jew who visited South America to examine its potential for German Jewish resettlement in late 1935. Ruppin, a committed Zionist and later the first professor of Jewish sociology at the Hebrew University (Jerusalem), published his report in the Hebrew press in Palestine, in five articles in Berlin's *Jüdische Rundschau,* in London's *Jewish Chronicle,* and later as a book.[16] The potential for German Jewish life in Brazil, according to Ruppin, was low. Eastern European Jews had succeeded because they worked as "salesmen on the installment system [who] go from house to house like peddlers in order to find customers, and it seems that the German Jews cannot very well compete in that respect with the East European Jews."[17] The two thousand German Jews who had immigrated to Brazil before October 1935 were having trouble getting the jobs they desired. The "immigrants were ignorant of the needs of the country and belong mostly to the commercial class. While skilled workers and artisans found remunerative work very quickly, this was much more difficult for the business people, who had at first to content themselves with subordinate and poorly paid positions."[18] Ruppin failed to mention that German Jews often refused to accept help from relief organizations operated by Eastern Europeans. In 1935, for example, only 494 of the 835 German Jewish refugees who migrated to Brazil went to the local HICEM (a joint refugee relief group) for help, even though the organization was finding jobs for about 75 percent of those who needed them.[19] Regardless of their reasons, as late as 1935 German Jewry found little cause to leave for Brazil.

Brazilian law did appear to make it difficult for German Jews in the liberal professions. Those with European professional degrees were not allowed to practice, and one immigrant aid group reported that the test to legalize a foreign medical degree was so difficult that "none— except a single dentist—is so far known to have passed."[20] Many German Jewish physicians were unable to obtain licenses and turned to other professions. Others affiliated with Brazilians in order to work officially in unrestricted areas of medicine while continuing their practice on the side. Evidence of this is found in the *Crónica Israelita,* published by the German Jewish Congregation of São Paulo, which was filled with advertisements for medical services by Jewish immigrant practitioners.[21] Yet extra-legal jobs were limited, and, according to Ruppin, "even in the event of relaxations in the legal immigration restrictions in the near future the economic prospects for German Jews, unless they have a capital of at least £1,000 are limited."[22]

Arthur Ruppin believed that Brazil would never accept more than the 835 German Jews it had in 1934. He was wrong: by 1936 twice that number had entered, representing a growing percentage of all Jewish immigrants to Brazil. Many who arrived before 1936 were young people, single or recently married, who later brought their parents and relatives to Brazil with *cartas de chamada,* official forms that allowed those resident in Brazil to buy prepaid passage for their relatives by providing them with an affidavit of support approved by the police in the city where an immigrant's sponsor lived and then legalized by the Department of Immigration of the Ministry of Labor, Industry, and Commerce.[23]

It was only when the Nuremberg Laws combined with an increasing difficulty in entering preferred nations of destination that German Jews began coming in greater numbers to Brazil. But just as political changes in Central Europe were leading Jews to realize that emigration might be the only means of survival, anti-Jewish attitudes in Brazil began to coalesce into formal anti-immigrant policies. European Jewish organizations, which only a year earlier had discouraged immigration to Brazil, now began to direct refugees there. *Brasilien: Als Aufnahmeland der Jüdischen Auswanderung aus Deutschland,* a privately published book, encouraged migration by explaining entrance requirements and describing the possibilities for German and German Jewish social acculturation and economic integration.[24] These groups also approached the Brazilian government to urge a more liberal attitude toward Jewish immigration, but the requests were generally rejected.

A perfect example of the clash of images, both between German and Eastern European Jews and between Brazilian elites and Jews in general, can be seen in the 1936 attempt by the JCA to open a new farming colony that would offer the Brazilian government the immigrants it wanted—farmers.[25] The JCA, it is worth remembering, had been formed in part to guarantee that Eastern European Jewish refugees would settle in the Americas (and thus outside of Central Europe), and thus its position as a negotiator of spaces for German Jews in Brazil was a new one.

No immigration plan was more carefully constructed than the one to create a German Jewish farming colony in Rezende, about 190 kilometers west of Rio de Janeiro. In July 1936 the JCA purchased a two-thousand-hectare plot, equipped the entire colony, and even found real farmers to settle it.[26] The project was carried out in consultation with the Brazilian minister of agriculture, who was invited to inspect the area. The JCA planned to recruit refugees from Germany who might "obtain admission into the country . . . [within] the Brazilian immigration restrictions."[27] By depositing a bond in a Rio de Janeiro bank, the JCA guaranteed that none of the 137 proposed families would become public charges, and the immigrants even managed to secure certificates of morality and capability from the Nazi government.[28] The minister of agriculture's blessing led the Department of Immigration to authorize visas, which, much to everyone's surprise, never arrived. Apparently, when the Department of Immigration informed the foreign minister, José Carlos de Macedo Soares, about the plans, he requested more information. Assuming that the foreign minister's request was a veiled sign of opposition, the Department of Immigration referred the matter to the Ministry of Labor, which canceled the authorization without ever informing the JCA.[29]

Opposition to the organized settlement of Jews at Rezende could be found throughout the government. Labienne Salgado dos Santos, a diplomat, did not "believe in either the sincerity of the organization [the JCA] or in the durability of the colony if it remains in the hands of Jews."[30] Filinto Müller, chief of the federal police, opposed all JCA plans, especially after intercepting a letter from a JCA employee to the organization's Paris headquarters that indicated the JCA was regularly bribing immigration officials to let refugee Jews with tourist visas enter Brazil.[31] Oliveira Vianna, an Aryanist ideologue and jurist closely linked to President Getúlio Vargas and at the time a consultant to the

Ministry of Labor, pointed to the few colonists who remained in the JCA's Quatro Irmãos colony as an argument for rejecting the visas.[32] Dulphe Pinheiro Machado, director general of the National Population Department (Departamento Nacional de Povoamento, or DNP), the Ministry of Labor's agency in charge of colonization, complained of "Jews . . . and other parasitical elements that constitute ethnic minorities and that upset the tranquility of the nations where they live."[33]

In December Agamemnon Magalhães informed the JCA that "the immigration of Jews to the property acquired . . . at Rezende would not be permitted."[34] No official reason was given, as the policy was kept hidden for fear of negative diplomatic repercussions. Relief groups were not fooled. Complaints of "anti-Semitic fascism" led the British ambassador, Sir Hugh Gurney, to broach the subject with President Vargas, who "fully recognizes the desirability of admitting agriculturists, particularly those with capital."[35] Even so, the visas were not granted. Others soon began putting pressure on Brazil. The diplomat Leo S. Rowe, director of the Pan-American Union (which became the permanent secretariat of the Organization of American States in 1948), pleaded with Oswaldo Aranha, Brazil's Minister of Foreign Relations, to do "a very great service which will be greatly appreciated."[36] The U.S. government entered the fray after determining that the new colony might provide a legal residence for Jews who had overstayed their visas.[37] The diplomatic attempts were fruitless. Visas for Jews, according to the foreign minister, simply "were not in accord with the present interests of the country."[38]

After more than two years of pressure from British and U.S. diplomats, the Brazilian government relented. In early April 1938 a different Rezende colony than the one envisioned finally opened. The settlers were already resident naturalized Brazilians and not new immigrants as originally planned. Thus the opening of the colony was played up as an example of how, with hard work on the land, foreign farmers could become "good" Brazilians. Ernani do Amaral Peixoto, Rio de Janeiro's federal interventor, visited the colony, and what he seemed to find "very agreeable" was that there were few Jews actually living there.[39] The non-Jewish residents of the city of Rezende agreed and held a mass in honor of the colonists.[40] An official press release on the opening of the colony focused on the humanitarian aspects of permitting the "purely Brazilian project" to open. No Brazilian tax money, the government emphasized, had been invested, and although "the colony is for 30 families . . . for now there are only 15."[41] The original plan to locate 137 families in the colony went unmentioned, as did the fact that houses had already been built for 80 families.

Amaral Peixoto's visit to Rezende was fairly big news: it was reported in most of Rio de Janeiro's newspapers and even made the front page of *O Carioca* and the *Correio da Manhã*.[42] Yet if the inter-ventor's visit was a mild propaganda opportunity for the regime, the arrival of President Vargas himself in May 1938 provided the Brazilian government, the JCA, and the Brazilian Jewish community with a chance to toot their own horns.[43] The weekly Yiddish *Idische Presse* (Imprensa Israelita) dedicated an entire issue to the story while the *Diário de Notícias* headlined "The Jew Returns to the Land."[44] While the president's expected visits to the fields, a colonist's home, and a school were uneventful, his brief, perhaps apocryphal, meeting with a young boy was significant. Demonstrating both a hope for assimilation and a distrust of the foreign, Vargas, for no apparent reason, asked the young boy, "Are you Hungarian?" "No, sir," responded the boy. "I am Brazilian."[45]

Confused images of Jews abounded in the press reports on the open-ing of the colony. In most cases, however, they reflected a vision of "the Jews" as both positive for development and negative for Brazilian soci-ety. A picture of one colonist in the *Diário de Notícias* that was labeled inaccurately "son of a Berlin banker" simultaneously led readers toward traditional anti-Semitic associations of Jews with wealth and a hope that such wealth might find its way into Brazil.[46] Rio de Janeiro's *A Noite* called the colony "a small homeland for those without a home-land," suggesting that Jews could never become Brazilian and that Rezende was a state within a state.[47] This was reinforced by constant references to the *Fazenda dos Judeus* (the plantation of the Jews). Those in government shared these views, and no refugees were actually given visas to settle in Rezende. When the JCA sent a group to exam-ine the colony in 1939, a visitor commented, "It is sad and significant to see the new houses fully furnished, on small vegetable, dairy, and fruit farms, fenced and equipped, standing empty and deteriorating."[48] In late 1942 Oswaldo Aranha even attempted to purchase five hundred hectares of the land as a horse-breeding farm.[49]

The JCA's attempt to play by the rules and regain governmental favor was a failure, but the refusal of the Vargas regime to grant visas to Jewish farmers suggests a number of points worth elucidating. Pre-conceived notions led many policymakers to reject the idea that Jews could be farmers. At the same time even those who believed in the efficacy of the agricultural training of the refugees saw the admittance of the group as both politically and culturally dangerous. Jewish immigrants, even if they were farmers, were not viewed as acceptable tillers of the soil but rather as undesirable Jews.

Images of Self and Other

In spite of the rejection of Jewish entry in the Rezende case, many German Jews did enter Brazil. Indeed, it was the new presence of German Jews that helped the established Eastern European community in its fight against anti-Semitism. The bourgeois background of the newcomers was less easily categorized as undesirable, in spite of their settlement in urban areas in contradiction to Brazilian immigration policy, which was geared toward farmers. Nativists, whose role in post-1930 Brazilian politics was critical, often directed their anger at Eastern European Jews, who were seen as both unproductive (because they were believed to spend all their time peddling) and unwhite. Yet the position of German Jews was less clear. They were highly acculturated, spoke languages common to non-Jewish immigrant communities in Brazil, and were moderate or conservative politically. German Jews were also viewed as highly educated, as skilled, and as arriving with capital to invest, and indeed this was often the case. As the non-Jewish Herbert V. Levy, at the time a young journalist (and later a federal deputy from São Paulo and director general of the financial newspaper *Gazeta Mercantil*), argued in his 1934 *Problemas actuaes da economia brasileira,* Germany's "anti-Semitic campaign offers [Brazil] the opportunity to receive . . . the best in the arts, in the sciences, in economics, in the letters [and] in all areas of cultural activity. . . . [German Jews] are of undeniable value to progress and cultural development."[50]

It is ironic that, while the established Eastern European Jewish community used images of German Jews to fight against anti-Semitism, German Jews themselves actively disassociated themselves from what they considered the culturally inferior established Eastern European community.[51] This, they believed, would prevent them from being categorized in negative ways by nativists who attacked Eastern European Jewish peddling and communal solidarity. German refugees were, in fact, part of the industrial European culture that many middle- and upper-class Brazilians wished to emulate. German Jewish organizations emphasized the teaching of Portuguese, something even the nativists had trouble criticizing. They also created institutions specifically aimed at promoting German social and cultural life, and among refugees there was rarely a declining attachment to German

high culture.[52] Herbert Caro, a lawyer and native of Berlin who helped
found the Brazilian-Jewish Cultural and Beneficent Society (SIBRA)
of Porto Alegre, translated Thomas Mann (who would also flee Germany) and Hermann Hesse for Editôra do Globo, a large publishing
house whose titles also included a great deal of European anti-Semitic
material.[53]

The "Jewish question" became increasingly complicated as large
numbers of Central European refugees entered Brazil. A number of
influential Brazilians, without abandoning restrictions, began to simultaneously support continued or expanded Jewish immigration. None,
however, proposed a completely open policy based on humanitarian
principles. Rather, like some Nazi policies in which certain Jews were
allowed to maintain their positions as long as they remained economically "useful," some diplomats and journalists argued that only
wealthy or skilled refugees should be permitted to enter the country.
Rio de Janeiro's well-established *Correio da Manhã* editorialized in
favor of an increased Jewish presence, noting that "the great exodus of
Jewish workers from Germany . . . would bring all their technical,
industrial and principally agricultural skills."[54] Ildefonso Falcão, the
Brazilian consul in Cologne, Germany, approached Foreign Minister
Afrânio de Mello Franco confidentially about the possibilities of giving immigrant visas to Germans "of the Semitic race who [formerly]
occupied public positions or were in the liberal professions."[55] In addition to their skills, thought Falcão, Jews would "bring part of their
capital because of a special concession made by the German government." Falcão did not reach his conclusion without a push; the Jewish
directors of some of Germany's largest industries, including Schürman
and Tietz A.G. (furniture) and the Ludolph Marx Group, had come to
the consul with formal proposals to establish similar firms in São Paulo
and Rio de Janeiro.[56]

The strong sense of Germanness that both was part of German Jewish culture and was emphasized by the status it brought in Brazil also
led to the creation of a very clear and separate German Jewish religious
sphere. German Jews generally followed the liberal tradition of wor-
ship, a form that grew out of the mid-nineteenth-century emancipation
and was based on the idea that Jews should be religious at home and
citizens in public. The liberal (*Einheitsgemeinde*) tradition, which
included religious services conducted in the national language, was
seen as inappropriate by many Jews whose economic and political situation in Eastern Europe had left them with a traditional form of wor-
ship. As early as 1934, Eastern European Jews accused German

refugees of being assimilationists and converts from Judaism. One woman who encountered this prejudice even suggested that the World Union for Progressive Judaism, a Jewish reform movement, establish a synagogue in Brazil, a situation that soon occurred.[57]

It was in the larger cities that the first large-scale German Jewish communal religious organizations were created. Although these new organizations were founded by German Jews of similar backgrounds, the differences among the existing Jewish communities affected the way in which they operated. In Porto Alegre, the German Jewish community created the SIBRA in July 1936 because of a conviction "within the circle of those Jews who speak German that there exists enough interest to create a social and cultural center."[58] Of the first two hundred members of the SIBRA, more than 75 percent were from Germany, with about one-third of the remainder from Austria or Hungary.[59] Unlike other German Jewish congregations in Brazil, however, the SIBRA was constructed within walking distance of the traditional Eastern European Jewish neighborhood of Bom Fim. This choice is significant, as it suggests that German Jews in Porto Alegre, perhaps because of the small size of the city and the Jewish population, hoped to create a unified community.[60] Unlike São Paulo and Rio de Janeiro, where friction between German Jews and earlier Eastern European arrivals ran high, German Jews in Porto Alegre integrated with members of the Eastern European community, who then associated themselves with the SIBRA.[61] The desire to create a unified Jewish community in Porto Alegre, however, did not indicate a declining attachment to German high culture, even among refugees from Nazism.

Unlike the SIBRA, the Jewish Congregation of São Paulo (Congregação Israelita Paulista, or CIP) was formed "with the expressed object of [helping] individual adjustment and collective [communal] survival."[62] The CIP was inaugurated in October 1936 when a young rabbi from Heidelberg was sent to conduct High Holy Day services for the German Jews resident in the city. Within a year Rabbi Fritz Pinkuss had moved permanently to São Paulo to help form the CIP, whose building was constructed far from the traditional Eastern European neighborhood of Bom Retiro. The CIP aggressively tried to re-create German Jewish religious and social life and actively disassociated itself from the established Jewish community.[63] In 1938 the directorate of the CIP created the Avanhandava Scout Troop, which, as Roney Cytronowicz and Judith Zuquim point out, became the pedagogical "key" to the formation of Jewish youth who were oriented toward elite Brazilian culture.[64]

All German Jewish communal organizations emphasized the teaching of Portuguese. This was based on a belief by most German Jews, many of whom were of bourgeois background, that one could be simultaneously a good Jew and a good citizen. Portuguese helped the German Jewish community integrate socially and economically. Integration was political as well, and the strong relationship between German Jewish leaders and Brazilian politicians often positively influenced the government's attitude toward Jewish refugees.

Conclusion

For most German Jews, the overseas struggle to maintain national and ethnic identity was a complex one. As participants in a premigratory culture that had suddenly shunned them, their experience abroad was one of constant differentiation, whether it be from German non-Jews or from other Jewish communities. The *Heimat* for German Jews was not that of the fiercely patriotic German non-Jews who had emigrated earlier. Germanness, which at the middle- and upper-class levels may have been only subtly contested prior to migration, radically divided Germans in their new Latin American homes.

While the lives of German Jews and non-Jews were very different throughout Latin America, the Brazilian case provides yet another twist on the story. Unlike other examples from the Americas, German Jewish refugees to Brazil found no established Central European base; rather, community power was held by Eastern European Jews who were both aggressive Yiddishists and Zionists. This lack of German Jewish institutional force changed the terms of cultural alliance as refugees rapidly realized that integration into local elite culture gave them numerous advantages. German Jewish leaders worked hard to assert their whiteness, their bourgeois status, and their Europeanness, and in many ways they were successful. When Brazil secretly closed its doors to refugees in 1938, Jews continued to enter. Indeed, Brazil's Jewish leadership (from all ethnic backgrounds) successfully manipulated images so that many refugees fleeing Europe were reconstructed as acceptable "German Jews." Almost ten thousand Jewish refugees entered Brazil between 1938 and 1942 as the Heimat abroad became Brazil at home.

NOTES

1. Jeffrey Lesser, *Negotiating National Identity: Immigrants, Minorities, and the Struggle for Ethnicity in Brazil* (Durham, 1999), 45–48; Jeffrey Lesser, *Jewish*

Colonization in Rio Grande do Sul, 1904–1925 (São Paulo, 1991); Jeffrey Lesser, *Welcoming the Undesirables: Brazil and the Jewish Question* (Berkeley, Calif., 1994), 180, appendix 2.

2. Louis H. Sobel (assistant secretary, American Jewish Joint Distribution Committee), "Jewish Community Life in Latin America," *American Jewish Year Book* 5706, no. 47 (Philadelphia, 1945), 119–40

3. B. D. Ansel, "Discord among Western and Eastern European Jews in Argentina," *American Jewish Historical Quarterly* 80 (1970): 153. See also Victor Mirelman, "Jewish Life in Buenos Aires before the East European Immigration (1860–1890)," *American Jewish Historical Quarterly* 48 (1978): 195–207.

4. Report by Dr. Ludwig Lorch of the Congregação Israelita Paulista dated November 1937. Archives of the American Joint Distribution Committee (New York City), hereafter AAJDC-NY, file #1091; Gilberto Freyre, "Brazilian Melting Pot: The Meeting of Race in Portuguese America," *Perspective of Brazil: An Atlantic Monthly Supplement* (1956): 8–12.

5. Jacob Lestschinsky, "Jewish Migrations, 1840–1956," in *The Jews: Their History, Culture, and Religion,* ed. Louis Finkelstein, vol. 2, 3d. ed. (New York, 1960), 1554; Egon and Frieda Wolff, *Os Judeus nos Primórdios do Brasil-República, visto especialmente pela documentação no Rio de Janeiro* (Rio de Janeiro, 1979).

6. Kurt Loewenstamm, *Vultos Judaicos no Brasil: uma contribuição a historia dos judeus no Brasil,* vol. 2, *Imperio, 1822–1899* (Rio de Janeiro, 1956), 25.

7. Between 1840 and 1900 the United States received about 875,000 Jews and Argentina about 27,000. Lestschinsky, "Jewish Migrations," 1536–96; and Mark Wischnitzer, *To Dwell in Safety: The Story of Jewish Migration since 1800* (Philadelphia, 1948), 295.

8. *American Israelite* (Cincinnati), Mar. 18, 1881, 300.

9. *Encyclopedia Judaica,* s.v. "Brazil" (Jerusalem, 1971), 1326.

10. Nachman Falbel, "Oswaldo Boxer e O projecto de Colonização de Judeus no Brasil," *Jornal do Imigrante* 10 (Dec. 1987–Jan. 1988): 18.

11. Leon Kellner, *Theodore Herzl's Lehrjahre, 1860–1895* (Vienna and Berlin, 1920), 142–44.

12. *Encyclopedia Judaica,* s.v. "Brazil," 1326. Sarah Bernhardt, who first visited Brazil in 1886, complains in her correspondence of yellow fever in Rio de Janeiro and that "rats and mice [are] everywhere." Cited in Arthur Gold and Robert Fizdale, *The Divine Sarah: A Life of Sarah Bernhardt* (New York, 1991), 225.

13. John Higham, *Strangers in the Land: Patterns of American Nativism, 1860–1925* (New Brunswick, N.J., 1955); Haim Avni, *Argentina and the Jews: A History of Jewish Immigration,* trans. Gila Brand (Tuscaloosa, Ala., 1991); Irving Abella and Harold Troper, *None Is Too Many: Canada and the Jews of Europe, 1933–1948* (New York, 1982).

14. Samuel Guy Inman, "Refugee Settlement in Latin America," *Annals of the American Academy of Political and Social Science* (May 1939): 183.

15. Haim Avni, "Patterns of Jewish Leadership in Latin America during the Holocaust," in *Jewish Leadership during the Nazi Era: Patterns of Behavior in the Free World,* ed. Randolph L. Braham (New York, 1985), 89.

16. *Jewish Chronicle* (London), supplement of April 1936, iv–vi; *Jüdische Rundschau* (Berlin), nos. 7, 11, 12, 13, and 15, published between Jan. 24 and Feb. 21, 1936. Artur Ruppin, *Los Júdios de America del Sur* (Buenos Aires, 1938).

17. *Jewish Chronicle* (London), supplement of April 1936, vi. All translations are my own unless otherwise noted.

18. *Jewish Chronicle* (London), supplement of April 1936, v.

19. Rapport de L'administration centrale au Conseil d'Administration (Report of the Central Administration of the Administrative Council of the Jewish Colonization Association), hereafter RACCA, 1935, 197. Archives of the Jewish Colonization Association, London, hereafter JCA-L.

20. Alfred Hirschberg, "The Economic Adjustment of Jewish Refugees in São Paulo," *Jewish Social Studies* 7 (1945): 37.

21. Alice Irene Hirschberg, *Desafio e Resposta: A História da Congregação Israelita Paulista* (São Paulo, 1976), 17. Complete collections of the *Crónica Israelita* can be found in the Biblioteca Alfred Hirschberg of the Congregação Israelita Paulista (São Paulo) and in microfilm at the American Jewish Archives (Cincinnati).

22. *Jewish Chronicle* (London), supplement of April 1936, vi.

23. Jewish Colonization Association, Bureau de Rio de Janeiro affilie a la HIAS-JCA-EMIGDIRECT, "Report for the year 1932." Séance du Conseil d'administration (Meeting of the Administrative Council), hereafter SCA (Mar. 16, 1933), 243–44. JCA-L.

24. Herbert Frankenstein, *Brasilien: Als Aufnahmeland der Jüdischen Auswanderung aus Deutschland* (Berlin, 1936).

25. Although entry quotas demanded that 80 percent of all immigrants to Brazil be farmers or rural workers, 1937 statistics published by the Brazilian Institute of Geography and Statistics (which was part of the Ministry of Foreign Affairs) show only 22 percent actually were. Instituto Brasileiro de Geografia e Estatística, *Brazil 1938: A New Survey of Brazilian Life* (Rio de Janeiro, 1939), 43–45.

26. For more on the birth and death of Rezende, see Avraham Milgram, "A Colonização Agrícola a Refugiados Judeus no Brasil, 1936–1939," in *Proceedings of the Tenth World Congress of Jewish Studies* (Jerusalem, 1990), 583–93.

27. RACCA-1937, 66. Arquivo Histórico Judaico Brasileiro, São Paulo.

28. "Rapport Sur L'Activité de la JCA (Dec. 1936–Jan. 1937). SCA (Feb. 1937) I, 131. JCA-L. Sir Osmond d'Avigdor Goldsmid (London) to Under Secretary of State (London) Apr. 29, 1937. SCA (June 29, 1937) I, 113. JCA-L.

29. Mr. Coote (Rio de Janeiro) to British Foreign Office (London), Sept. 23, 1937. O 371/2060 A 6925/78/6. Public Records Office, London, hereafter PRO-L.

30. Labienne Salgado dos Santos "Inconvenientes da Emigração Semita" attached to Ciro de Freitas Vale (Bucharest) to Aranha, Sept. 12, 1938, Maço 10.561 (741). Arquivo Histórico Itamaraty, Rio de Janeiro (Archive of the Brazilian Foreign Ministry), hereafter AHI-R.

31. Letter of Filinto Müller to Francisco Campos, Feb.5, 1938. Maço 10.561 (741). AHI-R.

32. Milgram, "A Colonização Agrícola," 585.

33. Dulphe Pinheiro Machado, Jan. 9, 1937. PRCNE-Serie Intercambio Comércial, Lata 174-No. 468—1936. Arquivo Nacional, Rio de Janeiro (Brazilian National Archives).

34. Hugh Gurney (British Embassy—Rio) to Anthony Eden (Principal Secretary of State—London), Dec. 31, 1936. FO 371/20604 A78/78/6, 15–17. PRO-L.

35. Gurney (Rio) to Mr. Troutbeck (London), Apr. 1, 1937. FO 371/20604 A2910/78/6. R.G. Gahagon (Foreign Office—London) to Sir Osmond d'Avigdor Goldsmid (London), Apr. 27, 1937. FO 371/20604 A2910/78/6. PRO-L.

36. Leo S. Rowe (Washington) to Aranha (Rio de Janeiro), Apr. 5, 1937. OA 37.04.05. Centro de Pesquisa e Documentação de História Contemporânea do Brasil, Fundação Getúlio Vargas, Rio de Janeiro (Center for Research and Documentation on the Contemporary History of Brazil).

37. Department of State Memorandum of Conversation between Alfred Houston, Laurence Duggan, and Mr. Manning (Division of American Republics), Feb. 16, 1938. 832.52 Germans/10 LH. National Archives and Record Administration, Washington.

38. Coote (Rio) to British Foreign Office (London), Sept. 23, 1937. FO 371/2060 A 6925/78/6. PRO-L.

39. *Diário Oficial—Estado do Rio de Janeiro,* Apr. 6, 1938.

40. Heinz Lewinsky, interviewed by Denise Simanke, [n.d.], Oral History Archives of the Instituto Cultural Judaico Marc Chagall, Porto Alegre.

41. *Diário Oficial—Estado do Rio de Janeiro,* Apr. 6, 1938.

42. *O Carioca* (Rio), Apr. 6, 1938; *Correio da Manhã* (Rio), Apr. 6, 1938; *A Opinião* (Rezende), Apr. 9, 1938; *A Lyra* (Rezende), Apr. 7, 1938.

43. "Exposição das demarches feitas pela Jewish Colonization Association junto ao Governo Brasileiro, com o propósito de trazer imigrantes agricultores para sua Fazenda de Rezende, Estado do Rio." PRRE. Box 27.586, Document 185660—1938. Arquivo Nacional, Rio de Janeiro.

44. *Idische Presse* (Imprensa Israelita—Rio), July 8, 1938; *Diário de Notícias* (Rio), Oct. 19, 1938.

45. *A Noite* (Rio), June 30, 1938.

46. *Diário de Notícias* (Rio), Oct. 19, 1938.

47. *A Noite* (Rio), June 30, 1938.

48. "Report of Mr. Tracy Phillips, Jan. 13, 1939," SCA (May 6, 1939) II. JCA-L.

49. JCA-Rio to Louis Oungre, JCA New York. Dec. 9, 1942. Fundo JCA, Box 14 (Diverse Correspondence re: Rezende, 1936–1944). Arquivo Histórico Judaico Brasileiro, São Paulo.

50. Herbert V. Levy, *Problemas actuaes da economia brasileira* (São Paulo, 1934), 104. When Levy was asked if ethnic solidarity might be a reason for his support of the entry of German Jews and his desire to prohibit Arab immigration, he replied that "neither [I] nor my close ancestors are Jewish." Herbert V. Levy, "A proposito de uma carta aberta ao Dr. José Maria Whitaker," in *As Vantagens da Immigração Syria no Brasil em torno de uma polêmica entre os Snrs. Herbert V. Levy e Salomão Jorge, no "Diario de São Paulo,"* ed. Amarilio Junior (Rio de Janeiro, 1935), 46.

51. Rabbi Fritz Pinkuss, interview by author, Aug. 19, 1986, São Paulo.

52. Jeffrey Lesser, "Diferencias regionales en el desarrollo histórico de las comunidades judeo-brasileñas contemporáneas: San Pablo y Porto Alegre," *Estudios Migratorios Latinoamericanos* 4 (1989): 71–84.

53. Bernhard Wolff, interview by author, July 21, 1986, Porto Alegre. Herbert Caro, "SIBRA 50 Anos," in *Sociedade Israelita Brasileira de Cultura e Beneficência, 1936–1986* (Porto Alegre, 1986), 48. Léons de Poncins, *As Forças Secretas da Revolução—Maçonaria e Judaismo* (Porto Alegre, 1931).

54. Oscar Messias Cardoso "A Emigração Israelita Através do Mundo," *Correio da Manhã,* Aug. 27, 1933. Cardoso apparently was unaware that the JCA was unable to find many Jewish farmers in Germany.

55. "Who's Who" (unsigned and undated diplomatic note). Hugh Gibson Collection, Box 99, Folder "Diplomatic Posts, Brazil (Rio de Janeiro) General." Hoover Institution Archives, Stanford, Calif. Ildefonso Falcão to Afranio de Mello Franco, June 27, 1933. EC/191/558/Reservado/1935/Annexo. Maço 10.561 (741). AHI-R.

56. Ildefonso Falcão to Afranio de Mello Franco, June 27, 1933. EC/191/558/Reservado/1935/Annexo. Maço 10.561 (741). AHI-R.

57. Sara Donceds (Rio de Janeiro) to Rabbi Louis I. Egelson (Union of American Hebrew Congregations, Cincinnati, Ohio), Jan. 30, l934. MSS Collection no. 16, Box 2, Folder 5—Brazil. American Jewish Archives, Cincinnati.

58. Bernhard Wolff, interview by author, July 21, 1986, Porto Alegre. Herbert Caro, "SIBRA 50 Anos," in *Sociedade Israelita Brasileira de Cultura e Beneficência, 1936–1986* (Porto Alegre, 1986), 7.

59. "Em Memória dos sócios falecidos e seus familiares, 1936–1986," Arquivo Bernhard Wolff (Porto Alegre).

60. Jeffrey Lesser, "Historische Entwicklung und regionale Unterschiede der zeitgenössischen brasilianisch-jüdischen Gemeinden: São Paulo und Porto Alegre," trans. Petra Möbius, in *Europäische Juden in Lateinamerika,* ed. Achim Schrader and Karl H. Rengstorf (St. Ingbert, 1989), 361–77.

61. For more on conflicts between German and Eastern European Jews in Brazil, see Jeffrey Lesser, "Continuity and Change within an Immigrant Community: The Jews of São Paulo, 1924–1945," *Luso-Brazilian Review* 25 (1988): 45–58.

62. Alice Irene Hirschberg, *e Resposta: A História da Congregação Israelita Paulista* (São Paulo, 1976), 17.

63. Rabbi Fritz Pinkuss, interview by author, Aug. 19, 1986, São Paulo.

64. Roney Cytronowicz and Judith Zuquim, *Avanhandava: A construção de um projeto para a juventude* (São Paulo, 1999), 25.

PART 3

Islands of Germanness

The diverse communities of ethnic Germans scattered across Central and Eastern Europe are the best-known groups in the German diaspora; they include settlements in Galicia, Volhynia, Bessarabia, Bukovina, the Volga, and Transylvania, to name a few of the most prominent. Certainly, these communities have occupied the most prominent position in domestic German debates about the *Auslandsdeutsche*. Ethnic German communities in Eastern and Central Europe date from different periods and have diverse political histories. Some (such as the Russian Germans or the *Siebenbürger Sachsen*) were the result of medieval or early modern emigration from the Holy Roman Empire to various destinations in Eastern Europe; others (such as the Sudeten Germans) were suddenly recast as "stranded communities" of ethnic Germans after the collapse of the Hapsburg Empire in 1918; a third group consisted of former citizens of the German Empire who lived in territories given to other nations after 1918 (such as the Germans in parts of Silesia who went to Poland after the war). In domestic German discussions, these varied groups were often referred to as *Sprachinseln* (which can be loosely translated as "islands of Germanness"), scattered across a sea of Slavic cultures.

The chapters on these heterogenous communities are presented together not only because these groups were all located in Europe but also because these chapters all show how ethnic Germans performed two functions within domestic German politics. First (like other diasporic German communities), their claims on Germany—or even their mere existence—were used by Germans to affirm notions of their own national character, even as ethnic Germans also challenged concepts of German citizenship. Ethnic Germans from Central and Eastern Europe played another role in German political debates as well: seen as legitimate objects of German concern, their existence strongly influenced German foreign policy after 1918 and often provided a rationale for Germany's claims on other nations' territories (the Sudetenland is one of the best-known examples).

After 1918 ethnic Germans in Central and Eastern Europe were drawn into increasingly problematic and complicated legal, political, and financial relationships with the German state. As Renate Bridenthal's chapter on the Russian Germans shows, far-flung political networks of ethnic Germans in Eastern Europe could exploit the German homeland's fascination with Germans abroad to obtain financial and logistical support from the German state. Pieter Judson's chapter, on the other hand, discusses German speakers in the Hapsburg lands and argues that the term *diaspora* must be used with caution (if at all) in discussing these groups before 1918. Before World War I, German-speaking nationalists in the Hapsburg Empire usually defined themselves without reference to the German Empire and did not see themselves as part of a diaspora. Only after 1918, as outsider minorities in the new Eastern European nation-states, did some German speakers begin to turn to the Reich. As Nancy Reagin's and Doris Bergen's chapters demonstrate, Germans in the Reich did initially see the Auslandsdeutsche in Eastern Europe as possessing an essentialized national character. But after the start of World War II, once millions of such ethnic Germans came under German control, ethnic and national categories "on the ground" were revealed as blurred and messy, and German military occupation authorities discovered that, in practice, ethnic identity could be labile, complex, or unclear in Eastern Europe. Nazi authorities' treatment of such ethnic Germans in occupied Europe was therefore often arbitrary and uneven, and the reaction of such *Volksdeutschen* to the Reich's policies varied widely. Stefan Wolff's chapter takes up the story of many of these groups after 1945, when—having fled or been expelled to West Germany—they continued to attempt to preserve their group identities and to influence German foreign policy, albeit now from within instead of outside Germany proper. As Wolff's contribution makes clear, the last chapter on the relationship between the state and ethnic Germans abroad has not yet been written, as Germany attempts to resolve the legacies and claims that the islands of Germanness left behind.

CHAPTER 8

Germans from Russia

The Political Network of a Double Diaspora

Renate Bridenthal

There are Germans whose dream landscape is not forests and mountains but wide open plains under a big sky. These are the Russian Germans, transplanted farmers whose origin was in the crowded Southwest German states in the eighteenth century but whose paradise and souls' *Heimat* became the Russian steppe, a paradise lost after a century and resought on the plains and pampas of North and South America. *Volk auf dem Weg,* the name of the newsletter of the Germany-based Landsmannschaft der Deutschen aus Russland, aptly captures their identity as colonists on the move, as economic migrants in the beginning and later as postwar transferred populations. In this chapter, I attempt to trace how this identity was constructed and maintained over the course of a century and a span of three continents by a select group of intellectuals, variously motivated to mobilize this far-flung constituency for a commonly understood interest.

Germans from Russia were land-hungry farmers who emigrated from the Southwest German states in the late eighteenth century as colonists to Russia. In 1763—enticed by special privileges, including tax and military exemptions, self-governance, and cultural autonomy—they accepted the invitation of the German-born tsarina Catherine the Great of Russia to settle hitherto uncultivated land along the Volga River and to model then-modern agricultural techniques to the surrounding Russian peasants. Others followed. In 1774 a victorious war against the Ottoman Empire brought the Black Sea area into the Russian Empire, opening more lands to such colonization. In 1803 a pioneering contingent from Swabia arrived in that region around the newly founded (1794) Odessa, followed by a larger immigration from Württemberg, Baden, Alsace, and the Palatinate upon special invitation in 1804 by Tsar Alexander I. Other land-hungry

German farmers settled in other parts of the Russian Empire in the early nineteenth century—Bessarabia, Wolhynia, and Transcaucus—alleviating social tensions in the German states.

There was no "German question" in Russia until the 1861 emancipation of the serfs, when their condition of indebtedness and resulting land hunger made a stark contrast with the prosperity enjoyed by German colonists, who, thanks to their privileges, had succeeded, especially in the Black Sea area, in acquiring ever more land for their burgeoning population.[1] This class distinction carried ethnic stereotypes, with Germans being accused of arrogance and clannishness. However, not until the establishment of a united German state in 1871 did suspicions of possible treason seriously raise a "German question." In the 1880s the Russian military began to fret over the security risk posed by these potential enemy aliens in the border areas, while the nationalist press agitated against the "peaceful conquest" by German property owners. Further inland, near the Black Sea, these Germans became scapegoats for the lack of land reform that disadvantaged Ukrainian and Russian peasants.[2]

Late-nineteenth-century state building and the accompanying rise in nationalism made Russo-German relations ever more precarious. Furthermore, Tsar Alexander II attempted to equalize the recently freed serfs with German colonists by removing the latter's century-old privileges. With this, the first of the Russian German *Volk* got on their *Weg.* Some went back to Germany. But more followed the lure of American railroad recruiters, who sought cheap labor and settlers for government-granted land.

In 1905 the outbreak of war and revolution in Russia stimulated further emigration. In the first year of World War I, Tsar Nicholas II sought to solve land hunger by expropriating the German colonists. He also threatened to deport them eastward, away from the possibility of serving as a fifth column for the advancing German army, as Stalin actually did in the next world war. Hence, the February Revolution of 1917 seemed to promise relief to the colonists, but the October Bolshevik Revolution brought many of them in on the side of the Whites. The defeat of the latter caused an exodus to Germany, a way station for many who continued on to North and South America. In all, from 1870 to 1920 an estimated 120,000 Russian Germans entered the United States, settling mainly in Dakota territory.[3] Those who remained in Russia had their private landholdings expropriated, and they either remained to work on the collective farms or moved into the cities and other professions. Early Soviet nationalities policy allowed the establishment of an Autonomous Volga Soviet Republic with cultural pre-rogatives for its German majority. It survived from 1924 to 1941, when Germany invaded again.

The next major exodus again followed on the heels of a German army retreat from Russia, this time after its defeat in World War II. While Stalin's deportations of German colonists from the Volga region had removed them from the military front, most of those in the Western Ukraine remained and either volunteered or were enlisted in the Nazi war effort. With the Nazi defeat, about three hundred thousand Russian Germans fled westward into Germany. Two-thirds of them were forcefully repatriated by the advancing Red Army; some thirty thousand fled abroad; and another seventy thousand remained in Germany.[4]

Finally, the dissolution of the Soviet Union in 1990 occasioned a huge mass exodus of about 1.5 million people claiming German descent and hence West German citizenship. Their integration into German society is a major contemporary problem addressed by social workers, social scientists, and historians and is complicated by the unification of the former two German states.

Remarkably, dispersion itself became a source of unique identity for these originally provincial and clannish farmers. This was largely due to the sustained efforts of an intellectual elite networking over time and space to represent the interests of its constituency and to try to mobilize it politically. Through pulpit, press, and research institutes, a few dedicated nationalists created and maintained an identity of these diasporic Germans, a *Volk auf dem Weg,* which persists to this day on the basis of a common ancestry.

The work of these nationalists was complicated by several factors. First, the Russian Germans formed no coherent unity before their displacement from Russia, having left Germany at different times and for different reasons and having settled far apart in different regions of Russia. They brought at best a local provincial patriotism with them, which took the form of naming their new villages after the ones they had left in Germany. Indeed, they brought the same names to the American frontier, and even now genealogical searches are done by village origin. Second, their further emigration abroad complicated the notion of "homeland." Most emigrants related emotionally to their particular settlement in Russia as *Heimat,* whereas Germany, the *alte Heimat,* was a constructed historical memory designed more to appeal to the state of Germany for help than to the colonists themselves. This cultural and mnemonic displacement particularly challenged the creation of a clear ethnic identity. Third, the dispersion of Russian Germans to the Western Hemisphere, where relative prosperity and pressures to assimilate attenuated their connection with both the Heimat and the alte Heimat, provided another obstacle to diaspora leaders.

In spite of all these difficulties, a cultural identity was forged. Here I trace, through a select number of individuals, three of the main networks that made possible a sense of commonality and attempted mobilization on behalf of the group as a whole. These are Johannes Schleuning, a pastor who used his church connections on behalf of nationalist unity; Karl Stumpp, a genealogist who put his training at the service of irredentist politics; the Sallet family of journalists, whose publications probably did the most for sustaining the links between Russian Germans across time, space, and changing political contexts; and Emma Schwabenland Haynes, an American descendant of Russian Germans, historian, and bridge between the Old World and the New World.

Johannes Schleuning, 1879–1962: God and the Volk: The Church Connection

The life of Johannes Schleuning spans the most disruptive period of Russian German history. His active involvement in most of its politics reveals the importance of the Protestant Church as an institution of this diasporic network. Although colonists subscribed to various forms of Christianity, Lutheranism was the most integral to German national identity. The Catholic Church was by definition more inclusive, and the Mennonites were more separatist. Religious divisions were often fierce, as were regional ones and possibly those of class, though the last has been underresearched.[5] It took a lot of conscious work to bring these various groups together, even as their histories converged in the twentieth century, and in this project the Protestant pastors were instrumental. A very important pastor for this project was Johannes Schleuning, who found in the church a ready living, lodging on his many travels, and a far-flung network of supporters for German cultural and national cohesion, bound as the Lutheran clergy were to the German language for textual exegesis and prayer.

The young Schleuning was intellectually ambitious, which was exceptional for a *Kolonistensohn.* He was educated at Dorpat University in Estonia, a major theological center for German Lutheranism in Russia but also an ideological battleground between emergent Russian and German nationalisms. A stronghold of orthodox Lutheranism and German national consciousness, the university's theological faculty provided young Schleuning with a new faith: Germanism (*Deutschtum*). The German people had been chosen by God; Schleuning swore to serve them body and soul.[6]

When radicalized Russian students took part in the revolution of 1905, Dorpat University was rent by conflict. The Russian government armed the German student fraternities, Schleuning among them, to defend the great landowning Baltic German barons who were threatened by their tenants and landless laborers.[7] But the turmoil sent many of the students fleeing "home" to Germany for the first time, where they were accepted into universities; Schleuning came to Greifswald with free tuition, bed, and board. He also visited Berlin, where he met with leaders of Baltic refugees and made his first bid for political leadership, hoping to link the Northern and Southern Germans in Russia, which became a lifelong goal.

In 1908, back in a stabilized and partially democratized Russia, Schleuning returned to the church, which he now saw as important for the formation of Volk consciousness among the dispersed Germans. In 1910 he assumed the post of assistant pastor in Tiflis, the capital of Georgia, where he was alarmed by the colonist youths' assimilative tendencies. To counter their Russification, he hired a dozen new German-speaking religion teachers and established secular programs of German culture through the *Deutscher Verein,* which he headed. He took over publication of the local newspaper, *Die Kaukasische Post,* bringing in Reich German editors, whose nationalist views caused the paper to be forbidden during World War I. Schleuning himself kept informed about struggles in "the motherland" by reading German newspapers and by visiting Germany again in 1911. Finally, he clarified his identity as a diasporic pastor with a mission to bridge the colonist, Baltic, and Reich Germans on behalf of *Deutschtumsarbeit* and sealed this resolve with his marriage to a Baltic German woman, a sister of a fraternity brother.[8] But the idyll was soon to end.

World War I intensified revolutionary movements everywhere; most dramatically, it brought down the Russian Empire. Class struggle assumed an ethnic edge in places. Not only were Germans invading, but an anti-German feeling had been growing among the population. The German colonists were envied for their acquisition of ever more land in the midst of a mass of indebted peasantry, fueling resentment especially in Bessarabia and the Black Sea area, where colonists owned at least twice as much land as their proportion in the population and employed landless peasants as agricultural labor.[9] And then the German armies arrived.

For Pastor Schleuning, it meant exile. His Germanophilism, as expressed in *Die Kaukasische Post,* and his programs for the Deutscher Verein were deemed to be support for the enemy; he was sent to Tobolsk in Siberia on his own recognizance. He was soon joined by his family and became connected to the local church, which provided him with remarkably pleasant memories of Sunday afternoons with other cultivated German exiles.[10] Had he remained near the front, things would have been much worse.

During this time German schools and newspapers were closed down, the language was forbidden in public places, and village names were Russified. Worst of all, within a broad band on the western front, a law of February 2, 1915, required Germans to sell all property acquired beyond the originally deeded land and to leave their relatively closed communities for mixed ethnic settlements in Siberia.[11] Only the war itself and ensuing revolution prevented full execution of this law.[12] While some embittered colonists did help the invading German army, most professed continued loyalty to the tsar, and about 250,000 of them served in the Russian army, mainly on the Turkish front.[13]

The revolution of 1917 engendered both hope and fear. On the one hand, the Provisional Government suspended the tsarist expropriation laws; on the other hand, landowners were potential targets in a sea of land-hungry peasants. Then the revolution went through many phases, further complicated by outside intervention. Colonist leaders scrambled to protect the interests of Russian Germans. In Moscow on April 20, 1917, the first meeting of all Russian Germans assembled eighty-six representatives from fifteen districts and founded the Association of Russian Citizens of German Nationality, which met again during August 1–3 as a congress, elected by local subgroups. Its goals were restoration of the right to Heimat, the return of expropriated properties, and freedom of religion and of cultural activity.[14] Before the October Revolution halted this experiment, Schleuning, freed by the Provisional Government from his Siberian exile, brought his assertive nationalism to it and made the delegates speak German rather than their more fluent Russian.[15] A week later, he was in Saratov at the Volga German Congress, which sought national self-determination. Schleuning attended all of its meetings and by July 1 had published the first edition of the *Saratower Deutsche Volkszeitung,* the first German-language newspaper since their prohibition. Sent far and wide to colonist settlements, it soon claimed eleven thousand subscribers but was shut down by the end of the year with the Bolshevik victory.

Civil war marked the next four years. In the Volga region, colonists resisted being drafted into the Red Army and the confiscation of their grain and livestock. In the Black Sea area, some collaborated with General Denikin's White Army.[16] Even the formally pacifist Mennonites resorted to arms when their properties were threatened.[17] In March 1918 the Treaty of Brest-Litovsk severed great swathes of Russian imperial territory and with it millions of German colonists in the Baltics, White Russia, Bessarabia, and Western Ukraine. Those remaining in Russia were given the option of selling their properties and emigrating within ten years. Germany itself became their last best hope.

In May 1918 Pastor Schleuning set out to *"meine Heimat, mein Volk"*—Germany—to seek help.[18] There he joined other clergy representing the various regions and denominations in addressing the Reichstag on behalf of resettling the Russian German colonists in the Reich. On a lecture tour through South Germany, he contacted the head of the newly founded German Foreign Institute (Deutsches Auslandinstitut, or DAI) in Stuttgart and worked with other Catholic and Protestant clergy to develop the image of a homogeneous ethnic group of two million *Volksdeutsche* in Russia. Thus, the diverse, closed, and sometimes contentious villages began to achieve a unifying identity, Russian Germandom, in the face of, and probably because of, persecution. Schleuning's mission, dating back to his Dorpat student days, was on the verge of realization.

By October Schleuning had brought his family to Berlin, where he worked full-time as head of the press section of the Association for Germans Abroad (VDA), helping to place former Russian German leaders and getting scholarships for refugee students.[19] But yearning to reestablish contact with Russia, he volunteered to reenter and make contact with the White Army. With agreement of the German Foreign Office, support of the VDA, a visa provided by the Interallied Commission, and a recommendation from the Russian Embassy to the counterrevolutionary General Denikin, Schleuning entered South Russia through the Dardanelles. The church connection provided him with bed and board wherever he went, but he was disappointed that the White Army refused to arm the local colonists. In the end, Schleuning found himself fleeing with all the rest, arriving home in November only to confront another revolution in Germany.[20]

Not only was Germany torn by revolution, but it soon found itself flooded with refugees and truncated territorially, with millions of German speakers left as minority islands in the successor states formed by the Paris Peace Treaties. The Weimar Republic's liberal laws of association led to the formation of dozens of self-help groups, some of them bitterly irredentist. Pastor Schleuning lost no time in organizing the Association of Volga Germans (Verein der Wolgadeutschen), made up of thousands who had left Russia.[21] Similar organizations formed for former colonists in the Black Sea region, Volhynia, Caucasus, and North Russia. In March 1919 these groups united in Berlin to form the Central Committee of Germans from Russia, headed by Schleuning and assisted by other clergy and businessmen.[22] Other such groups formed in the early 1920s, the loss of German state territory being compensated by more global claims of ethnicity. The head of the VDA observed that Germans were losing their state but gaining their Volk, and indeed VDA membership and activities peaked at this time.[23] Another important new organization was the DAI, established in Stuttgart in 1917 by a royal commission headed by the crown prince to strengthen the bonds of diasporic Germans with their homeland. It became a semipublic institution financed largely by the national government, with supplements by the state of Württemberg and private contributions, pioneering in the field of genealogy. The 1920s were also the heyday of *Ostforschung,* research about Germans abroad in universities and special institutes.[24]

But activists like Schleuning had a more practical agenda. The diasporic network of Russian Germans had to be expanded further afield. Offers of help in letters from relatives in the United States encouraged the association to organize aid from there. The clerical connection was an obvious one, so Schleuning set out on what became a sixteen-month lecture and fund-raising trip. On a whirlwind tour through Kansas, Nebraska, Colorado, Ohio, Iowa, California, Washington, Oregon, Illinois, Wisconsin, and North and South Dakota, and speaking sometimes two or three times a day, Schleuning raised about ten thousand dollars in cash and kind on the spot, with more to follow.[25]

But the most important result of the trip was the establishment of contact itself and the development of the notion that Russian Germans were a unique diaspora, a particular branch of Volksdeutsche, with a distinct identity to be maintained. Americans of Russian German descent representing local associations visited the colonies in Russia and the associations in Berlin. Other German minorities in Romania, Czechoslovakia, and Yugoslavia were tapped for aid for the famine-stricken Germans in Russia. In 1922 Prussia allowed a special mission,

Brüder in Not, to collect for them, although times were hard in Germany itself. And Schleuning wrote endlessly for the cause, including three books: *Geschichte der deutschen Kolonien an der Wolga, In Kampf und Todesnot,* and *Das Deutschtum in der Sowjetunion.*

Meanwhile, in 1924 the now stabilized Soviet Union allowed the establishment of an Autonomous Republic of Volga Germans, congruent with its resumption of diplomatic relations with Germany under the Treaty of Rapallo of 1922. Two-thirds of the republic's approximate population of five hundred thousand were Germans, but most of these refused to participate in government. The Soviet state was eager for capital, machinery, and expertise from Germany, but it heavily censored the literature that it deemed reactionary, including some of Schleuning's own writings.[26] Still, a cultural bridge of politically trusted Germans and Russian Germans sustained contacts between the two countries until the collectivization of the late 1920s brought such contacts to near collapse.

The collectivization of agriculture beginning in 1929 affected Germans very keenly, as they were disproportionately represented among kulaks, defined as farmers who produced a surplus beyond family needs and who employed labor and machinery.[27] Of these, some resisted forcibly, which resulted in either their death, deportation to the East, or their flight to the cities. The campaign against religion led to confiscation of church goods, and clergy considered subversive were deported in large numbers. Moscow was flooded with thousands of applicants for exit permits, but most countries suffering economic depression refused immigrants.[28] The famine of 1932–33 was denied by the Soviet government as hostile propaganda, with the result that little aid could get through at first. However, by 1934 money and packages from émigré and religious associations arrived and were distributed, often by pastors, although this aid was dubbed "Hitlerite."[29]

Schleuning's memoir, typical of his generation, grossly abbreviates the story of his life during the Nazi period into a mere twenty pages and fails to mention his early entry into the Nazi Party.[30] Nevertheless, he acknowledges accepting the post of Church Superintendent of Berlin Land I in 1934, which put him in charge of thirty-two pastors until 1945.[31] He also continued with the VDA, which worked with the churches before being Nazified and taken over by the SS-run ideologically racist Volksdeutsche Mittelstelle (VoMi).[32] The various Russian German émigré associations, including Schleuning's Association of Volga Germans, were unified in 1935 into the Verband der Deutschen aus Russland. In 1938 it too was subsumed by the VoMi and renamed

Verband der Russlanddeutschen (VRD) to indicate its ambition to include Germans still living in Russia.[33] Its organ became the *Deutsche Post aus dem Osten* (*DPO*), whose stated purpose was to mobilize "Russian Germandom" in all the world and to join it to the German *Muttervolk* under the leadership of Adolf Hitler.[34]

In fact, the *DPO* got reports from all over the world. The pastors' network alone brought a list of 280 Russian Germans living in Charbin, Manchukuo. A visiting schoolteacher reported on Russian German sharecroppers in Argentina.[35] At the VRD's June 1939 meeting in Stuttgart, reports from branches included Bulgaria, Yugoslavia, Argentina, and Brazil. An estimated two million Russian Germans were dispersed over the globe: roughly 400,000 in the United States, 200,000 in Canada, 250,000 in Brazil, and 150,000 in Argentina, with the remaining one million living mostly in Russia, making them the largest single group of Germans outside the Reich.[36]

In Germany itself, the VRD tried to expand its membership of about 1,500 by recruiting from the estimated 40,000 to 50,000 Russian Germans resettled in Germany from the former Russian Empire. The VRD's head, Adolf Frasch, complained that the Russian German tendency toward local, even village, particularism hampered efforts to elevate their broader Germanic consciousness.[37] One attempted lure was irredentism: nine million hectares of land worth seven billion gold marks were estimated to have been expropriated or abandoned; the *DPO* published a table of the acreage and asserted the legal claims of the former German colonists.

Eventually, the war cut off most contacts, and the Russian German organizations turned their attention to the Russian "homeland," hoping the invading German army would liberate it. We turn our attention next to another leading figure of the Russian German diaspora, one who had a different approach to networking.

Karl Stumpp, 1896–1982: The Family as Volk: Genealogy

If Schleuning was adventurous and sociable, always striding into an ever-widening world, Karl Stumpp was pedantic, an isolated researcher hunched over names and numbers, collating tables and charts and traveling only in the last instance. Seventeen years younger than Schleuning, Stumpp was born at Alexanderhilf, a German colony near Odessa, the gifted son of a farmer. He continued his higher education in Dorpat and in Odessa, and along with other young students he followed the retreating German armies of 1918 to Germany. He came to the University of Tübingen, where in 1922 he wrote a dissertation that was to define his life's work: "The German Colonies in the Black Sea Region." Equally important were the ties he formed with fellow émigré students, who became future colleagues as diaspora leaders. This "old boy" network included Georg Leibbrandt, his future superior in the SS, and Georg Rath, who became a pastor and major contact in the United States.[38] Newly married to another exiled Russian German, Stumpp accepted a post teaching in the German secondary school for girls at Tarutino in Bessarabia, which the peace treaties had transferred from Russia to Romania in 1918. For the next eleven years, he not only taught there but engaged in a variety of German nationalist extracurricular activities: he established a youth organization, trained choirs, lectured throughout Bessarabia on the history of the Germans in Russia, and began his monumental genealogical research.[39]

Stumpp's real opportunity came with Hitler's accession to power, which occasioned his move to Stuttgart, the informal headquarters of *Auslandsdeutsche.* There he found work as a business manager for the VDA, which in the ensuing two years increased its membership and treasury more than tenfold.[40] Its head, Hans Steinacher, had set up a research collective, the Volksdeutsche Forschungsgemeinschaften (VFG), in 1934 that gave special attention to German Americans, with a view to strengthening their ethnic consciousness by encouraging pen pals. Hitler Youth were enlisted for a letter-writing campaign and within a year had collected 15,680 addresses. Some thought the most reachable would be the relatively unassimilated Russian German farmers in western North Dakota, whose feebler connection to America was further frayed by dust bowl conditions and who, as agriculturalists, might be lured into returning as settlers of reconquered land.[41]

The VFG was an association of cultural researchers who worked together with the VDA, the Ministry of the Interior, the Nazi Party's Auslandsorganisation, and the Nazified DAI. In 1938 Stumpp found his niche there when the VRD merged into the DAI and made him director of its newly established research office on the Russian Germans, the Forschungsstelle des Russlanddeutschtums im Deutschen Ausland-Institut (FstR), in Berlin. A year earlier, he had joined the Nazi Party.[42]

In his first two years at the FstR, Stumpp went to work contacting Russian Germans all over the world. He wrote to Russian German publications abroad, announcing the establishment of the new research group, and succeeded in getting free subscriptions from several. His old Tübingen fraternity brother, Georg Rath, now a pastor in Nebraska and a member of the VRD, saw to it that he got the *Dakota Freie Presse,* to which Rath was a frequent contributor.[43] The pastoral connection was also valuable in providing access to congregations.

Stumpp's research was soon interrupted by the unfolding events of World War II. The secret agreement between Germany and the Soviet Union revising the Treaty of Paris on the Eastern Front included restoring Romania's Bessarabia to Russia. In 1921 a Romanian land reform law had expropriated properties over one hundred hectares, redistributing them to the landless, which made Bessarabian German landowners an embittered and hostile ethnic minority.[44] The advent of Soviet control in June 1940 was the last straw, as the occupying Red Army supported the agricultural laborers against the remaining landowners, who were now forced to sell their properties. In the summer of 1940, Stumpp, who had taught school in Bessarabia for eleven years, became one of several officials assigned to assist the transfer of Bessarabian Germans "home into the Reich." It was a windfall for later genealogical research. Stumpp was able to send about fifteen boxes of copied church registers to the DAI, intended to establish contacts with American relatives of the transferred Bessarabian German population.[45] In 1941 Stumpp and Heinrich Roemmich, his future collaborator in Russian German matters, visited one of several temporary camps for displaced Bessarabians to urge them to fill out forms tracing three generations, including those who had emigrated to America or elsewhere.[46] But an even larger task awaited Stumpp as war loomed.

Germany's territorial acquisitions led to some reorganization of the foreign affairs bureaucracy, and Stumpp's FstR came under the jurisdiction of the Political Section of the Nazi Ministry for the Occupied Eastern Territories, headed by Alfred Rosenberg. Rosenberg, a Baltic German who had fled the Russian Revolution of 1917, appointed Georg Leibbrandt as head of the Political Section. Like Stumpp, Leibbrandt was an émigré from the Odessa region and had also studied in Dorpat, as had both Schleuning and Stumpp. Having served as a translator for the invading German army in 1918, Leibbrandt joined its retreat to Germany and, like Stumpp, his classmate at the University of Tübingen, made Russian Germans his field of expertise.[47] He joined the Nazi Party in 1931, even before Hitler's accession to power.[48]

In 1935 Leibbrandt helped to unite the competing Russian German associations, such as Schleuning's Association of Volga Germans, into the unified VDR, with a view to instrumentalizing it for Germany's anticipated moves eastward.[49] With the German invasion of Russia in

June 1941, Leibbrandt chose his friend Stumpp to head a special action unit, designated Sonderkommando Dr. Stumpp, to follow the armies into Ukraine for the purpose of cataloging the German settlements there. The ethnographic reports thus compiled were intended in the first instance to locate Axis-friendly areas during the war, to underpin German administration of the occupied East, and to ascertain the value of previously German-owned properties with an eye to future compensation.[50] The collected material remains an important source even today for researchers of Germans in Russia, for Karl Stumpp was nothing if not thorough.

From November 1941 to March 1943, Stumpp's team of eighty people followed in the train of the killing operations of Einsatzgruppen C and D. Scouring the countryside, they prepared a series of village reports, of which about eighty remain extant, complete with property claims and genealogies evaluating the "Germanness," both biological and cultural, of the population. Those who passed the test might qualify to administer and re-Germanize the conquered territory. Those who failed the test, either because of mixed marriages with Ukrainians or because they were communists, were likely doomed.[51] The virtually empty columns tabulating the Jewish population of the villages remained unremarked upon, although there is little doubt that the team knew what the Einsatzgruppen were doing and that some of the Ukrainian Germans' "self-defense" groups even collaborated with them.[52] However, a mournful count was made of the disproportionately high number of ethnic German women and children in the villages, most of the able-bodied men having been either drafted, deported, or executed to prevent treason.[53]

In addition to the village reports, Stumpp wrote diaries from the fall of 1941 to the spring of 1942, recording his trip through Volhynia and Ukraine on the way to his headquarters in Dniepropetrovsk.[54] These are as startling for their omissions as for their observations. He was moved to see children celebrate their first German Christmas, was heartened when he saw the swastika flag flying on homes and public buildings, and grieved over the deportations and war losses of Russian Germans who reportedly welcomed the German army with tears in their eyes. But he coolly observed that colonists had moved into newly emptied Jewish homes and that some villages were now rid of Jews (*Judenrein*), to the relief of the locals who had complained of their cooperation with Bolshevik rule.[55]

Various other accounts indicate that the long-displaced colonists neither jubilantly greeted their "liberators" nor joined the partisans against them. Eventually, several hundred participated in executing Jews, but most seemed passive, perhaps fearful of retribution by either side.[56] As a group, they benefited from the Nazi occupation in that they received the homes and goods of murdered Jews and were otherwise generally favored over the local Ukrainian population.[57] But official German military reports found them seemingly ungrateful and unmotivated, wanting only to have their farms reprivatized, while the Nazi armies considered the collective farms at least temporarily more efficient.[58]

However, the usual competing agencies and agendas within Nazism caused Leibbrandt to fall out of favor, and so, with the loss of Leibbrandt as his sponsor, Stumpp's Kommando was dissolved.[59] In any case, the German armies were on the retreat and with them came an estimated one million Russian Germans from Ukraine into the formerly Polish territories of Warthegau and from there, with the Red Army advance, westward, "home," into the ever-shrinking Reich. In the spring of 1943, Stumpp himself returned to Germany, disillusioned and blaming the Nazi bureaucracy, of which he had been a part, for once again victimizing Russian Germans. Fearing retribution by the Russians, he went underground, working under an assumed name as a farmhand in Württemberg, before settling in Tübingen, where he was reunited with his family and employed as a teacher.[60]

There is a gap in Stumpp's biography until 1950, when he resumed his genealogical work with a reestablished émigré organization, the Landsmannschaft der Deutschen aus Russland (LDR). This brought him together with Johannes Schleuning, who had resumed his pastoral duties now in Helmstedt, and Stumpp's fellow Kommando Heinrich Roemmich, now a pastor in a suburb of Stuttgart. Together the trio led the LDR until one by one they died, with Stumpp going last. Until then, for the next thirty-two years, he was an indefatigable historian of the Russian German diaspora, producing several books and countless articles.[61] He edited the LDR's newsletter, *Volk auf dem Weg,* from 1951 to 1963. From 1954 on, he inaugurated and edited the society's annual *Heimatbücher,* which brought together information on the Russian German diaspora in Canada, Brazil, Argentina, Uruguay, Paraguay, Mexico, and the United States. The *Heimatbücher* also included poems, songs, stories, and memoirs in an effort to maintain a diasporic culture; its dependence on memories of historical injustice tended toward a culture of victimization.

The postwar organization of Russian Germans in Germany began tentatively. Concerned about irredentist tendencies and wishing to foster the expellees' integration into German society, the Allies only allowed them to meet under church auspices. Pastor Roemmich headed the first Protestant self-help committee for *Ostumsiedler* (East resettlers), a code designation of the approximately one hundred thousand refugee Russian Germans, who feared that clear identification would lead to their repatriation by the occupying Russian Army. Permitted by the Basic Law of the newly founded Federal Republic in 1949, such self-help committees were the basis of later *Landsmann-schaften* (homeland provincial societies), which lobbied for services, property compensation, and pensions.

A first task for these postwar exiles in Germany was to unify their various religious organizations and to create a more powerful organization that could challenge the laws that excluded from restitution those émigrés from socialist countries whose expropriations were not war conditioned but the result of socialist revolution. This effort led to the establishment of the Arbeitsgemeinschaft der Ostumsiedler (Working Group of East Resettlers) in April 1950 with Roemmich as head.[62] This was effectively the LDR, which so renamed itself in 1957. It included in its mission the representation of Russian Germans in Russia (where they were assumed to lack representation), which allowed Roemmich to accompany Chancellor Konrad Adenauer to Moscow in 1955.[63] Roemmich personally painstakingly researched Soviet social insurance laws, which became the basis for successful case-by-case legal appeals for pensions for Russian Germans in Germany.[64] He was awarded the *Bundesverdienstkreuz* first class (the Federal Republic's highest civilian honor) in 1964; Schleuning had received his in 1957.[65]

Irredentism became a more remote goal, though it did not disappear entirely. Both Roemmich and Stumpp continued to harbor such hopes, and *Volk auf dem Weg* kept reminding its readers of the large acreage previously held by German colonists in Russia. But the LDR was a rather puny member of the umbrella Bund der Vertriebenen (League of Expellees), in which the Sudeten and Silesian Germans figured most strongly.[66] The head of the Bund, Dr. Jaksch, irritatingly pointed out at an LDR meeting in 1964 that the League of Expellees always had to beg the federal government not to forget the Russian Germans in their humanitarian efforts.[67] And, indeed, the LDR leaders themselves were frustrated by the passivity of their putative constituency of about seventy thousand, of which only two thousand joined as members.[68] New arrivals, facilitated by a German-Soviet treaty of August 1970 allowing family reunions, in general did not join the LDR.[69] And the flood unleashed by the dissolution of the Soviet

Union raised huge social problems far beyond anything the LDR could handle. Its successors represent a revived Ostforschung, notably the Institute for German and East European Research in Göttingen, the East European Institute in Munich, and the German Society for East European Research in Berlin. In addition, various German organizations such as the Goethe Institute and the German Academic Exchange have taken up the torch of diasporic outreach by establishing educational and cultural programs for Germans in Ukraine. The Evangelical Lutheran Church in Germany has sent pastors to Ukraine to reestablish religious practices and to negotiate the return of church buildings and church property to Ukrainian Germans.[70] Archives of the former Soviet Union are now being opened for researchers and for claimants of compensation.[71] Some descendants have even returned as consultants for market-oriented agribusiness with the U.S. Agency for International Development.[72] And some have just gone back to visit their ancestral villages. In the United States, where Russian Germans helped to tame the Great Plains, the passion for seeking out genealogical roots in the late 1960s affected their descendants, too.

The Sallet Family and the *Dakota Freie Presse:* News of the Volk

When Germans from Russia, who were accustomed to living in isolated villages, first arrived in the United States in the late nineteenth century, they strove mightily to keep their hard-won long-standing cultural identity. But America had a transformative effect on all its immigrants. The first group of Russian Germans to arrive on the frontier was deceived by its expanse, mistaking the Great Plains for another fertile Great Steppe. Instead, the soil turned out to be rocky and recalcitrant, unbroken to the plow. Many a pioneer gave up and fled northward to Canada, westward to California, or even southward to Brazil or Argentina. Those who stayed had to give up the ethnic communities to which they were accustomed and to disperse under the conditions of the Homestead Act, which required residence on separate individual properties.

Although they clustered their homes as near to each other as possible, no tsarist Russification decree could have done more than this property law to threaten their cultural and familial ties. It took something extra to keep these in place.[73] Besides church services, that extra link was a weekly newspaper, the *Dakota Freie Presse* (*DFP*), which ran for eighty years (1874–1954) and served primarily Russian Germans. The historical insularity of the Russian Germans made this longevity possible, and, conversely, the newspaper fostered the insulation. By 1905 it had more subscriptions than any English-language newspaper in North Dakota and was referred to as the bible of Russian Germans and more recently as their "central nervous system."[74] Across the ocean, the DAI recognized its importance for the identity and cohesion of this group.[75] Its heart and soul was Friedrich Wilhelm Sallet, who bought the paper in 1903 and published it almost continuously until his death in 1932.

F. W. Sallet was not himself a Russian German. He was born in 1859 in East Prussia, apprenticed to a printer in Königsberg in 1872, and traveled to Russia and Sweden before coming to the United States at the turn of the century. Journalism was more than a business for him: the *DFP* became a mission. Sallet personally traveled around the settlements from time to time and commented genially on world affairs in his own special column, *"Betrachtungen"* (Sallet's views). He broadened the base of the newspaper from its original constituency of Black Sea Germans to include Volga Germans, engaging stringers in the various American states, as well as Canada, Russia, Germany—and even Argentina. The *DFP* published personal letters that not only helped far-flung families to keep in touch but also brought the economic and political news of their various host countries to other readers, helping them to decide whether or not to emigrate further. It paid attention to local and national affairs, discussed elections, and editorialized, for example, against Prohibition (along with most other German immigrants). By 1913 the *DFP* had twelve thousand subscribers and probably many more readers.[76]

This congenial activity was rudely interrupted by World War I. The Russian Germans, ingrown and slow to Americanize, became prime targets of suspicion.[77] Their support of neutrality in World War I did not help their case once the United States entered the war, even though they later bought war bonds and served in the army and its auxiliaries.[78] An admittedly biased source, Sallet's nephew Richard, who visited his uncle in the United States after the war, claimed that most Russian Germans were "completely on the side of Germany" in World War I. However, with Germany being a belligerent, 17,903 charges of treason by German Americans were brought to court nationwide, of which 5,720 led to convictions; in some places even physical violence was enacted against German immigrants. German-language church services and the teaching of German in schools were prohibited.

Newspaper subscriptions plummeted, and some newspapers folded altogether. Sallet ran ads begging his subscribers to pay up, and he offered bonuses of items like low-cost sewing machines and sweaters for new subscribers.[79] Sallet himself was briefly arrested in 1918 for having failed to file a translation of two articles in violation of a 1917 federal law that required such translation of all articles dealing with the war.[80] Nevertheless, the *DFP* did what it could to help readers' families in war-torn Russia by channeling remittances to relatives and friends of readers. Although only intermittently allowed there, the newspaper published letters that provided news of the revolution and such events as the Volga German Congress at Saratov attended by Schleuning (discussed previously).[81]

When armistice was agreed, the *DFP*'s headline read "The Breath of Freedom Wafts Powerfully throughout the World!" (*Der Freiheit Hauch weht mächtig durch die Welt*). Sallet added that the late president Woodrow Wilson deserved a monument for making the world safe for democracy. However, the final, signed peace treaty was another matter; the *DFP* excoriated the Treaty of Paris and bitterly blamed France and England, the continued existence of whose empires mocked Wilson's supposed war for democracy. Nevertheless, the newspaper resumed its work of connecting Russian Germans at home and abroad. A serialized history of German colonies in Russia by a stringer in Russia aimed to repair the damage done to cultural identity in the United States by the coerced assimilation of wartime, as well as by normal generational attrition.[82] The *DFP* offered a forum for the Russian Germans who had fled from Russia into Germany after the war, who were currently in holding camps, and who needed information about further emigration; here the letters columns were most useful. For immediate relief, the *DFP* facilitated the sending of money, clothing, and food from the United States, Canada, and even Argentina to Russia and Germany. Sallet personally solicited remittances, and his brother Daniel in Osterode, East Prussia, supervised their distribution there, including channeling some through Schleuning's Association of Volga Germans.[83]

Daniel's son Richard, who came to assist his uncle Friedrich in 1921, was different altogether. Born in 1900, he had enlisted in the warring German army as soon as he could and remained a fervent nationalist all his life. A 1925 photograph of him with his uncle shows a dapper, modern, young man in light-colored slacks, standing easily with his hands behind his back and smiling engagingly.[84] His uncle's fond references suggest he was more like a son than were his own three sons, and so Richard became managing editor of the *DFP* from 1923 to 1927. During these years, he not only wrote for the newspaper but also trav-

eled through the Midwest, contacting its readers and mapping the
Russian-German settlements, which later led to a book that provided
contacts for counterpart research in Germany and is still used as a reference.[85] He estimated some fifteen hundred such settlements with over
three hundred thousand inhabitants and deemed them to be more
effective colonizers of the American West than any other nationality.
He found these settlers to be very active in local and state politics,
observing that most Protestants were Republicans while most
Catholics were Democrats. They remained close to their churches and
were less likely than Reich Germans to participate in secular social
organizations. He observed the gradual Americanization of the young:
"In not too long a time the Russian-Germans as a strong ethnic component in the United States will belong to history."[86]

Richard Sallet retained a connection to the *DFP* until he negotiated
its sale in 1932, after his uncle's death, to the *National Weeklies,* which
gave it a new profascist editorial board, consisting of John Brendel and
H. E. Fritsch. Brendel was a Catholic Black Sea German who had fled
from the Russian Revolution to the United States. Fritsch was a Viennese who, after being briefly interned as an enemy alien, was deported
to Germany in May 1942 as part of an exchange of foreign journalists.[87] Under their editorship, the *DFP* supported Franco in Spain,
Mussolini in Italy, and Hitler in Germany all the way up to the entry of
the United States in World War II. It ran ads for English translations
of *Mein Kampf;* welcomed Germany's annexation of Austria and
Czechoslovakia; labeled Winston Churchill as "England's dictator";
endorsed Germany's invasion of Russia; and defended the Axis powers' "New Order" in Europe, with its racial hierarchizing of peoples.[88]
Regarding U.S. politics, it blasted universities, especially Columbia,
for being dominated by Jews and communists.

Meanwhile, Richard Sallet did not abandon the Russian German
constituency entirely. In 1932, still in the United States, he wrote a letter to the new German government proposing an exchange of German
communists for Germans in Russia, an idea approved by Schleuning in
Germany. When this failed, *DFP* editor John Brendel collaborated
with Sallet and Pastor Georg Rath of Nebraska, Stumpp's old university classmate and frequent contributor to the *DFP,* on a memorandum to the German government protesting alleged Bolshevik persecution of Russian Germans and petitioning it "to realize the emigration
and settle our brethren in the Eastern parts of Germany." The petition
was published in the *DFP* on May 25, 1933; collected an additional
twenty-six thousand signatures; and was sent to the VDA on August

13. From there, Russian German delegates, including Schleuning, took it to the Foreign Office, again to no avail.[89] At the same time, Brendel and Rath also issued an "Appeal for the Organization of a Central Committee of the German Russians in the United States" to cooperate with the German relief agency, Brüder in Not, in sending aid to the Germans in Russia and to establish closer relations with Russian Germans elsewhere and with their organizations in Germany.[90]

How well did the Russian German diaspora in the United States respond to these efforts to mobilize it on behalf of its original homeland? Not very well. Some Russian German leaders and groups objected to the petition. And then, while the *DFP* was their most widely read newspaper, there were others, such as *Der Staatsanzeiger,* that Brendel considered had "sold out to the communists."[91] Furthermore, natural attrition due to ongoing assimilation as well as political caution caused subscriptions to the German-language press to decline throughout the United States. The *DFP* shrank from a peak of 13,800 subscriptions in 1920 to 11,000 in 1935 to 5,400 in 1944.[92]

While there can be no sure answer as to subscribers' true opinions, a small sample of German-language newspaper readers in the United States made by the Works Progress Administration at the end of the Depression found that the majority interviewed claimed to be indifferent to or uninterested in the new Germany.[93] On the other hand, David Miller, a future organizer of the American Historical Society of Germans from Russia (examined later in the chapter), seeking to establish a national committee "to counteract the Nazi propaganda that is going through the German-Russian churches and the German-Russian communities," wrote: "The situation in the German-Russian communities is really quite serious. As you know, they read very little, they do not understand governmental or political affairs, and they have an inborn love and respect for anything that could be said to be German. As a matter of fact, a large group of them are pro-Hitler without knowing the reason."[94]

While we have no way of knowing how well founded Miller's fears were, the bombing of Pearl Harbor settled matters. Even the editors of the *DFP* turned on a dime. The headline on December 17, 1941, proclaimed: "Shoulder to Shoulder We Must Defend Our Nation." The *DFP* lasted another nine years after the war, edited by Joseph Gaeckle, one of the last old-timers who had been born abroad, in Bessarabia in 1874, but had long served in public office in North Dakota. Eventually, the *DFP* lapsed to fifteen hundred subscribers and disappeared in 1954 by consolidating with the *America Herold Zeitung.*[95]

Emma Schwabenland Haynes, 1907–84: The Circle Closes

If there was one person who did the most to bring the various threads of Russian German identity together, it was Emma Schwabenland Haynes, a founder of the American Historical Society of Germans from Russia and its representative to the LDR. As liaison between these two groups, she initiated a tighter collaboration than had ever existed before, closing the circle and bringing Schleuning, Stumpp, Leibbrandt, Roemmich, and even Sallet into a transatlantic network.

Born in Portland, Oregon, in 1907 to German immigrants from the Volga colonies, Emma Schwabenland took an early interest in the genealogy of her family and the history of the group as a whole. After completing her BA in 1927 at the University of Colorado, she wrote her MA thesis in 1929 there, titled "German Russians on the Volga and in the United States." In 1930–31, she was an exchange student to the University of Breslau, which invigorated her interest in Germany, and in 1934 she visited the Soviet Union primarily to see her father's hometown, which instilled in her an enduring interest in the fate of colonist descendants still there.

From 1931 to 1945, Schwabenland was a high school history teacher in Michigan City, Indiana. Still pursuing what would become her passion, she published a brief study, *History of the Volga Relief Society,* in 1941. But it was a quiet life, and so she must have been thrilled to see history being made when she became a translator for the Nuremberg war trials from 1945 to 1947. Looking back in 1968, she reminisced about her work there as "a combined receptionist and interpreter for the German defense counsel, in charge of the office to which the lawyers came for personal interviews with their clients."[96] What's more, in the sociable atmosphere of allied personnel in Nuremberg, she met her future husband, court reporter Thomas V. Haynes, embarking in 1948 on a late but companionably lasting marriage. After a brief return to the United States, they chose to remain in Europe until 1976, following his work to diverse places, settling in 1963 on the outskirts of Frankfurt on the Main.

For Emma Haynes, this life offered her inner historian and genealogist a golden opportunity. In 1959 she wrote "My Mother's People," followed in 1965 with "My Father and His People." Though neither was intended for publication, she pursued her family history, contacting Karl Stumpp at his home in Tübingen in 1964 and the LDR in Stuttgart. In 1967 she discovered that her father's first cousin had accompanied Schleuning back to Russia in 1919 and had survived after fighting with General Denikin's army against the Bolsheviks.[97] But the real chance for her to fully engage this interest came in 1968, when David Miller, a fellow alumnus of the University of Colorado and also a descendant of Germans from Russia, wrote to her with the intriguing proposal to establish an organization that would collect materials about this ethnic group. She was delighted; the ensuing American Historical Society of Germans from Russia (AHSGR) became the professional focus of the rest of her life.[98]

Haynes decided that her best role, as a resident in Germany, was as a representative of the AHSGR to the LDR, making them in effect sister organizations. They exchanged books, maps, and genealogical information. Haynes kept up a furious pace of correspondence. In the first half of 1973 alone, she wrote about five hundred letters, most of them researched responses to genealogical inquiries.[99] The two organizations hosted each other's officers as speakers at their conventions; most importantly, they established personal relationships, the one between Haynes and Stumpp being the most enduring and rewarding. She oversaw the translation and publication of his work and in 1971 convinced the AHSGR to bring him to the United States. A photograph from his visit shows him standing erect, wrapped in an Indian blanket, sporting a full white-feathered Indian headdress and smiling enigmatically.[100]

In 1981, on his eighty-fifth birthday, Karl Stumpp was made honorary president of the AHSGR, after a long-term stint as honorary chairman, in spite of the fact that painful knowledge of his Nazi past had broken open in 1973. Adam Giesinger, a Canadian member of the AHSGR who was writing a history of Germans from Russia, discovered the Ukrainian village reports made by the team of Sonderkommando Stumpp in the Library of Congress's holdings of captured German war documents. He reported that when Stumpp saw them on his visit he expressed surprised alarm and at first denied his participation. Haynes had seen the documents a year earlier and had known "for some time" even before 1971 that Stumpp had been in Russia with the German army. She wrote soothingly that he was probably just worried about being embarrassed and saw nothing "out of line."[101] While she deplored Stumpp's negative attitude about mixed marriages, she found it not unusual for his day. She thought his Sonderkommando was in Russia only to investigate Stalin's crimes, much as postwar American teams had investigated Nazi atrocities. She did not refer to his comments in the reports that some Ukrainian villages were now *judenfrei* (free of Jews). She believed his assertion that he had never joined the

Nazi Party, because, as she contended in another context, "I love Dr. Stumpp deeply and sincerely. . . . He is sweet and kind and fantastically generous. . . . It is inconceivable to me that he could have participated in Nazi atrocities in the Ukraine. . . . I wouldn't do anything to hurt him."[102]

Haynes never changed her mind; she must not have seen his party card on her 1974 visit to the Berlin Document Center in search of other material on Germans from Russia.[103] Her long collaboration with him on innocent genealogical projects had created an emotional blind spot. A few years later, she protected Stumpp from Israeli historian Meier Buchsweiler, going so far as to visit Israel to meet him. She wrote: "After all, I am very fond of Dr. Stumpp and I didn't want to be responsible for hurting his feelings in case Buchsweiler writes something derogatory about him. I'm sure that Buchsweiler is a careful historian, but he wouldn't be human if he weren't influenced by what the Nazis did to his people."[104] But after Stumpp's death, Haynes pragmatically advised Giesinger not to omit Stumpp's anti-Semitic statements from the book he was writing: "After all, somebody else could look up the reports, and your reputation as a scholar would be jeopardized if you left them out."[105]

All of Haynes's letters exude a courteous warmth, but no one else in the LDR won her heart like Stumpp. She wrote to Richard Sallet in 1969 in North Carolina, where he was teaching, and had the AHSGR send him a membership packet.[106] She was "on the best of terms" with George Leibbrandt but doubted that he should be invited to speak at an AHSGR convention, because of "so much controversy" about him.[107] Nevertheless, he was welcomed at the June 1974 meeting of the AHSGR in Fresno, California, which Mayor Ted Wills opened as a fellow descendant of Volga Germans. There Leibbrandt was defensive, having to explain the revealed contents of the Berlin Document Center that exposed his Nazi background. He took responsibility for the Ukrainian expedition but claimed it had had a purely welfare function.[108] He did not admit at this meeting that he also had been present, though in a minor role, at the Wannsee Conference of January 1942, which organized the Final Solution for European Jewry.[109]

By attending all the meetings of the LDR, Haynes also knew Roemmich, who had accompanied Stumpp in Ukraine, and in 1972 engaged him in the matter of Soviet German emigration.[110] The AHSGR could not have taken up such a political issue, as it was a tax-exempt organization hoping to become tax deductible.[111] But after visiting the Friedland refugee camp near Göttingen in 1973, Haynes attempted some individual action on behalf of further emigration.[112] She wrote to Secretary of State Henry Kissinger and to Senator James L. Buckley of New York, who had returned from a visit to the Soviet Union with about six thousand signatures of German family heads who wanted to emigrate to Germany. She supplied Senator Buckley with names of members of the AHSGR, of its North Dakota branch (later the independent Germans from Russia Heritage Society, or GRHS), and of a Mennonite group in Kansas.[113] She also engaged Ann Sheehy of the Minority Rights Group in London in a voluminous correspondence on the matter.

For the most part, Emma Haynes avoided overt political activity and held a steadfastly moderate position on most issues pertaining to Germans from Russia. Some of this was due to her childhood memories of anti-German hysteria during World War I, which made her hypercautious "for fear of giving offense."[114] But much of it was also due to her sense of fairness and to her training as a historian, seeking and sifting evidence carefully and striving for objectivity. Mentoring aspiring scholars, many of whom sought her out for advice, she meticulously edited their drafts and warned against interpretive extremes.[115]

Emma Schwabenland Haynes formed an important bridge between Russian Germans in the Old World and the New World. She pursued her mission until the last year of her life and maintained affectionate relationships with her many correspondents. In 1984 she sent all her correspondence pertaining to the AHSGR to Washington State University, where an ethnic studies program in Germans from Russia was being considered. It did not come into being, but her legacy was saved.

Conclusion

Personal relationships clearly formed the basis of this network of diaspora leaders. Their nationalist political activism drew them to one another in the kaleidoscope of institutions dedicated to Russian German interests. Karl Stumpp, Georg Leibbrandt, and Pastor Georg Rath met as students in Tübingen in the 1920s and cooperated for decades in Germany, Ukraine, and the United States. Daniel Sallet cooperated with Pastor Johannes Schleuning after World War I, and Richard Sallet contacted him in the 1930s. Stumpp, Pastor Heinrich Roemmich, and Pastor Schleuning ran the LDR in Germany after World War II. And Emma Schwabenland Haynes completed the circle in the 1970s by contacting virtually all of them and bringing the LDR and the American groups into closer association.

The relatively coherent identity that this transnational elite forged for Russian Germans depended intellectually on a nurtured historical memory of discrimination, multiple displacement, and dispossession. Institutionally, it depended on the support of Protestant churches, German Ostforschung institutes, a dedicated press, and genealogical associations. As a deterritorialized minority, Russian Germans had encountered repression in Russia, marginalization in Germany, and assimilative pressures in the United States. Lacking an economic or political base for hegemony, their intellectual elite lacked the resources for mass mobilization. Fatefully, they came to rely on successive manifestations of the German state to realize their goals. Political mobilization eluded all their efforts; a hopeless revanchism eventually yielded to nostalgia.

Today the communications revolution has enabled a general revival of ethnic links and ethnic historicism. Both American Russian German heritage societies maintain publications and Web sites; conduct tours to the German and Russian "homelands," as well as to Russian German settlements in South America; and participate in large annual meetings in Stuttgart. As yet, no well-defined new political leadership has emerged among the new arrivals in Germany. In the contemporary world of shifting sovereignties and fluid identities, the end of this chapter of German diaspora history has yet to be written.

NOTES

The research for this chapter was made possible in part by a grant from the Professional Staff Congress—City University of New York Foundation. Special thanks go to Michael M. Miller, bibliographer of the Germans from Russia Heritage Collection in the North Dakota Institute for Regional Studies, North Dakota State University, who generously opened his valuable collection to me. For the same reason, special thanks also go to Luis G. Vasquez, curator and reference archivist of the American Historical Society of Germans from Russia, and to Laila Miletic-Vejzovic, head of manuscripts, archives, and special collections of the libraries of Washington State University. Helpful critical readings were offered by Rebecca Boehling, Lisa DiCaprio, Marion Kaplan, Timothy Kloberdanz, Robert Moeller, Hanna Schissler, and, of course, my coeditors.

   1. In the Odessa area of Cherson, at 6 percent of the population, they came to own 19 percent of the land; in Jekatrinoslaw, at 5.4 percent of the population, they owned 25 percent of the land; in Taurien, at nearly 9 percent of the population, they owned 38 percent of the land; most dramatically, in Crimea, at 9 percent of the population, they owned 78 percent of the land. Ute Richter-Eberle, ed., *Geschichte und Kultur der Deutschen in Russland/UdSSR: Auf den Spuren einer*

Minderheit (Sigmaringen, 1989), 104. All translations are my own unless otherwise noted.

2. Dietmar Neutatz, *Die "deutsche Frage" im Schwarzmeergebiet und in Wolhynien* (Stuttgart, 1993), 436–38.

3. Richard Sallet, *Russian-German Settlements in the United States,* trans. LaVern J. Rippley and Armand Bauer (Fargo, N.D., 1974). Original German, Ph.D. diss., University of Königsberg, 1930.

4. Alexander Dallin, *German Rule in Russia, 1941–1945: A Study of Occupation Policies* (London, 1957), 292.

5. The most successful German colonists tended to assimilate: large landowners who lived far from the villages, city residents and intellectuals who had studied in Russian schools, and those aspiring to upward mobility through intermarriage. Their number cannot be determined, but the practice was condemned as abandonment by colonist newspapers. Neutatz, *Die "deutsche Frage,"* 379–80.

6. Johannes Schleuning, *Mein Leben hat ein Ziel: Lebenserinnerungen eines russlanddeutschen Pfarrers* (Witten, 1964), 180.

7. Schleuning, *Mein Leben,* 153.

8. Schleuning, *Mein Leben,* 190–229.

9. They often bought estates from impoverished nobles, evicted their tenants, and employed these people as agricultural laborers. Neutatz, *Die "deutsche Frage,"* 259, 265.

10. Schleuning, *Mein Leben,* 229–99.

11. David Rempel, "The Expropriation of the German Colonists in South Russia during the Great War," *Journal of Modern History* 4, no. 1 (1932): 49–67.

12. Benjamin Pinkus and Ingeborg Fleischhauer, *Die Deutschen in der Sowjetunion* (Baden-Baden, 1987), 50.

13. Boris V. Malinovskij, "Die deutschen Kolonisten als Teilnehmer an den Strafexpeditionen der österreichisch-ungarischen und deutschen Streitkräfte im Bewusstsein der ukrainischen Bevölkerung 1918," *Forschungen zur Geschichte und Kultur der Russlanddeutschen* (hereafter cited as *FGKR*) 7 (1997): 77.

14. Heinrich Roemmich, "Die Tragödie der deutschen Volksgruppe in Russland," *Heimatbuch der Deutschen aus Russland* (1958): 8.

15. Schleuning, *Mein Leben,* 325, 344.

16. Detlef Brandes, "Resistenz, Abwehr und Widerstand von Russlanddeutschen, 1917–1941," *FGKR* 4 (1994): 98.

17. Schleuning, *Mein Leben,* 535. Contemporary research on this is given by James Urry, "The Mennonites in Russia and the Soviet Union: Recent Perspectives from English Language Sources," *FGKR* 5 (1995): 129–68.

18. Schleuning, *Mein Leben,* 419, 433.

19. Schleuning, *Mein Leben,* 453. Schleuning was in the VDA's Hauptausschuss in 1925 and 1929. Bundesarchiv (hereafter BA) Koblenz, 57 (neu), no. 1016 and no. 1012 Box 2. The VDA was the successor, in 1908, to the German Schools Association (Allgemeiner Deutscher Schulverein) to preserve German culture outside the Reich by supporting schools, libraries, and students. It became increasingly nationalist and expansionist after World War I, moving close to the Deutscher Schutzbund, which contested the new state boundaries and developed

volksdeutsche ideology. Ernst Ritter, *Das Deutsche Ausland-Institut in Stuttgart, 1917–1945: Ein Beispiel deutscher Volkstumsarbeit zwischen den Weltkriegen* (Wiesbaden, 1976), 19–22.

20. Schleuning, *Mein Leben,* 482–579.

21. An estimated 120,000 Germans fled Russia during revolution, civil war, and German occupation, of whom half came to Germany and the rest continued to North and South America. Pinkus and Fleischhauer, *Deutschen in der Sowjetunion,* 156.

22. Schleuning, *Mein Leben,* 581–84.

23. Franz von Reichenau, head of the VDA, cited in Ritter, *Das Deutsche Ausland-Institut,* 13, 30.

24. There is a massive literature on Ostforschung relevant to this chapter, ranging from Michael Burleigh's *Germany Turns Eastwards* (Cambridge, 1988) to Michael Fahlbusch's *Wissenschaft im Dienst der nationalsozialistischen Politik? Die „Volksdeutschen Forschungsgemeinschaften" von 1931–1945* (Baden-Baden, 1999).

25. Some of the aid was quite idiosyncratic. In 1921, in a particularly rural twist, one group stubbornly insisted on sending over two thousand milk cows in three shiploads to Germany, although Herbert Hoover, head of the American Relief Association, had urged them to send condensed milk instead, as the cows were likely to die due to the shortage of fodder in Europe. La Vern J. Rippley, "Gift Cows for Germany," *North Dakota History* 40, no. 3 (1973): 4–15.

26. Nina E. Waschkau, "Kulturbeziehungen der Wolgadeutschen Republik mit Deutschland 1918–1933," *FGKR* 8 (1998): 115. See Pinkus and Fleischhauer, *Deutschen in der Sowjetunion,* 86–176, for a full treatment of the Volga Republic.

27. Where kulaks were about 4 to 5 percent of the majority population, they made up 15 percent of the German peasantry, which itself was only 1 percent of the total. A rough estimate yields about half a million thus dispossessed. Pinkus and Fleischhauer, *Deutschen in der Sowjetunion,* 103–6.

28. The German state relented slightly at the end of 1929 and accepted 5,583 peasants, who were placed in former POW camps before being shipped out to Canada, Brazil, and Argentina. Pinkus and Fleischhauer, *Deutschen in der Sowjetunion,* 185; J. Schleuning, *Die Stummen Reden: 400 Jahre evangelischlutherische Kirche in Russland* (Erlangen, n.d.), 123–24.

29. Victor Èencov, "Die deutsche Bevölkerung am Dnepr im Zeichen des stalinistischen Terrors," *FGKR* 5 (1995): 11.

30. Schleuning's National Socialist German Workers' Party (NSDAP) party card, no. 1734884, is dated April 1, 1933. Berlin Documentation Center, NSDAP Ortskartei, National Archives Microfilm Publication T 054, MFOK, Roll A 3340, Frame 2472.

31. Schleuning, *Mein Leben,* 605–7.

32. Rudolf Aschenauer, *Die Auslandsdeutschen: 100 Jahre Volkstumsarbeit, Leistung, und Schicksal* (Berg, 1981), 162.

33. Fahlbusch, *Wissenschaft im Dienst,* 594.

34. *Deutsche Post aus dem Osten* (hereafter cited as *DPO*), Mar. 1, 1936, 3.

35. *DPO,* Nov. 1936, 13–17.

36. *DPO,* Apr.–May 1939; inner cover has table of dispersion.

37. *DPO* June–July 1939, 5, 16.

38. Membership of the Tübingen Vereinigung ausländischer Studierender, winter semester 1920–21, BA Koblenz R 57, DAI, No. 1037, Heft 23.

39. Obituary by Adam Giesinger, "Dr. Karl Stumpp (1896–1982): A Life of Service to His People," *Journal of the American Historical Society of Germans from Russia* (hereafter cited as *JAHSGR*) 5, no. 1 (1982): 1–3.

40. Aschenauer, *Die Auslandsdeutschen,* 141, 158.

41. Unsigned document, initialed A.W. 11.5.40, in T-81, DAI, Roll 599, Frame 5386969.

42. Stumpp's NSDAP party card, no. 5973539, is dated May 24, 1937. Berlin Documentation Center, NSDAP Ortskartei, National Archives Microfilm Publication W 054, MFOK, Roll A 3340, Frame 0678. The 1939 party census elicited the information that Stumpp had previously been in the SA and was now entitled to a light-brown uniform, black boots, and an SA sports insignia. He identified his profession as "employee" (*Angestellter*). The information from the 1939 party census is on Roll A 3340, PC, 105.

43. Captured German War Documents, National Archives Microfilm T-81, DAI, Roll 632, Frame 5432060 and 5432098. The letters range from frame 5432053 to 5432137.

44. Eduard Krause, "Das Deutschtum in Bessarabien und seine Rücksiedlung ins Reich," September 10, 1940. Captured German War Documents, National Archives Microfilm T-81, DAI, Roll 633, Frame 5432767–69. Krause directed the FstR in Stumpp's absence.

45. Letter by Stumpp , Oct. 5, 1940, in BA Koblenz, R 57 (neu), no. 354.

46. Stumpp's form letter to various camps, Jan. (n.d.), 1941, Captured German War Documents, National Archives Microfilm, T-81, DAI, Roll 632, Frames 5432503–4; letter by Stumpp about the visit, Feb. 7, 1941, in BA Koblenz, R 57 (neu), no. 104.

47. Leibbrandt's dissertation was published as *Die deutschen Kolonien in Cherson und Bessarabien* (Stuttgart, 1926).

48. According to the NSDAP party census of 1939, Leibbrandt was member no. 830194 as of December 1, 1931. Berlin Documentation Center, National Archives, Roll A 3340-PC no. 059.

49. Ingeborg Fleischhauer, *Das Dritte Reich und die Deutschen in der Sowjetunion,* Schriftenreihe der Vierteljahrsheft für Zeitgeschichte no. 46 (Stuttgart, 1983), 33n.67. Leibbrandt's motivation is given by Fahlbusch, *Wissenschaft im Dienst,* 595.

50. Rosenberg's speech at a closed meeting, June 20, 1941, Document 1058-PS, *International Military Tribunal* 26. In it he claimed that the confiscated land in the Baltics was as large as East Prussia and in the Black Sea region as large as the states of Württemberg, Baden, and Alsace together.

51. Fahlbush, *Wissenschaft im Dienst,* 607 n316, observes that Fleischhauer minimizes the role of Stumpp and Leibbrandt in the Ukraine, while Meir Buchsweiler argues that it contributed to the extermination process, in his *Volksdeutsche in der Ukraine am Vorabend und Beginn des Zweiten Weltkriegs—ein Fall doppelter Loyalität?* (Tel Aviv, 1984).

52. Captured German War Documents, National Archives Microfilm, T-81,

DAI, Roll 606, Frames 5396969–7011; also Fahlbusch, *Wissenschaft im Dienst,* 609. Eric J. Schmaltz and Samuel D. Sinner, "The Nazi Ethnographic Research of Georg Leibbrandt and Karl Stumpp in Ukraine, and Its North American Legacy," *Holocaust and Genocide Studies* 14, no. 1 (2000): 28–64. The two authors of Russian German descent, in third-generation contrition (*Vergangenheitsbewältigung*), detail Stumpp's and Leibbrandt's complicity in the extermination of Jews in Ukraine. Sinner goes on to claim that Russian Germans were also victims of genocide in his published dissertation, *The Open Wound: The Genocide of German Ethnic Minorities in Russia and the Soviet Union, 1915–1949 and Beyond* (Fargo, N.D., 2000). Schmaltz has compiled an exhaustive, invaluable bibliography, *An Expanded Bibliography and Reference Guide for the Former Soviet Union's Ethnic Germans* (Fargo, 2003).

53. Buchsweiler, *Volksdeutsche in der Ukraine,* 288. Some details by region from Stumpp's village reports as well as from another set written by a Catholic priest, Father Nikolaus Pieger, in 1941 are given by Adam Giesinger, "The Black Sea Germans in 1941," *JAHSGR* 2, no. 1 (1979): 17–19.

54. Quartering the Kommando in Dniepropetrovsk allowed Stumpp to search the archives of that city, which had been the headquarters from 1800 to 1818 of the government office that had supervised the founding of the early Black Sea colonies. The census records for the colonies in 1816 became the basis for his book, *The Emigration from Germany to Russia, 1763 to 1862,* published with financial support from the American Historical Society of Germans from Russia in the United States. Giesinger, "Dr. Karl Stumpp," 1–2.

55. National Archives Microfilm, Captured German War Documents, T-175 Roll 580, Frames 00297–346.

56. Buchsweiler, *Volksdeutsche in der Ukraine,* 383, concludes that, while individual Russian Germans were fully complicit, the colonists formed no organized fifth column as such; see also 338–41.

57. For example, in Babi Yar, a site of mass executions, 137 trucks carried the clothing of murdered Jews to distribute to resident Germans, as testified by the commanding officer of Einsatzgruppe D at the Nürnberg war trials. Buchsweiler, *Volksdeutsche in der Ukraine,* 372. Richard Walth, who was invited by Stumpp to succeed him in the leadership of the LDR but declined, wrote that some Russian Germans objected to receiving stolen goods. But he is ambiguous on the question of German-Jewish relations in Ukraine: on the one hand, he claims they got along well on the basis of a shared language; on the other hand, he claims that Germans suffered especially from Jews who administered the process of collectivization. Richard H. Walth, *Strandgut der Weltgeschichte: Die Russlanddeutschen zwischen Stalin und Hitler* (Essen, 1994), 57–59, 70, 74.

58. Pinkus and Fleischhauer, *Deutschen in der Sowjetunion,* 270–79.

59. Rosenberg's official notice of Feb. 17, 1943, acknowledged Stumpp's "valuable work in difficult times." BA Koblenz, R 57 (neu), no. 859.

60. Giesinger, "Dr. Karl Stumpp," 2.

61. A list of Stumpp's writings would constitute another article. His major books include *The German Russians: Two Centuries of Pioneering,* trans. Joseph S. Height (Lincoln, Neb., 1964, 1967, 1978); *Das Schrifttum des Deutschtums in Russland* (a bibliography) (Stuttgart, 1958; Tübingen, 1971); and *Die Auswanderung aus Deutschland nach Russland in den Jahren 1763–1862* (Tübingen, 1972).

62. Heinrich Roemmich, "Die Entstehung und die Tätigkeit der Landsmann-schaft der Deutschen aus Russland e.V.," *Volk auf dem Weg,* June 1970, 2–3.

63. "Die Landsmannschaft der Deutschen aus Russland e.V.," *Heimatbuch,* 1973–81, 251.

64. Heinrich Roemmich, "Die Ablösung der Gründergeneration unserer Landsmannschaft," *Volk auf dem Weg,* May 1973, 1–2.

65. *Volk auf dem Weg,* Jan. 1964, 2; Schleuning, *Mein Leben,* 626.

66. Pertti Tapio Ahonen, "The Expellee Organizations and West German Ost-politik, 1949–1969" (Ph.D. diss., Yale University, 1999), exhaustively discusses the various expellee organizations and their party-political activities, showing how these hampered a more flexible *Ostpolitik* by the Federal Republic until détente in international relations and the chancellorship of Willy Brandt in 1969 ended much of their influence.

67. Reported in *Volk auf dem Weg,* June 1964, 3–5. Despite doubts as to the value of funding the tiny LDR, the Bundesministerium für Gesamtdeutsche Fragen supplied 25 percent of its income of DM 24,568 in 1957. The rest came from mem-bership dues, which were defined in part as subscriptions to *Volk auf dem Weg.*

68. Hans W. Schoenberg, *Germans from the East,* Studies in Social Life no. 15, ed. Günther Beyer and Martinus Nijhoff (The Hague, 1970), 317–18.

69. Pinkus and Fleischhauer, *Deutschen in der Sowjetunion,* 527.

70. Peter Hilkes, "Germans in the Ukraine and Their Place in the Framework of German-Ukrainian Relations: History and Perspectives," accessed March 1996, Web site of Germans from Russia Heritage Society, <http://www.lib.ndsu .nodak.edu/gerrus/hilkes.html>, accessed April 1998. Hilkes addresses the conven-tion "The Ukraine and Germany in the Twentieth Century," organized by the Ger-man Association of Ukrainian People and the Ukrainian Free University, March 13–15, 1996. Hilkes is a researcher at the East European Institute in Munich.

71. L. Krastova, "Overview of Archival Sources of the History of Germans of the Taurida Province (up to 1918) and Crimea (up to 1941)," *Newsletter of the American Historical Society of Germans from Russia,* no. 90 (spring–summer 1998): 12–14; Elizabeth M. Yerina, "Archives of the Former Autonomous Soviet Social-ist Republic of Germans on the Volga in Engels," *JAHSGR* 22, no. 1 (1999): 11–15.

72. *Newsletter of the American Historical Society of Germans from Russia* (win-ter 1996): 8, 12; see also Rodney Fink, "Life in the Agricultural Communities of Germans Living in Russia," *JAHSGR* 22, no. 1 (1999): 1–10.

73. Anthropology professor Timothy Kloberdanz at North Dakota State Uni-versity has written extensively about the local practices of Russian Germans in the Midwest. For the most exhaustive overview of and distinctions between the sub-groups, see his "Volksdeutsche: The Eastern European Germans," in *Plains Folk: North Dakota's Ethnic History,* ed. William C. Sherman et al. (Fargo, N.D., 1986), 119–81.

74. Anton H. Richter, "'Gebt ihr den Vorzug': The German-Language Press of North and South Dakota," *South Dakota History* 10, no. 3 (1980): 189–209, specifically 194–97. The anatomical description is offered by La Vern J. Rippley, "F.W. Sallet and the *Dakota Freie Presse,*" *North Dakota History* 59, no. 4 (1992): 2–21, specifically 2. Much of the biographical material on F. W. Sallet here is given in Rippley's article.

75. Sallet, *Russian German Settlements,* 93, citing the DAI's publication *Der Auslanddeutsche* in 1920.

76. Richter, "Gebt ihr den Vorzug," 197. It is difficult to calculate what percentage of the Russian German population this readership constituted. However, one calculation based on the 1920 census yields a figure of about one hundred thousand in North and South Dakota alone. George Rath, *The Black Sea Germans in the Dakotas* (Freeman, S.D., 1977), 333. Germans from the Volga region were more concentrated in Nebraska.

77. Elwyn B. Robinson, *History of North Dakota* (Lincoln, Neb., 1966), 286; William C. Sherman, *Prairie Mosaic: An Ethnic Atlas of Rural North Dakota* (Fargo, N.D., 1983), 50.

78. D. Jerome Tweton and Theodore B. Jelliff, *North Dakota: The Heritage of a People* (Fargo, N.D. 1976), 146.

79. *DFP,* 1917, passim.

80. Rippley, "F.W. Sallet," 11–15.

81. *DFP,* Nov. 13, 1917, 1.

82. *DFP,* 1919, passim.

83. *DFP,* Feb. 12, 1924, 7–8.

84. Rippley, "F.W. Sallet," 20.

85. Sallet, *Russian-German Settlements.*

86. Sallet, *Russian German Settlements,* 79, 95–97, 109.

87. La Vern J. Rippley, "A History of the *North Dakota Freie Presse*," *Heritage Review* 7 (December 1973): 12.

88. *DFP,* Feb. 10, 1933, 8; Sept. 23, 1938, 1; Nov. 25, 1938, 1.

89. "Memorandum and Petition to the German Imperial Government," in Georg Rath, *The Black Sea Germans,* 354, 399–401.

90. The appeal is reprinted in Rath, *The Black Sea Germans,* 401–2. As for Richard Sallet, he returned to Germany in 1933, became a legation counselor in the Foreign Service a year later, and finally joined the Nazi Party in 1938. Berlin Documentation Center, National Archives, NSDAP Zentralkartei, Roll A 3340—MFKL—0002. As propaganda attaché in the Germany Embassy in Washington, he also served as cultural contact for the Friends of the New Germany, an association of German Americans whose dues went to the Nazi Party. It was replaced in 1938 by the German American National Alliance, which in the Midwest entered the America First Committee, whose goal was to lobby Congress to remain neutral in war. Cornelia Wilhelm, *Bewegung oder Verein? Nationalsozialistische Volkstums-politik in den USA* (Stuttgart, 1998), 49–50, 251.

91. Rath, *The Black Sea Germans,* 354–55.

92. Karl J. R. Arndt and May E. Olson, *German-American Newspapers and Periodicals, 1732–1955* (Heidelberg, 1961), 421.

93. Jonathan F. Wagner, "Nazi Propaganda among North Dakota's Germans, 1934–1941," *North Dakota History* 54, no. 1 (1987): 15–24.

94. Letter, David Miller to Walter W. Land, Sept. 4, 1941. Emma Haynes Papers, Washington State University Library Special Collections (hereafter EHP), Box 6, Folder 79.

95. Rippley, "F.W. Sallet," 20–21.

96. Letter to David Miller, Sept. 24, 1968. EHP, Box 6, Folder 79. She relieved

Goering of rising to his feet when she entered the room and recalled his last words to her, thanking her for being kind to his wife and daughter.

97. Letter to David Miller, Nov. 15, 1968. EHP, Box 6, Folder 79.

98. The AHSGR held its first national convention in June 1970 but was soon torn by historical regional rivalries. Miller and Haynes were descendants of Volga Germans, but the North Dakotan descendants of Black Sea Germans, after some disputes, broke off to form a separate organization, since 1979 called the Germans from Russia Heritage Society. Haynes made several unsuccessful efforts to unify or at least to bridge the two groups; they remain separate to this day. Both offer genealogical services and organize trips to the German and Russian Heimat.

99. Letter to David Miller, June 3, 1973. EHP, Box 6, Folder 79.

100. Work Paper No. 2, Sept. 1971, North Dakota Historical Society of Germans from Russia, cover.

101. Letter to David Miller, Feb. 12, 1971. EHP, Box 6, Folder 79. Letter to Adam Giesinger, June 26, 1972. Haynes Collection (henceforth HC), at AHSGR.

102. Letters, Giesinger to Haynes, May 25, July 7, 1973; Jan. 13, 1974. Haynes to Giesinger, July 21, 1973; Feb. 12, Sept. 9, Sept. 18, Dec. 5, 1974. EHP, Box 6, Folder 75. Haynes to Gerda Walker, Oct. 31, 1974. EHP Box 7, Folder 85. Walker joined the AHSGR board as chair of the membership committee, with a special interest in genealogy.

103. Letter, Haynes to Giesinger, June 9, 1980, referring to her 1974 visit. EHP, Box 5, Folder 74.

104. Letter to Giesinger, Sept. 7, 1977. EHP, Box 5, Folder 74.

105. Letter to Giesinger, Jan. 31, 1984. HC, Box 5.

106. Letters to Miller, May 11, June 26, 1969. EHP, Box 6, Folder 79.

107. Letters to Walker, Oct. 7, 1972; Oct. 31, 1974. EHP, Box 7, Folder 85.

108. *Volk auf dem Weg,* June 1975, 1–2.

109. *In dem Strafverfahren Dr. Georg Leibbrandt und Dr. Otto Bräutigam.* BA, Kleine Erwerbungen, no. 655–4 Folge 1: Nachlass Otto Bräutigam. Landgericht Nürnberg-Fürth, 72Ks 3/50.

110. Haynes's own genealogical research, note to Berta Ohsohlin, geb. Schwabenland, n.d., refers to meeting Roemmich in 1967. HC, Box 3. Letter to Ann Sheehy, researcher with the Minority Rights Groups based in London, March 1, 1972. EHP, Box 7, Folder 83.

111. Letter, Ruth Amen to Richard Scheuerman, May 5, 1978. EHP, Box 7, Folder 82. Amen was president of the AHSGR and Scheuerman a Ph.D. candidate with political interests.

112. Letter to Sheehy, Mar. 14, 1973. EHP, Box 7, Folder 83.

113. Letter, David Miller to Haynes, Feb. 8, 1974. EHP, Box 6, Folder 79. Haynes to her brother Ray Schwabenland, Jan. 9, 1975. Box 1, HC.

114. Letter to LaVern Rippley, Apr. 17, 1975. EHP, Box 7, Folder 81.

115. Correspondence with Fred Koch, 1966–81. EHP, Box 6, Folder 78. Correspondence with Timothy Kloberdanz, 1971–81. EHP, Box 6, Folder 77. Correspondence with Richard Scheuerman, 1971–78. EHP, Box 7, Folder 82.

CHAPTER 9

When Is a Diaspora Not a Diaspora?

Rethinking Nation-Centered Narratives about Germans in Habsburg East Central Europe

Pieter Judson

With this chapter I want to encourage German historians to broaden their understanding of the term *German* beyond a nation-state-centered concept that for too long has privileged the German state founded in 1871 as the social, cultural, and political embodiment of a German nation. I suggest that communities in Habsburg East Central Europe, popularly constructed by German politicians and historians alike in the interwar period as diasporas, could not possibly have seen themselves in these terms much before 1918. When such communities did adopt a more nationalist identity in the post-1918 period, they usually referred back to prewar ideologies for guidance, traditions that had rarely made their relationship to Germany a necessary component of community identity. As a consequence of the national humiliations imposed by the Versailles and Trianon settlements, Germans in Germany tended increasingly to characterize such communities as "lost diasporas," eliding their fates with those of Germany's lost territories in West Prussia and Silesia. Not until the economically depressed 1930s, however, did Nazi propaganda and offers of support (cultural, political, and financial) to these hard-pressed communities succeed in creating a new self-understanding among them as diasporas of the German nation-state. Nazi annexations (Bohemia, Moravia, Silesia, Southern Styria) and attempted population transfers (Bukovina, South Tyrol) enabled these communities later and misleadingly to be remembered by community activists and historians alike as age-old diasporas, defined primarily by their relationship to Germany.

The use of this term *German diaspora* as an analytic tool requires a

critical acknowledgment of that concept's twentieth-century deriva-
tion from the related concept of the territorial nation-state. Like the
terms *nation, race,* or *ethnicity,* the term *diaspora* rests on historically
shifting ideological presumptions. This does not mean that ideas of
diaspora, just like those of race, nation or ethnicity, cannot produce
material and social effects. But it does require the social scientist to distinguish carefully between the ways in which nationalist ideologists
deployed the term *diaspora* (to argue for a necessary relationship
between those communities and the German state) and the ways in
which those communities understood their own identification as German. To use the concept *German diaspora* without interrogating its
potentially normative and nationalist presumptions risks reading contemporary forms of self- and group identification back onto its innocent subjects, for whom such forms of self-identification may have held
little meaning.[1]

For German historians in the twentieth century, the concept of German diasporas in East Central Europe seems to have embodied a com-
mon-sense logic. Substantial populations of German-speaking people
living outside of the German nation-state in Eastern Europe formed
diasporic communities that looked to Germany to reinforce a sense of
their own cultural identity, historical continuity, and sometimes political influence. Such communities were often understood both by themselves and by Germany as the product of successive waves of German
migration or colonization reaching back into the medieval period.
Local rulers, so the story went, had invited communities of German
artisans, merchants, and farmers to settle in particular regions of the
East, often giving these settlers a privileged legal position vis-à-vis local
Slavic populations. The concept of historic colonization underlying
much of the rhetoric about diasporas in the East often functioned to
reassure Germans in the new German state that their national identity
could be defined by a long history of economic success and cultural
superiority.[2]

Other authors in this volume demonstrate that the ways communities around the world defined themselves as German reflected contingent and situational conditions that shaped their particular assertions
of identity rather than some fundamentally authentic historic shared
identity. We should remember this caveat as we examine German-
speaking communities situated geographically much closer to Germany. Their very proximity to Germany made them useful pawns in
the foreign political dreams of ideologists hoping to realize an
expanded German nation-state after the defeat of 1918. In the post-1918

political landscape these communities may have occasionally flirted with a self-characterization as linked to the German nation-state. It was, however, their problematic place within new self-proclaimed nation-states, not their traditional ways of identifying themselves, that produced any such characterizations.

As difficult as it might be for us living in a globally nationalized world to imagine it, East Central Europeans who claimed membership in a German nation before 1918 often rejected any formal relationship to the German nation-state founded in 1871 and saw no contradiction in that choice. Confusion around this issue stems partly from the degree to which nationalists and their agendas in Germany itself dominated early writing about German diasporas, interpretations that were often unwittingly taken up by later historians. Confusion also results from the ways in which social scientists too often come to view their own categories for interpreting the past as having had significance for the contemporaries who lived them. When we consider those substantial communities of German speakers located in the Austrian half of the Dual Monarchy, where categories unrelated to our contemporary understanding of nation often shaped personal and community identity, the concept of diaspora takes on far different meanings. Here we find German nationalists who did not define themselves in relation to Wilhelmine Germany, who imagined their links with Wilhelmine Germany as comparable to their relations to German communities in other parts of Imperial Austria.[3]

This chapter will examine two linked phenomena: the implicit assumption that Central and Eastern Europeans categorized by a census as German speakers actually shared a common German identity and the largely post-1918 nationalist presumption that such groups formed diasporic communities that sought a relationship to the self-proclaimed German nation-state. Such German speakers often did not think of themselves as Germans before 1918, and even for committed nationalists, the demands of living in the anational Austrian Empire made the issue of any relationship to Wilhelmine Germany largely irrelevant.[4]

Both the experience of wartime occupation in the East and the catastrophic outcome of the war for Germany and Austria-Hungary helped intensify the popular interest in the Weimar Republic for communities of Germans living outside Germany. It created an entirely new potential for imagining the future of these Germans specifically in terms of their relationship to the German state, something that would have been impossible as long as the Habsburg monarchy existed. This popular obsession in Germany with the Germans of the East rapidly replaced interest in Germany's lost colonial empire, for example, as Lora Wildenthal has recently demonstrated in her work on German women's colonialist organizations. These groups, formerly devoted to the advancement of German settlement in Africa, often shifted their focus rapidly to the so-called lost German communities of Eastern Europe in the years following the war. The intensified promotion of *Ostforschung* in Germany and Austria, both in nationalist and academic circles after 1918, reflected a similar trend.[5]

The outcome of the war also produced a reconceptualization of the content and significance of German nationality among German-speaking communities in East Central Europe. At first German speakers often responded to the collapse of the Habsburg state by imagining that they could maintain their traditional community identity within the new states while shifting their loyalty from Vienna to rulers in the new capital. However, this option soon became impossible, given the ways that their new rulers conceptualized citizenship rights. German-speaking communities that had formerly existed within the multinational Habsburg state were absorbed, often forcibly, into new, self-styled nation-states that defined the term *nation* in narrow linguistic terms. Their new rulers quickly labeled these communities as either *Germanized nationals*—and capable of reintegration into the Czech, Polish, Slovene, or Italian nation—or as *German nationals*—and barred from membership in the new nation-state. This latter categorization often justified the forced expropriation of German community resources, the closing of German-language schools, and the banning of German voluntary associations, even if, as mentioned previously, those German-speaking communities offered declarations of loyalty to their new rulers.[6]

Several German-speaking communities found themselves forced for the first time to consider their own identities in terms of the German nation-state, a state that had meant little to them in the recent past. This was due less to some spontaneous growth in nationalist identity, loyalty, or renewed interest in *Heimat* among German speakers and more to the radical political, social, and economic structural changes brought about by the postwar order in Central and Eastern Europe. A reorientation of German speakers in the new Czechoslovakia, Poland, Romania, or Yugoslavia toward Germany was not automatic, and as an outcome it was in no way predestined. Several German speakers in these communities chose to emigrate or flee, and several also assimilated to the dominant language group of the new nation-state.[7] It is worth repeating that the policies of the new rulers, eager to create nations with which to people their new nation-states, produced a new sense of identity as "German diasporas" among these communities; this identity was not solely the initiative of the German speakers themselves. It was not foreordained that German speakers should in any way express a particular interest in, or feel any special relationship to, Germany, just as it was not foreordained that Czech or Polish nationalists should define national citizenship in their new states in narrow linguistic terms. Yet their sudden new status as second-class citizens, as *Germans* in Czechoslovakia, Italy, Poland, Romania, or Yugoslavia, made these German speakers more aware of possible links between their cultural forms of self-identification, a putative national identity, and the German nation-state.

Often at this moment after the war, German speakers in Habsburg East Central Europe became German nationals; their communities developed completely new identities that slowly reframed their interests in terms of their potential relationship to the German state.[8] Several other populations in the region experienced a similar reorientation of identity, among them those now identified as Hungarians in Czechoslovakia, Romania, and Yugoslavia; Ukrainians in the Soviet Union and Romania; and Jews everywhere (to name but a few). All found themselves defined by hostile governments as minority subaltern populations. They lived uneasily within self-styled nation-states as second-class citizens or as objects of forceful policies of assimilation, despite the legal guarantees of the minority protection treaties imposed on the new nation-states by the victorious powers.[9]

These communities of German speakers did have a legacy of rhetorical and organizational tools at their disposal for making sense of their new situation. These tools stressed the commonalties of German-language minority communities in East Central Europe and not their relationship to the German state. For almost three decades German nationalist activists had worked tirelessly to promote a sense of nationalist self-identification among different language groups throughout the Austrian half of the Dual Monarchy. Activists' efforts to promote national unity among Germans in Cisleithania, or even a serious belief in the importance of nation as such, had not always been successful, as we will see subsequently. Yet whatever their degree of success before the war, activists left a compelling potential legacy to those in the post-1918 world who sought strategies with which to understand their condition as national outsiders.

Nationalization and Its Limits in Pre-1918 Austria

The nationalization efforts that had dominated Austrian public life in the years before 1914 differed from apparently similar processes that characterized public life in self-styled nation-states like Germany, France, or Italy in the late nineteenth century. The Austrian state did indeed promote the kinds of administrative centralization and social integration associated with modernization processes elsewhere in Europe. Yet these policies did not involve the advancement of national identity to unify a disparate citizenry. Rather, the Habsburg state made Austrian identity dependent on the individual's (and later the group's) loyalty to the dynasty. Austrian patriotic symbols, rituals, and festivals served to highlight the overwhelming devotion of an admittedly culturally diverse population to its monarch. The state itself remained firmly anational, even as it worked to unify diverse populations. It did not wish to recognize the possible existence of nationalities either in statistical surveys or in policy-making.[10]

The liberal Austrian constitutions of 1848 and 1867 had recognized that differences in religion and in language constituted special cases for ensuring that institutions treat diverse individuals equally, and it was around the latter guarantee that nationalists built their movements.[11] Starting with Czech nationalists in the 1860s, each movement invoked the constitutional guarantee of linguistic equality for individuals both to define its own nationalist goals and to reform as many aspects of public life as possible. Language use both in the schools and in the bureaucracy provided the key legal fields for the activism pursued by a broad range of nationalist political movements. While their activism was designed to gain for each nation as large a share of state resources as possible (everything from the right to petition the civil service in one's own language to school funds for minority students to bilingual street signs), nationalists never sought to replace the Habsburg state with a series of nation-states. Indeed, nationalists often competed with each other rhetorically to assert their own nation's greater loyalty to the dynastic state. Ironically, by 1914, as Jeremy King has so aptly noted, anational Austrian law had been forced to recognize the existence of nations within Austria rather than the existence of individuals who spoke different languages. "In a trend with few European parallels," writes King, "the state began to become multinational."[12]

This "multinationalization" of society was the often unintended result of institutional agreements like the Moravian Compromise of 1905, which sought to diffuse conflict between Czech and German nationalists by removing national issues from the realm of politics. Resources and political competencies in Moravia would now be divided between the two sides: Germans and Czechs gained separate school systems, and they voted in separate curias (Czech and German candidates for political office no longer ran against each other). The requirement that all citizens self-consciously declare their adherence to one nation or the other produced an enormous if unintended nationalization of public life. Where before they might have considered themselves to be "Moravian" (and demand a bilingual, or Utraquist, education for their children), now Moravian citizens were forced to assume a national identity as Czechs or Germans.[13]

Not surprisingly, German nationalist activism throughout Austria had assumed an especially defensive quality from the start. It originated in the 1880s largely as a reaction against perceived legal and institutional inroads made by other linguistic groups at the expense of German speakers. German nationalism asserted a privileged place for the Germans within the empire on the basis of their cultural, economic, and occasionally numeric superiority. To justify German linguistic privilege, nationalists pointed to statistical evidence that German speakers paid proportionally far more taxes than anyone else in Austria did. They also promoted a particular cultural understanding of historic Habsburg expansion in the East as a German colonial or civilizing mission. This German nationalism did not, however, include irredentist yearnings for *Anschluss* with the *kleindeutsch* German state founded in 1871. To the contrary, most German speakers in Austria who even considered the matter desired little more than a formal political alliance for Austria-Hungary with Germany. Given a belief in their own historical mission in the East, given their overwhelmingly Catholic cultural bent, and given their perceptions of Prussia as culturally Protestant, most nationalists who even thought about the matter rejected the irredentist (and anti-Catholic) ravings of a Georg von Schönerer.[14]

If Austro-German nationalists rejected an identity defined in terms of their relationship to the Wilhelmine German nation-state, other aspects of German nationalist culture in Austria also undermined the notion of a necessary relationship to Germany. Two apparently contradictory tendencies helped ensure that German nationalists in Austria left Germany out of any nationalist or political mental equation. First, the traditional Austro-German liberal view dominant from 1848 through the 1870s (which survived in many forms down to 1945 and complicated later Nazi policy in the Sudetenland and the Protectorate) held that Germanness was an elite cultural quality that could in theory be adopted by other groups in Eastern Europe as they worked to improve themselves. In this view Germanness was linked neither to descent nor to a particular territory but rather to cultural capital. Liberals had expected that, even if other linguistic groups maintained their own folk traditions, they would educate their youth in German and that their education would assimilate these newcomers into the ranks of a larger German humanist elite. Although such a large-scale assimilation never came to pass, it meant that early German nationalism lacked the quality of territorialization found among some other nationalist movements in the empire.[15] Austro-Germans who even considered the matter were used to thinking of their nation as a quality rather than as a place, thus relativizing the importance of the Wilhelmine state founded in 1871. Later German nationalists had to create a link between the specific territory they claimed and their concept of Germanness.

The second point is that the critical importance of regional loyalties for German nationalists in Austria before 1914 often tended to relativize any potentially unique role that Wilhelmine Germany might play. Several interregional nationalist associations worked hard after 1880 to foster a sense of unity among communities of German speakers (and their territories) spread throughout Austria, but there is little evidence to suggest that they came close to accomplishing their goal. As Laurence Cole has recently demonstrated for the Tyrol, concepts of German national identity often served highly regionalist ends, assuming specific qualities that gave them little in common with concepts of Germanness in other parts of the monarchy. In the Tyrol, for example, German nationalism was defined primarily by loyalty to church, to dynasty, and to the particular provincial interests of the Tyrol vis-à-vis the centralizing state in Vienna. This put Tyrolean German nationalists bitterly at odds, for example, with their counterparts in Styria, for whom liberal anticlericalism played a crucial role in self-definition, or with Bohemian German nationalists, who viewed the central state as critical to the maintenance of their minority rights against majority Czechs.[16]

Even within the same province nationalist organizations might disagree on the fundamentals of identity. The Union of Germans in Bohemia (Bund der Deutschen in Böhmen), for example, promoted a racially anti-Semitic definition of the German nation while the German Union of the Bohemian Woods (Deutscher Böhmerwaldbund) remained open to Jewish membership and even sported a Jewish executive board member. The interregional German School Association (Deutscher Schulverein) recognized at least tacitly the important role Jewish private schools played in educating German-speaking children, where their minority status meant that the state did not fund a German-language school. The interregional Südmark, however, constructed Jews as the racial enemies of Germans. Farther to the east, the world of German nationalists in Galicia and the Bukovina was almost completely alien in its concerns to that of German nationalists in the West. Yet even among such apparently isolated German-speaking communities as those in the East, to which I will return later, German community identity did not rest on a concept of diaspora.[17]

If regionalist differences slowed the construction of a common German national movement or even a common sense of self-identification, a challenge admittedly faced by nationalists in the new Wilhelmine Reich as well as by those in Austria, other obstacles also stood in the way of making populations national.[18] Despite some twenty-five years of successful activism, by 1914 German nationalists consistently expressed frustration in their aim to achieve a unified and politically effective German identity among German speakers in Austria. What they had generally accomplished by 1914 was a considerable nationalization of white-collar professionals such as civil servants, teachers, service employees, and politicians at all levels of government, whose interests tended to be more directly impacted by nationalist legislation than those of other social groups.

This is particularly clear in the cases of teachers and civil servants. Changes over time in the state's linguistic requirements for positions in the local and regional civil service, for example, appeared adversely to affect the ongoing chances of educated German speakers to obtain such posts. German nationalists claimed that, as governments adopted new rules promoting bilingual administration in provinces like Bohemia, Moravia, or Styria—concessions, apparently, to Slav nationalist agitation—German-speaking candidates were increasingly disadvantaged. Slav candidates would more likely be selected for such posts, it was argued, because they were more likely to be competent in both their own languages and German, while Germans rarely learned a Slavic language.[19] These kinds of concerns shaped political agendas in turn. After 1890 German nationalists increasingly demanded administrative autonomy for purely German-speaking districts within bilingual provinces like Bohemia and Moravia in order to free as many local civil servant posts as possible from the supposedly onerous dual language requirement. In multilingual regions where administrative separation was not viable, nationalist organizations like the Südmark in fact changed their strategies by 1909 and began encouraging German speakers preparing for the civil service to take classes in a Slavic language.[20]

If such issues worried some segments of the population considerably, they do not appear to have resonated to the same extent with the majority of German speakers in the empire. Nationalists of all stripes had far less success mobilizing rural populations or the industrial working classes for specifically nationalist ends. National identity, often defined in urban bourgeois terms, had less immediate relevance to these groups, although it appears to have held a marginally greater significance to Czech-speaking workers and peasants than to their German-speaking counterparts.[21] German nationalists complained consistently about their inability to gain long-term support among both these social groups, although the nature of their own efforts made them more likely to succeed among peasants and the rural *Mittelstand* than among industrial workers.

In order to fortify existing rural German-speaking minorities against the gradual "incursions" of other populations, nationalists tried to strengthen existing minority communities by preventing the rise of conditions that promoted emigration or assimilation to another language group. It was not simply a question of avoiding foreclosures on Germans' farms by supplying cheap credit. It also meant promoting educational opportunities *in German* for rural youth and making sure that communities had a diverse population of artisans to serve their basic consumer needs. Several regional associations promoted the economic well-being of rural German-speaking populations by making cheap credit available to them, offering free classes on agricultural innovation, promoting job exchanges, and subsidizing the purchase of anything from fruit trees to farm implements. Yet for all of these efforts, it was not clear that nationalists had in fact succeeded in nationalizing the peasantry and the rural Mittelstand by 1914. In political terms their efforts did not always produce significantly greater numbers of nationalist voters in rural constituencies, for example. Nor did peasants necessarily understand the economic and educational efforts of the associations in primarily nationalist terms, though often in welfare terms.

Nationalists did not often attempt a comparable effort in majority German-speaking industrial regions, where, for example, Slav-speaking workers migrated in increasing numbers by 1900. The industrial working class in turn was largely politically loyal to the Austrian Social

Democratic Party, an organization theoretically opposed to the chauvinist interests of bourgeois nationalism. It was not so much their nationalism that may have prevented German nationalists from making inroads into socialist political support, however, but rather their unwillingness to address issues of concern to working-class Austrians. A series of articles published by the organization Südmark in 1909 recognized this nationalist inability to speak to the concerns of industrial workers and warned that, without a mass base to lend it credibility, German nationalism could not achieve the political influence it hoped to gain within the empire: "Whenever we demanded of the German worker that he subordinate his class to his *völkisch* interests . . . these so-called völkisch interests often proved to be the class interests of the mighty who [at that time] dominated the German parties."[22] In the final years before the outbreak of war, a few initiatives to organize unions and parties that would bring German workers into the nationalist movement took shape, but their successes were limited to very specific regions.[23]

German Identities

As previously noted, German nationalist activists rarely mentioned relations with Germany as a defining or even an important issue. Their self-identification did not flow from the explicit belief in a significant relationship to Germany but rather from the situation of German speakers in Austria. While there might exist a self-styled German nation-state to the north and west of Cisleithania, the fact remained that over ten million German speakers lived under Habsburg rule and many considered themselves part of a larger German nation that was not defined by the territory of Wilhelmine Germany. An examination of the way nationalist organizations defined their goals demonstrates that when German nationalists thought about the German nation it was in a way that did not privilege Germany. And as much as the wartime alliance between Germany and Austria-Hungary sparked the collective imagination of Austro-German nationalists, causing them to reimagine their present and future relationship to the Wilhelmine Reich, this did not in most cases spur a revaluation of the special concerns of Austro-Germans.[24]

In 1912 the combined membership of regional and interregional German nationalist associations in Austria (including Bosnia-Hercegowina) stood at some 560,000.[25] The largest and best known of these organizations was the interregional German School Association, which counted some 200,000 members. Founded in 1880 the association saw its work very much in terms of updating, so to speak, a traditional German colonial or settler presence in Eastern Europe. Its mission statement deplored the recent losses by Germans to Slav and Italian peoples in an imagined demographic battle on the linguistic frontier. The German School Association proposed to minimize further losses by funding German-language schools for linguistically mixed communities whose German-speaking population was too small to qualify them for a state-funded German-language school.[26]

German School Association literature spoke in terms of losses and gains for a larger German nation, but one that was rarely defined by political boundaries. Instead, the association focused its efforts on the issue that supposedly united all German speakers in Austria: their role as guardians of a cultural frontier. The association defined this frontier, however, in terms of its cultural and historic relationship to Vienna and not in terms of any relationship to the Wilhelmine Reich. Association writers occasionally analyzed Wilhelmine German attitudes or policies toward so-called Polish incursions in East Prussia, for example, but always for comparative purposes and never to suggest that Austro-Germans somehow *belonged* to Germany. Furthermore, when writers traced the historic origins of German communities in Bohemia, Galicia, or the Bukovina, among others, they referred to German migrations in terms that emphasized their regional origins (Swabia, Bavaria, Saxony) and played the notion of the Wilhelmine Reich as a point of origin. Thus, despite the very different linguistic composition of their respective populations, Germany and Austria were treated in the pages of the German School Association magazines as sibling German states with complementary missions in Europe.

Another issue helped shape the sense of Austro-German identity negatively as it might relate to Wilhelmine Germany. Several Czech nationalist organizations consistently accused their German nationalist opponents of constituting advance columns for Reich German penetration. Reich Germans, it was insinuated, funded the German School Association. Such accusations implied that any popularity enjoyed by the association was illusory, the creation of powerful foreign interests. Czech nationalists hoped to diminish any sense of legitimacy or popularity that might attach to the German School Association in Bohemia by implying that it was a foreign organization largely funded from across the border.[27]

Over its almost forty-year existence the German School Association built or offered financial support to hundreds of kindergartens, primary schools, and advanced schools for boys and girls throughout the empire. The association was careful, however, to avoid any rhetoric that might imply a mission to Germanize. It always defined its purpose in defensive terms, to remedy losses, strengthening the nation through German-language schooling so that no German children would be lost to another nation. The association was happy to accept students of Czech or Slovene parentage who wished their children to obtain an education in German, but it refuted accusations that it proselytized or pressured parents to enroll their children in its schools.[28] Czech and Slovene nationalists who supported the work of similar organizations of their own in turn accused the German School Association of outright Germanization. Both German and Czech nationalists constantly battled over children in linguistically mixed communities, complaining that employers and landlords exerted undue pressure on parents to enroll their children in the wrong school. This competition had the unintended if salubrious effect of dramatically increasing the numbers of schools, particularly in rural areas, and raising the general level of literacy and education among those populations where nationalist competition was at its fiercest.[29]

Other nationalist organizations focused their efforts on securing the economic survival of German communities as well. How these organizations defined both their purpose and the specific problems they hoped to address reveals a great deal about their imagined relationship to a larger German nation. In Habsburg East Central Europe the supposed language frontiers (*Sprachgrenze*) mentioned previously, where speakers of two or more languages lived in close proximity to each other, were usually imagined to be located in rural regions. Within these areas the towns tended to have a German-speaking plurality, while speakers of other languages dominated the surrounding rural areas (thus the German linguistic term *Sprachinsel,* or "language island," to describe such communities, which the editors of this volume have translated as "islands of Germanness"). In fact, *mixed-language regions* might be a more appropriate term for these areas, since their inhabitants generally could communicate in more than one language and families often included speakers of both languages. Such familial and social mixing was anathema to most nationalists, who saw it as a sign of demographic weakness. If an individual were bilingual, then what would prevent him and his children from crossing over to the other side?[30]

Clearly an education in the appropriate language would help to prevent this national tragedy. So would the economic measures mentioned previously, those designed to keep rural communities viable and to prevent the enemy nation from practicing a kind of nationalist blackmail by means of boycotts or hostile housing policies. Both sides in such situations justified their own use of boycotts or selective housing in defensive terms, and both worked to prevent the other from gaining an economic upper hand. It is difficult to say with any certainty whether local populations paid much attention to nationalist exhortations to boycott. In addition to promoting economic stimulants (anything from local tourism to the fruit trees and farm implements), these associations also engaged in charitable activities, handing out Christmas presents to the poor, collecting clothing and food for the winter, or creating small local libraries. They constantly extended their realm of activism, attempting to nationalize all aspects of private and public life and thereby to realize the separation between cultures that they claimed already existed. These efforts became increasingly ambitious after 1900, so much so that in many cases the associations overstepped the very limits of their defensive origins in order to proclaim aggressive new projects.[31]

The Union of Bohemian Germans extended the demographic metaphor to the issue of German orphans supposedly raised in Czech orphanages and thus lost to the German nation. The union built private orphanages to save German children for the nation. Several other regional organizations followed the union's example, although most relied more on the less expensive option of "orphan colonies," villages where children were lodged with German foster parents. The Südmark, operating primarily in Styria, Carinthia, and Krain, targeted a series of villages to the north of the Styrian city Marburg for German settlement. A large majority of Marburgers spoke German, but the city itself was cut off demographically from the German-speaking territory to the north by a swathe of rural villages inhabited both by Slovene speakers and a minority of German speakers. The Südmark hoped eventually to use its settlement program to Germanize the area directly to the north of Marburg and thus connect the "island" city to the German "mainland." The organization bought properties as they became available and sold them at reduced rates to farmers and artisans (largely Protestants from Württemberg in the German Reich, a fact that created unanticipated problems in overwhelmingly Catholic villages). Other regional organizations, such as the Nordmark (operating in Silesia), attempted to emulate this settlement program.[32]

In both these cases nationalist associations adapted the rhetoric of a tradition of German colonialism and settlement to more modern ends.

If, according to this rhetoric, Germans had been invited to colonize areas of Eastern Europe centuries ago because their economic habits and cultural superiority were recognized by local rulers, modern Germans too must pursue a similar cultural mission to prevent uncultured barbarians from ruining Austrian civilization. Here we must be careful to note the situational uses of colonial and settlement rhetoric on all sides. German historians may be surprised to learn that Slavic nationalist groups also engaged in discourses of colonialism and cultural superiority against the Germans when it suited their purposes. In particular, Czech nationalists portrayed Czech migrants to German areas as courageous colonizers, settling new regions within the lands of the Bohemian crown. Czech nationalists took every opportunity to tout their own cultural achievements and to contrast their own status as a modern *Kulturnation* to the often uncultured, loutish, and violent behavior of German nationalists.[33] At other times, Czech nationalists liked to characterize the activities of their German nationalist rivals in terms of a brutal colonial relationship between Germanizing colonizer and Czech colonized. Some German nationalists too constructed their mission, as we have seen, in terms of bringing culture to a benighted East. At other times Germans might lament the fate of helpless German minorities at the hands of invading Czech colonizers who overturned traditional existing social relations. The legacies of these tropes are particularly apparent among some Czechoslovakian Sudeten Germans in the 1930s and, interestingly, reemerge with particular vehemence after their annexation to Germany in 1938. Sudeten German leaders and organizations frequently demanded special treatment for their followers due to their recent history of colonization, both real and imagined, at the hands of the merciless Czech nation-state.[34]

Every one of these claims reflected a strategic use of existing rhetorical opportunities, although it should be clear that both those opportunities and the significance of the rhetoric reflected changed realities after 1918. While those categorized as German nationals after 1918 may have suffered under their new rulers, we should not accept the often self-contradictory claims of either side on this issue as an accurate reflection of social, economic, and cultural relations in the Austrian Empire. Nor should we accept the ludicrous thesis that under the empire one side reproduced the kinds of relations that characterized European colonialism outside of Europe in its treatment of the other side. To do so would be to fall into the trap laid for us by nationalists themselves, to believe the myths about this earlier period propounded by German nationalists in post-1918 Germany or Slavic nationalists in the successor states. We do not have to look far for evidence that social relations among so-called nations were not as simple as the nationalists implied. The testimony of the latter provides plenty of evidence for the challenges faced by nationalists in a frustratingly nonnationalist world. Both the Union of Germans in Bohemia and the Südmark, for example, experienced considerable difficulties in realizing their nationally more aggressive schemes, difficulties that suggest the fundamental chasm that separated nationalist claims about society from reality. When both the league and its Czech nationalist counterparts actually investigated their own orphan placement programs, they occasionally found that a supposedly reliable foster family was in fact raising the child in the wrong language or that the family's knowledge of the national language was woefully inadequate. Families needing the extra funds simply claimed to be German or Czech, without perhaps grasping the freighted meaning of such an assertion. Similarly, the Südmark experienced more than a little difficulty in determining whether a candidate for a farm was in fact an "authentic German" or simply a German-speaking opportunist looking for a good deal.[35]

This set of problems reflects a larger contradiction faced by all nationalist organizations in the empire, one whose dimensions are illustrated by nationalist activism around the imperial census. Every ten years the empire carried out a census that included questions about language use. Nationalists liked to claim that language use as documented in the census indicated a form of national self-identification, and activists for each nation struggled to raise its census numbers relative to the others.[36] German nationalists claimed, for example, that those who listed German as their language of daily use in the census questionnaires *were* in fact Germans. More often than not, however, nationalist organizations spent their sizeable resources trying to convince German speakers themselves to *become* Germans. Their broad construction of German identity that included everyone who listed German on the census often papered over even deeper contradictions, since some nationalist organizations, for example, denied membership in the nation to Jews who claimed German as their language of daily use in the census. Nationalists might well refer to nations as if they were easily recognized and defined phenomena. Reality suggested that, to the extent that they existed at all, nations were remarkably ill-defined, unstable entities.

Although nationalist organizations claimed to strengthen the threatened border or island populations of Germans in particular, most of them functioned in regions that were geographically not very far removed from majority German-speaking regions of Austria (and Germany). There were some exceptions to this norm, one of which is particularly instructive regarding the question of diaspora and identity: the Association of Christian Germans in the Bukovina (Verein der christlichen Deutschen in der Bukovina). This organization tells us something about how German nationalists on the eastern periphery of the empire understood their Germanness and in particular how they imagined a relationship to the rest of a German nation. Unlike German nationalists in the other contested regions, nationalists in the Bukovina, Galicia, or Bosnia-Herzegowina could trace their very existence to relatively recent migrations. In Galicia the power of the traditional Polish elite and its largely uncontested policy of Polonization, particularly in regard to education, meant that German nationalists there organized late and in relatively small numbers. German speakers had made up 5 percent of the Galician population in 1880, but by 1910 that number had shrunk to just over 1 percent. Local German nationalist efforts succeeded more easily among Galicia's German Protestant communities than among German-speaking Catholic ones, since Polish identity was intrinsically defined by a Catholic religious identity.[37]

In the more interesting case of the Bukovina one could argue that no linguistic group was socially or historically dominant, although some were more dominant than others. The Bukovina was in fact Austria's "most multicultural" province. Once the Bukovina had gained administrative independence from Galicia after 1848 (and again in the 1860s), the former Polish elite became a tiny and relatively powerless minority (3.5 percent) next to a majority of Ukrainian (Ruthene) speakers (38 percent) and Romanian speakers (34 percent), followed by a significant German-speaking minority of over 20 percent. The German-speaking presence in the Bukovina dated from as recently as the 1780s, when under Joseph II German farmers had migrated east to regions recently annexed from Romanian boyars and divided by the Habsburgs with the Ottomans. Already in the early nineteenth century the cities and larger towns of the Bukovina had a particularly large German-speaking presence. In Czernowitz, the capital, 47 percent of the inhabitants reported German as their language of daily use in 1900. Here also the government established a German-speaking university, thanks to the tireless efforts of a (Romanian-speaking) parliamentary deputy from Czernowitz, Constantine Tomaszcuk. Both the new university and the provincial administration served as something of a magnet for an educated German elite. Once the administration of the Bukovina had been separated from that of Galicia, the German language became one of the two official provincial administrative languages, next to Romanian (Ukrainian was later added to the official list of official provincial languages as well). Business in the Diet was generally conducted in German or Romanian.

These structural factors help to explain what may seem paradoxical: that in a place geographically so far removed from other German communities in the empire, German speakers felt little need for connection either with each other or with a possible imagined German homeland back in the West. Most German-speaking communities in the Bukovina had little sense of belonging to a larger national community at all, despite their relatively recent arrival there. This is partly because rural Bukovina remained relatively cut off from the towns until well into the twentieth century. German-speaking farmers lived in unconnected rural communities dispersed throughout the Bukovina. The more urbanized and educated German speakers were primarily Jews, who constituted well over half of those statistically categorized as German speakers in the province. Non-Jewish German speakers, university professors, white-collar workers, and some merchants formed more of a German social community in cities like Czernowitz but do not seem to have viewed themselves as constituting a diaspora. This resulted from the fact that German speakers exercised proportionally as much (if not more) influence in provincial political and social affairs as did any other group. And unlike the situation in the rest of Austria, a sense of pragmatism rather than ideology or mutual suspicion characterized political relations between Jewish and Gentile German organizations in the Bukovina. In fact, relations among nationalist groups in the Bukovina were generally more manageable than elsewhere in the monarchy. Since no one group held a majority in the Diet, the German speakers often played a pivotal role allied either with the Romanian nationalists (most of the time) or with the Ruthenes.

For this reason, an interesting tension seems to mark accounts by German nationalist writers in the West of the Association of Christian Germans in the Bukovina. The former often presented the organization to their readers as if its very raison d'être lay in a bitter conflict that divided Germans and Jews in a barbarous eastern setting. In writing about the origins of this organization, for example, the anti-Semitic German nationalist *Deutsche Volkszeitung in Reichenberg* saw the association's mission as the liberation of so-called Aryan Germans in the Bukovina from the financial thrall in which Jewish moneylenders held them. The organization itself, however, claimed that its appellation of Christian was meant to differentiate it from Jewish Germans as much as its appellation of German functioned to differentiate it from Catholic Poles. It treated Jews as fellow German speakers who were, however, organized in a different set of social and cultural networks.[38]

The efforts of the association, founded and led largely by professors at the university in Czernowitz, focused on raising the educational opportunities for German speakers in a region that suffered from some of the highest illiteracy rates in the empire. In particular, the association hoped to encourage rural Germans to send their children to higher institutions of learning by providing housing and social support to youth from the country who attended the urban middle and high schools and the university in Czernowitz. The association also founded a chain of rural credit unions to battle peasant indebtedness to usurers, which was indeed high, but as far as I have been able to determine, its literature never associated Jews explicitly with this particular problem. In fact, the literature published by the association makes no mention at all of Jews, Jewish associations, or anti-Semitism.

The association made clear that it wished to inculcate German speakers with an understanding of their place in a larger German nation. Viewed from the perspective of Czernowitz, Kimpolung, or Radautz, however, that larger German nation often seems to have referred to a collectivity of German speakers within the Bukovina itself, as the easternmost outpost of the German nation within Austria. The association's literature made no mention of Germany. Organizers did not conceive of themselves defensively as a threatened island of German culture in a sea of barbarous Slavs and Romanians the way German nationalists in the West often portrayed them. The association promoted a sense of German pride of place in the Bukovina, depicting the society as a microcosm of Austria, a community admittedly made up of several nations. This type of identification clearly grew out of the circumstances created by Imperial Austrian rule, a form of rule that did not define a privileged majority nation against minority populations in this region.[39]

After World War I, when Romania gained control over the Bukovina, the organized German community attempted to deal with the new government in the familiar terms to which it had become accustomed under the Austrian Empire. German leaders expected that their schools and cultural and political organizations would continue to flourish in a multicultural province of Romania, and they saw no contradiction between their identities as Germans and their necessary loyalty to a Romanian state. Although the new regime officially accepted the written demands made upon it by elected representatives of the

German community in 1918, government policy toward minority schools and cultural organizations became increasingly repressive during the interwar period. It was largely as a result of this growing repression and of fears about the proximity of the Soviet Union that many in the Bukovina's German community turned to Nazi Germany for support. A growing factionalism in the 1930s divided German community institutions, pitting those who demanded a "völkisch renewal" of the community and political orientation toward Nazi Germany against those who continued to seek accommodation with the Romanian state. With the invasion of the region by the Soviet Union in June 1940, the German community largely agreed to its resettlement in occupied Poland and later Germany.[40]

After 1918

When German nationalists in East Central Europe sought rhetorical and organizational models to deal with their new and unprecedented situation after 1918, they generally turned to the strategies that seemed to have served them well under the Habsburg monarchy. This required a renewal of self-help organization, appeals to the international community for justice, and implicit attempts at accommodation with the new national governments. Since they saw themselves more as legitimate players on the local political scene than as threatened outposts of an embattled Germany, they did not immediately redefine their activism in relation to Germany. Their adoption of prewar ways of thinking about the nation, derived from experience in a multicultural empire, made it difficult for these communities to redefine themselves successfully in terms of a necessary relationship to the Weimar or Nazi German state. So too did the apparent economic weakness and political isolation of that German state in the early 1920s. This was as much the case with a group as politically influential as the so-called Sudeten Germans in Czechoslovakia as it was with smaller minority communities in Yugoslavia, Poland, and Romania, although the latter were often subjected to greater violence and more punitive state measures than were the Sudetens.

Economic depression brought a greater nationalist radicalism in the successor states in the 1930s. Traditional conservative regimes found themselves pressured to assert their nationalist credentials more aggressively or face challenges from restive populist movements. To many German observers, with their minority status perspective in the successor states, the accession of the Nazis to power in Germany seemed to reflect a powerful national renewal that might serve as a forceful ally in pursuing their minority rights. This suggested potentially new avenues of redress that had not previously been available. Nowhere was this more clearly the case than in Czechoslovakia, where under pressure from a badly failing economy German speakers deserted their traditional parties for Henlein's Nazis. And yet even here the old legacies of a different kind of nationalism continued to shape local concerns and demands made by German communities. Some Sudeten German activists in the 1930s who supported a full annexation of the Sudetenland claimed that the broader German-speaking population in Czechoslovakia had *so little understanding* of the importance of its German identity that within a generation all sense of its German national identity would be lost. Once Germany had annexed the Sudetenland and asserted protectorate status for the rest of Bohemia-Moravia, Sudeten leaders continued to cast their particular demands on the state in terms that referred to debates from the Habsburg past. Thus in demanding that schoolteachers in particular not be called up to the Wehrmacht, German nationalists in the Sudetenland maintained that the *Volk* was not yet fully German and required an education in its own identity. Echoing the nineteenth-century characterization of the schoolteacher as the instrument of the nation in the face of Czech attacks, activists claimed that, with German teachers serving in the ranks, the Volk would be left to the mercy of Czech-speaking teachers. As late as 1941, German nationalists in Bohemia still felt the nation had not adequately been forged![41]

Is it possible that we can only truly speak of German diasporas in Habsburg East Central Europe as an important element of memory after the brutal expulsions of 1945? In a sense the expulsions created the German diaspora communities within Germany that had not previously existed as such. I have argued that the vibrant communities of German speakers that dotted the landscapes of pre-1918 Habsburg Europe did not constitute German diasporas in the narrow sense because they did not define themselves in terms of a relationship to a German state. While they often may have seen themselves as German by 1914, we must be careful to locate exactly what that appellation actually meant to them. It seems yet another irony that Imperial Austria, a state that produced so much German nationalist activism, also produced a sense of German identity so unconcerned with its potential relationship to its German nation-state neighbor.

The Habsburg state enabled battling nationalists to live in extreme tension with one another even as it offered a powerful guarantee for the survival of each. This assertion has become something of a cliché, and it should not be confused with the notion that an idealized Habsburg state functioned justly in every situation or that despite all appearances to the contrary the state had somehow "solved" its nationalities problems. Still, in order to promote its own survival the Austrian state had no choice but to dispense a kind of proportional justice to the increasingly important nationalists who peopled its territories. In doing so it unknowingly legitimized the existence of nations in the public sphere. Yet it did so in a context that promised to protect the rights of each. This promise in turn fueled nationalist activism, since some remote area of public life always remained that required further reform. This promise also framed the terms of nationalist political activism in ways that would have been impossible in the context of a nation-state. An understanding of how people viewed the significance of *nation* within this kind of framework remains elusive to us. It is close to impossible for inhabitants of our own nationalized world either to recapture or to understand what "nation" might have meant in a nonnationalized world.

While nationalist activism appeared to dominate politics in the Austrian Empire by 1914, this had not necessarily produced a mass society of nationalized individuals. Outside the political system, which was admittedly awash in nationalist activism, it is simply not clear to what extent people adopted or acted upon nationalist forms of self-identification. The concept of an Austro-German border identity promoted by nationalist associations and popular authors, for example, did not necessarily reflect the actual experience of those who lived in linguistically mixed regions, unless political agitation had shaped the inhabitants' views of their own situation. Even where nationalism clearly dominated social and cultural life, as it did in Bohemia, regional concerns often shaped particular forms of German self-identification, and this made these forms different to the point of unrecognizable to Germans from different regions. National identity only made sense if cast in a way that highlighted regional concerns and traditions. Whether or not German speakers in Austria explicitly proclaimed it, their Germanness was fundamentally defined by their *Austrianness* as well as by their particular region, not by their imagined relationship to Wilhelmine Germany. After all, even the Bohemian German politicians who in 1918 opposed their annexation by the new Czechoslovakia demanded to remain a province of German Austria (Deutsch Österreich), and not Anschluss with Germany. To speak of the Germans in the Austrian Empire as constituting a self-conscious unified group, therefore, is a problematic venture, to say the least. To speak of German diasporas before 1918 is even more problematic.

The term *German diaspora* as it is applied to communities in Habsburg East Central Europe (and perhaps others) must refer somewhat to the self-understanding of these communities. And these communities existed in a world where German identity, to the extent that it held meaning for people, did not refer to the German nation-state. If, therefore, interwar German nationalist politics in East Central Europe were constructed in Brubaker's triangular terms (diaspora–host nation—Germany), it is the rise of this new way of conceiving nationalist politics that requires further explanation. New attitudes and approaches to nationalist activism and identity management had to be forged. They were not simply given by the political situation. If Germans in formerly Habsburg Central Europe came to see their identities defined in terms of a relationship to the German state, then that development must be explained; it cannot simply be presumed. As German historians reexamine Germany's relationship to its Eastern neighbors, they will need to do this from a perspective of the East itself and not simply from the perspective of the West.

NOTES

1. Rogers Brubaker has usefully pointed to the dangers involved when we move from treating groups as descriptive or analytic categories to accepting them as something real. See "Ethnicity without Groups," *Archives Européènes de Sociologie* (May 2002): 163–89.

2. Interest in these German-speaking communities of Eastern Europe flourished within the limited boundaries of nationalist and sometimes specific religious circles in the Wilhelmine Kaiserreich. Ronald Smelser, *The Sudeten Problem, 1933–1938:* Volkstumspolitik *and the Formulation of Nazi Foreign Policy* (Middletown, Conn., 1975), 14–69; Michael Burleigh, *Germany Turns Eastwards: A Study of Ostforschung in the Third Reich* (Cambridge, 1988). A typical example of such writing in the 1930s is Erwin Barta and Karl Bell, *Geschichte der Schutzarbeit am deutschen Volkstum* (Dresden, 1930). Barta and Bell, both German nationalist activists from Austria, recounted the history of German nationalist organizing in communities in Habsburg Austria as a prelude to understanding these communities as diasporas of the larger German nation-state.

3. See the useful recent survey of German literary, cultural, and political texts by Jörg Kirchhoff, *Die Deutschen in der Österreichisch-Ungarischen Monarchie: Ihr Verhältnis zum Staat, zur Deutschen Nation und ihr Kollektives Selbstverständnis (1866/67–1918)* (Berlin, 2001).

4. The 1910 census counted 9,950,678 people in the Austrian half of the Dual Monarchy who listed German as their preferred language of daily use (*Umgangsprache*), 35.58 percent of the total population. Peter Urbanitsch, "Die Deutschen in Österreich. Statistische-deskriptiver Überblick," in *Die Habsburger Monarchie, 1848–1918*, vol. 3, *Die Völker des Reiches,* ed. Adam Wandruszka and Peter Urbanitsch (Vienna, 1980), 38, table 1.

5. On the social, cultural, and political effects of German wartime occupation and activism on the Eastern front, see Vejas G. Liulevicius, *War Land on the Eastern Front: Culture, National Identity, and German Occupation in World War I* (Cambridge, 2000); Paul Weindling, *Epidemics and Genocide in Eastern Europe, 1890–1945* (Oxford, 2000); and Lora Wildenthal, *German Women for Empire, 1884–1945* (Durham, N.C., 2001), especially 172–200. For the subtle transformations in ideological positioning after 1918, see Barta and Bell, *Geschichte der Schutzarbeit.*

6. See Irina Livezeanu's exemplary analysis of the Romanian takeover of the Bukovina in *Cultural Politics in Greater Romania: Regionalism, Nation Building, and Ethnic Struggle, 1918–1930* (Ithaca and London, 1995), 49–87. See also Arnold Suppan, "Untersteierer, Gottscheer, und Laibacher als deutsche Minderheit zwischen Adria, Karawanken und Mur (1918–1948)," in *Deutsche Geschichte im Osten Europas: Zwischen Adria und Karawanken,* ed. Arnold Suppan (Berlin, 1998); Helmut Rumpler and Arnold Suppan, eds., *Geschichte der Deutschen im Bereich des heutigen Slowenien 1848–1941* (Vienna and Munich, 1988); Jeremy King, *Budweisers into Czechs and Germans: A Local History of Bohemian Politics, 1848–1948* (Princeton and Oxford, 2002); and Johann Wolfgang Brügel, *Tschechen und Deutsche, 1918–1938* (Munich, 1967).

7. For examples, see King, *Budweisers,* 158–68; Arnold Suppan, "Lage der Deutschen," in *Geschichte der Deutschen,* ed. Rumpler and Suppan, 173–75.

8. Karl F. Bahm, "The Inconveniences of Nationality: German Bohemians, the Disintegration of the Habsburg Monarchy, and the Attempt to Create a 'Sudeten German' Identity," *Nationalities Papers* 27, no. 3 (1999): 377–99; Pieter M. Judson, "Frontier Germans: The Invention of the *Sprachgrenze*" in *Identität-Kultur-Raum: Kulturelle Praktiken und die Ausbildung von Imagined Communities in Nordamerika und Zentraleuropa,* ed. S. Ingram, M. Reisenleitner, and C. Szabo-Knotik (Vienna, 2001), 85–99; Rogers Brubaker, *Nationalism Reframed: Nationhood and the National Question in the New Europe* (New York, 1996). Brubaker examines the triangular quality that characterized the relationship of Eastern European German communities to Germany and to their host states in the interwar period. In an otherwise thoughtful book Brubaker's characterization of prewar nationalism among those communities is badly flawed. He proposes that German nationalism in pre-1918 Austria was irredentist in nature, a commonly held belief about Austro-Germans that the sources do not confirm (115–16).

9. Hungarian minorities in Czechoslovakia, Yugoslavia, and Romania had a strong sense of a diasporic relationship to the Hungarian state. The situation of formerly Austrian or Hungarian Jews in Poland or Romania was particularly complicated by the fact that their religious identity defined them out of the nation in those states. Especially in Romania but also in Poland, religious belief defined the

particulars of national identity. Many Austrian Jews in Galicia and the Bukovina considered their own identity in terms of allegiance to the anational imperial state that they rightly perceived had protected them from Polish, Romanian, or Ukrainian anti-Semitism. In Czechoslovakia Jews could choose to identify themselves as part of the Czech nation or they could even choose to list themselves simply as Jews in the census (often a means of diminishing the number of those who reported themselves as Germans in the interwar period). However, both the German and Czech nationalist movements were often characterized by anti-Semitism both before and after 1918, making national identification for Jews more difficult. On Jewish dilemmas in post-1918 Eastern Europe, see Hannah Arendt, *The Origins of Totalitarianism* (New York, 1958), chapter 9; Marsha L. Rozenblit, *Reconstructing a National Identity: The Jews of Habsburg Austria during World War I* (Oxford and New York, 2001).

10. On imperial attempts to create dynastic patriotism, see Daniel Unowsky, "Reasserting Empire: Habsburg Imperial Celebrations after the Revolutions of 1848–1849," in *Staging the Past: The Politics of Commemoration in Habsburg Central Europe, 1848 to the Present,* ed. Maria Bucur and Nancy M. Wingfield (West Lafayette, Ind., 2001), 13–45.

11. See Gerald Stourzh, "Die Gleichberechtigung der Volksstämme als Verfassungsprinzip, 1848–1918," in *Die Habsburgermonarchie, 1848–1918,* vol. 3, *Die Völker des Reiches,* ed. Adam Wandruszka and Peter Urbanitsch (Vienna, 1980), 975–1206; see, more generally, Stourzh's excellent *Die Gleichberechtigung der Nationalitäten in der Verfassung und Verwaltung Österreichs, 1848–1918* (Vienna, 1985). On the bureaucracy, see Karl Megner, *Beamte: Wirtschafts- und sozialgeschichtliche Aspekte des k.k. Beamtentums* (Vienna, 1986); Karl Hugelmann, ed., *Das Nationalitätenrecht des alten Österreich* (Vienna and Leipzig, 1934). On the conflict over schools, see Hannelore Burger, *Sprachenrecht und Sprachengerechtigkeit im österreichischen Unterrichtswesen, 1867–1918* (Vienna, 1995).

12. King, *Budweisers,* 114.

13. On the Moravian Compromise, see Horst Glassl, *Der Mährische Ausgleich* (Munich, 1967); Robert Luft, "Die Mittelpartei des mährischen Grossgrundbesitzes 1879 bis 1918: Zur Problematik des Ausgleiches in Mähren und Böhmen," in *Die Chance der Verständigung: Ansichten und Absätze zu übernationaler Zusammenarbeit in den böhmischen Ländern 1848–1918,* ed. Ferdinand Seibt (Munich, 1987), 187–244; T. Mills Kelly, "Taking It to the Streets: Czech National Socialists in 1908," *Austrian History Yearbook* 29 (1998): 93–112; Pieter M. Judson, *Exclusive Revolutionaries: Liberal Politics, Social Experience, and National Identity in the Austrian Empire, 1848–1914* (Ann Arbor, Mich., 1996), 262–64.

14. For a full summary of the literature on literate Austro-German attitudes toward Wilhemine Germany, see Kirchhoff, *Die Deutschen.* For a careful statistical analysis of German speakers' tax contributions and so-called national property in Bohemia, see Heinrich Rauchberg, *Der nationale Besitzstand in Böhmen,* 2 vols. (Leipzig, 1905). On Schönerer, see Andrew Whiteside, *The Socialism of Fools: Georg Ritter von Schönerer and Austrian Pan-Germanism* (Berkeley and Los Angeles, 1975). While statistics on tax payment confirmed German preeminence in the economy, another form of statistic meant to measure cultural superiority; those

measuring literacy, for example, favored the Czechs. See, for example, Adelbert Rom, "Der Bildungsgrad der Bevölkerung Österreichs und seine Entwicklung seit 1880 mit besonderer Berücksichtigung der Sudeten- und Karpathenländer," *Statistische Monatsschrift* 19 (1914): 589–642.

15. Czech states' rights nationalism, for example, insisted on the territorial integrity of Bohemia, Moravia, and Austrian Silesia. Peter Bugge, "Czech Nation-Building, National Self-Perception, and Politics, 1780–1914" (Ph.D. diss., University of Aarhus, 1994), especially 103–20; Bruce Garver, *The Young Czech Party, 1874–1901, and the Emergence of a Multi-Party System* (New Haven, 1978), 49–60.

16. Laurence Cole, *"Für Gott, Kaiser und Vaterland": Nationale Identität der deutschsprachigen Bevölkerung Tirols, 1860–1914* (Frankfurt am Main, 2000). On Bohemia, see Jan Křen, *Die Konfliktgemeinschaft: Tschechen und Deutsche, 1870–1918* (Munich, 2000).

17. Lawyer Israel Kohn of Budweis/Budějovice served on the Böhmerwaldbund's executive board from 1884 until his death in 1917. Deutscher Böhmerwaldbund, "Bundesleitungsmitglieder 1884–1934," in *Fünfzig Jahre Deutscher Böhmerwaldbund* (Budweis, 1934), 2. On the issue of Jewish schools and the German School Association, see Pieter M. Judson, "'Whether Race or Conviction Should be the Standard': National Identity and Liberal Politics in Nineteenth-Century Austria," *Austrian History Yearbook* 22 (1991): 76–95.

18. On the challenges of regionalism in Wilhelmine Germany, see Celia Applegate, *A Nation of Provincials: The German Idea of Heimat* (Berkeley, Calif., 1990); Alon Confino, *The Nation as Local Metaphor: Württemberg, Imperial Germany, and National Memory, 1871–1918* (Chapel Hill, N.C., 1997); Thomas Serrier, "'Deutsche Kulturarbeit in der Ostmark': Der Mythos vom deutschen Vorrang und die Grenzproblematik in der Provinz Posen (1871–1914)," and Günter Riederer, "Zwischern 'Kilbe,' 'Coiffe,' und Kaisergeburtstag: Die Schwierigkeiten Nationaler und regionaler Identitätsstiftung in Elsass-Lothringen (1870–1918)," both in *Die Nationalisierung von Grenzen: Zur Konstruktion nationaler Identität in sprachlich gemischten Grenzregionen,* ed. Michael G. Müller and Rolf Petri (Marburg, 2002), 13–34, 109–36.

19. On the general problem of nationalism and the civil service, see Megner, *Beamte,* especially 245–58. By 1910 the number of Bohemian provincial civil servants of Czech-speaking background far outstripped their relative percentage in the Bohemian population. See Hugelmann, *Das Nationalitätenrecht,* 355.

20. See the articles "Mittel und Wege zur Erhaltung des deutschen Beamtenstandes in den bedrohten Gebieten" and "Deutscher Beamten-Nachwuchs im Kampfgebiete" in *Mitteilungen des Vereins Südmark* (*MVS*) 1909, 3–7.

21. For a suggestive comparison of the relative successes of Czech and German nationalists in appealing to working-class or peasant audiences, see Karl F. Bahm, "Beyond the Bourgeoisie: Rethinking Nation, Culture, and Modernity in Nineteenth-Century Central Europe," *Austrian History Yearbook* 29 (1998): 19–35.

22. *MVS,* Feb. 1909, 41–42. This and all other translations in this chapter are my own unless otherwise noted. See also Bahm, "Beyond the Bourgeoisie." In some industrialized regions (e.g., Marburg/Maribor in Styria) German nationalist strategies were clearly more effective than in others (Bohemia, Silesia), as comparative census data suggests.

23. On the German Workers Party (Deutsche Arbeiter Partei), which elected three deputies to the Austrian Parliament in 1911, see Lothar Höbelt, *Kornblume und Kaiseradler: Die deutschfreiheitliche Parteien Altösterreichs, 1882–1918* (Vienna and Munich, 1993), 242–47; Harald Bachmann, "Sozialstruktur und Parteientwicklung im nordwestböhmischen Kohlenrevier vor dem Zusammenbruch der Monarchie," *Bohemia* 10 (1969): 270–86; and Andrew Whiteside, *Austrian National Socialism before 1918* (The Hague, 1962).

24. Kirchhoff, *Die Deutschen,* 171–202.

25. *Deutsches Jahrbuch für Österreich. Anschriftenwerk in Berufen selbstständig tätiger Deutschösterreicher* (Vienna, 1913). This edition describes each of the associations and lists membership and financial statistics.

26. Austrian school law required the presence of an average of forty school-age children over a three-year period in order to qualify that community for a government-funded school in a given language. Both the Czech and German School Associations built schools in communities with too few children and hoped that their efforts would eventually produce enough children to require the government to assume funding responsibilities for their schools. On policy and its administration, particularly where language was concerned, see Burger, *Sprachenrecht und Sprachengerechtigkeit,* especially 100–111.

27. Articles and reports in the publications of the Czech School Association or the Czech National Association for the Bohemian Woods consistently raise the issue of funding and suggest that the German School Association and other nationalist organizations were controlled by foreign (German) interests. See frequent examples from the *Zpráva o činnosti Národní Jednoty Pošumavské,* 1906, 1907, 1908, 26–27, and the *Věstník Ústřední Matice Školské* (Prague, 1908).

28. See the essay on the three different categories of children served by the German School Association in *Der Kampf ums Deutschtum* 2 (1913): 24–29. For a similar essay see *Der getreue Eckart: Halbmonatschrift für das deutsche Haus,* 1908, 252. Attitudes among non-German speakers toward the issue of German schooling varied by region and occasionally by community. In Southern Styria and Carinthia, for example, Slovene-speaking parents often believed that a German-language education would bring greater social and employment opportunities for their children and the German School Association did little to discourage this belief. See Maria Kurz, "Der Volksschulstreit in der Südsteiermark in der Zeit der Dezemberverfassung" (BA thesis, University of Vienna, 1986).

29. Since nationalists worked so hard to delineate and prove the differences that separated their two imagined communities (one had culture, the other didn't), they were unlikely to recognize the large number of schools created by their competition as a benefit. This competition created work for Austria's highest administrative and supreme courts (*Verwaltungsgerichthof* and *Reichsgericht*), whose judges constantly ruled on cases involving language, parents, and schools in the period 1890–1918. See Stourzh, "Die Gleichberechtigung," and Burger, *Sprachenrecht und Sprachengerechtigkeit.*

30. On the dangers of bilingualism, see, for example, J. Zemmrich, *Sprachgrenze und Deutschtum in Böhmen* (Braunschweig, 1902), 7–10. The concept of a language frontier was an ideological construction created by nationalists in the 1880s that imagined an uneasy coexistence of two cultures fundamentally opposed

to each other and engaged in a zero-sum struggle to the death. Cultural mixing among peoples within a given region (for many different reasons, such as personal or economic) in fact often constituted a norm that nationalists preferred not to recognize. See Judson, "Frontier Germans."

31. On the boycott movements, see Catherine Albrecht, "The Rhetoric of Economic Nationalism in the Bohemian Boycott Campaigns of the Late Habsburg Monarchy," *Austrian History Yearbook* 32 (2001): 47–67. On competitive charitable giving and Christmas gifts, see *Der Kampf ums Deutschtum*, 1913–12, 25.

32. On nationalist orphanages, see *Bericht über die Thätigkeit des Bundes der Deutschen in Böhmen* (Prague, 1907–10); *MVS*, 1910, 57. On the Südmark see Eduard Staudinger, "Die Südmark: Aspekte der Programmatik und Struktur eines deutschen Schutzvereins in der Steiermark bis 1914," in *Geschichte der Deutschen*, ed. Rumpler and Suppan, 130–54; Pieter M Judson, "Connect the Dots: The Südmark Frontier Settlement Program" in *Teachers, Tourists, and Terrorists: Nationalizing the Language Frontier in Habsburg Central Europe, 1880–1925*, manuscript. On other colonization efforts, see *Deutsches Jahrbuch für Österreich*. Most provincial organizations could not raise the enormous sums that a serious settlement program required.

33. On the Czech nationalist self-image as colonizers in German-speaking regions of Bohemia, see K. Vitvera, *Cous od Začatku České Kolonisace* (Prague, 1907) (Published by the Národní Jednota Severočeské); *České Menšiny a Menšinové Školství* (Prague, 1911); and Mark Cornwall, "The Struggle on the Czech-German Language Border, 1880–1940," *English Historical Review* (September 1994): 914–51.

34. On Sudeten Germans' demands for special treatment at the hands of the Third Reich because of disabilities suffered under the interwar Czech regime, see Volker Zimmermann, *Die Sudetendeutschen im NS Staat* (Munich, 1999); and Ralf Gebel, *Heim ins Reich! Konrad Henlein und der Reichsgau Sudetenland,1938–1945* (Munich, 1999).

35. On the orphan problem, see Dr. Karl Schücker, *Waisenheim des Bundes der Deutschen in Böhmen. Jahrbuch der Deutschen Jugendfürsorge in Böhmen* (Prague, 1909), 21. On Südmark problems with settlers' authenticity, see *MVS*, 1907–8, 288–89.

36. For a detailed analysis of the politics of the census, see Emil Brix, *Die Umgangssprache in Altösterreich zwischen Agitation und Assimilation* (Vienna, 1982).

37. For population statistics (and for subsequent paragraphs) on Galicia and the Bukovina, see Wandruszka and Urbanitsch, eds., *Die Habsburger Monarchie, 1848–1918*, vol. 3, 38, table 1.

38. On the organization and its relations with Jews in the Bukovina, see *Deutsches Jahrbuch für Österreich*, 208; *Deutscher Kalender für die Bukowina*, 1903, 1904, 1910; and Franz Lang, ed., *Buchenland Hundertfünfzig Jahre Deutschtum in der Bukovina* (Munich, 1961).

39. The association promoted links to other Eastern (Hungarian) communities of German speakers, such as those in Transylvania and the Banat, founding the Association of Carpathian Germans in 1910. See Emanuel Turczynski, "Das

Vereinswesen der Deutschen in der Bukovina," in *Buchenland,* ed. Lang, 113.

40. Turczynski, "Das Vereinswesen," 118–19, reproduces the Germans' memorandum of November 17, 1918. A provisional Romanian government in the Bukovina agreed to fourteen of the fifteen demands (the exception was the demand to maintain the German-language status of the university in Czernowitz). A week later, representatives of the German Council (Deutscher Volksrat) voted overwhelmingly for annexation by Romania. Subsequent Romanian policy in the realm of education is analyzed superbly by Livezeanu, *Cultural Politics,* chapter 2. On the internal conflicts of the 1930s and the resettlement in 1940, see Turczynski, "Das Vereinswesen," 123–30.

41. On debates over Sudeten German identities, see Tara E. Zahra, "Custody Battles: Nationalizing Childhood in Bohemia and Moravia, 1900–1945" (Ph.D. diss., University of Michigan, 2005); see also Zahra, "Reclaiming Children for the Nation: Germanization, National Ascription, and Democracy in the Bohemian Lands, 1900–1945," *Central European History* 37 (2004): 499–541. For examples cited by Zahra of Sudeten Germans demanding teacher exemptions from Wehrmacht service, given the alleged need to recolonize a weakened German community, see *Meldungen aus dem Reich,* Nr. 37, Jan. 8, 1940; Bundesarchiv R 58/ 145 F. 1–1 SD Bericht, Dec. 1, 1939; *Meldungen aus dem Reich,* Nr. 333, Nov. 9, 1942, p. 5008; Karlsbad, June 12, 1941, an Herrn Reichsminister des Innern from Regierungspräsident in Karlsbad Bundesarchiv, R 1501 127122, *Reichsministerium des Innern, Grenzlandfürsorge Sudetenland,* Regierungsbezirk Karlsbad p. 128, I/5 a. 1225/41.

CHAPTER 10

German *Brigadoon*?

Domesticity and Metropolitan Perceptions of
Auslandsdeutschen in Southwest Africa and
Eastern Europe

Nancy R. Reagin

In the 1950s play and movie *Brigadoon,* a Scottish village, wrapped in mist and isolated from the world by magic, is rediscovered by the twentieth century. The modern people who enter the village are delighted to find that its inhabitants have preserved the values, dress, dialect, and lifestyle of an earlier time. The German *Sprachinseln* of Eastern Europe were never wrapped in mist, but they were effectively ignored by public opinion in what became Imperial Germany for most of the nineteenth century. This chapter examines their "rediscovery" during the early twentieth century (especially during the interwar period), juxtaposing the depiction of gender roles and family life within these communities with metropolitan (i.e., Reich German) discussions of German settlers' homes in Southwest Africa during the same period. In both Southwest Africa and Eastern Europe, ethnic Germans were surrounded by non-German majorities. For metropolitan Germans, both groups possessed an essentialized Germanness that was thrown into relief by their non-German surroundings, and this core identity was supported by and expressed within the private sphere.

Within the area that later became Germany, before the mid-nineteenth century there was much less official interest in, and popular awareness of, the varied communities of ethnic Germans scattered outside of Germany and Austria-Hungary than would be the case after 1918.[1] By 1900, however, an awareness of these so-called Germans abroad had become part of the contentious articulation of a German national identity. The public exhibited a taste for popular depictions of Germans abroad who exemplified German national character in their

new surroundings: both as individuals—explorers and scientific inno-
vators—and in distinct ethnic German communities, which allegedly
improved the culture of the surrounding area.[2] Ethnic Germans whose
ancestors had departed from different sections of the Holy Roman
Empire for destinations outside of the Kaiserreich and the Hapsburg
Empire were increasingly seen as part of a German diaspora and were
offered the chance to claim German passports after 1913.[3]

Awareness of the "Germans" abroad thus played an important role
in the articulation of German national identity. With the exception of
migrants to the United States (who, it was widely acknowledged,
assimilated fairly quickly), Wilhelmine writers insisted that German-
speaking communities (subsequently labeled *Auslandsdeutschen*)
remained culturally and often geographically separate within their host
cultures.[4] Indeed, seen from the vantage point of Imperial Germany,
the backdrop of a foreign setting usually served to throw the essential
Germanness of migrants into high relief. The focus in this chapter is on
the domestic and gendered aspects of these depictions of Germans
abroad. When Germanness was defined by contrast with a foreign culture, what characteristics were ascribed to German women? How did
domestic practices and symbols supposedly help create and reproduce
German identity in Africa and Eastern Europe? What role did such
gendered attributes allegedly play in preserving Auslandsdeutsche
communities?

Although later writers would present them as intrinsically German,
many of the domestic practices discussed here only emerged within
Germany during the mid-nineteenth century, as part of a process of
class formation and differentiation. The introduction of new household technologies during the nineteenth century, and the increasing
tendency of urban households to purchase what they needed from the
market rather than producing goods themselves, resulted in new standards and routines in household management among the urban bourgeoisie.[5] High standards of cleanliness and household order, along
with a fixed routine for the performance of housework and the thrifty
management of household resources, now helped define social hierarchy and membership among the German bourgeoisie.

The new standards of household management were reflected in and
promoted by a flood of new advice literature and organizations for
bourgeois housewives.[6] The cleanliness, order, fixed routine, and cozi-
ness of middle strata households were attested to by such markers as
snow-white curtains, a well-ordered cabinet filled with sparkling white
linens, meticulously kept household account books, flowers on the

table, and a thrifty *Küchenzettel* (the week's menu plan) with its Sunday roast and cake.[7]

The lack of such domestic practices, by contrast, stigmatized working-class households. Working-class housewives' supposed deficiencies in cleanliness and order were proof of their inferiority and even degradation in the eyes of bourgeois observers. Descriptions of the filth and misery of the hovels of the working poor filled the writings of Wilhelmine social reformers and philanthropists, who usually attributed the poverty and dirt of working-class homes to their inhabitants' moral shortcomings. Working-class women became the objects of bourgeois missionary impulses after 1880, as middle-class reformers tried to popularize bourgeois approaches to housekeeping.[8]

What was bourgeois in Germany, however, was simply "German" abroad: in foreign settings, the markers that served to differentiate the bourgeoisie at home now symbolized ethnic or even racial identity as a whole.[9] By the same token, domestic disorder and dirt became associated with foreign women rather than with the working poor in Germany's cities. In Wilhelmine popular magazines and housewives' publications, it was a truism that no foreign woman kept house as well as German *Hausfrauen*.[10] When German authors of the varied genres discussed later thought of ethnic German women abroad, then, it was usually against a preestablished backdrop, an assumption that foreigners could not keep house as well as Germans.

We turn first to the household management of women who migrated to Germany's African colonies, especially to German Southwest Africa. The domestic adventures of such women were popularized for the metropolitan audience in a variety of publications, including memoirs and travel literature written by immigrants, the widely read illustrated weekly *Kolonie und Heimat* (the organ of the Women's League of the Colonial Society), and the large body of popular fiction produced after 1905 about Germany's colonies.[11] Such sources, along with newspaper accounts, provided German readers with their chief sources of information about Germans in Africa.[12] Although *Kolonie und Heimat* and similar publications began to find audiences in the years before World War I (the best-selling novel *Peter Moors Fahrt nach Südwest* was first published in 1907, and excerpts from popular colonial publications were reprinted in Imperial German school textbooks), works on German colonial life (especially fiction) reached their highest point of popularity during the 1920s and 1930s, after Germany had lost its colonies.[13]

This literature thus grew at the same time as the explosion in the research on ethnic German communities in Eastern Europe, which I will discuss later. Like the colonial literature, works on Germans in Eastern Europe appeared before 1914 but grew rapidly in number after 1918; during the prewar period, most such publications focused on ethnic Germans who lived in the Russian Empire. In the case of Eastern Europe, the enormous increase during the interwar period in the amount of ink spilled on ethnic Germans was of course related to the change in the status of those who had lived within the Hapsburg Empire. Before 1918 ethnic German enclaves were scattered across East Central Europe and were often seen as outposts in a Slavic environment. But within the Hapsburg Empire, Germans were the single most influential ethnic group and German was the language of both the civil service and the military. After 1918 such ethnic Germans became vulnerable ethnic minorities in some parts of East Central Europe, whom metropolitan Germans perceived as endangered Sprachinseln, and thus a much more interesting research subject. After 1918 ethnic Germans in both Southwest Africa and Eastern Europe were thus seen as enclaves of Germanness surrounded by non-Germans, no longer under the protection of a German state.

Accounts of German housewives in Africa of course included descriptions of their African servants and the African dwellings, which usually surrounded the German homestead and provided a sharp contrast to German housekeeping.[14] African homes were described as "huts" or "hovels," lacking the doors, windows, separate rooms for different activities, and straight lines that characterized European homes. In their memoirs, German female migrants commented disparagingly about African homes and the cleanliness of their inhabitants. Maria Karow, who kept house for her invalid sister in Southwest Africa for two years, later published a memoir that described the lifestyle and character of her sister's servants in some detail. She wrote that the homes of all Africans resembled "molehills," without proper doors or ventilation.[15] Margarethe v. Eckenbrecher, who worked as a teacher for decades in Southwest Africa, also compared the typical African home to "an enormous, gray-brown molehill. The entrance is a small opening, covered with a thornbush, animal pelts, sacks, or sometimes a door."[16]

Because of the shortage of German brides, many colonists had supposedly been compelled to marry African or mixed-race women; such women were also stigmatized as wasteful, inferior housekeepers.[17] But when a settler married a German housewife and brought her to his farm, she supposedly introduced metropolitan standards of cleanliness and order. Clara Brockmann, who lived in Southwest Africa for some years, later wrote in her publications for a metropolitan audience that

> without the presence of a Hausfrau . . . a farm cannot become *heimisch,* because only [her presence] secures German ways and customs, and a German family life. . . . [I knew a bachelor farmer whose animals throve but whose] house and rooms were in terribly neglected condition. . . . [After his bride arrived from Germany] the unkempt dwelling was transformed into an inviting rural home. In the kitchen and courtyard everything was well organized, and the garden bloomed. . . . [T]he rooms now resembled the comfortable abodes of the homeland.[18]

Painstaking cleanliness, above all, was both a marker of ethnic identity abroad and a reminder of the homeland. Maria Karow wrote that when she visited the homes of several artisans who had migrated there, "Their wives greeted me and showed me with pride their households, in which everything was so clean that it gleamed. If the African servants had not been there, I would have thought myself in Germany."[19]

Several authors described how a German housewife began almost immediately to outfit her home with the objects that symbolized good housekeeping at home, especially white curtains and embroidered, framed proverbs on the walls. One writer wrote that as soon as a woman arrived "there begins a hammering and washing. . . . muslin curtains and blindingly white linens give the house the stamp of a German home. . . . now the wash is conscientiously scrubbed twice with soap, boiled, and bleached on the lawn; after being ironed, it is put— now snow white—in the linen cabinet."[20]

Seen from the outside, the homes and (in larger settlements) the communities of Germans in Africa were presented as resembling those of the orderly small towns of the homeland. Travel writers and novelists described towns laid out with straight, wide streets, clean public spaces, and homes in good repair, contrasting German settlements with "dirty" British-ruled Mombasa (in Kenya) and Zanzibar. In his survey of German colonies, *Auf deutschem Boden in Afrika,* Paul Kollmann compared German-ruled Dar-es-Salaam with British Zanzibar.

> Viewed from the harbor, the city . . . gives the impression of a development of German villas . . . [with] pretty houses, built mainly of sparkling white lathe and plaster. . . .What a difference between Dar es Salaam and Zanzibar! Like day and night! . . . [In Zanzibar]

everywhere dilapidated houses . . . everywhere dirt in the streets. . . . in harsh contrast to what we see on *German* territory . . . *here* cleanliness prevails to the extreme; tree-lined streets, all the buildings with their decorative exteriors [and] solid and cozy furnishings.[21]

Cleanliness and European-style domesticity helped to define racial identity and to justify European hegemony throughout the colonial world, as Ann Stoler and other scholars have made clear.[22] But as the comparison of British Zanzibar and German Dar-es-Salaam indicates, for many of those who wrote about or participated in German colonization in Africa, extreme cleanliness and a certain approach to domestic management signified not only whiteness but also Germanness: a broad sense of German ethnic identity that transcended formal citizenship. This conclusion is also supported by the literature on the Eastern European Auslandsdeutschen that was produced during the same period.

Like the novels, memoirs, and travel literature that depicted German colonial life, works on Auslandsdeutschen (especially communities of ethnic Germans in Eastern Europe) began to appear in large numbers first during the Wilhelmine period and reached their apogee during the Weimar and Nazi periods. But the work produced after 1918 about Germans who lived in so-called Sprachinseln in Eastern Europe was incomparably more vast than the literature on German colonists. Indeed, it is far too enormous to be mastered in one lifetime. To offer one example, a bibliography that focuses solely on works on the Donauschwaben of Central Europe (themselves only a fraction of the Sprachinseln) contains over eight thousand listings for publications on this one area, the bulk of which appeared during the interwar period. Eastern European Auslandsdeutschen were indeed a hot scholarly topic within Germany during the interwar period, for reasons discussed in greater detail later. These publications included heavy, serious academic tomes by geographers, historians, linguists, and ethnographers; coffee-table books or travel literature aimed at a popular audience; amateur research of varying quality published by a host of local historical associations; and popular magazines from the interwar period, such as *der Auslandsdeutsche* and *der Volksdeutsche* (which had its own publication for youths, the *Roland-Blätter*).

This ethnographic gold lode was not a chance formation; it was funded and sponsored by a network of organizations and bureaucratic institutions. Some were *Vereine* that were the pillars of the pan-Germanist *völkisch* movement and the broader middle-class nationalist subculture, such as the Verein für das Deutschtum im Ausland, the Alldeutscher Verband, the Ostmarken Verein, the Deutsche Kolonialgesellschaft, and religious organizations for Germans abroad such as the Gustav-Adolf Verein. More serious academic research was often produced by scholars associated with one of a number of think tanks devoted to Auslandsdeutschen. The most prominent of these was the Deutsche Auslandsinstitut in Stuttgart, but research was also sponsored by the Institute for Eastern European History in Vienna and the Seminar for Eastern European History and Ethnography in Berlin. Many members of these institutions were connected to the voluntary associations listed previously. Both academic institutions and popular nationalist associations were funded and supported by the German government (the Verein für das Deutschtum im Ausland, or VDA, had particularly close ties to the German Foreign Office) and prominent German industrialists.[23]

During the Wilhelmine period, most of these voluntary organizations were smaller than the size they would later become, and there was a good deal of overlap between early German colonial boosters and those who were interested in ethnic Germans in Eastern Europe and elsewhere. The German academics and businessmen who mingled in these associations hoped that both German colonies and ethnic German communities in other nations would help to increase German exports and that ethnic Germans abroad would act as mediators between German businesses and foreign markets.[24] After 1918 membership in these organizations grew dramatically: the interwar period was the heyday of associations concerned with ethnic Germans abroad. The largest such group, the VDA, grew from forty-two thousand in 1909 to almost one million by 1925 and to over two million by 1929.[25]

At the same time, the purpose and focus of these publications shifted from economic boosterism to an openly revanchist focus on German claims in Eastern Europe, using such research to support the expansion of Germany's boundaries and influence in Central and Eastern Europe. As Michael Burleigh has noted about the scholarly publications on Eastern Europe during this period, German academics saw scholarship "as a means of substantiating 'rights'" and justifying revisions to the Treaty of Versailles.[26] Writers in both popular and scholarly interwar publications spoke of Sprachinseln and *Sprachgrenzen,* implying that linguistic boundaries should be equated with national boundaries, and used terms such as the *Kampf um die Erhaltung der Sprachinseln.* Their work often depicted the oppression of ethnic Germans in Eastern Europe, arguing that, at best, Auslandsdeutschen faced pressures that might submerge their ethnic islands; at worst, they faced open persecution, even torture or rape.[27] Awareness of ethnic Germans abroad and the perils they allegedly faced, fund-raising for them, and publicity about them thus became a core part of popular German nationalism after World War I. The Sprachinseln abroad were in fact incorporated into the larger nationalist vision of the *Volksgemeinschaft*.

Establishing claims meant surveying boundaries, and this literature used a variety of markers—deriving from agricultural, economic, religious, educational, and domestic life—to demarcate lines between the Auslandsdeutschen and surrounding host cultures. These works devoted considerable space to the crafts, guilds, and agricultural practices of ethnic German communities, including painstaking map after map of the layouts of fields and villages, which argued for the superior productivity, industriousness, and technological sophistication of ethnic German farmers and artisans. Ethnic German men were thus depicted as more hard working, dedicated, and orderly than their non-German counterparts.

But intermingled with the discussion of masculine workplaces were discussions of domestic spaces and practices, which made analogous claims for ethnic German women and their families. Academic and especially popular publications were fascinated with the daily lives and homes of Auslandsdeutschen and reproduced photographs, drawings, and elaborate descriptions of their clothing (*Trachten*), dialects, neighborhoods, domestic architecture, furniture, domestic decorative arts, holiday customs, and family life, including the division of work within the family and inheritance patterns.

As in Africa, the *Ostforscher* argued that German settlements in East Central Europe (which they sometimes referred to as *Volksboden,* that is, landscapes that bore an intrinsically German stamp) were distinguished by their clean streets, laid out in straight lines. Ethnic German homes were supposedly characterized by elaborate gables and straight lines; they, too, were kept in good repair.[28] One ethnologist's 1933 description of ethnic German villages in the Banat region of Romania was typical: "the German settlements are distinguished by their exemplary cleanliness and order, as seen in the neat cobbled streets and their clean courtyards, which sharply sets them apart from the homes of the other ethnic groups."[29] The vocabulary used to describe Slavic homes (whether Romanian, Russian, or Polish), however, was strikingly reminiscent of contemporary depictions of African households in Southwest Africa: Slavic families invariably lived in irregular, badly kept "huts," sometimes smoky or infested by vermin. Many books simply reproduced photographs of supposedly representative ethnic German and Slavic houses, which formed a striking contrast. One ethnologist claimed that the homes of "natives" in the Balkans were

> huts [that] consist of one, or at most two rooms. . . . their kitchens are blackened with smoke and covered with soot, because they are not designed to prevent the fires from smoking. . . . There is no furniture: chairs, benches, beds, and cabinets are unknown. One simply sleeps on a straw mat on the floor. . . . [When the Germans first came to this area] they were quartered in the dirty, smoky rooms of the Jews and Serbs, and became vermin-infested. Therefore they immediately built primitive huts for temporary use [until their houses were finished], which, according to their custom, they kept painstakingly clean.[30]

As in Africa, ethnic German housewives and their household management in Eastern Europe (especially their alleged penchant for order and sparkling white sheets, curtains, and so forth) were used to define—in gendered terms—German national identity and superiority. Through such domestic rituals and symbols, one writer wrote, women among the Volga Germans maintained a bridge between the old *Heimat* and the new. Such housekeeping, he concluded, passed on to their children the values of "a love for order, cleanliness, and a higher standard of living," qualities that represented a uniquely German heritage.[31]

Around the world, and especially across Eastern Europe, ethnic German homes were described as standing out from those in surrounding cultures by virtue of their cleanliness and the snow-white linens and aprons produced by Auslandsdeutsche housewives. In Southeastern Europe, one writer described the parlor (*gute Stube*) of the typical ethnic German household.

> On either side of the room are beds, each with its large down-filled quilt, covered with white duvets. . . . by the window is a cabinet, which is covered with a snow-white cloth, produced by the housewife herself. . . . the floor is wooden, and is thoroughly scoured once a week. Over the windows, we see small white, homemade embroidered curtains.[32]

German farms in Galicia, another wrote, "have lovely houses . . .
which are distinguished by an impressive degree of cleanliness. . . .
[Even the local Poles acknowledge] that the Germans are thriftier and
harder working than the Poles, and that their homes are cleaner."[33]
Another writer described a group of ethnic German young women
going to church in Romania: "I watched the group of young women in
their lovely traditional costumes. Sparkling white embroidered aprons
fluttered around each tall, slim figure. Each one had tightly braided
hair, and wore a satin *Borte* [headdress] from which fell long silk rib-
bons, flowing over the pure white, heavily embroidered shirt."[34] In
Dobrudja an ethnologist described the gute Stube of a typical ethnic
German home: "[This room] contains the best furniture and linens. . . .
clean, bright curtains hang in the windows, and the walls are richly
decorated with pictures, photographs, and framed sayings. . . . [There
is invariably also] a large bed [*Paradebett*] which displays five feather
pillows, each encased in a snow white, embroidered covering. . . .
Almost without exception, all houses and rooms are meticulously
orderly and clean."[35]

Expressions like *gute Stube, Paradebett,* and *Kachelofen* (an oven
decorated with ceramic tiles) were frequently used to describe Auslandsdeutsche homes: these were familiar, cozy domestic items and
terms familiar to metropolitan Germans. And readers were assured
that, although much else might have changed in Eastern Europe over
the centuries, domestic details had been relatively unchanging and
hence were implicitly timeless. Many academic works—such as the
multivolume, monumental *Handwörterbuch des Grenz- und Ausland-
deutschtums*—documented change over time in various ethnic German
communities' economic organizations, legal institutions, and arts and
literary life, but these works argued that lifestyle and domesticity, in a
broad sense, remained unchanged. Thus, the *Handwörterbuch* included
successive sections for each community, chronologically organized for
different periods, which traced historic change and development in the
public sphere among ethnic Germans in each region. Private life was
treated in an enormous section on *Hausform und Wohnweise* in the
very first chronological segment for each community (which might
cover the early modern period or the nineteenth century); in subsequent segments, the information for each topic in the public sphere was
updated, but for Hausform und Wohnweise, readers were always
referred back to the section in the opening segment. Private life thus
evidently stood outside of historic change, even as the nations in which
German communities were located were divided and reorganized. And

the roots of domestic practices could be traced back to the German-speaking parts of the Holy Roman Empire, according to this literature. Scholars claimed that Trachten, domestic architectural forms, and dialects could be clearly shown to have derived from whatever section of the Holy Roman Empire these people's ancestors had come from; costumes, expressions, and holiday customs from early modern Pflalz or Rhineland—swept away by modernization in Germany—still allegedly lived on in the Sprachinseln.

Descriptions like these (and many more examples could be offered here) must have reassured German readers about the essential Germanness of such qualities as cleanliness, order, and well-organized household management, and the broader domestic customs and practices to which they were linked, by showing how such characteristics survived for hundreds of years even in isolated ethnic German settlements in Russia or off in the African bush. These depictions of Germans abroad thus could be—and were—used as a mirror by Germans at home to reflect what they saw as the essence of their national character, and this character was often defined in gendered terms. Women—especially in their roles as housewives—served as vehicles for the expression and maintenance of German ethnic identity: imagined housewives in communities that, as described, bore a striking resemblance to völkisch Brigadoons.

The discussion of what constituted Germanness was not limited to popular publications, however, and its importance went beyond the realm of pure discourse. These German communities of Eastern Europe in particular, so-called Sprachinseln, were romanticized and popularized in the consciousness of the German public and most especially within conservative German bourgeoisie. The awareness of these communities, and the images associated with them, were taken up and carried forward by Nazi theorists and policymakers as well.

After 1939, as Nazi leaders attempted massive reorganization of the map and populations of Eastern Europe, these interwar fairy tales had an increasingly important impact on the implementation of German policy. During World War II, Nazi bureaucrats in occupied Eastern Europe, strongly influenced by the work of interwar academics, attempted to sweep up, sort through, and categorize millions of Auslandsdeutschen or *Volksdeutschen,* trying to assess the depth and degree of their Germanness in order to assign citizenship, and to re-Germanize those who had fallen away from the ideal standards depicted in the earlier works on these communities. Hundreds of thousands of ethnic Germans were taken from their homelands and brought to occupied Poland to create a new border region populated largely by Auslandsdeutschen.[36]

In the interwar literature, the Sprachinseln had usually been described as implicitly separate from their host cultures and their German identity seen as unambiguous. But the reality of documenting and resettling so many people revealed that it was often difficult to draw clear ethnic lines. Too many people with some claim on German citizenship had mixed ancestry, or came from mixed or assimilated communities, and often spoke German badly or not at all. Nazi bureaucrats never did develop a uniform standard for assessing whether applicants from Eastern Europe were completely German. Many of the evaluators relied upon so-called biological characteristics (hair and eye color). If applicants for citizenship possessed these physical criteria but lacked social characteristics considered German (such as language ability, orderliness, and cleanliness), these could be taught after citizenship was granted.[37]

But there was no single bureaucracy that controlled all decisions relating to the Volksdeutschen across the disorganized panorama of occupied Eastern Europe. From one nation to the next, sometimes even from one *Gau* to the next in what had been Poland, different agencies and Nazi bureaucrats employed diverse and conflicting criteria. When the ancestry of so-called Volksdeutchen was unclear, or their Germanness was called into question for other reasons (a faulty command of the German language, for example), then many bureaucrats (from the Volksdeutsche Mittelstelle or from Reichskommissar für die Festigung des Deutschtums) relied upon social characteristics and behaviors.[38] Among these, practices and characteristics associated with domesticity could play a particularly important role in evaluating the Germanness of female applicants. Applicants could be and were denied citizenship, or given it on probation only, if they had dirty homes; in cases where the applicant's home life was unclear, Nazi bureaucrats might send social workers or women from the NS Frauenschaft to inspect the applicant's housekeeping and general domesticity.[39] A clean home, with white linens, was sometimes taken as a guarantor of German ancestry—an ironic tribute to the impact of the interwar literature that I have discussed.

Even those whose alleged citizenship, ethnicity, and race had been certified, and who had been resettled from Eastern Europe to the Wartheland (as one section of Poland was renamed), often had to have their housekeeping and homes re-Germanized to meet the ideal standards of the imaginary Hausfrau. A good part of the work of the NS

Frauenschaft in occupied Poland was to re-Germanize the homes of
Poles who had been deported to the East before the new Volksdeutsche
"settlers" arrived. Teams of women and girls from the Bund deutscher
Mädel would stand by as the SS cleared out Polish farmers and their
families from their homes, making sure that Polish women did not
smuggle small domestic items with them: the entire inventory of
kitchen goods and linens were to be preserved for the new occupants.
Then the teams of women would go to work, scrubbing away the "Polish dreck," whitening the walls, hanging white curtains, and putting
out flowers. Only then were the new "German" settlers brought to
these homes.

But members of the NS Frauenschaft soon found that the domesticity, and hence Germanness, of many ethnic German women was ques-
tionable. The internal correspondence of the Nazi women assigned to
Poland shows that they established a scale of Germanness that guided
their work with Volksdeutsche families, on which they ranked and
compared the Baltic Germans, Bukovina Germans, Galician Germans, and so forth, in terms of their housekeeping abilities and the
clarity and purity of their German dialects. The resettled Germans
from the Dobrudja, for example, were highly regarded, since their German was still "pure" and their houses were kept clean and orderly.
Such settlers were praised for giving formerly Polish homes a new
"German look."[40] One press release claimed that the resettled women
"took up their work quickly and many homes quickly developed a
German appearance. Windows were washed, and everywhere one
quickly noted the hand which set things in order."[41]

But other female advisors from the "old Reich" were disappointed
to see that many of the resettled families had "lost" their domestic German attributes, including not only their language but also any claim to
superior housekeeping. The Galician Germans, for example, were
alleged to prefer to speak Polish instead of German and to be disor-
derly, dirty housekeepers. Advisors from the NS Frauenschaft and
Deutsches Frauenwerk set up kindergartens, cooking courses, and
domestic science courses to "re-Germanize" their charges' housekeeping and child-rearing practices. A number of Nazi women's groups
sent social workers to inspect ethnic German homes and to encourage
women to meet higher standards of order and cleanliness, although
these women usually had increased duties in the fields and stables after
their husbands and sons had been drafted. Reports sent back to Berlin
by such advisors complained repeatedly about the "primitive lifestyle
and knowledge of housekeeping" of ethnic German women and noted

that "we simply cannot assume anything [about their knowledge of housekeeping], and must teach them even the simplest recipes and rules of cooking." Another advisor noted that "The news quickly spread [through the district] that I expected to see well-ordered rooms and clean, not torn clothing [when I paid house calls] . . . and I believe that I did have some influence in this area."[42] The resettled families had to be taught how to celebrate a "German-style" Christmas and to sing new hymns.[43] In short, the NS Frauenschaft attempted to resocialize ethnic German housewives, re-creating the pan-German domesticity that had been vividly described in the interwar literature produced by Ostforscher and writers for the popular nationalist audience.

German national identity has been an ongoing construction project since the early nineteenth century. Drawing the lines that demarcated the German Empire from "greater Germany" (as it was called in the mid-nineteenth century), redrawing the map of Central Europe after 1918 (often showing in ghostly gray, or with dotted lines, the border zones that "ought" to be within German boundaries), and then successively revising Germany's borders and identity after 1933 meant that both academics and popular nationalist writers were forced to scramble to constantly revise their definitions and works.[44] These fluctuations, and the problematic and fluid concept of German identity itself, made the establishment of a stable core of Germanness all the more necessary for metropolitan German audiences. The core of Germanness that allegedly existed among all ethnic Germans justified expanding national boundaries, as Germany's rulers aspired to encompass all true Germans within a German state. Domesticity helped define such a core identity for many Germans, which explains why it figured so strongly in interwar discussions of Eastern European Volksdeutschen and in Nazi policies toward resettled ethnic Germans after 1939. In the midst of other challenges and revisions to German national identity, the patterns, practices, and attributes of daily, domestic life helped to define German normalcy. Domesticity was an essential quality that would allegedly never change, even as so much else was swept clean away.

NOTES

This chapter (along with other works that I have published) benefited from a careful reading by the members of the German Women's History Study Group. I am particularly indebted to coeditor Krista O'Donnell, who generously shared many of her Southwest African sources with me. I am also grateful to Benjamin Lapp and the outside readers recruited by the University of Michigan Press, whose judicious suggestions also helped to improve this piece. All translations in this chapter are my own unless otherwise specified.

1. See Gerhard Weidenfeller, *VDA. Verein für das Deutschtum im Ausland. Allgemeiner Deutscher Schulverein (1881–1918). Ein Beitrag zur Geschichte des deutschen Nationalismus und Imperialismus im Kaiserreich* (Frankfurt, 1976), 37–44.

2. See Kirsten Belgum's examination of the depiction of Germans abroad in the popular illustrated magazine *Gartenlaube,* "A Nation for the Masses: Production of German Identity in the Late-Nineteenth Century Popular Press," in *A User's Guide to German Cultural Studies,* ed. Scott Denham, Irene Kacandes, and Jonathan Petropoulos (Ann Arbor, Mich., 1997), 163–80.

3. Rogers Brubaker, *Citizenship and Nationhood in France and Germany* (Cambridge, Mass., 1992), 117–19.

4. The provenance of the term *Auslandsdeutschen* is not entirely clear. It evidently first came into widespread usage within Germany during the public discussions that led to the passage of the 1913 citizenship law. Before World War I, the term was almost always used to refer to ethnic Germans who lived outside both Germany and the Hapsburg Empire (where German speakers were, of course, the dominant group and were not a minority in the same sense as they were in Russia, for example). After 1918, when ethnic German communities were "stranded" by the collapse of the Hapsburg Empire and rendered true ethnic minorities, the term *Auslandsdeutschen* was increasingly applied to almost all ethnic Germans who resided outside of Germany, Austria, and Switzerland. For a discussion of the background usages of this term, see Howard Sargent, "Pioneer or Delinquent? Images of the German Abroad in the Debate over Citizenship Law," paper presented at the conference "The *Heimat* Abroad: The Boundaries of Germanness," Center for European Studies, New York University, November 19–20, 1999; see also Brubaker, *Citizenship and Nationhood,* 114–20.

5. For the changes in household management that accompanied urbanization and the introduction of new household technologies and the articulation of new standards of hygiene, cleanliness, and order in bourgeois households during the mid-nineteenth century in Germany, see my article "The Imagined Hausfrau: National Identity, Domesticity, and Colonialism in Imperial Germany," *Journal of Modern History* 73 (March 2001): 54–86. See also Margarethe Freudenthal, *Gestaltwandel der städtischen, bürgerlichen, und proletarischen Hauswirtschaft zwischen 1760 und 1910* (Frankfurt and Berlin, 1986), 95–112; and Marion Kaplan, *The Making of the Jewish Middle Class: Women, Family, and Identity in Imperial Germany* (New York, 1991), 33–35.

6. See Reagin, "The Imagined Hausfrau" and *A German Women's Movement: Class and Gender in Hanover, 1880–1933* (Chapel Hill, 1995), 71–98. See also Kirsten Schlegel-Matthias, *"Im Haus und am Herd": Der Wandel des Hausfrauenbildes und der Hausarbeit 1880–1930* (Stuttgart, 1995). For a discussion of the advice literature and housewives' organizations that promoted these housekeeping standards, see Annabel Weismann, *Froh erfülle deine Pflicht* (Berlin, 1989); Inga Wiedemann,

Herrin im Hause: Durch Koch- und Haushaltsbücher zur bürgerlichen Hausfrau (Pfaffenweiler, 1993); Siegfried Bluth, *Der Hausfrau gewidmet: Ein Beitrag zur Kulturgeschichte der Hausfrau* (Weil der Stadt, 1979); and Gisela Framke and Gisela Marenk, eds., *Beruf der Jungfrau: Henriette Davidis und Bürgerliches Frauenverständis im 19. Jahrhundert* (Oberhausen, 1988). The association of household cleanliness with social differentiation and hierarchy was, of course, not confined to Germany, as the literature on the emergence of the bourgeoisie in other European cultures makes clear.

7. See Reagin, "The Imagined Hausfrau"; Sibylle Meyer, *Das Theater mit der Hausarbeit: Bürgerliche Repräsentation in der Familie der wilhelminischen Zeit* (Frankfurt, 1982).

8. Reagin, *A German Women's Movement,* 73–97; Ute Frevert, "Fürsorgliche Belagerung. Hygienebewegung und Arbeiterfrauen im 19. und frühen 20. Jahrhundert," *Geschichte und Gesellschaft* 11 (1985): 420–46; Kathleen Canning, *Languages of Labor and Gender: Female Factory Work in Germany, 1850–1914* (Ithaca, 1996), 122–25, 150. These attempts to "reform" working-class housekeeping were, of course, not limited to Germany but rather were popular throughout the Western world during the nineteenth century; in the United States such programs went under the rubric of "Americanization."

9. See Jean and John Comaroff, "Homemade Hegemony: Modernity, Domesticity, and Colonialism in South Africa," in *African Encounters with Domesticity,* ed. Karen T. Hansen (New Brunswick, N.J., 1992), 37–74.

10. These ubiquitous depictions of foreign housewives (e.g., the recurring cliché that English women left all their housework to their servants and that American women spent their time shopping) are the subject of Reagin, "The Imagined Hausfrau."

11. For memoirs and travel literature written by women who had been to Africa, see Clara Brockmann, *Die deutsche Frau in Südwestafrika: Ein Beitrag zur Frauenfrage in unseren Kolonien* (Berlin, 1910); Else Sonnenberg, *Wie es am Waterberg zuging: Ein Beitrag zur Geschichte des Hereroaufstandes* (Berlin, 1905); Ada Cramer, *Weiss oder Schwarz: Lehr- und Leidensjahre eines Farmers in Südwest im Lichte des Rassenhasses* (Berlin, 1913); Margarethe v. Eckenbrecher, Helene v. Falkenhausen, Stabsarzt Dr. Kuhn, and Oberleutnant Stuhlmann, *Deutsch-Südwestafrika. Kriegs- und Friedensbilder* (Leipzig, 1907); Helene v. Falkenhausen, *Ansiedlerschicksale: Elf Jahre in Deutsch-Südwestafrika 1893–1904* (Berlin, 1905); Margarethe v. Eckenbrecher, *Im dichten Pori; Reise- und Jagdbilder aus Deutsch-Ostafrika* (Berlin, 1912) and *Was Afrika mir gab und nahm: Erlebnisse einer deutschen Frau in Südwestafrika* (Berlin, 1940); and Maria Karow, *Wo sonst der Fuss des Kriegers trat. Farmerleben in Südwest nach dem Kriege* (Berlin, 1909). For a discussion of German colonists in popular Wilhelmine and Weimar fiction, see Joachim Warmbold, *Germania in Africa: Germany's Colonial Literature* (New York, 1989); and Sibylle Benninghoff-Lühl, "'Ach Afrika! Wär ich zu hause!' Gedanken zum Deutschen Kolonialroman der Jahrhundertwende," in *Afrika und der Deutsche Kolonialismus: Zivilisierung zwischen Schnapshandel und Bibelstunde,* ed. Renate Nestvogel and Rainer Tetzlaff (Berlin, 1987), 83–100. Since German Southwest Africa attracted by far the largest number of migrants (it had the most

"suitable" climate and geography), the bulk of published memoirs, books, and articles was concerned with Germans in this colony.

12. For a broader history of the migration of women to German Southwest Africa, see Krista E. O'Donnell, "The Colonial Woman Question: Gender, National Identity, and Empire in the German Colonial Society Female Emigration Program, 1896–1914" (Ph.D. diss., SUNY Binghamton, 1996); see also Lora Wildenthal, *German Women for Empire, 1884–1945* (Durham N.C., 2001); and Florence Herve, ed., *Namibia: Frauen mischen sich ein* (Berlin, 1993).

13. See Warmbold, *Germania in Africa*, 80–92, 144–45; and Benninghoff-Lühl, "'Ach Afrika!'," 85–89.

14. Comments on the poor personal hygiene of Africans were ubiquitous in travel literature and memoirs. See, for example, Karow, *Wo sonst der Fuss,* 33–34, and Brockmann, *Die deutsche Frau in Südwestafrika,* 25–28. During the precolonial era, Africans throughout Southern Africa used pastes made of various oils and muds on their skins to protect themselves against insects and the sun and also because safe supplies of water for washing were often not available. See Timothy Burke, *Lifebuoy Men and Lux Women: Commodification, Consumption, and Cleanliness in Modern Zimbabwe* (Durham, N.C., 1996), 24–25; see also Comaroff, "Homemade Hegemony"; and Nancy Rose Hunt, "Colonial Fairy Tales and the Knife and Fork Doctrine in the Heart of Africa," in *African Encounters,* ed. Hansen, 143–71.

15. Karow, *Wo sonst der Fuss,* 154. Tim Burke notes the ways in which racism led whites to attempt to segregate and isolate themselves physically. Whites were so convinced that Africans were dirty and were so revolted by contact with them that they often went to astonishing lengths to avoid touching anything that had come into contact with natives, such as breaking teacups that visiting African teachers had drunk from or scrubbing chairs that Africans had sat on. See Burke, *Lifebuoy Men,* 21.

16. Eckenbrecher, *Was Afrika mir gab und nahm,* 27, 32. Eckenbrecher added later, however, that these homes were kept tolerably clean, an admission that sets her apart from other writers.

17. For a persuasive discussion of why German settlers might have in fact preferred to marry local women, see O'Donnell, "The Colonial Woman Question," 46–49.

18. Brockmann, *Die deutsche Frau in Südwestafrika,* 3–6.

19. Karow, *Wo sonst der Fuss,* 128.

20. Emmy Müller, "Die deutsche Frau in der Südsee," *Kolonie und Heimat* 3 (1910): 6–7. Other writers also noted how they hung white curtains and *Andenken* as one of their first acts after arriving; see Sonnenberg, *Wie es am Waterberg zuging,* and Falkenhausen, *Ansiedlerschicksale.* Considering the difficulties of maintaining a metropolitan standard of hygiene in Southwest Africa (such as the lack of running, or often any clean, water; the extremely dusty conditions; and the termites) one may be skeptical about such claims. But of the writers surveyed here, only Falkenhausen ever admitted to a less-than-German standard of cleanliness; the others all asserted that they were able to reproduce *heimische* standards of cleanliness and order.

21. Paul Kollmann, *Auf deutschem Boden in Afrika: Ernste und heitere Erleb-nisse* (Berlin, 1900), quoted in Warmbold, *Germania in Africa,* 158; italics in origi-nal. See Warmbold, *Germania in Africa,* 158–63, for other writers' descriptions of the exceptional cleanliness of German colonies.

22. See, for example, Ann L. Stoler, "Carnal Knowledge and Imperial Power: Gender, Race, and Morality in Colonial Asia," in *Gender at the Crossroads of Knowledge: Feminist Anthropology in the Post-Modern Era,* ed. Micaela di Leonardo (Berkeley, Calif., 1991); Burke, *Lifebuoy Men;* and Hansen, *African Encounters with Domesticity.*

23. For discussions of these right-wing voluntary associations, academic insti-tutions, and their links to government agencies and German business leaders, see Michael Burleigh, *Germany Turns Eastward: A Study of Ostforschung in the Third Reich* (Cambridge, 1988); Weidenfeller, *VDA;* Ernst Ritter, *Das Deutsche Aus-lands-Institut in Stuttgart 1917–1945: Ein Beispiel deutscher Volkstumsarbeit zwis-chen den Weltkriegen* (Wiesbaden, 1976); Walter v. Goldendach and Hans-Rüdiger Minow, *'Deutschtum Erwache!' Aus dem Innenleben des staatlichen Pangermanis-mus* (Berlin, 1994); and Pieter Judson, *Exclusive Revolutionaries: Liberal Politics, Social Experience, and National Identity in the Austrian Empire, 1848–1914* (Ann Arbor, Mich., 1996).

24. See Goldendach, *'Deutschtum erwache!,'* and Weidenfeller, *VDA.*

25. See Goldendach, *'Deutschtum erwache!,'* 129, and Weidenfeller, *VDA,* 325.

26. Burleigh, *Germany Turns Eastward,* 29.

27. Weidenfeller, *VDA,* 51–55, 131.

28. See Burleigh, *Germany Turns Eastward,* 25–26. Lyrical descriptions of eth-nic German fields and streets, which are always described as *schnurgerade* (laid out in very straight lines), abound in descriptions of ethnic German communities. See, for example, Raimund Kaindl, *Die Deutschen in Galizien und in der Bukowina* (Frankfurt, 1916), 128–32; Irmgard Pohl, *Deutsche im Südosten Europas: Vorposten des Volkstums* (Leipzig, 1938), 55–57; and Maria Kahle, *Deutsches Volk in der Fremde* (Oldenburg, 1933), 9–10.

29. See Carl Petersen et al., eds., *Handwörterbuch des Grenz- und Auslands-deutschtums,* vol. 1 (Breslau, 1933–35), 242.

30. Pohl, *Deutsche im Südosten Europas,* 55, 57. This description is somewhat more vehement than those of other writers (probably because it comes from 1938— the strong anti-Semitism is not typical of earlier literature), but it combines all the stereotypes about Slavs presented by earlier authors. For the inability of Slavs and Southeastern Europeans to get rid of vermin, see also "Leben der deutschen Frau im Orient," *Die Welt der Frau* 35 (1909); the prevalence of fleas and lice throughout Romania recurs in Ilse Obrig, *Guter Mucki, nimm auch mit: Eine Reise zu den Aus-landsdeutschen in Rumänien* (Stuttgart, 1938). See also Raimund Kaindl, *Deutsche Art—treu bewahrt* (Vienna, 1924), 57.

31. Jakob Stach, *Die deutschen Kolonien in Südrussland,* (Prischib, 1905), 97–99.

32. Karl Kraushaar, *Sitten und Bräuche der Deutschen in Ungarn, Rumänien, und Jugoslavien* (Vienna, 1932), 12–13.

33. Kaindl, *Die Deutschen in Galizien,* 159, 161.

34. Kahle, *Deutsches Volk in der Fremde,* 34.

35. Paul Traeger, *Die Deutschen in der Dobrudscha* (Stuttgart, 1922), 146.

36. See Dietmut Majer, *"Fremdvölker" im Dritten Reich* (Boppard am Rhein, 1981), 215–20, 419–26; Elizabeth Harvey, "'Die Deutsche Frau im Osten': 'Rasse,' Geschlecht, und Oeffentlicher Raum im besetzten Polen, 1940–44," *Archiv für Sozialgeschichte* 38 (1998): 191–214; and Doris L. Bergen, "The Nazi Concept of 'Volksdeutsche' and the Exacerbation of Anti-Semitism in Eastern Europe, 1939–1945," *Journal of Contemporary History* 29 (1994): 569–82.

37. See Isabel Heinemann, "Himmler's Search for 'Good Blood': Racial Selection/Germanization in the Occupied East," paper presented at the annual conference of the German Studies Association, Atlanta, October 1999.

38. See, for example, Bundesarchiv (hereafter BA) Berlin, R 69, Einwanderer Zentralstelle Litzmannstadt, Bd. 302, Regelung von Staatsangehörigkeitsfragen—Richtlinien.

39. Private communication from Doris Bergen, Oct. 6, 1999. For more on the arbitrary evaluation of those who applied for categorization as "Volksdeutschen" during World War II, see Bergen's chapter in this volume, which extensively discusses the criteria used to assign citizenship and racial categorization.

40. See BA, R 49 Reichskommissar für die Festigung des Volkstums, Nrn. 3045 and 3062 for materials relating to the work of the NS Frauenschaft and the Deutsches Frauenwerk with resettled ethnic Germans. Some of this material consists of press releases, which, of course, described the new "German" homes in usually glowing terms. But these volumes also include internal reports, which assessed the shortcomings and lack of "Germanness" of resettled women in much franker terms as well.

41. BA, R 49 Reichskommissar für die Festigung des Volkstums, Nr. 3045, Bd. 1, p. 148.

42. From reports in BA, R 49, Nr. 3053, p. 93, and Nr. 3045 Bd. 1, p. 137.

43. BA, R 49, Nr. 3062, p. 71.

44. A popular example of this ongoing revision is Gottfried Fittbogen's *Was jeder Deutsche vom Grenz- und Auslandsdeutschtum wissen muss,* which went through numerous editions during the 1930s; as the author admitted in the introduction to one edition, he could hardly keep up with the changes. See the ninth edition of his *Was jeder Deutsche vom Grenz- und Auslanddeutschtum wissen muss* (Berlin, 1938), 7.

CHAPTER 11

Tenuousness and Tenacity

The *Volksdeutschen* of Eastern Europe,
World War II, and the Holocaust

Doris L. Bergen

A 1938 memorandum of the German Reich chancellery defined *Volksdeutsche* as people whose "language and culture" had "German origins," although they were not citizens of Germany.[1] The German word *Volksdeutsch,* however, carries overtones of blood and race captured neither in that bland definition nor in the English translation "ethnic Germans." According to German experts in the 1930s, about thirty million Volksdeutsche lived outside the Reich,[2] at least ten million of them in Eastern Europe: Poland, the Baltic states, Ukraine, Hungary, and Romania.[3] The twin Nazi goals of purification of the so-called Aryan race and spatial expansion, particularly eastward,[4] ensured that the Volksdeutschen in Eastern Europe occupied a special place in German plans.[5] But what of the ethnic Germans themselves? What part did they play in World War II and the Holocaust?

The postwar statement of a married couple from Pusztavam, Hungary, illustrates some of the forms that ethnic German participation could take. The handwritten document, signed by both husband and wife, describes the massacre of Jews in their hometown on October 16, 1944. The couple's house, the man recalled, was about five hundred meters from a small hill.

There ten people at a time had to undress. Only then did they realize that they were going to be shot. No one had told my wife and me about it. But all of a sudden there was so much crying and screaming that we could hear it even in our own beloved home, where a group of neighbors had gathered. All of them heard how those poor people begged not to be shot and promised to help fight for Germany. The whole population of Pusztavam was outraged about what was happening. But they could do nothing against the SS soldiers. They were real devils. . . . Later the SS soldiers went to the Jews' homes and took away all of their baggage and their clothes. Those things were distributed among members of the *Volksbund* [an ethnic German organization].[6]

In contrast to many Germans in the fatherland, that man and woman, like their counterparts in Poland, Yugoslavia, and Ukraine, were not separated geographically from the shooting pits and killing centers of the Holocaust; they lived next door. The Volksdeutschen, as the Pusztavam report shows, were witnesses to and beneficiaries of genocide; other sources present them as perpetrators and, less frequently, as resistors.

The account of events in Pusztavam, like many similar records, assumes obvious distinctions—between ethnic Germans and Jews, on the one hand, and Volksdeutsche and *Reichsdeutsche* (Germans from Germany), on the other. Reality, it turns out, was often less clear-cut, particularly in the early stages of the war. Over decades and in some cases centuries, German-speaking settlers in the East had intermarried with their neighbors. Many had changed their religious allegiances, adopted or adapted cultural practices, abandoned the German language, or transformed it in ways alien to the German ear. Nazi authorities used a combination of cumbersome bureaucracy and simple arbitrariness in their attempts to sort out this ethnic mix to their advantage. The results often disappointed proponents of racial purity. Such confusion in turn contributed both to the insecurity of people defined as ethnic Germans and to the vulnerability of those designated outside that privileged group: most notably Jews and Slavs.

By now it is customary to speak of ethnicity—like gender, race, and so much else—as constructed. And, indeed, like those other "facts" of social life, ethnicity is neither inherent nor somehow natural but rather erected and maintained by people through a complex interplay of social, ideological, and political forces. That something is constructed by no means makes it impotent or irrelevant. To the contrary, myth and manipulability not only can coexist with but can reinforce powerful social divisions. In the case of the Volksdeutschen, ethnicity took on life-and-death significance in the context of a regime and a war based on notions of race, racial purity, and the reordering of Europe along lines of "blood." The rest of this chapter explores the relationship between constructed ethnicity and actual genocide in Eastern Europe during World War II. What does it mean to call the notion of

Volksdeutsch tenuous? How did that ambiguity shape ethnic German involvement in the crimes of the Third Reich—as perpetrators, opponents, and casualties?

Centrality and Tenuousness of the Concept of Volksdeutsch

The concept of Volksdeutsch played a crucial role in National Socialist notions of race and space. Nazi racial policy had two sides. On the one hand, it involved eradication of people deemed impure—Jews above all, Gypsies, and certain mentally or physically handicapped people—as well as enslavement and "reduction" of purported *Untermenschen* such as Slavs; on the other hand, it meant promotion of those people identified as valuable Aryans. In the East, the second half of this dual policy meant locating ethnic Germans and designating them the beneficiaries of genocide. In October 1939, Hitler charged Heinrich Himmler, the man who would orchestrate the implementation of the destruction of the European Jews, with the task of administering the web of organizations and regulations set up to identify, reeducate, and resettle the Volksdeutschen.[7] In much the same way as Nazi authorities made laws and institutions to define and deal with Jews, they constructed a complex bureaucracy to handle ethnic Germans.[8]

In the self-referential system of Nazi thought, the mere existence of the Volksdeutschen provided some legitimation for the murder of millions of other people. The idea that ethnic Germans would inherit the homes and possessions of people whom Nazi ideology defined as unworthy of life made the so-called struggle for *Lebensraum* more concrete. At the same time, the notion that pure Germans had somehow been trapped outside the Reich and forced to suffer under alien rule provided Hitler's forces with a pretext to overrun Eastern Europe. Ethnic Germans constituted at least a potential fifth column,[9] as well as an integral part of the massive resettlement schemes that made up the Nazis' "new European order."[10] If the Volksdeutschen had not existed, Nazi ideologues might have invented them. And in some very significant ways, they did precisely that.

Nazi ideology assumed ethnic Germans to be easily identifiable—from their appearance, language, habits of living, and qualities, such as cleanliness, willingness to work hard, and devotion to National Socialism.[11] But when German authorities tried to implement policies regarding the Volksdeutschen, they found the concept to be full of contradictions, unclarity, and absurdities. Was language to be the definitive criterion? Many Jews outside the Reich also spoke German, and many people who qualified as Volksdeutsche did not. Was blood the dividing line? Even inside the Reich, "German blood" proved impossible to establish, as the Nuremberg Laws, with their reliance on religious distinctions, demonstrated.[12] And religion itself? Ethnic Germans came from varied backgrounds, including Lutheran, Catholic, Baptist, and Mennonite. No single criterion proved satisfactory to delineate this important group.

Contemporaries did not fail to notice the many difficulties associated with defining Volksdeutsche. When the Ministry of Justice proposed a new marriage law, it planned to prohibit German citizens from marrying foreigners. Drafters of the law wanted to make an exception for ethnic Germans, but "the difficulty of delineating ethnic Germans in a clear and unambiguous way" persuaded them not to do so.[13] Sometimes vagueness took more dramatic forms. In August 1941 the Nazi murder squad Einsatzgruppe B reported from Smolensk that it had located a number of ethnic Germans. According to the report, however, intermarriage had so alienated those people from their roots that their claim to Germanness was now tentative at best. Despite that admission, the Einsatzgruppe considered it in Germany's "ethnic-political interests" to carve out a special status for those dubious Volksdeutschen. Accordingly, the Einsatzgruppe requested additional allocations of food and preferential treatment with regard to housing for the group.[14] For Nazi purposes, the existence of people who could be labeled *Volksdeutsche* was more important than the cultural or racial authenticity of such claims.

Throughout the war, offices all over occupied and incorporated Eastern Europe busied themselves with the task of assessing, cataloging, and educating the Volksdeutschen. German officials used all kinds of methods, ranging from elaborate orange cards with questions about the shape of individuals' eyelids and chins to the designation of entire villages as ethnic German settlements to tests of political reliability. There were even SS inspectors who assessed the racial potential of the fetuses of pregnant slave laborers in Germany. If the fetus was ruled "desirable," the woman was required to carry the pregnancy to term and submit the child for "Germanization"; if it was found "undesirable," she was forced to abort. Files of the SS Race and Settlement Office's Wiesbaden branch contain the records of one particular inspector for early 1945. He traveled across Southwestern Germany to appraise the claims to Germanness of people from Ukraine, Poland, and other parts of Europe. His report for January 1945 praised the "cleanliness and diligence" of a young female candidate for Germanization from the Banat and evaluated the racial potential of several fetuses.[15] Bureaucracies in Prague, Berlin, Lodz, and elsewhere pursued their own programs to identify and advance ethnic Germans.[16]

All such efforts notwithstanding, instead of finding pockets of pure Germanness preserved in the East, observers from the Reich often discovered ethnic Germans who had been influenced by the culture of their neighbors, even in some cases their Jewish neighbors. A German Protestant visitor to colonies of Volksdeutschen in Poland remarked that their language reflected a "Jewish jargon."[17] Some ethnic Germans had even married Jews. In 1944 the resettlement program for Volksdeutschen in Galicia encountered such a case. An ethnic German woman who had divorced her Jewish husband applied for resettlement. The SS questioned whether she or her children qualified for inclusion in the program. It was Himmler who ultimately decided that the mother could be accepted for resettlement without the two children. They could only enter Germany as charges of the Reichssicherheitshauptamt (Reich Security Headquarters), and only if they were sterilized.[18] On the list of Nazi priorities, destruction of Jews outranked promotion of Volksdeutschen.

Volksdeutsche as Perpetrators

Often, however, the two goals of furthering ethnic Germans and annihilating Jews dovetailed. The work of Götz Aly draws direct links of policy between ethnic Germans and the Holocaust. Nazi measures regarding the Volksdeutschen, Aly argues, set the timing of genocide, as authorities rushed to remove Jews and Slavs to make space for ethnic German resettlers.[19] Archival and published sources go even further, attesting to the fact that some of the Volksdeutschen in Eastern Europe contributed far more than silent acquiescence to the betrayal and murder of their Jewish neighbors. Bands of ethnic German men— most notably the Selbstschutz, or ethnic German militia, in Poland— killed at least ten thousand Jewish and Christian Poles in the first weeks of the war.[20] The SS recruited heavily from among ethnic Germans: certain units like the Prinz Eugen consisted almost exclusively of Volksdeutschen.[21] Ethnic German men formed an important part of the staff of killing centers and labor camps all over Eastern and Central Europe. Jewish memoir literature describes individual ethnic Germans who stole Jewish property, participated in Nazi-sponsored pogroms, and turned in Jews who tried to pass as Aryans.[22]

It may not always have been clear who was to count as an ethnic

German, but one aspect of the definition remained constant: members of that group were the official beneficiaries of genocide. In theory at least, they received the goods stolen from those deemed unworthy to occupy space in the new Nazi order. That distinction served to clarify the dichotomy between ethnic Germans and their neighbors. Any doubts about who was an ethnic German disappeared once the non-Volksdeutschen in a community had been expropriated and expelled to the benefit of those classified as Volksdeutsch.

When Germans and their helpers deported and murdered Jews or evicted Polish Gentiles, they reassigned the properties left behind to ethnic Germans who either came from the region in question or had been resettled there.[23] The Einsatzgruppen that slaughtered Jews in the Soviet Union in 1942 also distributed "loot, cattle, and harvesting machines" to the ethnic German population, "making available the houses and belongings of Jews and so on."[24] At Himmler's order, various agencies distributed to the people identified as ethnic Germans under the Nazis' resettlement program clothing and household effects seized from Jews who had been killed in death camps and elsewhere.[25] Jewish belongings, from thermos bottles to baby carriages, mirrors, and sunglasses, were collected for the Volksdeutschen. Instructions to relevant agencies reminded them to remove the Jewish star from all clothing.[26] Once in possession of Jewish belongings, the ethnic Germans retained a vested interest in promoting the Nazi cause. Nazi racial policy had given them what they had, and their continued claim to those possessions rested on the racist assumptions inherent to the National Socialist worldview.

Jews who experienced expropriation witnessed how greed increased the ranks of their antagonists. Many of the most eager predators, some Jewish observers noted, the newly minted ethnic Germans, were in fact their old Polish or Ukrainian neighbors. A Jewish survivor from Radomsko recalled a Polish druggist who declared himself a Volksdeutscher in order to take over a family enterprise that manufactured paints and dyes.[27] Another survivor from the same town suggested that a Ukrainian family simply "became Volksdeutsche" in order to claim the flat of a Jewish man who collected antiques.[28] An official report submitted to the Foreign Office in April 1944 confirmed that, in Hungary, the "sanitizing actions" of invading German troops engaged in the "solution of the Jewish question" had indeed had very favorable material effects for ethnic Germans there.[29] Under the Nazi program of incentives, opportunism of all kinds swelled the Volksdeutschen ranks. A Polish survivor describes members of the Selbstschutz as "people from our town, Poles." With the Nazi presence, she said, they "suddenly heard the call of their German blood! Mostly they were scum: ex-jailbirds, card-sharps, thieves, petty (and not so petty!) crooks."[30]

Nazi policies regarding the Volksdeutschen exacerbated anti-Semitism and polarized ethnic relations by stirring up greed for possessions seized from Jewish and other victims. But there were other, less obvious ways that the concept of "ethnic Germanness" fostered hatreds. The very tenuousness of the notion, which one might expect to have mitigated its destructive effects, in fact served to worsen the plight of Jews and Slavs in Eastern Europe. Given the difficulties of defining *Volksdeutsche,* those who aspired to membership found the easiest way to prove themselves as good Germans was to show that they were good Nazis. And the most effective way to establish Nazi credentials was by endorsing and actively implementing attacks on the enemies of the Reich. Enlisting in the SS,[31] participating in pogroms, and laying claim to Jewish property could all be means to that end.[32]

For their part, Nazi authorities openly distorted the definition of *Volksdeutsche* in order to expand the ranks of the SS. In April 1944 German officials in Hungary announced that ethnic Germans there would perform their military service in the Waffen-SS. The Germans accompanied that decision with a new, broader definition of *Volksdeutschen.* The Hungarian government had based its count of 720,000 on the assumption that ethnic Germans were those who identified themselves as such and were recognized by the ethnic German leadership. Nazi authorities opted to dispense with any formal definition at all, basing the decision instead on an interview with the individual in question. In this way, the Germans reported, they could add several hundred thousand people to the original count of Volksdeutschen in Hungary.[33]

Nazi authorities used negative incentives as well to encourage ethnic German participation in the regime's crimes. Recognizing that uncertainty and insecurity increase manipulability, they constantly altered rules and regulations, making ethnic Germans aware that they could lose their status if they fell out of favor. In May 1941 SS authorities announced that ethnic Germans in the Baltic states who had not registered for the first resettlement program in 1940 could no longer be considered for government service. By passing up the earlier opportunity to cooperate, SS officials reasoned, those people had demonstrated a deficient commitment to Germanness.[34]

In August 1941 Einsatzgruppe B in Smolensk asked the military not to issue permanent identification papers for ethnic Germans, so that the option of reassessing an individual's status would remain open.[35] The *Deutsche Volksliste* begun in 1941 was to gather information on ethnic Germans and to divide them into four categories, ranging from the "pure and politically clean" specimens of category one to the "renegades" of category four, who had to be won back to Germanness. Members of all four groups qualified for resettlement. Politically undesirable men and women, however, could be locked up. Moreover, SS and police officers were to supervise the Germanization process; in cases where parents neglected the Germanic training of their offspring, the children were to be taken away and given to other homes.[36] In February 1942 Himmler himself ordered that people of German ancestry who failed to register themselves on the Deutsche Volksliste could be sent to concentration camps.[37] The rewards of Germanness, it was clear, were only for those Volksdeutschen who proved loyal, active partners in the Nazi project.

Volksdeutsche as Opponents of Genocide

In formal and informal ways, the special status of the Volksdeutschen implicated many of them in genocide. At the same time, at least some ethnic Germans used their privileged positions to assist their neighbors and to oppose the regime. Much more research is needed before definitive conclusions can be made in this regard. But it is both ironic and telling that all of the examples of ethnic German opposition I have found so far involve individuals who were themselves integrated into the Nazi system.

Best known no doubt is Oskar Schindler, a Volksdeutscher from what had been Czechoslovakia. As an ethnic German, Schindler benefited materially from the expropriation and expulsion of Polish Jews and Gentiles; in turn, he used his new wealth and influence to rescue over one thousand Jews.[38] In her documentary film, *Diamonds in the Snow,* Mira Reym Binford points out that the Polish woman in Bendzin who hid her was also an ethnic German. As the mother of two members of the SS, that woman received extra rations. She used at least some of them to save the life of a young Jewish girl. Her motivations, it appears, were simple; she loved children and could not bear the thought of them suffering.[39]

Ethnic Germans even more directly implicated in genocide performed acts of opposition and assistance as well. In some of these cases, motives seem to have been less than altruistic, but the results for those whose lives often hinged on such small demonstrations of humanity could nonetheless be decisive. Leon Weliczker Wells, a Polish Jew who survived a number of other camps, indicates that, although ethnic German guards were not necessarily any more humane than their counterparts from the Reich, they at least could be bribed.[40] That corruptibility in turn made it possible to deal with them.

Personal accounts from family members of Holocaust survivors confirm the activities of ethnic German rescuers and helpers within the Nazi camp system. One man, the son of Holocaust survivors from Poland, told me about his father's encounter in Auschwitz with an ethnic German from his hometown. The father was a prisoner, the Volksdeutscher a guard. The guard arranged to meet his acquaintance secretly in a corner of the camp. There he gave him some warm clothes and food, items the Jewish man believes were crucial to his survival. He never saw that guard again.[41] A Romanian Jewish survivor told a similar story. Imprisoned in a labor camp, he and a group of others were assigned to work in a stone quarry. Sick and half-starved, they knew they could not survive more than a few days in that backbreaking detachment. Marching to the quarry, some of the prisoners heard their putatively German guard muttering to himself in Romanian. They recognized him as a Volksdeutscher who, although not willing to address them directly, nevertheless understood everything they said. He also grasped their desperation. Instead of forcing them to haul the heavy stones, he allowed them to snare rabbits, which they cooked and ate. The two weeks on that detail, that survivor insists, gave him the extra strength to live through the most deadly winter of the war.[42]

Nazi sources confirm the opposition activities of individual ethnic Germans. Records of the special court (*Sondergericht*) in Bromberg/ Bydgoszcz, for example, include the case of an ethnic German man from the Sudetenland who was employed as an armaments worker in territories incorporated from Poland. He was accused of neglecting his responsibilities and allowing faulty grenades to be produced. It is not clear whether he set out to sabotage the German war effort, but it is evident that his German bosses found him suspect because he spoke Czech and Polish to his subordinates, even to those who knew German.[43] As the files demonstrate, German authorities worried a great deal about bonds of sociability and familiarity between Volksdeutschen and people with whom they often had more in common than with Germans from the Reich.[44]

Ties to neighbors and knowledge of languages other than German made Volksdeutsche potentially good contacts for opposition efforts.

But the tenuousness of the category itself meant that they, unlike Germans from the Reich, could be punished with expulsion from the *Volk.* At least one woman in Poland lost her privileged status as an ethnic German when she was convicted of helping her grandson desert the Wehrmacht. Even the intercessions of her daughter—a German citizen—and her son-in-law—a German military officer—were of no avail.[45] Although such accounts are few and scattered throughout the vast record of World War II, they need to be included in the history of the Volksdeutschen. Those exceptions serve as a reminder of both the possibility of human decency and the danger of creating rigid categories that preclude recognizing the enormous variation of human experience.

The Volksdeutschen as Casualties of Brutalization

Nazi authorities consistently proved to be more concerned with destroying Jews and expanding German power in the East than with maintaining the purity of some ideology of Germanness. Sometimes those priorities worked to the advantage of ethnic Germans, at least in the short term. More often, however, they subjected the Volksdeutschen too to the arbitrary and brutal power of a regime that many of them endorsed themselves.

In early 1940 the minister of the interior announced that, in the interests of the fatherland, Volksdeutsche should be defined as generously as possible. Political reliability was not to play a role.[46] Himmler took expansion of the category even further. Sometime in 1940–41 he ordered the Germanization of "racially valuable Poles." If sufficient numbers of suitable ethnic Germans were not on hand, that program implied, Hitler's underlings could simply make more. Himmler tried to lure Poles into the scheme with promises of property and economic advancement, presumably at Jewish expense.[47]

Loose definitions served the interests of Nazi population policies but left those defined as Volksdeutsch open to criticism. Although Nazi rhetoric praised the ethnic Germans as paragons of Aryan purity and National Socialist loyalty, treatment of the Volksdeutschen often reflected contempt. Reich authorities of all kinds griped about Volksdeutschen, who they said lacked proper German qualities: diligence, cleanliness, sexual self-control, and the ability to speak German.[48] Already in 1941 military reports included complaints about ethnic German soldiers whose German language skills were not up to par.[49] In 1944 SS officials in the Wartheland grumbled that the Volksdeutschen sent from Russia spoke only Polish, Russian, or Ukrainian and had forgotten how to work.[50] Other *Gau* authorities protested that the ethnic Germans they were expected to resettle lacked proper German family values. As soon as their husbands were out of the picture, one reporter carped, the women took up with Ukrainians and Poles. The men, the account continued, were no better; they slept with Polish women and assumed the cultural habits of Poles, while the youth were lazy and promiscuous.[51]

Many inside the Reich viewed the "brothers and sisters" from outside its borders as second- or third-rate Germans at best. In November 1944, for example, reports from the Volksdeutsche Mittelstelle, the Nazi office in charge of ethnic German affairs, lamented that in some parts of Germany "people tried to relegate the Germans from the Southeast [Volksdeutsche from the Balkans] to the table with the alien workers and the prisoners of war."[52] Amid rivalry for increasingly scarce housing, food, and security, snobbery, prejudice, and abuse flourished.

Disputes about who actually counted as Volksdeutsch and to what they were entitled proved to be as chronic as the Nazi passion for ethnic and racial purity. Even on the brink of defeat, officials bickered over individual cases. The resulting insecurity complicated the lives of ethnic Germans in myriad ways. An intriguing illustration of both tenacity and ambiguity involved two Polish sisters. One received ethnic German status; the other did not. As of April 1944 Johanna and Danuta W. lived and worked near Kassel. Although their parents were "pure Polish," they applied for Germanization (*Eindeutschung*).[53] Authorities in Cholm approved Johanna's application, but their Lublin counterparts rejected Danuta's. When her son by an SS man received Volksdeutsch status, Danuta, backed by her employer, SS *Standartenführer* Richter, requested review of her case.[54]

Richter called Danuta hardworking and expressed the hope that "German girls" too would possess such properties.[55] That endorsement, along with a note of support from the Race and Settlement Office in Berlin, failed to produce the necessary papers.[56] The only reason given for rejecting Danuta was that "she did not look so good." Her status caused practical problems because the sisters lived together. Under the terms of Nazi racial law, ethnic Germans such as Johanna were to eschew all social contact with Poles like Danuta whose passports were stamped with a "P."[57] By September 1944, despite a hefty correspondence in which conflicting photographs of Danuta changed hands and her boss stressed the value of her "German soul,"[58] nothing had been resolved. Authorities in Lodz requested copies of Johanna's papers,[59] and the Krakow Race and Settlement office got involved as well. In the shuffle, some of Johanna's documents went missing and Danuta's files fell prey to conditions at the front.[60] Further details are unknown.

As the story of Danuta W. indicates, the designation *Volksdeutsch* continued to be sought after by outsiders and protected by insiders, even as the German war effort fell apart. Nazi authorities might have been uncertain about what constituted ethnic Germanness, but they did not waver when it came to enforcing that category. Indeed, instead of abating as the situation at the fronts deteriorated, Nazi interest in the fine points of ethnic definition seemed to increase. Perhaps the struggle to locate and relocate Volksdeutsche, like the effort to kill the Jews, was one part of the war where success still seemed possible. And no doubt Germans assigned to tasks in that area of endeavor found it more attractive to stay put and try to prove their usefulness than face the alternative: assignment to the front, where the enemy was likely to be armed.

The combination of tenacity and uncertainty that characterized the Nazi approach to the Volksdeutschen proved disastrous for many ethnic Germans at the end of the war. Official determination to the cause promoted an illusion of impending victory and generated similar resolve on the part of many ethnic Germans who continued up until the end to associate themselves with Nazi war aims. Certainly some ethnic Germans joined the partisans or tried to melt back into the Polish or Hungarian mainstream.[61] After years of Nazi domination, however, Central European ethnicities were no longer as flexible as they once had been. Insistence on the firmness of the category of Volksdeutschen created a concrete identity out of what had been rather fluid and tenuous and promoted a deadly polarization of ethnic relations that outlasted Nazi control in Europe.

Ethnic stereotypes can develop a self-perpetrating dynamic; they come to make sense to people because they have no alternative ways to interpret reality and because it is in their interest to believe themselves superior. Such self-delusion backfired for some Volksdeutschen. Many were so blinded by their stake in German victory that they lost touch with reality. In his memoirs, Charles Kotkowsky, a Polish Jew, describes the dazed, self-defeating behavior of the ethnic Germans he knew in the final phases of the war. In 1944 Kotkowsky was a slave laborer in a glassworks near Warsaw. The factory, presumably stolen from its former owners, was directed by a Pole of German origin; his son and three other ethnic Germans supervised the Polish Jewish and Gentile work force.

By July 1944 everyone in the factory anticipated a Russian offensive at the Vistula, and the Volksdeutschen feared for their lives.[62] Hoping for protection from the Polish Gentiles, they turned to the Jews, appointing only Jewish watchmen to guard the fence and sound the alarm in case of trouble. Members of the Jewish underground acquired some of those positions and from them performed acts of sabotage. Caught in their own racial assumptions, the Volksdeutschen attributed those deeds to "Polish bandits" and responded by strengthening the Jewish guard contingent.[63] Some Jewish slave workers thus got guns and practice using them, skills they brought to the Warsaw Uprising.[64]

Such confusions and delusions had very real repercussions for the Volksdeutschen. Through the haze of denial, ethnic Germans could persist in their illusion of victory while their situation became more and more precarious. In 1944, when Nazi authorities made belated attempts to evacuate ethnic Germans, many refused to move. After Romania capitulated in August, the German military had to force the Volksdeutschen to leave northern Transylvania.[65] In Serbia-Banat, only about 10 percent of the ethnic Germans left in October 1944.[66] Despite threats from the local Serbs, when orders came to evacuate the Batschka on October 6 and 7, 1944, of the approximately 240,000 ethnic Germans there, a "not unsubstantial number" decided to stay.[67]

By refusing to leave or deciding too late to do so, the Volksdeutschen left themselves vulnerable to attack from Soviet forces as well as from their Polish, Serbian, Hungarian, and Ukrainian neighbors. Vacillation and confusion had repercussions for ethnic Germans' remembering and forgetting as well. Recent misery tends to supplant the memory of earlier hardships, and vivid events push vaguer recollections aside. Accordingly, ethnic Germans' postwar narratives generally skipped over the war, alluded to its chaotic final phase, and then began in earnest with the concrete event that marked the onset of their victim status: arrival of the Red Army. This tendency too became formalized in the official record: questionnaires sent to ethnic Germans in the late 1940s and 1950s from authorities in the Federal Republic asked them to begin their testimony by noting when and from which direction Soviet troops marched into their communities.[68] Thus after the war, many Volksdeutsche nurtured and embellished their memories of lost homes and lost peace with their neighbors. But Hitler, National Socialism, and the Germans in general did not appear in those laments. Instead, ethnic Germans blamed their misery, real and imagined, on the Soviets and their henchmen. Accounts of victimization by the communist hordes and their diabolical fellow travelers generally proved flexible enough to absorb memories of suffering in the Nazi past.

The story of the ethnic Germans of Eastern Europe is a story of a concept enlisted in the cause of brutality. The Volksdeutschen themselves were not untouched; even they, the favorite children of the thousand-year Reich, experienced the imperiousness of that regime firsthand. Many of them suffered terribly, not only at the hands of the Red Army and their angry neighbors but also as a result of Nazi policies themselves. Götz Aly describes the string of broken promises that typified state treatment of ethnic Germans from the East.[69] Many Volksdeutsche spent one and even two years in camps waiting for farms or businesses to become available, that is, for their Polish Gentile or Jewish owners to be deported or murdered.[70] Jews bore the full brunt of a brutal worldview based on rigid ethnic and racial divisions, but even the Volksdeutschen experienced effects of that ruthlessness.

Official correspondence demonstrates how ethnic Germans became casualties of the brutalization of public life in Nazi-occupied Europe. In January 1945, the Arbeitsamt (Labor Office) in Dillenburg informed the SS Race and Settlement Office in Wiesbaden that a Polish woman laborer wished to terminate her pregnancy, now in the fourth month. SS authorities forbade an abortion on the grounds that the mother was a racially desirable "part German," the father "tolerable." When the couple resisted Germanization, however, the SS official declared them of no interest; he would consider the child valuable only if it were separated from its parents. The pair agreed to apply for Germanization but dragged their feet, arguing that because they came from Kalisch they were already Germans. The SS man was furious. That attitude, he complained, was typical of those "waiting to see what developments in the East will bring."[71] His final word on the case expressed the utter cynicism characteristic of Nazi ethnic policy. "It cannot be in our interest," he wrote, "to leave for the Polish world human material [*Menschenmaterial*] such as this case represents, in particular with respect to the German blood that is on hand here. In situations such as this, in my opinion, there must be only two possibilities: either extermination [*Vernichtung*] or absorption into Germandom [*Deutschtum*]."[72]

Conclusion

By the end of the war, the category of Volksdeutsch had changed from something fluid and tenuous into a rigid classification, loaded with vested interests and replete with massive implications. During the war, the definition of *Volksdeutschen* had contributed to the vulnerability of Jews and the polarization of the ethnic situation in Eastern Europe. Afterward, in some sense, the Volksdeutschen reaped what they and their Nazi backers had sown. Often their Polish, Ukrainian, and Serbian neighbors did not ask about individual behavior but rather judged them all as part of a compromised group.

As Robert Moeller has observed, the Volksdeutschen developed another kind of relationship to the Holocaust after the war: through implicit and explicit comparisons, they appropriated Jewish suffering and claimed it as analogous to their fate at Soviet hands.[73] By the end of the 1950s, that version of events had been enshrined in an eight-volume collection of testimonies, sponsored by the Federal Ministry for Expellees, Refugees, and Victims of War.[74] Popular novels, historical studies,[75] films, and a flood of memoirs echoed the portrayal of the Volksdeutschen as the victims par excellence of a war that Germans liked to remind the world had been hell for everyone. That version of the past, in turn, served to conceal not only ethnic German participation in the crimes of the Third Reich but the ways that Volksdeutsche too had been casualties of Nazi brutalization.

NOTES

Since 1992 I have presented papers on related topics at the Southern Historical Association, the German Studies Association, the University of Vermont, the University of Florida, the conference on mourning at the University of Chicago, the American Historical Association, and the University of Göttingen. I am grateful to fellow panelists, commentators, and members of the audience on all of those occasions for questions and suggestions. My research on the Volksdeutschen has been generously supported by the German Academic Exchange Service, the University of Vermont, the Max-Planck-Institut für Geschichte in Göttingen, the University of Notre Dame, the German Marshall Fund of the United States, and the Alexander von Humboldt Foundation. Thanks also to Geoffrey Giles, Alan Steinweis, and Eduard and Valentine Peters for their help. This chapter first appeared as "The '*Volksdeutschen*' of Eastern Europe, World War II, and the Holocaust: Constructed Ethnicity, Real Genocide," in *Germany and Eastern Europe: Cultural Identities and Cultural Differences,* ed. Geoffry Giles and Keith Bullivant, *Yearbook of European Studies* 13 (1999): 70–93.

1. Hans-Heinrich Lammers, "Betrifft: Formulierung der Begriffe 'Deutschtum im Ausland, Auslandsdeutscher und Volksdeutscher,'" Jan. 25, 1938, Bundesarchiv Potsdam (hereafter BA Potsdam), 51.01/23905. All translations are my own unless otherwise specified. Many of the files I used in the Bundesarchiven have since been moved to different locations.

2. "Brüder in der Fremde," *Glaube und Heimat: Bilder-Bote für das evangelische Haus* 3 (Mar. 1935): 22; Politisches Archiv des Auswärtigen Amts Bonn (hereafter AA Bonn), R 82089. For background, see Anthony Tihamer Komjathy and Rebecca Stockwell, *German Minorities and the Third Reich: Ethnic Germans of East Central Europe between the Wars* (New York, 1980); Martin Broszat, *Nationalsozialistische Polenpolitik, 1939–1945* (Stuttgart, 1961); Meir Buchsweiler, *Volksdeutsche in der Ukraine am Vorabend und Beginn des Zweiten Weltkriegs, ein Fall doppelter Loyalität?* (Gerlingen, 1984); and Richard Blanke, *Orphans of Versailles: The Germans in Western Poland, 1918–1939* (Lexington, Ky., 1993).

3. Hans-Joachin Goetz, "Eidesstattliche Erklärung," Oct. 3, 1947; Institut für Zeitgeschichte Munich (hereafter IfZ Munich), NO 5321.

4. Eberhard Jäckel, *Hitler's Weltanschauung: A Blueprint for Power*, trans. Herbert Arnold (Middletown, Conn., 1972); Gerhard Weinberg, "The World through Hitler's Eyes," in *Germany, Hitler, and World War II: Essays in Modern German and World History*, ed. Gerhard L. Weinberg (New York, 1995), 32–35.

5. Valdis O. Lumans, *Himmler's Auxiliaries: The Volksdeutsche Mittelstelle and the German National Minorities of Europe, 1939–1945* (Chapel Hill, N.C., 1993).

6. Statement signed Andreas Leitner and Anna Leitner née Freidman, Bundesarchiv Koblenz (hereafter BA Koblenz), Ost-Dokumentation 16 Ung./31. See also "Pusztavam Schicksal 1944," Amberg, Jan. 27, 1961, 1, BA Koblenz, Ost-Dokumentation 16 Ung./31.

7. "Erlaß des Führers und Reichskanzlers zur Festigung deutschen Volkstums, vom 7. Oktober 39," BA Koblenz, R18/5468/fiche 1. On Himmler, see Richard Breitman, *The Architect of Genocide: Himmler and the Final Solution* (New York, 1991).

8. Key regulations regarding the Volksdeutschen include the following: Himmler: "Erlaß über die Überprüfung und Aussonderung der Bevölkerung in den eingegliederten Ostgebieten vom 12. September 1940"; "Verordnung über die Deutsche Volksliste und die deutsche Staatsangehörigkeit in den eingegliederten Ostgebieten vom 4. März 1941"; Ministry of the Interior, "Erlaß vom 13. März 1941 I c 5425/41/500c Ost"; and "Erlaß des Führers und Reichskanzlers vom 7.10.1939." All are discussed in Heinrich Himmler, "Allgemeine Anordnung Nr. 12/g über die Behandlung der in die Deutsche Volksliste eingetragenen Personen." Feb. 9, 1942, BA Koblenz, R18/5468/fiche 2/153–60.

9. Margot Hegemann, "Die Deutsche Volksgruppe in Rumänien—Eine Fünfte Kolonne des deutschen Imperialismus in Südosteuropa," *Jahrbuch für Geschichte der UdSSR und der Volksdemokratischen Länder Europas* 4 (1960): 371–84. For other perspectives on ethnic Germans in Romania, see Wolfgang Miege, *Das Dritte Reich und die deutsche Volksgruppe in Rumänien, 1933–1938: Ein Beitrag zur nationalsozialistischen Volkstumspolitik* (Frankfurt a. M., 1972); and Bernd G. Längin, ed., *Rumäniendeutsche zwischen Bleiben und Kommen* (Bonn, 1990).

10. Robert L. Koehl, *RKFDV: German Resettlement and Population Policy, 1939–1945: A History of the Reich Commission for the Strengthening of Germandom* (Cambridge, Mass., 1957).

11. See, for example, G[ünther], "Der deutsche Nationaltag," *Deutscher Bote in*

Norwegen, Nachrichtenblatt der deutschen Behörden, Gemeinde u. Vereine (Oslo), no. 7, April 1934, 45, AA Bonn, R 61681.

12. Raul Hilberg, *The Destruction of the European Jews,* vol. 1, rev. ed. (New York, 1985), 67.

13. Dr. Gurtner, Reich Ministry of Justice, "Verabschiedung des Gesetzentwurfs über die Eheschließung Deutscher mit Ausländern durch die Reichsregierung," BA Potsdam, 51.01/23544, 3.

14. Der Chef der Sicherheitspolizei und des SD, Aug. 29, 1941, "Ereignismeldung UdSSR. Nr. 67 (copy), 10–11. This is part of the report of Einsatzgruppe B, Standort Smolensk, IfZ Munich, NO 2837.

15. SS-Oberscharführer Reinhold Ratzeburg: "Dienstreisebericht 2/45," Wiesbaden, Jan. 28, 1945, Hessisches Hauptstaatsarchiv Wiesbaden (hereafter HHStA Wiesbaden), 483/7360, 1–2.

16. See, for example, records of the Deutsche Umsiedlungs-Treuhand GmbH, Berlin, involving 1944 and 1945, BA Potsdam, 17.02, e.g., files 118–19, 494–95.

17. Gerda von Klitzing, "Bei unseren Brüdern in Polesien und Wolhynien," *Glaube und Heimat* 38, Sept. 17, 1933; AA Bonn 82088; see also "Kleine Mitteilungen," *Posener Evangelisches Kirchenblatt* 6 (March 1934): 245, AA Bonn, R 82088.

18. SS-Obersturmbahnführer (signature illegible) to Reichskommissar für die Festigung deutschen Volkstums—Stabshauptamt—Schweiklberg/Post Vilshofen Ndb., Feb. 10, 1944, IfZ Munich, NO 5342.

19. Götz Aly, *"Endlösung": Völkerverschiebung und der Mord an den europäischen Juden* (Frankfurt a. M., 1995), 41, 167.

20. Christian Jansen and Arno Weckbecker, *Der „Volksdeutsche Selbstschutz" in Polen 1939/40* (Munich, 1992); Eva Seeber, "Der Anteil der Minderheitsorganisation 'Selbstschutz' an den faschistischen Vernichtungsaktionen im Herbst und Winter 1939 in Polen," *Jahrbuch für Geschichte der sozialistischen Länder Europas* 13, no. 2 (1969): 3–34.

21. See Robert Herzog, *Die Volksdeutschen in der Waffen SS* (Tübingen, 1955); see also Reichsführer SS, *Aufbruch: Briefe germanischer Kriegsfreiwilliger der SS-Division Wiking* (Berlin and Leipzig, 1943).

22. For example, Volksdeutsche appear as perpetrators in memoirs by Alexander Donat, *The Holocaust Kingdom: A Memoir* (New York, 1965); Leon Weliczker Wells, *The Death Brigade (The Janowska Road)* (New York, 1963); and Adina Blady Szwajger, *I Remember Nothing More: The Warsaw Children's Hospital and the Jewish Resistance* (London, 1990).

23. See Edgar Hoffmann, "Eidesstattlicher Erklärung," Sept. 3, 1947; IfZ Munich, NO 5125.Hoffmann; see also SS-Brigadeführer Greifelt and Dr. Winkler, head of Haupttreuhandstelle Ost, "Einzelfragen des Osteinsatzes" [undated; probably late 1940], IfZ Munich, NO 5149.

24. Security Service, "Ereignismeldung UdSSR Nr. 95," Sept. 26, 1942, section titled "Einsatzgruppe D. Standort Nikolajew," IfZ Munich, NO 3147.

25. Himmler to Chef des SS-Wirtschafts-Verwaltungshauptamtes, SS-Obergruppenführer Pohl, and to Chef des Hauptamtes Volksdeutsche Mittelstelle, SS-Obergruppenführer Lorenz, Oct. 24, 1942, IfZ Munich, NO 606.

26. SS-Brigadeführer und Generalmajor der Waffen-SS Frank to Leiter der Verwaltung des K.L. Auschwitz, Sept. 26, 1942, IfZ Munich, NO 724, 4.

27. Stefania Heilbrunn, *Children of Dust and Heaven: A Collective Memoir* (Johannesburg, 1978).

28. Heilbrunn, *Children of Dust,* 70.

29. H. Hezinger, Volksdeutsche Mittelstelle, to Legationsrat Dr. Reichel, Auswärtiges Amt, Berlin, May 22, 1944, IfZ Munich, NG/d 5351–5460.

30. Heilbrunn, *Children of Dust,* 71.

31. See the report which noted with approval the reclassification of a family from Poland as new Volksdeutsche. The report added that this family had three sons who were eager to join the SS as soon as their ethnic German status was approved. See SS-Oberscharführer Reinhold Ratzeburg, "Dienstreisebericht 2/45," Wiesbaden, Jan. 28, 1945, HHStA Wiesbaden, 483/7360, 1–2.

32. Doris L. Bergen, "The Nazi Concept of '*Volksdeutsche*' and the Exacerbation of Anti-Semitism in Eastern Europe, 1939–45," *Journal of Contemporary History* 29 (1994): 569–82.

33. H. Hezinger, "Monatsbericht April 1944 über die Lage in den Deutschen Volksgruppen," Volksdeutsche Mittelstelle, 22 May 1944; IfZ Munich, NG/d 5351–5460.

34. SS-Brigadeführer Greifelt, "Vorgang: Übernahme von Flüchtlingen aus den Baltenländern in den öffentlichen Dienst," May 16, 1941, BA Potsdam, 51.01/23952.

35. Chef der Sicherheitspolizei und des SD, "Ereignismeldung UdSSR. Nr. 67, 10–11," Aug. 29, 1941, IfZ Munich, NO 2837.

36. Reichsführer SS und Chef der Deutschen Polizei, Reichskommissar für die Festigung Deutschen Volkstums, "Betrifft: Behandlung der in Abteilung 4 der Deutschen Volksliste eingetragenen Personen," Feb. 16, 1942, BA Koblenz, R 18/5468/fiche 2/161–66.

37. Himmler, "Allgemeine Anordnung Nr. 12/g."

38. See Thomas Keneally, *Schindler's List* (New York, 1993).

39. *Diamonds in the Snow,* dir. Mira Reym Binford, PBS documentary, 1990.

40. Wells, *Death Brigade.*

41. Personal information from Alan Steinweis (Lincoln, Neb.).

42. Personal information from Ginni Stern (Burlington, Vt.).

43. See 1944 case against Duschek, Archiwum Pánstwowe w Bydgoszczy (hereafter AP Bydgoszcz), 80/1341.

44. For a fascinating account of the complex relationship between at least one ethnic German and his Slavic neighbors, see Eberhard von Cube, *Überleben war alles: Aufzeichnungen eines baltischen Umsiedlers von 1939 bis 1946* (Luneburg, 1986).

45. See case of Franziska Burnicki, before the Sondergericht, Bromberg, 1944, AP Bydgoszcz, 80/1203.

46. Reichsminister des Innern und den Herrn Reichsminister für Volksaufklärung und Propaganda, I Ost 1107 II/39/4021, Jan. 4, 1940, BA Potsdam, 51.01 RKM/23912.

47. Goetz, "Eidesstattliche Erklärung," 5–6.

48. See, for example, Nationalsozialistische Deutsche Arbeiter Partei (NSDAP) Reichsleitung, "Ansiedlung weiterer Rußlanddeutscher im Gau Wartheland,"

Hauptamt für Volkstumsfragen, Bad Ischl-Kaltenbach, July 20, 1944; BA Koblenz R 59/65/fiche 3/132–36.

49. See "Heerespsychologischer Bericht Nr. 11," Berlin, June 7, 1941, no. 103/41, Bundesarchiv-Militärarchiv Freiburg, RH 15/115, 65–68.

50. NSDAP Reichsleitung, "Ansiedlung weiterer Rußlanddeutscher."

51. NSDAP Reichsleitung, "Ansiedlung weiterer Rußlanddeutscher."

52. Anton Scherer, ed., *Unbekannte SS-Geheimberichte über die Evakuierung der Südostdeutschen im Oktober und November 1944 sowie über die politische Lage in Rumänien, Ungarn, der Slowakei, im Serbischen Banat und im "unabhängigen Staat Kroatien"* (Graz, 1990), 39.

53. SS-Sturmbannführer Pfefferberg, Höhere SS- und Polizeiführer im Bereich des Wehrkreises IX, to the Rasse und Siedlungshauptamt-SS, Aussenstelle, Litzmannstadt, Kassel, Apr. 15, 1944, United States Holocaust Memorial Museum Archive (USHMMA), RG 15.021M, reel 6, folder 38, p. 77.

54. SS- und Polizeiführer im Distrikt Lublin, Volksdeutsche Mittelstelle, der Kreisbeauftragte, to the Rasse- und Siedlungsamt, Litzmannstadt, Lublin, Apr. 17, 1944, USHMMA, RG 15.021M, reel 6, folder 38, p. 79.

55. Hans-Joachim Richter, Arolsen, June 6, 1944, USHMMA, RG 15.021M, reel 6, folder 38, p. 81.

56. Schwalm, Chef des Rasse- und Siedlungshauptamtes-SS: Der Stabsführer, to Leiter der Außenstelle L'Stdt, des RUS-HA-SS, SS-Stubaf. Dongus, Berlin, June 29, 1944, USHMMA, RG 15.021M, reel 6, folder 38, p. 86.

57. Höhere SS- und Polizeiführer im Bereich des Wehrkrieses IX, Der SS-Führer im Rasse- und Siedlungswesen, to Rasse- und Siedlungshauptamt-SS Aussenstelle, Litzmannstadt, Arolsen, July 6, 1944, USHMMA, RG 15.021M, reel 6, folder 38, p. 87.

58. RuS Außenstelle, Litzmannstadt, to SS-Standartenführer Hans-Joachim Richter, Arolsen/Waldeck, Litzmannstadt, July 8, 1944; Richter, Arolsen, July 13, 1944; Richter to the Rasse- und Siedlungshauptamt, Nebenstelle Litzmannstadt, Arolsen, June 6, 1944; Richter to Sturmbannführer Dongus, RuS, Außenstelle, Litzmannstadt, Arolsen, July 13, 1944; SS-Hauptsturmführer, Der Stabsführer der Außenstelle, RuS, to Richter, Litzmannstadt, July 19, 1944; all in USHMM, RG 15.021M, reel 6, folder 38, pp. 88–92.

59. SS-Hauptsturmführer, RuS, to the Höhere-SS- und Polizeiführer "Fulda-Werra," Kassel, Sept. 1, 1944; SS-Führer im RuS, to RuS Aussenstelle, Litzmannstadt; and Richter to RuS, Litzmannstadt, Arolsen, Sept. 4, 1944, USHMMA, RG 15.021M, reel 6, folder 38, pp. 94–96.

60. SS-Hauptsturmführer, Chef der Sicherheitspolizei und des S.D., Einwandererzentralstelle, to RuS, Aussenstelle Litzmannstadt, Cracow, Nov. 21, 1944, USHMMA, RG 15.021M, reel 6, folder 38, p. 103.

61. For one case where partisans were described as of German background, see SS Lublin, "Fernschreiben Ia Tgb. Nr. 572/44 g," Lublin, June 7, 1944, USHMMA, RG 15.027M, reel 2, file 13, pp. 30 and reverse.

62. Charles Kotkowsky, "Remnants: Memoirs of a Survivor," manuscript, 88–89; USHMMA, RG 10.045, fiches 1–5: 57–94.

63. Kotkowsky, "Remnants," 92.

64. Kotkowsky, "Remnants," 94.

65. Scherer, ed., *Unbekannte,* 7.

66. Scherer, ed. *Unbekannte,* 9.

67. Scherer, ed. *Unbekannte,* 15.

68. "Fragebogenberichte zur Dokumentation der Vertreibung der Deutschen aus Ost-Mitteleuropa (Gemeindeschicksalsberichte)," BA Koblenz, Ost-Dokumentation 1.

69. Aly, *Endlösung,* e.g., 176–77, 242–43.

70. A list of Nazi abuses toward ethnic Germans appears in K. Rüb, "Denkschrift über die Not der Umsiedler," manuscript (Stuttgart, July 28, 1945); BA Potsdam, 17.02/295. For letters of complaint from ethnic Germans, see records of the Deutsche Umsiedlungs-Treuhand-Gesellschaft, BA Potsdam 17.02/108, 137, 147; and records of the Einwandererzentralstelle, Rasse und Siedlungsamt, Aussenstelle Litzmannstadt, USHMMA, RG 15.021M, reel 6.

71. Arbeitsamt Dillenburg, Jan. 2, 1944 [should be 1945]; response from SS-Sturmbannführer Rödel, Höhere SS- und Polizeiführer Rhein/Westmark, SS-Führer im RuS - Wesen, to Reichsärztekammer, Bezirksstelle Gießen/Lahn, Wiesbaden, Feb. 15, 1945; Rödel to Jugendamt des Landkreises Dillenburg, Feb. 16, 1945; Rödel to NSDAP Gauamtsleitung Hessen, Amt für Volkswohlfahrt Frankfurt/Main, Feb. 16, 1945; and orange cards (Hauptuntersuchung) for the Lisiaks, Feb. 2, 1945; all in HHStA Wiesbaden, 483/11374.

72. Rödel to Gauamt für Volkstumsfragen, Feb. 15, 1945, HHStA Wiesbaden, 483/11374.

73. Robert Moeller, "War Stories: The Search for a Usable Past in the Federal Republic of Germany," *American Historical Review* 101, no. 4 (1996): 1008–48.

74. Theodor Schieder, ed., *Dokumentation der Vertreibung der Deutschen aus Ost-Mitteleuropa,* vols. 1–8 (Göttingen, 1954–61).

75. See, e.g., Alfred M. De Zayas, *Anmerkungen zur Vertreibung der Deutschen aus dem Osten,* 2d ed. (Stuttgart, 1987); *The German Expellees: Victims in War and Peace* (New York, 1993); *Nemesis at Potsdam: The Anglo-Americans and the Expulsion of the Germans: Background, Execution, Consequences,* rev. 2d ed. (London, 1979); and *Zeugnisse der Vertreibung: Mit bisher unveröffentlichten Bilddokumenten* (Krefeld, 1983); for a more balanced account, see Wolfgang Benz, ed., *Die Vertreibung der Deutschen aus dem Osten: Ursachen, Ereignisse, Folgen* (Frankfurt a. M., 1985).

CHAPTER 12

The Politics of Homeland

Irredentism and Reconciliation in the Policies
of German Federal Governments and
Expellee Organizations toward Ethnic German
Minorities in Central and Eastern Europe,
1949–99

Stefan Wolff

Today ethnic German populations live in four countries in Western Europe and in sixteen countries in Central and Eastern Europe. Their historical origins, size, status, and degree of integration and assimilation differ greatly, not just between East and West but also within each of these broadly defined geographic regions. Numerically, their size has significantly decreased during this century, especially since the end of World War II. Right after 1945 about twelve million ethnic Germans either fled or were expelled from their homelands, primarily in Poland and Czechoslovakia, and since then about another four million ethnic Germans have left their homelands in Central and Eastern Europe and settled in the Federal Republic.

During the cold war period, the issue of German minorities was secondary to many other problems arising from the East-West divide and the need to prevent a military confrontation between the two blocs. After the collapse of communism in 1989–90, however, this question gained new prominence in the relationship between Germany and countries in Central and Eastern Europe, particularly in Poland and the Czech Republic. As I will explore in greater detail in this chapter, the relationship between the Federal Republic and her neighbors has never been completely free from strains over minority and border issues. Yet, the dramatic political changes at the beginning of the last decade have opened fundamentally new opportunities for both the federal government and expellee organizations.

The Loss of Homeland, 1945–55

The major problems facing German policymakers after World War I had been the territorial truncation of German territory and the reparations to be paid to the Allied powers. An additional and novel challenge presented itself after 1945. Ethnic Germans, in particular from Central and East European countries, were expelled or fled from their traditional settlement areas, such as in Poland and Czechoslovakia, or were deported to forced labor camps in the Soviet Union, as it happened in Romania and Yugoslavia. In any event, ethnic Germans were subjected to systematic popular and state discrimination as a result of the atrocious occupation policies of the Nazis during the war, in which many of them had actively participated.[1] Although this wave of repression and expulsion ended by the early 1950s and the citizenship rights of ethnic Germans were gradually reinstated, their situation was still not considered satisfactory by the West German government, partly because they suffered all the "usual" disadvantages of life under communism and partly because residual bitterness from the German occupation left them vulnerable to continued discrimination.

In the early years of its existence, the Federal Republic, however, was preoccupied with other issues both domestically and in its external relations. Domestically, the rebuilding of social and economic life, including the integration of over eight million refugees and expellees, took priority.[2] On the international stage, German Chancellor Adenauer had set a foreign policy agenda whose foremost aim was to ensure the integration of the country into the Western alliance.

This process of integration into the West, which provided a path to political security, economic recovery, and gradually also social prosperity, was the preferred option of the overwhelming majority of the population and politicians. Yet, at the same time, the Western alliance as a symbol of postwar developments signaled, at least temporarily, an acceptance of the status quo, which, given the German borders in 1949, found significantly less public support. While it was generally accepted that neither Alsace and Lorraine nor the Sudetenland could be rightfully claimed by Germany, the fixing of the German-Polish border along the Oder-Neisse line was renounced in public by West German politicians of almost all political backgrounds, including the chancellor and his cabinet ministers. Simultaneously, however, it was equally clear that the federal government was in no position to offer a credible political approach as to how to revise the German-Polish border. Not only was this contrary to the interests of all four Allied powers of

World War II, but West Germany itself no longer had a common border with Poland. Despite the claim of the Federal Republic to be the sole representative of the German people, it was a matter of political reality that the East German state, in violation of the Potsdam Agreement, had officially recognized the new border in a treaty with Poland in July 1950.

This unfavorable position, however, did not prevent political activists among the expellees from keeping the issue of expulsions and of the territorial losses Germany had incurred after 1945 on the domestic political agenda of the Federal Republic. Expellees and refugees had not only suffered the trauma of being forced from their ancestral homeland, but they also arrived in devastated and underdeveloped areas of rural Bavaria, Lower Saxony, and Schleswig Holstein. With an official ban on expellee organizations in place in all three western occupation zones until 1949, refugees and expellees began to organize themselves at the local level only and often in close association with churches. Initially, there was a duality in their organizational structure. The Central League of Expelled Germans (Zentralverband der vertriebenen Deutschen; from 1951 on, Union of Expelled Germans, Bund vertriebener Deutscher, or BvD) concerned itself primarily with social and economic issues of integration and compensation, while regional-cultural associations (*Landsmannschaften*) focused on the preservation of the expellees' distinct geographic identities, including their traditions, customs, and culture. In August 1949, nine of them, which were organized at the federal level or in the process of doing so, formed the Coalition of Eastern German Regional-Cultural Associations (Vereinigung der ostdeutschen Landsmannschaften, or VoL). Four of the Landsmannschaften joined the BvD in 1951 but retained their membership in the VoL. A first attempt to overcome this dualism failed later in 1951. Thus, the VoL pursued its own organizational consolidation, admitted further regional-cultural associations of expellees from Southeastern Europe, changed its name to League of Regional-Cultural Associations (Verband der Landsmannschaften, or VdL) in August 1952, and began to establish its branches in each of the federal states of West Germany.

The political agenda of the various expellee organizations had been laid down in the 1950 Charter of the German Expellees. This fundamental document has guided expellee demands and policies ever since and is a vivid expression of the identity of expellees as a particular group in West German postwar society, united by their collective experiences of suffering and their desire to correct the wrongs of expulsion.

In the charter, the expellees proclaimed their willingness to forgo revenge and retribution, to support the creation of a united and free Europe, and to contribute to the reconstruction of Germany and Europe. On this basis, they demanded complete equality in West Germany, a distribution of the costs and consequences of the war among the entire German population, integration into all occupational groups in the German economy, and the inclusion of the expellees in the European reconstruction effort. Although their demands were focused on integration in West Germany, the expellees also insisted on their right to their homeland and demanded that this be recognized as a fundamental human right.[3] And here lies the key to understanding what united people from the most diverse geographical, professional, social, and political backgrounds: "To separate human beings by force from their homeland means to kill their spirit. We have suffered and experienced this fate. Therefore, we feel called upon to demand that the right to one's homeland be recognized and implemented as a God-given basic right of all humankind."[4]

Yet, their articulation of a common suffering and loss of homeland initially did not result in a common political platform. Between 1948–49 and 1952 two wings fought for political leadership within the broad spectrum of expellee and refugee organizations. One wing focused on the so-called national principle and made the recovery of the lost homeland its political priority. Oriented toward the political far right, it did not manage to generate sufficient electoral support. In contrast, the political party—the Union of Expellees and Disenfranchised (Bund der Heimatvertriebenen und Entrechteten, or BHE; after November 1952, Gesamtdeutscher Block-Bund vertriebener Deutscher)—gained public recognition and spectacular electoral support by addressing the specific social and economic interests of the expellees in the Federal Republic. Their successes, however, resulted in a gradual decline of the BHE: the greater the social and economic integration of the expellees, the less this population group felt the need for a distinct political party. The BHE's failure to form a permanent and stable coalition with other smaller center parties meant that it fell below the 5 percent threshold in the federal elections in 1957 and again in 1961 after it had been absorbed within the All-German Party (Gesamtdeutsche Partei, or GDP). Despite its short existence, the BHE facilitated and supported the contribution of the German refugees and expellees to the social, political, and economic development of postwar West Germany.[5] However, throughout the period between 1945 and 1990, the shared loss of homeland and feelings of suffering continued to be essential components of the expellees' identity in the Federal Republic, shaping expellee organizations in West German civil society, as they began to develop a foreign policy agenda of their own.

Maintaining the Homelands from Afar, 1955–90

By the mid-1950s, it had become clear to activists in both the BvD and the VdL that the representation of expellee interests could become more efficient if they created a single organization within which the separate entities could pool their resources. By October 1957 this process was completed, and the Union of Expellees—United Regional-Cultural Associations and State Organizations (Bund der Vertriebenen—Vereinigte Landsmannschaften und Landesverbände, or BdV) formed. It consisted of twenty regional cultural associations,[6] eleven state organizations (one in each of the federal states at the time, with five new ones being founded after German unification in 1990), and seven special interest groups.[7] The organization's main publication, *German Eastern Service* (*Deutscher Ostdienst,* or *DOD*), published a statement by the first president of the BdV, Hans Krüger, in which he defined the mission of his organization as being a mediator between East and West. Krüger further asserted that

> In the spirit of a humanist-Christian worldview, in the spirit of the best eastern German cultural traditions, in the spirit of Leibniz, Kant, Herder and Lessing, the expellees not only renounce revenge and retribution, but they seek reconciliation of the seemingly irreconcilable in order to prepare the ground for a peace of law and justice. This noble attitude gives them the right to demand justice for themselves and for all expellees and refugees in the world.[8]

As the Charter of the German Expellees of 1950 had also made clear, Krüger emphasized the right of the expellees to their homeland, their right to self-determination, and their claim to contribute to the peaceful coexistence of all peoples in freedom.[9]

By the mid-1950s, when Germany's integration into the Western world had been assured by her membership in the North Atlantic Treaty Organization (NATO) and the precursor institutions of today's European Union, the German government could turn eastward again. As a result of public pressure and political lobbying by the various expellee organizations, the Federal Republic committed itself to a for-

eign policy vis-à-vis the communist countries in Central and Eastern
Europe that, while avoiding an official recognition of established borders, implicitly accepted the status quo for the time being. This policy
shift included humanitarian efforts to improve the situation of ethnic
Germans in these countries. The possibilities of direct involvement,
however, were extremely limited throughout this period until 1989 so
that the major goal of German foreign policy toward ethnic German
minorities in Central and Eastern Europe was to negotiate agreements
with the states with ethnic Germans that would allow the latter to emigrate to Germany.[10] A precondition for this was the establishment of
diplomatic relations with the relevant states in the Eastern bloc, a
necessity recognized by the expellee organizations as well. In his 1958
contribution to the first issue of *DOD,* Krüger noted that an "isolated
German *Ostpolitik* and with it the realization of the political goals of
the expellees with respect to their homeland are impossible. Both
depend on the correct analysis of the geopolitical situation, and they
have to be executed in consideration of the policy of the western bloc.
. . . Geopolitically, they depend on political détente between East and
West."[11]

The first step in this direction taken by the federal government was
the Soviet-German Treaty of 1955, followed by a verbal agreement in
1958, according to which all those persons of ethnic German origin
who had been German citizens before June 21, 1941, were entitled to
repatriation to the Federal Republic.[12] Treaties with Poland (1970) and
Czechoslovakia (1973) followed, both of which specifically addressed
the sensitive issue of borders, confirming that the German government
of the day respected the territorial status quo. In both treaties, the sig-
natory states assured one another of respect for each other's territorial
integrity and affirmed that neither had territorial claims against the
other.[13] Nonetheless, rulings of the German Constitutional Court in
1973, 1975, and 1987 rejected any suggestion that the treaties with
Moscow and Warsaw violated the assertion of Germany's Basic Law,
which defined German territory by its 1937 borders. While this interpretation pleased the BdV, it did not have a practical impact on the
foreign policy of the federal government, nor did it give the BdV more
opportunities to become more actively involved in foreign policy matters. On the contrary, the insistence of the BdV's leading officials that
the border question remain open led to serious disputes with the federal government in the 1980s. The political impotence of the expellee
organizations became strikingly obvious in 1985, when the motto for
the twenty-first annual meeting of the Silesian expellees was changed

from "Forty Years of Expulsion—Silesia Remains Ours" to "Forty Years of Expulsion—Silesia Remains Our Future in the Europe of Free Peoples" after a personal intervention by Chancellor Kohl. By the same token, in 1987 Herbert Hupka, the chairman of the Landsmann-schaft Schlesien, lost his safe seat on the Christian Democratic Union (CDU) list for the federal elections.

Expellee organizations' lack of political power, however, was offset by a stronger public interest in social and cultural issues from the late 1980s onward, particularly at local levels. Activists, including many who had already been born in the Federal Republic, began to commit more time and funds to helping ethnic German resettlers from Central and Eastern Europe (*Aussiedler*) integrate within German society; to preserving their own cultural heritage and traditions (supported by a special government program for the promotion of Germanic culture from Eastern Europe initiated in 1988); and to developing and increasing cross-border human contacts with Czechoslovakia and Poland and other states with ethnic German minorities in Central and Eastern Europe.

In general, the period between 1955 and 1989–90 was characterized by the attempt to promote coexistence between East and West, against the background of the political realities of the cold war. This did not leave the West German government any other option than to facilitate the emigration of ethnic Germans from Central and Eastern Europe to the Federal Republic, which included primarily ethnic Germans from the Soviet Union, Romania, and Poland. German policy toward ethnic Germans in Central and Eastern Europe was thus not very proactive between 1945 and 1989.[14] In part, this was because such a policy had always been suspected of a hidden revisionist agenda not only by the states in which ethnic German minorities lived but also by many West Germans; and in part, it was because remaining in their homelands was not the preferred option of most ethnic Germans in Central and Eastern Europe, nor was it seen as an acceptable alternative by the federal government.

The Challenge of New Opportunities, 1990–97

The General Context of German Policy toward Ethnic German Minorities in Central and Eastern Europe after 1990

The transition to democracy in Central and Eastern Europe provided an entirely different set of new and enlarged opportunities for Germany's policy toward German minorities in Central and Eastern Europe. On the one hand, democratization meant the granting of such basic rights and liberties as the freedoms of speech, association, and political participation, allowing ethnic Germans in their homelands to form their own parties, stand for election, and actively advance the interests of their group. On the other hand, it also meant that there were no longer any restrictions on emigration, and given the experience of the past, many ethnic Germans, particularly in Poland, Romania, and the Soviet Union and its successor states, seized this opportunity and emigrated to Germany. Both developments required a measured and carefully considered policy response from Germany—domestically to cope with the enormous influx of ethnic Germans and internationally to assure the neighboring states in Central and Eastern Europe of the inviolability of the postwar borders, while simultaneously supporting German minorities at qualitatively and quantitatively new levels and ensuring their protection as national minorities. All this had to happen within the framework of general German foreign policy premises, such as the support for the transition to democracy and a market economy, the creation of a new collective security order embracing all states in Europe, and respect for international law and human rights.

The Domestic Response: Restriction of Immigration

The most important legislation passed in response to the vast increase in the numbers of ethnic Germans[15] leaving their homelands to migrate to Germany was the 1993 War Consequences Conciliation Act. Entitlement to German citizenship, formerly automatic, was revoked under this act. Ethnic Germans now had to prove ethnic discrimination in their homelands and a long-standing affinity to German culture, language, and traditions in order to qualify. Furthermore, the annual intake of ethnic Germans was limited to the average of the years 1991 and 1992 within a 10 percent margin, that is, a maximum of about 250,000 people. Since before this, in 1990, a bill had been passed that required ethnic Germans to apply for admission to Germany from their homelands, the annual intake could effectively be restricted to these quotas. In 1996 authorities introduced a language test as a way of ensuring applicants' affinity to German language and culture. Together these changed regulations have considerably reduced the immigration of ethnic Germans to the Federal Republic—from around 220,000 each year between 1993 and 1995, the immigration figures dropped to 178,000 in 1996 and 134,000 in 1997. In 1998 just over 100,000 ethnic Germans immigrated, while in 1999 their number crept up slightly to 104,916. However, by 2000 the number of ethnic Germans immigrating to the Federal Republic was below 100,000 for the first time in more than a decade and has remained there since.[16]

The External Response: Creating an Alternative to "Repatriation"

Realizing that the changed conditions after 1990 required a fundamentally different foreign policy approach, the German government integrated its policy toward ethnic German communities in Central and Eastern Europe into the wider framework of its efforts to promote democracy, prosperity, and security in Central and Eastern Europe. Given the ethnopolitical demography of the region with its many national minorities, latent border disputes, and interethnic tensions, it was obvious that the role of minorities would be a crucial one in two ways. The ultimate test of successful democratization would have to include an assessment of whether or not members of national minorities, individually and collectively, were entitled to full equality and the right to preserve, express, and develop their distinct identities in their homelands. Furthermore, it would not be possible to create a viable collective security system without settling existing ethnic and territorial conflicts and establishing frameworks within which future disputes could be resolved peacefully. Taking these assumptions as a starting point, the German government concluded that national minorities could play a crucial part in bringing about results in these two interrelated processes.[17] The federal government sought to create partnerships with the Central and East European states and the German minorities living there that, as expressed in international treaties and bilateral agreements,[18] would promote the government's "overall foreign policy concept of a European peace policy of reconciliation, understanding, and co-operation."[19] Cultural, social, and economic measures to support ethnic German minorities, although primarily "aimed at an improvement of the living conditions of ethnic Germans in their homelands," would naturally benefit whole regions and their populations independent of their ethnic origin and thus promote interethnic harmony and economic prosperity while strengthening the emerging democratic political structures.[20] Thus, by creating favorable conditions for the integration of ethnic Germans into the societies of their homelands as citizens with equal rights, the German government hoped to provide an alternative to emigration.[21]

Not all of the projects, however, have been successful. In the early stages, there was a general lack of coordination because the German government was still formulating a comprehensive policy toward ethnic Germans in Central and Eastern Europe and was only just beginning to adapt to the new conditions created by the sudden collapse of communism. Millions of deutsche marks were pumped into large-scale projects, such as the construction of houses for the settlement of ethnic Germans near St. Petersburg; yet, once the money had been allocated, there was little or no monitoring of the progress of the project nor any assurance that these projects would increase the willingness of ethnic Germans to remain in their homelands. Even closer to home, the Association for Germans Abroad (Verein für das Deutschtum im Ausland, or VDA) had been enmeshed in a financial scandal about the misuse of twenty-two million deutsche marks allocated to it by the federal Ministry of the Interior, which the VDA was supposed to spend on funding support programs for ethnic Germans in Central and Eastern Europe.

It came as no surprise that the new Red-Green coalition government began to reconceptualize German policy toward ethnic Germans abroad soon after it came to power. In 1999 it decided to abandon all large-scale investment plans since these projects did not have any measurable success in persuading ethnic Germans not to emigrate to Germany. Instead, plans were drawn up (and have since then been gradually implemented) to direct resources toward self-help projects, in particular through providing seed funding for small and medium-size businesses, and to improve the services offered by the community centers for ethnic Germans abroad (*Begegnungsstätten*) to increase training and vocational qualification programs, to provide more after-school German classes, to fund initiatives by community organizations, and to intensify social work with young ethnic Germans. Furthermore, the government decided to support these efforts primarily within Russia and Poland.[22] Aid programs for German minorities in other countries, such as Romania or the Baltic Republics, were not phased out but rather scaled back and concentrated on social work, and the new federal government, too, realizes that these programs are an important instrument of a foreign policy aimed at "the peaceful and tolerant coexistence of various national groups" in states with ethnic German minorities.[23]

The restructuring and partial reconceptualization of Germany's policy toward ethnic Germans in Central and Eastern Europe are driven by the desire for greater effectiveness, on the one hand, and by the need to decrease spending in all areas in order to consolidate the federal budget, on the other. For the period from 2000 to 2003, annual cuts of twenty-six million deutsche marks have been proposed for "Measures in Support of German Minorities in Their Homelands."[24]

While expellee organizations generally acknowledged the need for structures that are more efficient, and accepted that spending cuts in the area of policy toward ethnic Germans abroad could not be completely avoided, they particularly criticized the new concept for the promotion of the "German Culture of Eastern Europe."[25] The main criticisms were not directed at the proposed budget cuts of around eight million deutsche marks (out of currently forty-three million deutsche marks annually) but at the plans for restructuring the entire network of organizations and institutions involved in the preservation of expellee culture and cross-border cultural cooperation with the former homelands. The new concept envisioned the consolidation of such organizations and institutions on a "broad regional basis"—Northeastern Europe (Pomerania, East and West Prussia, parts of the former Soviet Union, and Baltic Republics), Silesia, Sudetenland, and Southeastern Europe. Despite the fact that there were numerous inconsistencies in the previous scheme of administering the cultural work of expellee organizations, including the costly duality of institutions at many levels, the proposed centralization was more likely to undermine the basis of this cultural work, most of which had been carried out by expellees and Aussiedler. The government's justifications for the centralization initiative claimed that expellee organizations had not adjusted to the post-1989 geopolitical changes, let alone reflected them in their work. Moreover, the policy presumed that, for reasons of advanced age, the actual expellees of 1945 to 1950 could and should no longer be the main activists of cultural exchange.[26] These developments were uncomfortable reminders of past ideological battles and cast a shadow of doubt at the commitment of the new federal government to continue the cooperation with expellees in the process of reconciliation between Germany and the countries in Central and Eastern Europe in which German minorities live.

Two Case Studies: Germany's Relationship with the Czech Republic and Poland

In Germany's relationship with Czechoslovakia, and after 1993 with the Czech Republic, territorial issues never played a part at the intergovernmental level, because all West German governments after 1949 had accepted, at least implicitly, the formula of "Germany within the borders of 1937" as the Allied powers had expressed it in the London Protocol of September 1944.[27] More important was the channeling of humanitarian aid to support the remaining ethnic Germans in Czecho- slovakia and above all to facilitate a comprehensive process of recon- ciliation. Because of the political role played by the German minority during the interwar period and their subsequent expulsion from the Sudetenland, bilateral relations have never been completely free from certain strains and have sometimes been affected negatively by the problems created by the presence and activities of the Sudeten German expellees in the Federal Republic.

After years of negotiations, the German-Czech Declaration of Janu- ary 21, 1997, was the lowest common denominator the two govern- ments could find on the two most critical issues—the role of the Sude- ten Germans in the breakup of Czechoslovakia in 1938 and their collective victimization and expulsion after the end of World War II. The German government accepted the responsibility of Germany in the developments leading up to the Munich Agreement and the destruction of Czechoslovakia, expressed its deep sorrow over the suffering of Czechs during the Nazi occupation of their country, and acknowledged that it was these two issues that prepared the ground for the postwar treatment and expulsion of members of the German minority in the country. The Czech government, on the other side, regretted the post- war policy vis-à-vis ethnic Germans, which resulted in the expulsion and expropriation of a large section of the ethnic German minority, including many innocent people. Both governments agreed that the remaining members of the ethnic German minority in the Czech Republic and the expellees and their descendants would play an impor- tant role in the future relationship of the two countries and that the support of the ethnic German minority in the Czech Republic was a matter of mutual interest. In order to fulfill this interest, a joint Ger- man-Czech Future Fund was created, to which Germany contributed about 140 million deutsche marks and the Czech Republic about 25 million deutsche marks. One of the fund's goals was determined as sup- port of the ethnic German minority in the Czech Republic.

Historically, the problems between Germany and Poland have been much more complex in comparison to those between Germany and Czechoslovakia or the Czech Republic. German oppression of Poles had been fiercer and lasted longer than that of the Czechs, and the number of expellees from Poland (about nine million) exceeded those from the Sudetenland (about three million) by far. In addition, the so- called former *Ostgebiete* had only been placed under provisional Polish administration by the communiqué of the Potsdam conference in 1945, while a permanent settlement of their status was to be resolved in a later peace treaty. Thus, the relationship with Poland had a somewhat higher priority on the German foreign policy agenda, especially in relation to German unification. The German minority always figured prominently in the formulation of policy objectives within Germany's policy vis-à-vis Poland. As early as 1989 a joint declaration by the German chancellor and the Polish prime minister acknowledged the existence of a population of German descent in Poland and the need to protect its cultural identity.

Today, the relations between Germany and Poland have their legal basis in a bilateral treaty of 1990, in which the Federal Republic explicitly guaranteed the Oder-Neisse line as the common border, and in the 1991 Treaty on Good Neighborly Relations and Cooperation. To secure a legal framework for the development of the ethnic German minority in Poland was only one part of German foreign policy. This goal has been complemented by substantial material aid for ethnic Germans in the areas of culture and education (responsibilities of the Foreign Office), economic reconstruction (the responsibility of the Ministry of the Interior), and social and community work (responsibilities of the German Red Cross, and, before 1990, also through the Ministry of Inner-German Affairs). Material aid had already been committed to the ethnic German minority before 1989 but in comparatively smaller proportions. The changes in Poland in 1989–90 allowed the allocation of larger funds, through different channels and for new purposes (see table 1). Geographically, material support has always been primarily directed to the Upper Silesian region.

TABLE 1.   German Financial Support for Ethnic Germans in Poland, 1987–94

	AA	BMI	DRK	BMfiB
1987	—	—	2.5	2.6
1988	—	—	2.4	3.7
1989		—	2.8	5.5
1990	5.5	6.8	3.3	5.3
1991		24.2	3.1	—
1992	3.5	26.5	1.4	—
1993	6.5	25.7	1.1	—
1994	6.5	25.3	1.4	—

Source: *Bundestagsdrucksache* 13/1036.

Note: Since 1994, the combined annual average of all funds made available to the ethnic German minority in Poland has been around twenty-five million deutsche marks. All figures in millions of deutsche marks. AA = Foreign Office; BMI = Ministry of the Interior; DRK = German Red Cross; BMfiB = Ministry of Inner-German Affairs.

Funding in the educational and cultural sector has included a variety of activities. The German government has provided staff support to improve the quality of German language instruction in Poland. The number of teachers sent to Poland has increased from just 1 in 1989 to 111 in 1994. In addition, four federal government–sponsored experts on German language teaching have been working in Poland since 1994; the German Academic Exchange Service has been funding twenty-six lecturers at Polish universities; and the Goethe Institute has supplied eight lecturers for the further training of Polish teachers of German. Since 1993 members of the ethnic German minority in Poland have also had access to a special grant program to study in Germany for a period of up to twelve months. The federal government also provides partial funding for the television and radio broadcasts and print media of the German minority and supplies German newspapers and magazines to the cultural and political organizations of the minority.

The Ministry of the Interior has also channeled financial aid to various ethnic German minority associations in Poland. The annual amounts increased from 4.7 million deutsche marks in 1991 to 5.8 million in 1992 and then dropped to 5.7 million and to 5.4 million deutsche marks in 1993 and 1994, respectively. A far larger amount of money, however, has been spent on projects to support the economic recovery of the areas in which members of the ethnic German minority live, thus benefiting not only the minorities but also these regions and the rest of the population as a whole. Efforts here were concentrated on improvements in infrastructure, for example, water supply systems, and on promoting small businesses and private farms. Funding of such projects increased from 700,000 deutsche marks in 1991 to 8.7 million deutsche marks in 1994 and again to 14.8 million deutsche marks in 1996. For the distribution of these funds, the federal government uses the Foundation for the Development of Silesia and partly funds three staff positions there. The German government has also provided funds for various social welfare projects, including the improvement of medical services in Upper Silesia and the creation of a network of centers to care for the elderly.

Irredentism or Constructive Reconciliation?
A New Opportunity for the Expellees

The collapse of communism came as unexpectedly for the expellee organizations as it did for the German government. Yet, the government's perception of the opportunities arising from the dramatic events in 1989–90 was rather different from that of the expellees, and there were also different reactions within the BdV. German government policy—which was to achieve the unification of the two German states at the price of abandoning all territorial claims and formally accepting the borders of East Germany as those of the united Germany—was seen as unacceptable and treacherous by many in the leadership of the BdV. Instead, activists of the organization tried to stage a referendum in Poland under the motto "Peace through Free Choice" (*Frieden durch freie Abstimmung*). This raised completely unrealistic hopes among many members of the ethnic German minority in Poland, particularly in Upper Silesia, where the response to the signature campaign in support of the referendum had been strong. These hopes were dashed when Chancellor Kohl declared at an event celebrating the fortieth anniversary of the Charter of the German Expellees in 1990 that the recognition of the Oder-Neisse line as Germany's eastern frontier was the price that had to be paid for the reunification with East Germany.

For historical reasons, the question of where the borders should be drawn between the Federal Republic and Czechoslovakia or the Czech Republic had never been as controversial as that of the territorial boundaries between Germany and Poland. But the rhetoric of expellee activists from the Czech lands has, if anything, been more aggressive than that of their Polish counterparts. This became particularly obvious in a 1991 collection of essays written by leading figures of the Sudeten German community on the obligation of the Sudeten Germans vis-à-vis their homeland.[28] In one of the essays, Harry Hochfelder, a member of the Sudeten German Council and the Sudeten German Academy of Sciences and Arts, demanded that the "restitution [of property] has to be handled in such a way that the ethnic group [of Sudeten Germans] can exercise unlimited political sovereignty in its homeland. Certainly there will be resettlement of the non-German population currently living in the area, for which incentives have to be made available, but which must not be forced."[29] Roland Schnürch, vice president of the Federal Assembly of the Sudetendeutsche Landsmannschaft, asserted the claim of some Sudeten Germans to Czech territory even more forcefully. He "decisively" rejected the "belonging of the Sudetenland to any Czechoslovak state." From this, he concluded that "the border question has not been solved yet."[30] Another contributor, Willi Wanka, a member of the advisory committee on foreign affairs of the Sudeten German Council, insisted that, "without the return of the Sudeten areas to the Sudeten Germans, there will be no resolution of the Sudeten German question."[31]

Extremist demands of this kind were not popular with either the German or the Czech (and Polish) governments. Subsequently, more moderate voices and more conciliatory approaches have also emerged. As early as 1993 the leadership of the BdV, at that time still dominated by the "old guard" around Herbert Hupka and Herbert Czaja, acknowledged the positive steps taken by the Polish government to improve the situation of ethnic Germans in Poland.[32] Erika Steinbach, the chairperson of the BdV since May 1998, gave a speech to students at the Charles University in Prague that declared that, five decades after the end of World War II, "coming to terms with the past cannot be about guilt and retribution. . . .We have to face the history of this century together in order to build a peaceful and prosperous future." She even accepted the critique of the Czech ambassador to Germany that it was painful for Czechs to hear her use the term *expelling states* (*Vertreiberstaaten*). She emphasized that today's Czech Republic is a democracy that has not expelled any Germans; yet, she insisted that the Czech Republic, as much as Germany, had to accept the legacy of the past. More importantly for the particularly sensitive relationship with the Czech Republic, Steinbach reassured her listeners that, although the expellees loved their ancestral homelands, "they respect the dignity of the people living there now. And they do not want . . . that other people will ever be expelled."[33] The new Red-Green government has also recognized this shift toward moderation. In her address at the twenty-fifth anniversary of the Cultural Foundation of the German Expellees, the chairperson of the Culture and Media Committee of the Bundestag, Elke Leonhard of the Social Democratic Party (SPD), emphasized that nobody had the right to "discredit as revanchism the legitimate interests of the expellees in the preservation of their culture and the public acknowledgment of their fate: territorial questions that could affect national rights are no longer an issue."[34]

However, two issues—while not directly contradicting these statements—continue to influence German-Polish and German-Czech relations: the restitution of property, or adequate compensation for it, and the right for expellees to return to their homelands. Both of these questions have strong political implications. The demand for property restitution (or compensation) entered a new phase during the summer of 1999, when the Sudeten German Regional-Cultural Association decided to support the filing of a collective court case in the United

States against the Czech state and when ethnic German resettlers from Poland who left the country between the 1950s and 1970s brought their case for restitution or compensation to the Polish Supreme Court.[35] At the same time, the BdV and the Sudeten German Landsmannschaft have demanded on several occasions that Czech and Polish accession to the European Union (EU) be made dependent upon the restitution of property to expellees or their adequate compensation. Chancellor Schroeder of Germany made it clear in March 1999 that he would not support Sudeten German property claims and that his government did not intend to make any claims itself.[36] Expellee organizations have nevertheless persisted in their attempts to link EU membership for Poland and the Czech Republic to a satisfactory resolution of the property question, often pointing to the examples of Hungary and Estonia, both of which introduced legislation to this effect. One side effect of this approach by the expellees is the fact that the remaining ethnic German minorities in Poland and the Czech Republic find themselves in an increasingly awkward position in their homelands. In this context, one of the leading activists of the ethnic German minority in Poland, Henryk Kroll, a member of the Polish Sejm, asked the BdV chairperson, Erika Steinbach, in October 1999 publicly to drop the demand to make restitution or compensation for the expellees a condition of EU membership.

The most controversial and potentially most explosive issue in German-Czech relations is the so-called Beneš Decrees, which dealt with the confiscation of German (and Hungarian) property in Czechoslovakia and citizenship issues in relation to members of the two ethnic groups. Here, too, a number of opportunities have arisen on several levels—bilaterally as well as on the European stage—and they have been exploited by expellee activists. In April 1999 a resolution was passed by the European Parliament in which its members called "on the Czech Government, in the same spirit of reconciliatory statements made by President Havel, to repeal the surviving laws and decrees from 1945 and 1946, insofar as they concern the expulsion of individual ethnic groups in the former Czechoslovakia." Prior to this resolution of the European Parliament, the U.S. House of Representatives passed a resolution on October 13, 1998, in which members of the House demanded that the formerly communist countries in Central and Eastern Europe "return wrongfully expropriated properties to their rightful owners or, when actual return is not possible, to pay prompt, just, and effective compensation, in accordance with principles of justice and in a manner that is just, transparent, and fair." In the 2000 resolution of the European Parliament on the status of negotiations on the Czech Republic's membership application, the European Parliament stated that it "welcomes the Czech government's willingness to scrutinise the laws and decrees of the Beneš Government dating from 1945 and 1946 and still on the statute books to ascertain whether they run counter to the EU law in force and the Copenhagen criteria."[37]

The first European Parliament resolution was immediately seized upon by a group of members of the German Bundestag who proposed a motion, cosponsored by the Christian Democratic Union/Christian Socialist Union (CDU/CSU) parliamentary party, in which the federal government was asked "to take appropriate action in the spirit of the [resolution of the European Parliament] . . . on its own and in collaboration with the other EU member states and the institutions of the EU." A counter-motion was introduced by the parliamentary parties of SPD and Alliance 90/The Greens in October 1999, in which the Bundestag was asked to welcome the statement by Chancellor Schroeder and Czech minister-president Zeman of March 8, 1999, that "neither government will reintroduce property issues [into their bilateral relationship] either today or in the future." This motion received a majority vote both at committee stage and after a parliamentary debate in June 2000, while that of the CDU/CSU parliamentarians was rejected.[38]

Also at the bilateral level, German dismemberment and occupation of Czechoslovakia, which cannot be separated from the events after 1945, and the expulsions have been dealt with both in the 1992 German-Czechoslovak treaty and the 1997 German-Czech Declaration and in a number of other official statements by both governments. Yet, comments by Czech prime minister Miloš Zeman on the Sudeten Germans being "traitors" and "Hitler's fifth column," however, considerably soured relations between the Czech and German governments in early 2002, leading to the cancellation of a planned visit to the Czech Republic by the German chancellor. The German minister of the interior's contribution to the debate has also been controversial: in his address to the Sudeten German Day in May 2002, Otto Schily of the SPD called on the Czech Republic to eliminate the Beneš decrees from its legal order but also reiterated his government's policy that none of this implied a demand for compensation or restitution of property. Edmund Stoiber, the conservative challenger of current federal chancellor Gerhard Schroeder, declared that his party insisted on a repeal of the Beneš decrees prior to the Czech Republic's EU accession because their continued existence contravened the Copenhagen criteria for EU membership. In contrast to the current government, Stoiber continued, a government led by him would seek a resolution of past issues rather than ignore them. The astonishing capacity that the expulsion of the Sudeten Germans has to affect Czech-German relations thus not only is a matter of bilateral and international relations but also plays a part in domestic politics. As much as government and opposition in Germany have traded blows over the issue in the run-up to the general elections in September, it has also been a topic for Czech domestic preelection politics. On the same day that Stoiber demanded the strict application of the Copenhagen criteria, Zeman declared during a memorial act at the former concentration camp of Theresienstadt/Terezin that the expulsion had fulfilled the Sudeten Germans' desire, as they had wanted to go "home to Germany" (*heim ins Reich*) anyway. Czech minister of the interior Stanislav Gross, Vice Premier Vladimir Spidla, and leading opposition politicians justified the postwar expulsions as contributing to European peace and stability after 1945. Zeman and Spidla have since also acknowledged that a humanitarian gesture toward Germans who were expelled unjustly should be considered. Yet, the insistence that this would affect at most one hundred people already bore the seeds of new confrontation.

In contrast to the thus rather stormy relationship between Germany and the Czech Republic, the relations between the latter and the EU seem more stable for the time being. In April 2002, EU enlargement commissioner Günter Verheugen and Zeman issued a joint statement in which they acknowledged that "there has been much public discussion on some of the Czechoslovak Presidential Decrees of 1945, and on some of the ensuing Czechoslovak legislation of the immediate postwar period" but also insisted that "as was the case with measures taken by other European countries at that time, some of these Acts would not pass muster today if judged by current standards—but they belong to history." This policy is widely supported by governments across Europe, in particular also because a Czech Constitutional Court ruling of March 1995 established that Presidential Decree No. 108/45 (on the confiscation of property) was a unique act that "for more than four decades has established no legal relations and thus no longer has a constitutive character" in the Czech legal system; that is, it is no longer valid or applicable. In February 1999 the Czech government stated in its Foreign Policy Concept that the decrees were "extinct," a view that was subsequently also adopted by the Czech parliament. Officials at all levels have thus managed to find ways out of the dilemma created by the high aspirations that the EU has in terms of human rights and acts committed after World War II that contradict these norms. For obvious reasons, such a difficult balancing act is unlikely to please everyone involved, but the commitment of all governments and the EU commission to leave the past behind and move on to a common future is in the general spirit of post-1990 developments of reconciliation rather than confrontation.[39]

Likewise, the right for expellees to settle in their homelands also gained prominence in the political debate about the accession of Poland and the Czech Republic to the EU and the expected extension of EU principles, including the freedom of mobility, to the two countries, thus giving all current EU citizens, including German expellees and their children and grandchildren, a legal right to settle and acquire property in Poland and the Czech Republic, which has caused considerable unease in Poland and the Czech Republic. However, it is rather unlikely that large numbers of expellees or their children and grandchildren would actually take up such an opportunity.[40]

Nevertheless, relationships with both countries have improved significantly at lower and less formal levels. This has taken the form of communal partnerships between towns in the Federal Republic and in the former homelands of expellees, especially in former East Prussia, Upper Silesia, and the Czech Republic, in which expellees are often actively involved.[41] Increasingly, the various expellee organizations have made efforts to foster dialogue with their homelands at various levels. Joint workshops have taken place in Germany, Poland, and the Czech Republic, bringing together officials and activists from both sides to explore the past and, even more importantly, to discuss ways of how to build the future. Similarly, expellees have visited their former hometowns and villages to assess the specific needs of these regions and to initiate aid programs.[42] Even less formally, many expellees and their children and grandchildren have gotten involved individually in projects to facilitate the reconstruction of their former homelands after decades of communism, most of them without any intention of resettlement, border revisions, or the like. Expellees from East Prussia have started an initiative for the preservation of cultural monuments in their former homeland, while Sudeten German expellees have contributed to the reconstruction of many churches in the Czech Republic and have initiated exchange projects with their former homeland communities.[43] From this perspective, the work of the refugees, expellees, and their children has made a significant and positive contribution to Germany's policy toward ethnic German minorities in Central and Eastern Europe after 1990: it has fostered reconciliation and has been a part of the efforts to improve the living conditions of ethnic German minorities in their homelands. In particular, the former of these two assertions is still a matter of debate even within Germany. However, there seems to be growing consensus that the involvement of expellees has, especially after 1989–90, complemented the reconciliation policy of German governments. As Germany's minister of the interior, Otto Schily, put it, "Contrary to frequent prejudice, the overwhelming majority of German expellees have actively participated in the process of reconciliation between the European nations, and they continue to do so today."[44]

Outlook: The Future of Germany's Policy toward Ethnic Germans in Central and Eastern Europe

The democratization of the formerly communist societies in Central and Eastern Europe opened new opportunities for Germany's policy toward ethnic German minorities in Central and Eastern Europe. A number of factors complemented each other during this period in a unique fashion: increased possibilities for supporting ethnic German minorities in their homelands; the need to do so in order to halt the mass exodus of ethnic Germans to the Federal Republic; the desire of the German expellees to become involved in this process; and the genuine interest of the former communist countries in improving their relationship with Germany, which was seen as an important stepping-stone toward membership in the EU and NATO. Germany's firm intention to bridge the gap between cultures and across historical enmities could only be realized through reconciliation and mutual understanding. Part of this was the inevitable unconditional recognition of the borders with Poland and Czechoslovakia. Yet, the joint future of Germany and its eastern neighbors could not be secured without addressing the situation of ethnic German minorities in these countries and the suffering of the postwar refugees and expellees. On the basis of numerous treaties and within the framework set out by the 1990 Copenhagen Declaration of the Conference on Security and Cooperation in Europe, Germany and Poland and Germany and the Czech Republic have developed relationships that allow their governments to tackle the issue of minority rights and support from Germany for ethnic Germans and to include representatives of the minorities and the expellee organizations in this process. Yet, for historical as well as contemporary reasons, this has remained a very sensitive problem. German policy toward ethnic Germans abroad, therefore, has always only been one part of a more comprehensive foreign policy approach toward its eastern neighbors that aims at a stabilization of democracy and the creation of a market economy in these countries. These achievements will provide a wider social, political, and economic framework within which harmonious interethnic relationships can develop, which will inevitably benefit ethnic German minorities as well.

The inclusion of expellee organizations in this process has been vital, despite the difficulties it has occasionally caused. For the success of the reconciliation process, it is essential that the human dimension in the relationships between Germany and its neighbors to the east be not ignored. Only the joint efforts of the ethnic German minorities, the population of the states of which they are now citizens, and the expellees will provide a framework within which the further cooperation with, and integration of, the countries in Central and Eastern Europe with ethnic German minorities will not reopen old wounds but will instead pave the way to a secure and prosperous future.

Notes

1. Ethnic Germans in the Soviet Union had been deported to the Central Asian Republics from their settlements in the European parts of the country after Hitler Germany's attack in 1941.

2. By 1949 about 7.6 million refugees and expellees had arrived in the western zones of occupation; by 1953 it was 8.4 million. The total number of refugees and expellees was around 12 million, with approximately 3.5 million of them being resettled in what was to become the German Democratic Republic.

3. The existence of such a right has recently been recognized by the United Nations. On May 28, 1995, the UN high commissioner for human rights, José Ayala-Lasso, affirmed in a message to the German expellees that "the right not to be expelled from one's ancestral homeland is a fundamental human right." Translated from Hochkommissar für Menschenrechte der Vereinten Nationen, *Grußbotschaft an die deutschen Vertriebenen vom 28. Mai 1995.* All translations in this chapter are my own unless otherwise specified.

4. "Charta der deutschen Heimatvertriebenen, gegeben zu Stuttgart am 5. August 1950," *Kulturelle Arbeitshefte* 22 (1995): 15

5. While this may seem to be self-promotional propaganda by the BdV, it is actually an almost literal translation from a speech by the German minister of the interior, Otto Schily, a Social Democratic Party member, delivered on the fiftieth anniversary of the BdV on May 29, 1999. Otto Schily, "Die Erinnerung und das Gedenken findet ihren Sinn in dem Willen für eine bessere Zukunft," Rede auf der Festveranstaltung zum 50. Jahrestag des Bundes der Vertriebenen am 29. Mai 1999 im Berliner Dom, transcript in possession of the author.

6. German Balts; Banat Swabians; Berlin—Mark Brandenburg; Bessarabia Germans; Bukovina Germans; Germans from Danzig; Dobrudja and Bulgarian Germans; Danube Swabians; Carpathian Germans; Lithuanian Germans; Upper Silesian Germans; East Prussians; Pomerania; Russian Germans; Sathmar Swabians; Silesia, Lower and Upper Silesia; Transylvanian Saxons; Sudeten Germans; Weichsel-Warthe; and West Prussia.

7. Industrialists, youth, students, women, track athletes, the deaf, and farmers.

8. Hans Krüger, "Leitartikel in der Erstausgabe des Deutschen Ostdiensts," reprinted in *Deutscher Ostdienst* 40, no. 1–2 (Jan. 9, 1998): 3–4 (quote is from 3).

9. Krüger, "Leitartikel," 3.

10. The agreements between West Germany and some of the states in Central and Eastern Europe with ethnic German minorities for the repatriation of ethnic Germans included financial arrangements setting "per capita fees" to be paid by the federal government. Average figures of annual emigration of ethnic Germans after 1950 are as follows: 1955–59: 64,000; 1960–64: 18,000; 1965–69: 26,000; 1970–74: 25,000; 1975–79: 46,000; 1980–84: 49,000, 1985–86: 41,000; 1987: 78,000.

11. Krüger, "Leitartikel," 4.

12. This, however, solved only a part of the problem, since it included only the Germans of the northern territories of former East Prussia, the so-called Memel Germans, and those ethnic Germans who, in the aftermath of the German-Soviet treaty of 1939, had been resettled to the territories then occupied by Germany from the Baltic states, Galicia, Volhynia, Bessarabia, and the Northern Bukovina but found themselves again on Soviet territory at the end of the war. Thus, it did not cover the by far largest group of ethnic Germans who had migrated there, mostly in the eighteenth and nineteenth centuries.

13. Cf. *Bulletin der Bundesregierung* (1970): 1815, 1973, 1631.

14. After the change in government in Germany in 1982, there were some modest attempts to achieve a recognition and protection of ethnic Germans as a minority in Poland. However, it was only in 1989 that a joint declaration of the two heads of government, Mazowiecki and Kohl, stated that both governments would allow persons who were of German or Polish origin or saw themselves as part of either of these traditions or cultures to preserve, express, and develop their distinct ethnic identities.

15. In 1988, over 200,000 ethnic Germans "returned" to Germany; by 1989, it was already 377,000; and in 1990, the numbers of ethnic German immigrants to the Federal Republic peaked at 397,000.

16. This drop has two further reasons apart from legal restrictions—many ethnic Germans who have successfully applied for citizenship but have not yet exercised their option to migrate to Germany are holding this option in reserve. In addition, the majority of people from Romania and Poland who had wanted to leave had already done so in the late 1980s and early 1990s, so that the demand from these countries is now greatly reduced.

17. Cf. *Bundestagsdrucksache* 13/10845; *BMI-Pressemitteilung* May 18, 1999; and *BMI-Pressemitteilung* June 14, 1999.

18. The key international agreements in this context are the 1990 Copenhagen document of the Conference on Security and Cooperation in Europe and the

Council of Europe's Framework Declaration on minority rights. Bilateral treaties exist between Germany and Poland, the Czech and Slovak Republics, Hungary, Romania, and Russia. Major bilateral agreements were concluded with Ukraine and Kazakhstan.

19. *Bundestagsdrucksache* 13/3195.

20. Cf. *Bundestagsdrucksache* 13/3428 and *Bundestagsdrucksache* 13/1116.

21. Cf. *Bundestagsdrucksache* 13/3428.

22. Cf. *BMI-Pressemitteilung* Sept. 1, 1999; *BMI-Pressemitteilung* Aug. 10, 1999; and *BMI-Pressemitteilung* June 25, 1999.

23. Cf. *BMI-Pressemitteilung* July 2, 1999 and *BMI-Pressemitteilung* Oct. 21, 1999.

24. The total of the various budget titles had peaked in 1997 at almost 115 million deutsche marks, not including the payments made to various expellee organizations to support their activities in Central and Eastern Europe (5.1 million deutsche marks) and also not including institutional funding for the BdV (24.8 million deutsche marks) before it was cut down to 85 million deutsche marks in 1998 and 75 million deutsche marks in 1999. From 1998 to 1999, there was however a significant increase in institutional funding for the BdV to 42 million deutsche marks. These cuts account for around 1 percent of the total savings in the federal budget in 2000, decreasing to around 0.5 percent by 2003.

25. "Deutsche Kultur des östlichen Europas" is the title of a special subgroup in the federal chancellory's Department of Culture and Media, which has been created only since 1998. The former term, "German Culture of the East" (Deutsche Kultur des Ostens), is no longer used.

26. Cf. Andreas Rossmann, "Der kalte Krieger. Unter Ideologieverdacht: Naumann und die Vertriebenenkultur," *Frankfurter Allgemeine Zeitung,* Aug. 28, 1999; and Reinhard Müller, "Nichts als Erinnerung? Wie die Bundesregierung das kulturelle Erbe der Vertriebenen tilgen will," *Frankfurter Allgemeine Zeitung,* Sept. 23, 1999.

27. Otto Kimminich, "Völkerrecht und Geschichte im Disput über die Beziehungen Deutschlands zu seinen östlichen Nachbarn," *Aus Politik und Zeitgeschichte* 28 (1996): 28–38 (quote is from 33).

28. Rolf-Josef Eibicht, ed., *Die Sudetendeutschen und ihre Heimat. Erbe—Auftrag—Ziel* (Wesseding, 1991).

29. Harry Hochfelder, "Über die Ziele sudetendeutscher Politik," in *Die Sudetendeutschen,* ed. Eibicht, 50–59 (quote is from 58).

30. Roland Schnürch, "Konsequenzen sudetendeutscher Heimatpolitik," in *Die Sudetendeutschen,,* 83–94 (quote is from 83).

31. Willi Wanka, "Mit dem Blick auf eine wahre Lösung. Anmerkungen zur Sudetenfrage," in *Die Sudetendeutschen,* ed. Eibicht, 74–82 (quote is from 75).

32. Marian Dobrosielski, *Deutsche Minderheiten in Polen* (Hamburg, 1992), 144.

33. All quotes are from Erika Steinbach, *Tschechen und Deutsche—Der Weg in die Zukunft,* Vortrag vor Studenten der Karlsuniversität in Prag, Mar. 17, 1999, available at <http://www.bund-der-vertriebenen.de/politik.htm>.

34. Elke Leonhard, *Die Verantwortung der Politik für die gesamtdeutsche Kultur,* Festrede aus Anlass des 25 jährigen Bestehens der Kulturstiftung der deutschen Vertriebenen am June 14, 1999.

35. While the legal situation of both groups of claimants is different, their action was, to some extent, triggered by a resolution of the U.S. House of Representatives in 1998 urging "countries which have not already done so to return wrongfully expropriated properties to their rightful owners or, when actual return is not possible, to pay prompt, just and effective compensation, in accordance with principles of justice and in a manner that is just, transparent and fair," 105th Cong., 2d Sess, H. RES. 562 (HRES 562 IH).

36. *Bundeskanzleramt Pressemitteilung* Mar. 9, 1999.

37. European Parliament, 1999, "Resolution on the Czech Republic's membership application to the European union and the state of negotiations," (COM[1999] 503—C5-0026/2000—1997/2180[COS]). See also House of Representatives [105th Cong., 2d Sess.], "House Resolution No. 562," [HRES 562 IH], 1998; and also European Parliament, 2000, *Resolution on the Regular Report from the Commission on the Czech Republic's Progress towards Accession* (COM[98]0708 C4–0111/99).

38. Deutscher Bundestag, "Antrag der Abgeordneten Hartmut Koschyk, Christian Schmidt (Fürth), Karl Lamers, Peter Hintze und der Fraktion der CDU/CSU: Versöhnung durch Ächtung von Vertreibung," *Bundestagsdrucksache* 14/1311, June 29, 1999; and Deutscher Bundestag, "Antrag der Fraktionen SPD und Bündnis 90/Die Grünen: Weiterentwicklung der deutschtschechischen Beziehungen," *Bundestagsdrucksache* 14/1873, Oct. 26, 1999.

39. See Joint Press Statement of Prime Minister Zeman and EU Commissioner Verheugen, April 11, 2002. available online at <http://www.czechembassy.org/wwwo/mzv/default.asp?id=11191&ido=6569&idj=2&amb=1> (accessed April 23, 2002). See also Judgment Pl. US 14/94 of the Constitutional Court of the Czech Republic in the Name of the Czech Republic, available online at <http://www.concourt.cz/angl_verze/doc/p-14–94.html> (accessed Sept. 1, 2004); see also Beschluss des Abgeordnetenhauses des Parlaments der Tschechischen Republik zu den Dekreten des Präsidenten der Republik, April 24, 2002, available online at <http://www.czechembassy.org/servis/soubor.asp?id=1996> (accessed April 30, 2003).

40. The interest of most expellees in their former homelands is mostly nostalgic returning to the places of their (childhood) memory as tourists (*Heimwehtouristen*) rather than as permanent resettlers.

41. One such example is the twinning arrangement between former Preussisch Holland (now Paslek), the town of Hürth in Germany, and the local association of expellees, many of whom originally came from Preussisch Holland/Paslek. The agreement covers a range of areas, including the preservation of cultural monuments, cooperation in historic research and in the area of culture, promotion of contacts in the fields of tourism and business, humanitarian aid, and support for exchange programs. For further details, see *Deutscher Ostdienst* 40, no. 25 (June 19, 1998): 6–7. Another noteworthy case is that of the town of Ratibor in Upper Silesia. Here expellees became actively involved in the construction of a wastewater facility, and the chairman of the Landsmannschaft Schlesien, Herbert Hupka, for years a target of communist propaganda, was awarded the town's honorary medal for his efforts. Another example is the organization Aid for You (Hilfe für Euch), based in Kiel, Germany, which since 1984 has supported ethnic Germans in former East Prussia, primarily with food and clothing.

42. This, very often, takes very basic forms. The donation campaign "Notopfer Königsberg" of the BdV state organization North Rhine-Westphalia, for example, funded the provision of running water for one family, of winter food for the cow of another family, and the repair of roofs of several houses.

43. The sculptor Walter Grill, to name just one prominent case, has organized several exhibitions of his work and that of his colleagues in his former hometown of Karlsbad/Karlovy Vary. According to him, the personal contact with people living in the former Sudetenland now has managed to overcome many prejudices and fears on both sides. According to Grill, "[F]or an artist, home will be wherever he can freely practice his art." Quoted in David G. Rock and Stefan Wolff, eds., *Coming Home to Germany? The Integration of Ethnic Germans from Central and Eastern Europe in the Federal Republic* (Oxford, 2001).

44. Schily, "Die Erinnerung," Available at <http://www.bmi.bund.de / nn_122054/Internet/Content/Nachrichten/Reden/1999/05/Die_Erinnerung_und_ das_ Gedenken_findet_Id_19498_de.html> (accessed Sept. 1, 2004).

Contributors

Doris L. Bergen is associate professor of history at the University of Notre Dame. She is author of *Twisted Cross: The German Christian Movement in the Third Reich* (1996) and *War and Genocide: A Concise History of the Holocaust* (2003) and editor of *The Sword of the Lord: Military Chaplains from the First to the Twenty-First Century* (2004). Her work has been supported by fellowships from the Alexander von Humboldt Foundation, the German Academic Exchange Service, the German Marshall Fund of the United States, and the Center for Advanced Holocaust Studies at the United States Holocaust Memorial Museum.

Renate Bridenthal is emerita professor of history at Brooklyn College of the City University of New York. Her previous publications have been mainly in women's history, notably as coeditor of and contributor to *Becoming Visible: Women in European History* (1977, 1987, 1998), *When Biology Became Destiny: Women in Weimar and Nazi Germany* (1984), and *Families in Flux* (1989). Her recent research interest is in German ethnicity abroad, particularly among Russian Germans.

Tobias Brinkmann is lecturer in history at the University of Southampton, England. He has been a research fellow at the Simon-Dubnow Institute for Jewish History and Culture in Leipzig, Germany, and taught in the American Studies and History Departments of the University of Leipzig. He is currently completing a book on immigrants and transmigrants in Berlin during the 1920s. His recent publications include several book chapters and journal articles on migration, modern Jewish history, and cultural history, as well as his book, *Von der Gemeinde zur "Community": Jüdische Einwanderer in Chicago, 1840–1900* (2002).

Jürgen Buchenau is associate professor of history at the University of North Carolina at Charlotte. He is the author of *In the Shadow of the Giant: The Making of Mexico's Central America Policy, 1876–1930* (1996) and *Werkzeuge des Fortschritts: Eine deutsche Händlerfamilie in Mexiko von 1865 bis zur Gegenwart* (2002), recently published in English as *Tools of Progress: A German Merchant Family in Mexico City* (2004). He has received numerous grants and awards, including a fellowship from the National Endowment for the Humanities for his work on the German diaspora in Mexico. He is currently working on a book on the Mexican revolutionary leader Plutarco Elías Calles.

Norbert Götz is assistant professor of Nordic history at the University of Greifswald. His research interests are international relations, civil society, political ideologies, and the welfare state. He has recently published *Ungleiche Geschwister: Die Konstruktion von national-sozialistischer Volksgemeinschaft und schwedischem Volksheim* (2001) and coedited the volume *Civil Society in the Baltic Sea Region* (2003).

Pieter Judson is professor and chair of the History Department at Swarthmore College. His *Exclusive Revolutionaries: Liberal Politics, Social Experience, and National Identity in the Austrian Empire, 1848–1914* (1996) won the Herbert Baxter Adams prize of the American Historical Association in 1997 and the Austrian Cultural Forum's book prize for 1998. He is also the author of *Wien Brennt! Die Revolution von 1848 und ihr liberales Erbe* (1998), coeditor of *Constructing Nationalism in Habsburg Central Europe* (2004), and has written numerous articles and reviews on nationalist political cultures, regional history, and tourism in Habsburg Central Europe.

Thomas Lekan is assistant professor of history at the University of South Carolina in Columbia. His book on German and European environmental and urban history, *Imagining the Nation in Nature: Landscape Preservation and German Identity, 1885–1945* (2003), has just appeared. He is currently coediting with Thomas Zeller a volume of essays dedicated to German environmental history entitled *Germany's Nature: Cultural Landscapes and Environmental History.* His current research focuses on the environmental and cultural significance of nature tourism in modern Europe, as well as the comparative evolution of German and U.S. environmental perception and ecological movements.

Jeffrey Lesser is professor of history and director of the Latin American and Caribbean Studies Program at Emory University. He is the author of *Negotiating National Identity: Minorities, Immigrants, and the Struggle for Ethnicity in Brazil* (1999), winner of the best book prize from the Brazilian Section of the Latin American Studies Association. His *Welcoming the Undesirables: Brazil and the Jewish Ques-*

tion (1994) won the best book prize from the New England Council on Latin American Studies. Lesser is also the editor of *Searching for Home Abroad: Japanese-Brazilians and Transnationalism* (2003) and *New Approaches to Brazilian Studies* (2001), as well as coeditor of *Arab and Jewish Immigrants in Latin America: Images and Realities* (1998). He is currently studying discrimination and transnational identity among Brazilians of Asian descent.

Krista (Molly) O'Donnell is associate professor of history at William Paterson University. Her research has been funded by the Fulbright Commission and examines organized German women's colonization in Namibia. She is the author of several articles on German colonialism and the construction of colonial community. She is completing her monograph, *Women and Empire: Gender and Community in German Southwest Africa, 1896–1933* (forthcoming).

Nancy R. Reagin is professor of history and the director of the Women's and Gender Studies Program at Pace University in New York. She is the author of *A German Women's Movement: Class and Gender in Hanover, 1880–1933* (1995) and of numerous articles on the history of prostitution, housewives' organizations, and consumption. She is currently completing a second monograph on gender and German national identity between 1871 and 1945.

Howard Sargent currently works for the National Education Association in Washington, D.C. Sargent's research in the history of German citizenship laws has been supported by a Fulbright Fellowship in Berlin from 1995 to 1997 and a stipend from the Institute for European History in Mainz in 1998. Prior to joining the NEA in 2002, he worked at the Library of Congress and the Woodrow Wilson Center for Scholars.

Stefan Wolff trained as a political scientist and is now a reader in politics at the University of Bath in England. He specializes in the prevention, management, and settlement of ethnic and religious self-determination conflicts and in post-conflict reconstruction of deeply divided and war-torn societies. Wolff has also published extensively on issues related to the German question, including *German Minorities in Europe: Ethnic Identity and Cultural Belonging* (2000), *Coming Home to Germany: The Integration of Ethnic Germans from Central and Eastern Europe in the Federal Republic* (2002, with David Rock), and *The German Question since 1919: Analysis with Key Documents* (2003).

Index

Adam, Walter, 71
Adenauer, Konrad, 201, 288
Adler, Liebmann (rabbi), 122
Africa/Africans, 2, 3, 40, 47, 49–50, 52, 53,
    54–55, 250–53. *See also* German South-
    west Africa (GSWA)
Afro-Germans, 16, 46, 52–55
AHSGR. *See* American Historical Society
    of Germans from Russia
Alexander I (tsar), 187
Aliens Law, 32
Alldeutscher Verband (ADV or Pan-Ger-
    man League), 25–28, 254
Allgemeines Landrecht (ALR), 19
All-German Party (Gesamtdeutsche Partei
    or GDP), 290
Alsace-Lorraine, 2
Aly, Götz, 271–74, 280
America Herold Zeitung (newspaper),
    206
American Historical Society of Germans
    from Russia (AHSGR), 208–10
Anarak Peixoto, Ernani do, 174–75
Anderson, Benedict, 8
Arangha, Oswaldo, 174
Arbeitsgemeinschaft der Ostumsiedler
    (Working Group of East Resettlers),
    201
Argentina, 87, 105, 171, 196, 200
Aryan Germans, 236
Aschheim, Steven, 131
Asia/Asians, 2, 31, 53
Asociación de Ayuda Social de la Colonia
    Alemana (Social Assistance Associa-
    tion of the German Colony), 104
Assimilation, 3–4
    in Mexico, 102–5
Association for Germans Abroad. *See*
    Verein für das Deutschtum im Ausland
    (VDA)

Association of Volga Germans. *See* Verein
    der Wolgadeutschen
Auslandsdeutsche, 7, 62, 66, 185, 249, 253,
    256, 258, 262
Auslandsorganization der NSDAP (For-
    eign Organization of the NSDAP),
    62–64, 99, 100, 197
Deutsches Wollen (journal), 64
    intentions of, 63–64
Aussiedler, 3–4, 7, 31, 33–34, 62, 287,
    293–95, 309
Austria, 2, 226, 237
    Austrofascist movement, 71
    Deutscher Schulverein (German School
        Association), 227, 229–31
    and Volksgemeinschaft, 70–72
Austrian Social Democratic Party, 228–29
Austro-German nationalists, 224–29
Autonomous Republic of Volga Germans,
    189, 195
Avanhandava Scout Troop, 178
Avila Camacho, Manuel, 100, 101
Avni, Haim, 171

Bade, Klaus, 12
Baiersdorf, Jacob, 115
Balkans, 7, 256
Baltic Germans, 260
Barkai, Avraham, 112, 130
Basic Law, 201, 292
    Article 116, 30–31
Basters, 44–45
Bavaria, 112, 113, 230, 289
Bayerischer Staatsanzeiger (newspaper),
    73–74
Belgium, 153
Bell, Richard Manga, 52–53
Beneš Decrees, 303–4
Bergen, Doris, 4, 11, 65, 186
Bergh, Henry, 146

Bethmann-Hollweg (German chancellor), 29

Bildung, 8, 10, 12, 41, 124, 128

Binford, Mira Reym, 274

Bismarck, Otto von, 22–25, 70, 92, 148, 161

Bismarckian Germany, citizenship/emigration in, 22–25

Blood and Soil (*Blut und Boden*), 143, 155–56, 162

B'nai B'rith, 117–19, 129, 132

Bohemia, 113, 219, 227, 230, 234, 240

Bohemian German nationalists, 226

Bohle, Ernst Wilhelm, 62

Böker family, and Hispanization of names, 90

Boxer, Oswald, 170

Brazil, 65, 87, 101, 105, 196, 200

   Brazilian-Jewish Cultural and Beneficent Society (SIBRA), 177–78

   communal religious organizations, 178

   envisioning, by Central European Jewry, 169–76

   German Jews in, 167–83

      and anti-Semitism, 176–77

      Germanness of, 177–78

      integration of, 168–69

   and professional degrees, 172

   immigration policies, 177

   Jewish Congregation of São Paulo, 172, 178

   Jewish immigration to, 167–68

   Rezende colony, 173–76

Brazilian-Jewish Cultural and Beneficent Society (SIBRA), 177–78

Brazilian Volksgemeinschaft, 66–68

Brechtel, Rudolf, 103

Brendel, John, 205

Brentano, Lorenzo, 120

Bridenthal, Renate, 4, 11, 186

Brinkmann, Tobias, 83–84, 89

Brothers and Strangers (Aschheim), 131

Brubaker, Rogers, 6–7, 8, 22

Brüder in Not, 195, 206

Buchenau, Jürgen, 4, 84

Buckley, James L., 210

Bukovina, 185, 219, 227, 230, 235–38

Bukovina Germans, 260

Bulgaria, 196

Bund der Deutschen in Böhmen (Union of Germans in Bohemia), 226

Bund der Heimatvertriebenen und Entrechteten (BHE or Union of Expellees and Disenfranchised), 290

Bund der Vertriebenen (BdV or Union of Expellees—United Regional-Cultural Associations), 291–92, 301

Bund vertriebener Deutscher (BvD or Union of Expelled Germans), 289

Burleigh, Michael, 254

Canada, 87, 171, 200, 202

Cannstatter Volksfest, 161

Cárdenas, Lázaro, 97, 100

Carinthia, 232

Caro, Herbert, 177

Carranza, Venustiano, 97–98

Casino Alemán (Deutsches Haus), 91

Catherine the Great (tsarina), 187

Catholic Church, 6, 93, 169, 190, 225

Central and Eastern Europe, 7, 9, 31, 111, 133, 156, 220–21, 248–49, 253–61, 267–81, 293–95

   restructuring of Germany's policy toward ethnic Germans in, 296–97

Central Committee of Germans from Russia, 194

Central League of Expelled Germans (Zentralverband der vertriebenen Deutschen), 289

Charter of German Expellees (1950), 289, 291

Chicago Eifelverein, 148–49

Chicago German (newspaper), 160

Chile, 87

China, 40

Christlich Demokratische Union Deutschlands (CDU or Christian Democratic Union), 32–33, 304

Christlich Soziale Union (CSU or Christian Social Union), 304

Chronik, Isaak (rabbi), 115–16

CIP. See Congregação Israelita Paulista

Citizenship laws, 15, 17–39

   continuities/new directions, 30–35

   and German-Jewish immigrants in U.S., 120–22

   history of, 28

Coalition of Eastern German Regional-Cultural Associations (Vereinigung der ostdeutschen Landsmannschaften or VoL), 289

Colegio Alemán, 93–95, 101, 103–4
Colonies
    domestication of, 44
    transformation into *Heimat,* 42, 252–53,
        255–56
Congregação Israelita Paulista (CIP), 172,
    178
Conzen, Kathleen Neils, 143–44
Copenhagen Declaration of the Conference
    on Security and Cooperation in
    Europe (1990), 307
Correio da Manhã (newspaper), 175, 177
Cremer, J. C., 148
Crónica Israelita (newspaper), 172
Cytronowicz, Roney, 178
Czaja, Herbert, 302
Czechoslovakia, 65, 71–72, 153, 194, 222,
    231–34, 239, 288, 292–93, 302–5,
    307
    Germany's relationship with, 297–300
    and Volksgemeinschaft, 72–73
Czech Republic, 303–7

Dakota Freie Press (*DFP*) (newspaper),
    202–6
Davis, Ethelyn C., 95–96
Denikin, General, 193
Denmark, 2
Der Kampf (journal), 73
Der Staatsanzeiger (newspaper), 206
Deutsche Front (German Front), 74–75
Deutsche Gesellschaft (German Society),
    115
Deutsche Kolonialgesellschaft (DKG or
    German Colonial Society), 25, 27,
    43–44, 254
Deutsche Post aus dem Osten (*DPO*) (news-
    paper), 196
Deutscher Ostdienst (*DOD* or *German East-
    ern Service*) (magazine), 291–92
Deutscher Schulverein (German School
    Association), 227, 229–31
Deutscher Verein (German Association),
    191
Deutsches Ausland-Institut (DAI or Ger-
    man Foreign Institute), 152, 197–98,
    254
Deutsches Zentral Comitee für die Russ-
    ischen Juden (German Central Com-
    mittee for Russian Jews), 170
Deutsche Volksgemeinschaft in Mexiko

(DVM or German Volksgemeinschaft
    in Mexico), 63
Deutsche Volkszeitung in Reichenberg
    (newspaper), 236
Deutsche Zeitung von Mexico (newspaper),
    93, 96
Deutschtum im Ausland, 62
Diamonds in the Snow (documentary), 274
Diário de Notícias (newspaper), 175
Diaspora, 5–6, 11, 219–20, 241
Diaspora (journal), 5–6
Díaz, Porfirio, 91–94, 96
Die Deborah (newspaper), 126
Die Kaukasische Post (newspaper), 191
Die Nation (newspaper), 68–69
Diepgen, Eberhard, 34
Diner, Hasia R., 112, 114, 132
Dollfuß, Engelbert, 71
Dual citizenship, campaign against, 33

Eastern European Jews, and Brazil, 170
Echeverría, Luis, 103
Eckenbrecher, Margarethe v., 251
Eifel/Eifelverein, 148
Einbürgerungsrichtlinien, 30–31
Einhorn, David, 126–29
Einsatzgruppe, 270, 272–74
El Anfora, 98
England, 92
Erzberger, Matthias, 48
Ethnic Germans. See *Auslandsdeutsche;
    Aussiedler; Volksdeutsche*
Ethnocultural model, 25, 27
Evangelical Lutheran Church in Germany,
    202
Expellee organizations. See *Heimatver-
    triebenenverbände* (expellee organiza-
    tions)

Fabri, Friedrich, 24
Fahrmeir, Andreas, 20
Falcão, Ildefonso, 177
Faust, Albert, 145 47, 156–57
Fazenda dos Judeus, 175
Federal Ministry for Expellees, Refugees,
    and Victims of War, 281
Felsenthal, Bernhard, 114, 122, 127–29
Fichte, Johan Gottlieb, 73
Flaggenstreit, 98–99
Fletcher, Henry P., 96, 98
Fletcher, Yael Simpson, 52

Foreign Organization of the NSDAP.
  See Auslandsorganization der
  NSDAP
France, 2, 92, 224
Frankel, Zacharias, 124
Frankfurt Assembly, attempt to create Ger-
  man nation-state, 21–22
Franzel, Emil, 73–74
Frasch, Adolf, 196
Frauenbund der Deutsche Kolonialge-
  sellschaft (Women's Union of the Ger-
  man Colonial Society), 43
Freie Demokratische Partei (FDP or Free
  Democratic Party), 32
Frick, Wilhelm, 157
Fritsch, H. E., 205

Gabaccia, Donna, 6
Gaeckle, Joseph, 206
Galicia, 185, 227, 230, 235–36
Gastarbeiter, 30–31
Geiger, Abraham, 124, 127, 130
General Prussian Legal Code (Allgemeines
  Landrecht or ALR), 19
German Aid Society, 115
German Americans, 4, 59, 60, 86, 141–47,
  150–52, 157–62
  in Chicago, 119–22, 125–30, 141–43,
    148–50, 160–61, 202–4
  cultural landscape, 147
  farmers, 145–47
  Heimat, 147–48
  identity before 1914, 143–50
  social life of, 148–49
  "special gifts" of, 144–45
  and temperance movement, 144
German Colonial Society. *See* Deutsche
  Kolonialgesellschaft (DKG)
German Confederation, 18
German Constitutional Court, 292
German-Czech Declaration, 298
German Democratic Republic, 9
German diaspora, 5–6, 9, 15, 17–39, 83,
  219–47
  after 1918, 238–41
  German identities, 229–38
  nationalization in pre-1918 Austria,
    224–29
  use of term, 219–20, 241
German domestic practices/housekeeping,
  I, II, 45, 249–52, 255–61

re-Germanizing of homes during World
  War II, 259–60
*German Eastern Service (Deutscher Ost-
  dienst or DOD)* (magazine), 291–92
German Element in the United States, The
  (Faust), 145
German Foreign Institute. *See* Deutsches
  Ausland-Institut (DAI)
German-Jewish immigrants in U.S., 111–40
  Civil War, 120–22
  anti-Jewish prejudice during, 121
  colonial Jewry, use of term, 111
  first Jews in America, 111
  German associations, 113–15
  rabbis/Jewish businessmen's involve-
    ment in, 115
  German community, as loose ethnic net-
    work, 119
  German Jews, use of term, 112
  Jewish community in Chicago, 117–19
  B'nai B'rith, 117–19
  congregations/associations, 118–19,
    132
  residential mobility among, 119
  Jewish immigrants in Chicago, 114–17
  Jewish leaders in Chicago, and the Ger-
    man community, 116–17
  Jewish Reformers, 123–26, 133
  Kehilat Anshe Maarab (KAM) (Men of
    the West), 125
  in nineteenth century, 112–14
  origins of reform in Chicago, 122–30
  use of German as spoken language,
    113–14
German Jews, 8, 30, 64, 83
  in Brazil, 167–83
  in the United States, 112–17, 119–34
  use of term, 111–12, 131–33
German National People's Party
  (Deutschnationale Volkspartei), in
  Austria, 70
Germanness, 4, 8–12, 24, 42, 65, 112, 114–17,
  133–34, 199, 226, 240, 249, 251, 260–61,
  270, 273–74, 276
  preservation of, 2
  use of term, 4
German Red Cross, 299
German School Association. *See* Deutscher
  Schulverein
German Southwest Africa (GSWA), 40–42,
  44–48

barring of interracial marriage/
    intercourse/cohabitation,
    40–41
German citizenship and equal treatment
    in the colonies, 46–47
men's attitudes toward European
    wives/homemakers, 47
natives and nonnatives, 41, 250
Germans
    Afro-Germans, 16, 46, 54–55
    Baltic Germans, 260
    Black Sea Germans, 7
    Bukovina Germans, 260
    Galician Germans, 260
    in Mexico, 85–110
    Reich Germans, 230, 248
    Russian Germans, 4, 185, 187–218
    Sudeten Germans, 72, 185, 233, 238–39,
        304
    Ukrainian Germans, 199, 202
    use of term, 4
    Volga Germans, 7, 209, 256
German states. See *Länder*
Germany
    acquired colonies, 40
    anti-Semitic/anti-Slavic prejudices, and
        citizenship policies, 26
    citizenship laws, 15, 17–39
    German Foreign Office (Auswärtiges
        Amt), 28–29, 152, 254
    German Interior Ministry, 28, 300
    German Naval Office, 28–29
    and mixed-race persons, 41–42
    North German Confederation, citizen-
        ship law (1870), 23
    race policies, comparison with other
        European empires, 49
    unification, 18, 92
Gesamtdeutsche Partei (GDP). *See*
    All-German Party
Gierke, Otto, 70
Giesinger, Adam, 208
Gleichschaltung, 161
Goethe Institute, 202
Golinelli, Angelo, 47
Götz, Norbert, 8, 10, 16
Grant, Ulysses S., 122
Greenebaum, Henry, 115–16
Gross, Stanislav, 305
Gurney, Hugh, 174
Gustav-Adolf Verein, 254

Haake, Heinz, 158–60
Habsburg Empire, 7, 11, 72, 185, 238–40
    and Austrian identity, 224
Härtung, Carl, 148–50
Hawgood, John, 146
Hayes, Rutherford B., 93
Haynes, Emma Schwabenland, 190, 207–10
Haynes, Thomas V., 207
Hecker, Friedrich, 120–21
Heimat (homeland), 1–2, 8, 11, 12, 42, 44, 45,
        187
    defined, 141
    German metaphors of, 54
    loss of, 288–91
    maintaining from afar, 291–93
    mobilization of sentiment in World War I
        and Weimar Republic, 150–55
    politics of, 287–312
    sociability, 161
Heimat abroad
    local promotion of, 141–66
    use of term, 77
Heimatbrief (newsletter), 159–60
Heimatbücher, 200
Heimatvertriebenenverbände (expellee orga-
        nizations), 9, 289–92, 297, 302–3, 308
Henlein, Konrad, 72, 239
Herero-Nama war (1904–7), 42
Herzl, Theodore, 170
Hess, Rudolf, 155
Hesse, Hermann, 177
Heuer, Friedrich, 47
Himmler, Heinrich, 157, 269, 271–72, 274
Hirsch, Emil G., 115–16
Hitler, Adolf, 3, 8, 30, 63, 67–68, 72, 84, 99,
        205, 269, 276, 279
Hitler Youth, 197
Hochfelder, Harry, 301
Hofbrauer, Josef, 73
Huici, Blanca, 103
Hungary, 7, 71, 112, 178, 289–92, 297, 302–3,
        308
Hupka, Herbert, 293, 302

Idische Presse (Imprensa Israelita) (news-
        paper), 175
Illinois Staatszeitung (newspaper), 114, 117,
        119, 132
Imhof, Kurt, 69
Institute for Eastern European History, 254
Israelite (newspaper), 126

Italian diaspora, 6
Italy, 224
Italy's Many Diasporas (Gabaccia), 6
Ius sanguinis, 27–29, 97
Ius solis, 27–28, 97

Jaksch, Wenzel, 74, 201
Jewish Advance (newspaper), 114
Jewish Colonization Association (JCA), 167, 173–75
Jewish Congregation of São Paulo. *See* Congregação Israelita Paulista (CIP)
Jewish diaspora, 10
Jewish German-Americans, use of term, 132
Jewish Reform Association, 127
Jews of Chicago, 120–22, 125–26
Joseph II (emperor), 235
Juárez, Benito, 91–92
Judson, Pieter, 7, 11, 186
Jung, Jacob Leo, 148

Kaiserreich (Wilhelmine Germany), 2, 11, 15, 16, 23–24, 26–27, 30, 34, 50, 70, 84, 151, 221, 227, 229, 240
Karow, Maria, 251
Kehilat Anshe Maarab (KAM or Men of the West), 125–26
Khoi, 44
King, Jeremy, 224
Kissinger, Henry, 210
Kleindeutschland, 70, 113
Know-Nothings, 120
Koehler, Arthur, 67
Kohl, Helmut, 32, 293, 301
"Kol Kore Bamidbar" manifesto, 127–28
Kolonie und Heimat (magazine), 43–55, 250
  editorial policy toward miscegenation, 43–45, 54
  fixation on image of "trouser niggers," 51–52
  and Rehoboth Baster community, 44–45
  and rhetorical distance between home and colony, 44
Korrespondenzblatt (newsletter), 171
Koselleck, Reinhart, 19, 68
Kotkowsky, Charles, 278
Krüger, Hans, 291–92
Küchenzettel, 249–50
Kulaks, 195
Kulturlandschaft, 142, 147
Kulturnation, 8, 10, 141, 233

Lamprecht, Karl, 147
Länder (German states), 7, 18, 188
  citizenship/emigration in, 22–25
  citizenship laws in, before unification, 18–22
  praxis of Volksgemeinschaft, 61–62
  waves of transatlantic emigration, 22–23
Landrat, 48
Landsmannschaft der Deutschen aus Russland (LDR or Regional-Cultural Association of Germans from Russia), 200–202
Latvia, 75
  German-Baltic Volksgemeinschaft, 75
  and subnational concept of Volksgemeinschaft, 75–76
Law on Emigration Matters (1897), 151
League for German Culture (Liga pro cultura alemana), 63
League of Bohemian Woods (Deutscher Böhmerwaldbund), 226–27
League of Regional-Cultural Associations (Verband der Landsmannschaften or VdL), 289
League of the Germans in Romania (Verband der Deutschen in Rumänien), 76
Leibbrandt, Georg, 197–99, 210
Lekan, Thomas, 9, 10, 83, 86
Leonhard, Elke, 302
Lesser, Jeffrey, 10, 84, 100
Levy, Herbert V., 176
Liberal Reforma (Mexico), 88
Liga pro cultura alemana (League for German Culture), 63
Lincoln, Abraham, 120
London Protocol (September 1944), 298
López Portillo, José, 103
Löwenthal, Richard, 73
Lutheranism, 93–95, 190

Machado, Dulphe Pinheiro, 174
Magalhães, Agamemnon, 174
Mann, Thomas, 177
Marburg, 232
Maximilian (Habsburg prince), 87–88, 91
Mayer, Leopold, 125
Mbida, Johann, 52
Mello Franco, Afranio de, 177
Mendelssohn, Moses, 123
Metzler, Franz, 66–67

Mexico, 200
Club Alemán, 102
Colegio Alemán, 94, 101, 103–4
Deutsche Zeitung von Mexico (newspaper), 93
German churches, efforts to promote, 94–95
German Club, 102
German colony, 4, 85–110
    assimilation, 102–5
    assimilationist phase, 86
    and cosmopolitan elite in Porfirian Mexico, 93
    marginalization of, 104
    population/institutions, 93
    reaction to news of Hitler's appointment as chancellor, 99
    schools, 94
    self-segregation of, 95–96
    stages of national identity, 86
    U.S. focus on destruction of, 101
German immigration, 87
German merchants, 88–89
    and Mexican Revolution, 97
    and Porfirian/Imperial era, 92–93
immigration law, 97
immigration restrictions, 102
linguistic conventions, 90
political/social environment, 87–88
Meyer, Michael A., 114–15, 123, 125
Miller, David, 206, 208
Miller, Randall, 143
Ministry of Inner-German Affairs, 299
Miscegenation
    colonial problem of, 45–46, 50
    German debate over, 41, 54
Mittelstand, 228
Mixed-language regions, 231
Moeller, Robert, 281
Moravia, 219, 224–25, 227
Moravian Compromise (1905), 224
Mosse, George L., 124
Müller, Filinto, 173
Multinationalization, 224–25
Munich Agreement, 298

Nadel, Stanley, 112, 132
Napoleon (Bonaparte), 2, 123
National Population Department (Departmento Nacional de Povoamento or DNP) (Brazil), 174

National Socialist Party of Germany (National Socialist German Workers' Party [Nazi Party] or NSDAP), 58, 60–62, 67, 69, 70, 155–56, 269, 279
Nationalsozialistische Frauenschaft (Nazi Women's League), 259–61
Nationalstaat, 22
Naturalization policies, 32
Nazi Foreign Organization. *See* Auslandsorganization der NSDAP
Nazi Party. *See* National Socialist Party of Germany
Nazis/Nazi era, 18, 59, 239
    citizenship laws, 16
    collection/distribution of Jewish belongings for, 272–73
    fetal examinations for racial potential, 270
    and German Volksgemeinschaft, 60–61
    proclamation of supranational Volksgemeinschaft, 60–61
    and racial purity, 268
    use of Volksgemeinschaft concept against Austria, 71
    Volksgemeinschaft, 30
Neue Schweiz (New Switzerland) movement, 69–70
Nicholas II (tsar), 170, 188
Niessen Deiters, Leonore, 48
Nordmark, 232
North Atlantic Treaty Organization (NATO), 291
North German Confederation, citizenship law (1870), 23
Nuremberg Laws, 172

O Carioca (newspaper), 175
O'Donnell, Krista (Molly), 10, 16
Ostforschung, 194, 202, 222
Ostgebiete, 298–99
Ostjuden, 131, 134
Ostmarken Verein, 254

Palestine, 171
Pan-German League. *See* Alldeutscher Verband (ADV)
Paraguay, 200
Partei des Demokratischen Sozialismus (PDS or Party of Democratic Socialism), 33
Pedro II (Dom), 169

Pénétration pacifique, 154
Peter Moors Fahrt nach Südwest, 250
Plural diasporas, 6
Poland, 76, 112, 153, 185, 222–23, 238, 259, 268, 270–71, 275–76, 288, 292, 293–94, 307
  Germany's relationship with, 297–300
Political Section of the Nazi Ministry for the Occupied Eastern Territories, 198
Porter, Katherine Anne, 89
Portugal, 111
Pratt, Mary Louise, 86
Provincial League (Rhineland), 154
Prussia, 19–23, 194–95, 219, 225
  citizenship law (1842), 21
  citizenship reforms, 19–20
  history of, 2–3
Prussian Law of 1842, 25

Rath, Georg, 197–98, 205, 210
Reagin, Nancy, 4, 11, 186
Rehoboth Basters, 44–45
Reichsausschuß für Volksgesundheitsdienst (Reich Committee on Public Health Service), 63–64
Reichsbürgergesetz, 30
Reichsdeutsche (Reich Germans), 230, 248, 268
Reichstag, 48–49
Reichswanderungsamt (RWA or Reich Emigration Office), 151–52
Renard, Edmund, 155
Rheinländer in aller Welt program, 160
Rhenish Regional History Institute, 154
Rhenish Republic, 154, 159–60
Rhineland Tourist Bureau, 159
Riehl, Heinrich, 142
Roemmich, Heinrich, 200
Romania, 194, 222–23, 235, 237–38, 255, 257, 267, 279, 288, 293–94
  and Volksgemeinschaft, 76
Rosenberg, Alfred, 198
Rosenthal, Julius, 115
Rowe, Leo S., 174
Ruppin, Arthur, 171–72
Russia, 131, 187–88, 191–92, 277
Russian Germans, 4, 185, 187–218
  American Historical Society of Germans from Russia (AHSGR), 208–10

Dakota Freie Press (DFP) (newspaper), 202–6
Dorpat, 191, 196, 198
emigration, 188–90
"German question" in Russia, 188
Germans from Russia Heritage Society, 211
Haynes, Emma Schwabenland, 190, 207–10
Leibbrandt, Georg, 197–99, 210
Rath, Georg, 197–98, 210
Roemmich, Heinrich, 198–201, 209, 210
Sallet family, 202–6
Schleuning, Johannes, 190–96, 210
Stumpp, Karl, 196–202, 210
Russian Jews, 170
  use of term, 131

Saarländer Verein (Saarländ Association), 149
Salgado dos Santos, Labienne, 173
Sallet family, 202–6
Salomon, Edward, 115, 121
Sargent, Howard, 10, 12, 16
Saxony, 230
Schily, Otto, 32–34, 304, 307
Schleswig-Holstein, 2
Schleuning, Johannes, 190–96, 200, 210
Schroeder, Gerhard, 303–4
Schurz, Carl, 146
Schuschnigg, Kurt, 71
Schwabenverein (Association of Swabians), 149–50, 161
Seminar for Eastern European History and Ethnography, 254
Sheehy, Ann, 210
Sheffer, Gabriel, 5
SIBRA. *See* Brazilian-Jewish Cultural and Beneficent Society
Siebenbürger Sachsen, 60, 283
Silesia, 2, 219
Soares, Jóse Carlos de Macedo, 173
Social Democratic Party. *See* Sozialdemokratische Partei Deutschlands (SPD)
Sollmann, Wilhelm, 73
South Tyrol. *See* Tyrol
Soviet-German Treaty of 1955, 292
Soviet Union, 12, 223, 238, 293–94
Sozialdemokratische Partei Deutschlands

(SPD or Social Democratic Party of Germany), 32, 73, 302
Spain, 111
SPD/Green coalition government, 32–33, 296
Spidia, Vladimir, 305
Sprachgrenzen, 231, 254
Sprachinseln (islands of Germanness), 1, 185, 231, 248, 254–55, 259
SS Volksdeutsche Mittelstelle. *See* Volksdeutsche Mittelstelle of the SS (VoMi)
Staatsvolksgemeinschaft, 66–67
Steinacher, Hans, 197
Steinback, Erika, 302–3
Stoecker, Helene, 48
Stoler, Ann, 49
Stumpp, Karl, 190, 196–202, 208, 209, 210
  and support for Hitler, 197
Styria, 219, 227, 232
Sudeten Germans, 72, 185, 233, 238–39, 304–5
Südmark, 227, 229, 232, 234
Süd-Ost (newspaper), 76
Swabia, 230
Switzerland, 68–70
  and Volksgemeinschaft, 68–70

Tirpitz, Alfred von, 29
Tomaszcuk, Constantine, 235
Trade diasporas, 5, 85
Tragedy of German-America, The (Hawgood), 146
Transylvania, 185
Treaty of Brest-Litovsk, 193
Treaty of Rapallo (1922), 195
Treaty of Versailles, 3, 254
Treaty on Good Neighborly Relations and Cooperation (1991), 299
Turner, Frederick Jackson, 147
Tyrol (South Tyrol), 219, 226
Tyrolean German nationalists, 226

Ukraine, 188, 193, 199–200, 202, 208–10, 223, 235–36
Ukrainian Germans, 199, 202, 272, 279
Ullmann, Hermann, 153–54
Unabhängiger Orden Treuer Schwestern (Independent Order of True Sisters), 119
Unification, 18–22

citizenship laws in German *Länder* before unification, 18–22
Union of Bohemian Germans, 232, 234
Union of Expelled Germans (Bund vertriebener Deutscher or BvD), 289
Union of Expellees and Disenfranchised (Bund der Heimatvertriebenen und Entrechteten or BHE), 290
Union of Expellees—United Regional-Cultural Associations (Bund der Vertriebenen or BdV), 291–92, 301
United Hebrew Relief Association (UHRA), 118–19, 121, 129, 132
United States, 92, 105, 171, 200
  focus on destruction of German colony, 101
  German-Jewish immigrants, in Civil War, 120–22
  Jewish Reform movement, 133
Uruguay, 200

Vargas, Getúlio, 173–75
VDA. *See* Verein fur das Deutschtum im Ausland
Verband der Deutschen aus Russland (VRD or League of Germans from Russia), 195
Verband der Deutschen in Rumänien (Association of Germans in Romania), 76
Verband der Russlanddeutschen (League of Russian Germans), 196
Verband Deutscher Reichsangehöriger (VDR or League of German Citizens), 96
Verein der Wolgadeutschen (Association of Volga Germans), 194, 198, 204
Verein für das Deutschtum im Ausland (VDA or Association for Germans Abroad), 9, 152–54, 158, 193–94, 197, 254, 296
Vereinigung der ostdeutschen Landsmannschaften (VoL or Coalition of Eastern German Regional-Cultural Associations), 289
Vianna, Oliveira, 173–74
Volga, 185
Volga Germans, 7, 209, 256
Volhynia, 185
Volk auf dem Weg (newsletter), 187, 188–89, 200

Volksbund für das Deutschtum im Ausland
    (People's Union for Germanness
    Abroad), 62
Volksdeutsche, 62, 99, 186, 193–94, 258–61
    as casualties of brutalization, 276–80
    centrality and tenuousness of the concept
        of, 269–71
    collection/distribution of Jewish belong-
        ings for, 272–73
    distortion of term by Nazis, 273
    and the Holocaust, 268, 274–75
    marriage to foreigners, 270
    as opponents of genocide, 274–76
    opposition activities of, 275–76
    as perpetrators, 271–74
    tenuousness/tenacity of, 267–86
    use of term, 267
Volksdeutsche Forschungsgemeinschaften
    (VFG), 197
Volksdeutsche Mittelstelle of the SS
    (VoMi), 157–58, 195–96, 259
Volksgemeinschaft, 8, 10, 16, 30,
    58–59
    in Austria, 70–72
    in Czechoslovakia, 72–73
    in Latvia, 75–76
    national concept of, 59, 65–66
    in North America, 59
    in Romania, 76
    subnational concept of, 59, 75–76
    supranational concept of, 59–65
    in Switzerland, 68–70
    use of term, 58
Volksgruppen in Europa (League of Ger-
    man Communities in Europe), 72
Volksliste, 65, 274
Volkstrachten, 53–54
Volkstum (German character), 66
Volk und Arbeiter (*People and Workers*)
    (Jaksch), 74
von Kollenberg, Rüdt, 99

von Mentz, Brigida, 105
von Ranke, Leopold, 124
von Schiller, Friedrich, 150
Vorposten (journal), 73

Wächtler, Fritz, 156–57
Wannsee Conference, 209
War Consequences Conciliation Act (1993),
    294
Wars of Unification, 22
Weimar Republic, 7, 9, 67, 98, 150, 155, 194,
    221
Wells, Leon Weliczker, 275
Wels, Otto, 74
White, A. D., 145
Wildenthal, Lora, 222
Wilhelm II (kaiser), 25, 96
Wilhelmine Germany. *See* Kaiserreich
Wilson, Woodrow, 151
Wise, Isaac Mayer (rabbi), 126, 129, 130
Wolff, Stefan, 11, 186
Women, and German identity, 1, 11, 42–43,
    45, 48
World War I, 3–4, 9, 11, 70, 83, 96, 97, 142,
    237, 255, 288
    and German American Heimat clubs,
        150–51
    and Russian Germans in the U.S., 203
World War II, 61, 65, 76, 100, 189, 258,
    267–68, 287

Yugoslavia, 194, 196, 222–23, 238, 268, 288

Zeman, Miloš, 304–5
Zender, Michael, 151
Zentralverband der vertriebenen Deutschen
    (Central League of Expelled Germans),
    289
Zimmer, Oliver, 68–69
Zimmermann Telegram, 98
Zuquim, Judith, 178